THE
JEWS

Also by Ben M. Freeman

Jewish Pride: Rebuilding a People

Reclaiming Our Story: The Pursuit of Jewish Pride

BEN M. FREEMAN

THE JEWS

An Indigenous People

First published in February 2025 by No Pasaran Media
This edition published in the USA in September 2025

Copyright © Ben M. Freeman 2025

The moral right of Ben Maxwell Freeman to be identified
as the author of this work has been asserted in accordance with
the Copyright, Designs, and Patents Act 1988.

All rights reserved. No part of this publication may be reproduced or
transmitted in any form or by any means, electronic or mechanical including
photocopying, recording, or any information storage or retrieval system,
without prior permission in writing from the publishers.

ISBN 9781917523677

Also available as an ebook: 9781917523684
and as an audiobook: 9781917523691

Typeset by Typo•glyphix
Cover design by simonlevyassociates.com
Index by Dr. Laurence Errington
Project management by Whitefox
Printed in Canada
Distributed in the USA by Itasca Books, Minneapolis, MN, USA

Photography credits

Ben M. Freeman: Gary Swart
Rabbi Isaac Choua: Phelia Barouh
Yaffa Tegegne: Jenni Fellegi
Vlad Khaykin: Jennifer Winfrey
Dr. Efrat Sopher: Robert Shack
Dr. Winston Pickett: Adam Pickett

I dedicate this book to the Jewish people and our indigenous relationship with Eretz Yisrael, and to my parents, Sarah and Malcolm, from whom I first learned of my deep connection to Israel.

CONTENTS

Acknowledgments		ix
Maps		x
Foreword: Dr. Einat Wilf		xvii
Prologue		xxi
Introduction		1
Chapter 1	A History of the Jews and our Land: In The Beginning	25
Chapter 2	A History of the Jews and our Land: Two Kingdoms	55
Chapter 3	A History of the Jews and our Land: Post-Exilic Israel	83
Chapter 4	A History of the Jews and our Land: The End of Jewish Sovereignty	103
Chapter 5	A Study on Jewish Indigeneity	123
Chapter 6	A Study on Jewish Indigeneity Continued	153
Chapter 7	An Interview with Rabbi Isaac Choua	183
Chapter 8	An Interview with Yaffa Tegegne	195
Chapter 9	An Interview with Vlad Khaykin	205
Chapter 10	An Interview with Dr. Efrat Sopher	217
Chapter 11	An Interview with Dr. Winston Pickett	227
Chapter 12	The Jews: An Indigenous People	237
Notes		266
Index		301
About the Author		312

The following individuals provided invaluable support and guidance in completing this work, and for that, I am deeply grateful:

Gary Swart
Dr. Winston Pickett
Rabbi Jeremy Rosen
Rabbi Isaac Choua
Tracey Allen MBE

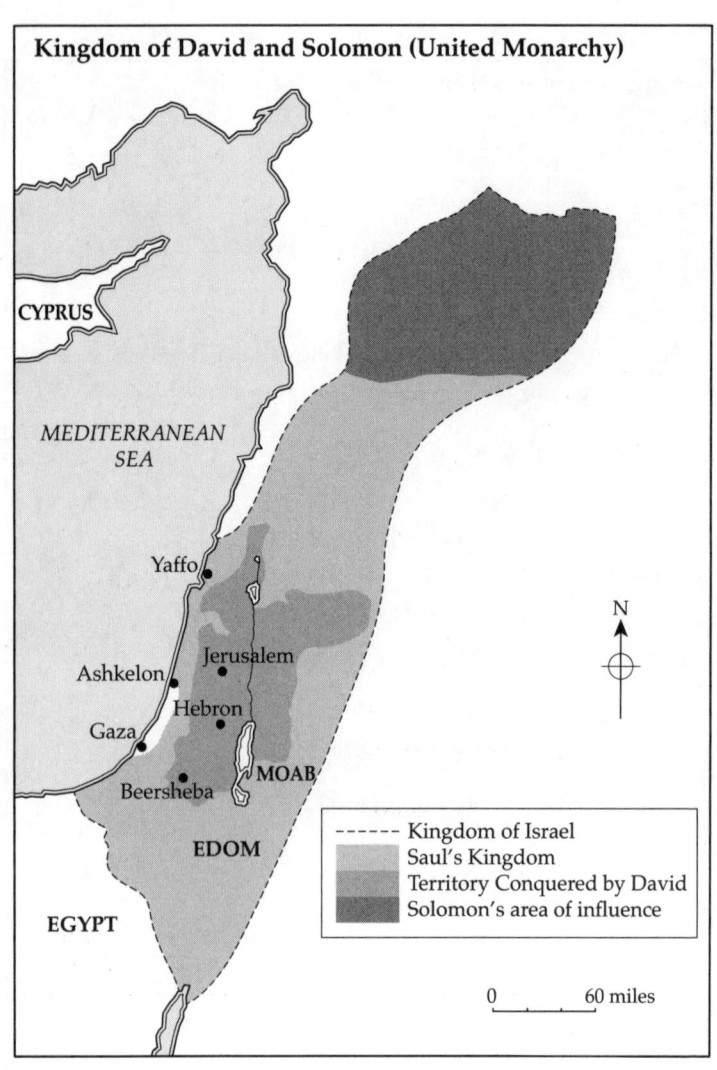

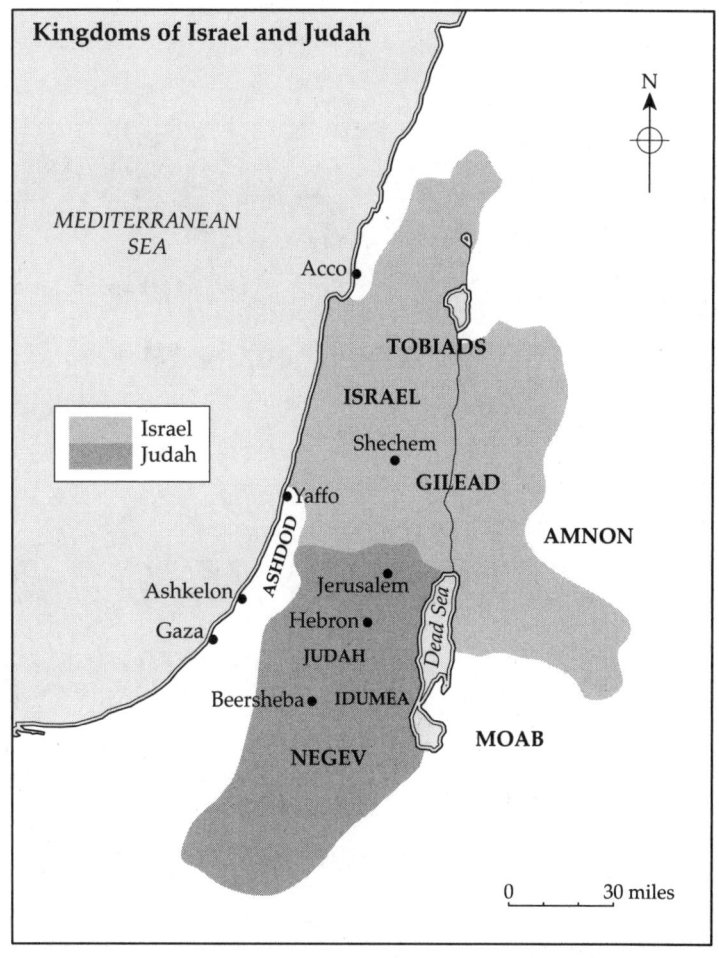

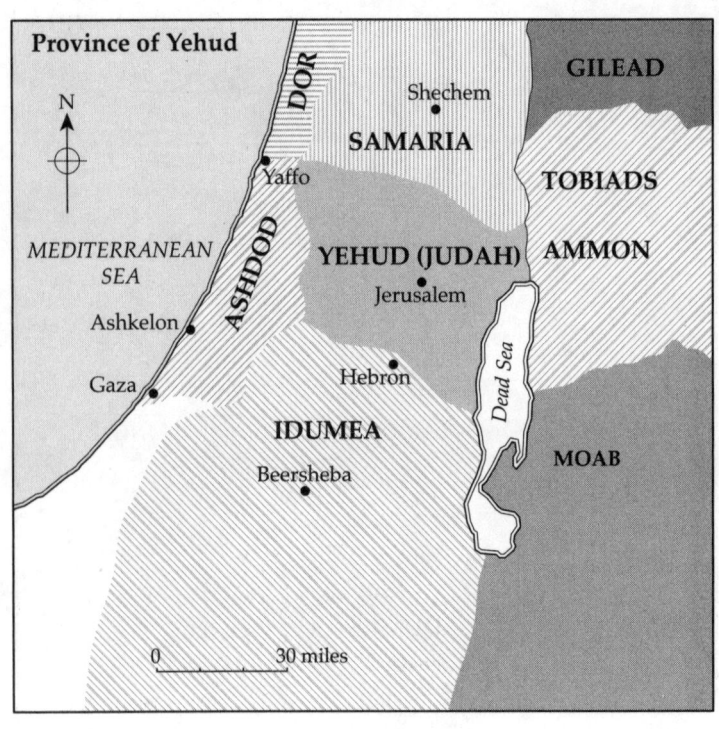

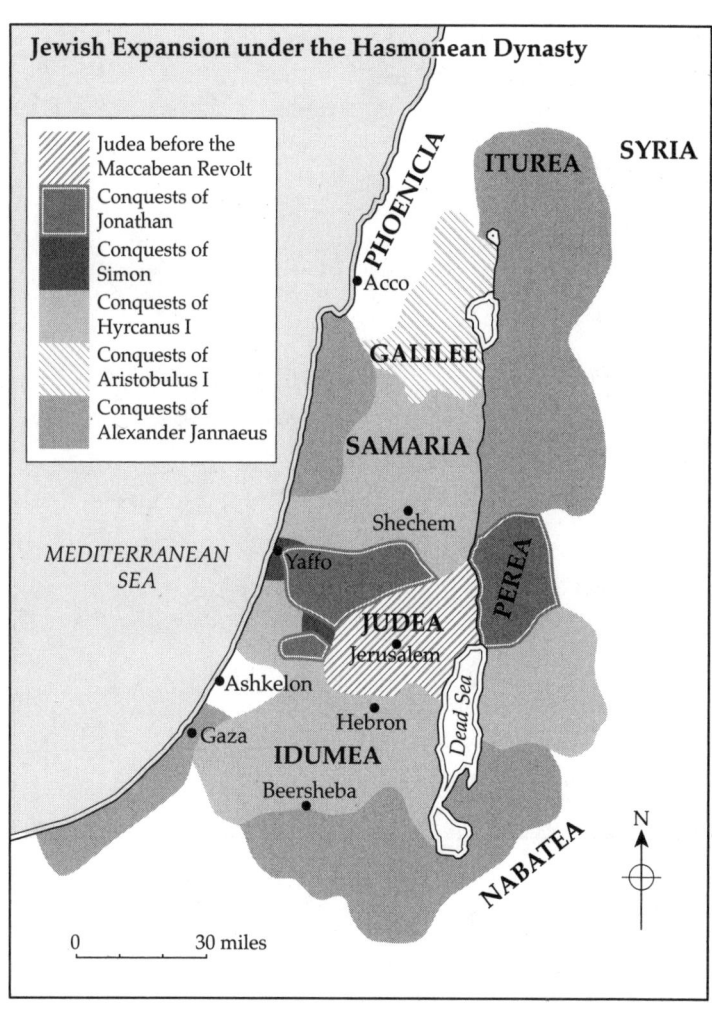

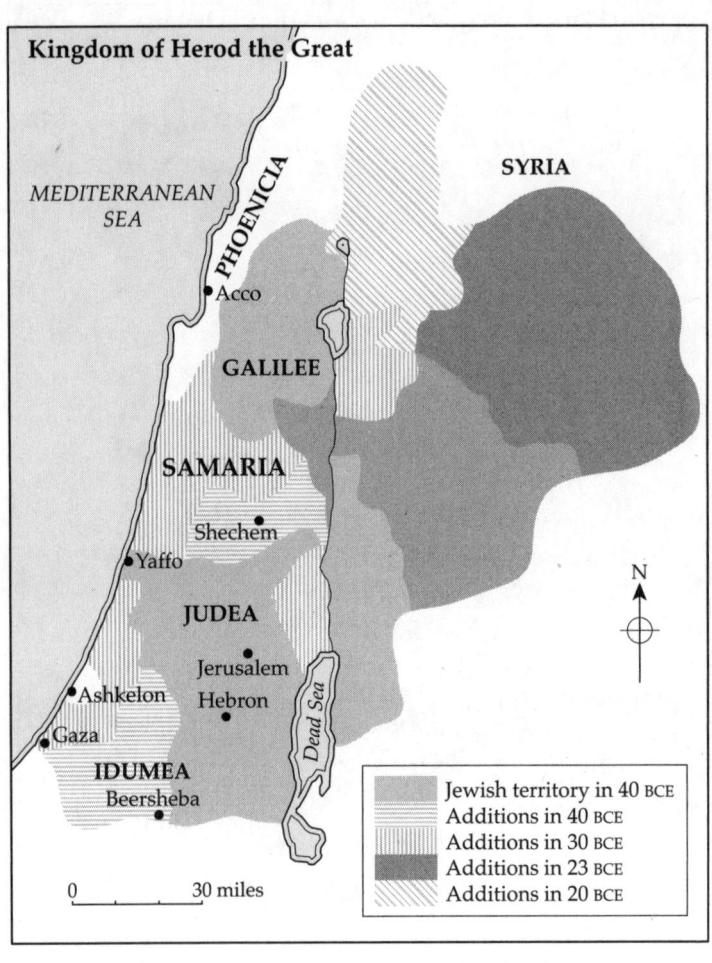

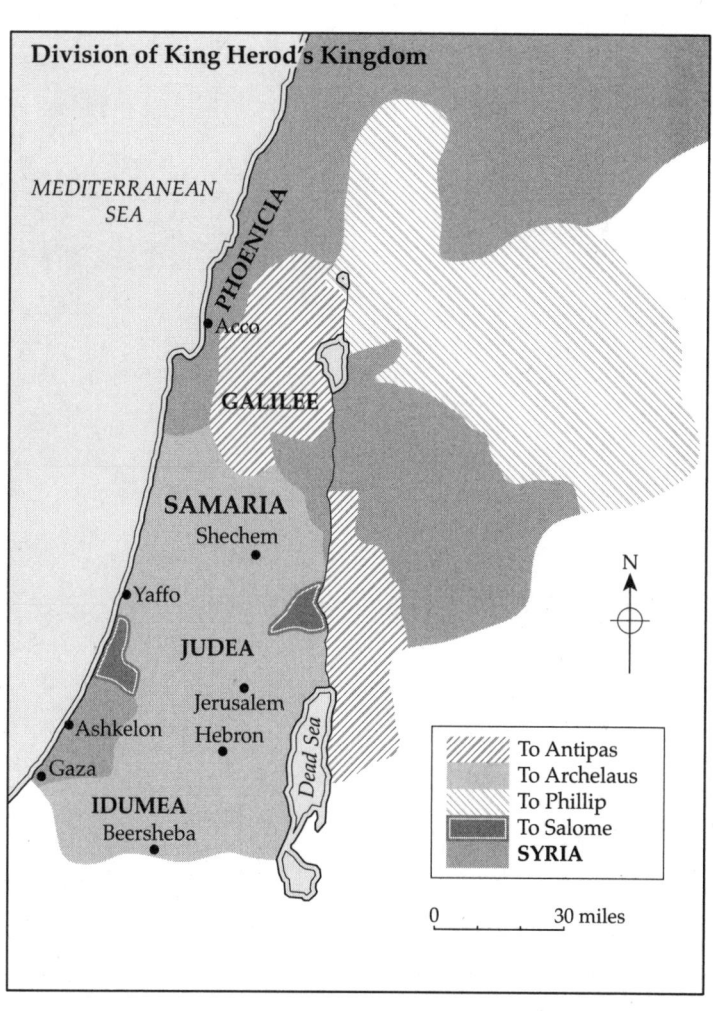

FOREWORD: DR. EINAT WILF

For decades, but particularly since October 7, 2023 and the subsequent global rise in antisemitism, the Jewish people and various aspects of Jewish identity have been under attack. Jewish history is being deliberately rewritten, erased, and hijacked, and the Jewish people are being defined by a hostile world in order to retroactively justify the hostility. As part of this ongoing attack, the central feature of the deep Jewish connection to the Land of Israel is being erased. This makes it urgent that Jews stand against these efforts and insist on the foundations of the Jewish story. It is precisely why *The Jews: An Indigenous People* by Ben M. Freeman enters this conversation at such a critical moment in Jewish history.

Ben goes back to the basics, reminding us all that Jewish indigeneity is a vital concept, not just for the past and present, but for the future of the Jewish people and the future of the Jewish people in their state and in this world. With a powerful and unapologetic voice, Ben continues his mission to build Jewish pride, rooted in the centrality of Jewish peoplehood to the Jewish identity. As with his previous writings, he refuses to let the non-Jewish world define the Jewish story, especially when that story is deliberately diminished, distorted, and erased.

As the culmination of his Jewish Pride trilogy, this book empowers Jews to see themselves as the modern inheritors of an ancient and proud civilization. It confronts the inaccurate and Christian-framed understanding of Judaism as simply an unrooted faith. To be Jewish, regardless of where one lives, is to be rooted in the Land of Israel, in the stones of Jerusalem, and in the language of Hebrew.

While the Jewish connection to the Land of Israel was once widely accepted and respected, it has been under assault since it became clear that Jews have developed the gall to actually expect political rights of self-determination that express their indigenous connection to the land. But after decades of a concerted and, unfortunately, successful campaign, rooted in Soviet propaganda, to posit Zionism as synonymous with the world's evils, and the creation of what I have to term Palestinianism, as the ideology that deliberately erases and supersedes the Jewish connection with the land, Jews are no longer viewed as a people native to the Levant, and are misrepresented as a mere religious group and, in a bizarre inversion, a colonial force with no indigenous claim to the land.

Ben's work reasserts a truth that has been obscured in recent years: Jews are not foreign interlopers who wandered into the Middle East to seize land. At their core, and regardless of the Diaspora, Jews are Levantine. The Levant is where Jews originated, developed, and remained rooted physically, spiritually, and culturally for thousands of years. As Ben makes clear, it is possible to have multiple identities; to live in the Diaspora does not diminish Jewish indigeneity.

Most importantly, in this book, Ben reminds us that to be indigenous, even according to the legal definition, is not simply to live in a place for a long time; rather, it is to have one's entire culture, calendar, rituals, language, idioms, and sacred time connected to one land and one land only. In this sense, the Jews are not just indigenous to the Land of Israel, they epitomize what it means to be indigenous.

Regarding the power of this book in the non-Jewish world, to accept Jewish indigeneity is to understand that Israel, as a Jewish state, is the modern political expression of an ancient bond between a people, an entire culture, and a land. As long as this bond is denied, the prospects for peace are null. The path to peace depends on acceptance of Jewish indigeneity, on the flipping of the false prism of Jews as foreigners to the land, to the true one of Jews as indigenous. This ideology, which I have come to term "Arab Zionism"—the Arab and Islamic political, cultural, and theological embrace of the Jewish people's right to self-determination in its ancestral homeland—is the only idea and attitude that would bring true peace to the region. For peace to be achieved, Arabs and Muslims must recognize, through their own religious texts and traditions, the deep and undeniable Jewish connection to the Land of Israel. From this recognition must come an understanding that Zionism and the State of Israel are not foreign impositions or colonial projects, but the modern manifestations of ancient Jewish indigeneity. Only on this basis can true peace be built.

Arab Zionism is an affirmation of the Jewish people's inherent right to self-determination in their indigenous homeland, rooted within a proud Arab and Muslim historical framework. This understanding is essential to fostering genuine coexistence, mutual respect, and lasting peace. A future in which Jews and Arabs live with dignity, security, and shared purpose depends on this recognition.

Just as this book is essential for the Arab world and the journey toward peace, it is equally vital for Jews around the globe who are on a road of self-discovery. It gives Jews, and our non-Jewish allies, the language to better articulate who we are, and our deep connection to the Land of Israel.

As Ben advocates, Jews must continue the work of decolonization. In 1948, we decolonized our indigenous land after 2,000 years of foreign rule. But the decolonization Ben calls for is internal, a mental and cultural liberation. Jews must come to understand their identity free from the distortions imposed by non-Jewish societies, distortions that constantly demand that Jews reshape themselves as the price of acceptance. We must stand tall and proud, defining our Jewishness through a Jewish lens. *The Jews: An Indigenous People* is a guide to that self-liberation.

In writing this book, Ben M. Freeman has given its readers a gift. It is a gift to Jewish readers who refuse to minimize their Jewishness and are searching for a way to live with pride and authenticity, and it is a gift to non-Jewish counterparts seeking to understand what it truly means to be Jewish.

My hope is that this book will shift the conversation, both within and beyond the Jewish community, that it will spark change and lead us toward healing. Modern Jews are the contemporary heirs of an ancient civilization, and it is time we understood it, embraced it, and claimed it.

PROLOGUE

"Don't forget the pomegranate!" my mother, Sarah, called after my father, Malcolm, who had been tasked with collecting fruit for Rosh Hashanah, the Jewish New Year.

As we often did, we were hosting friends for a celebratory meal at our home, and the pomegranate held particular significance. Along with wheat, barley, grapes, figs, olives, and dates, it makes up the *Shivat Haminim*—the seven species of fruit (featured on the cover of this book) mentioned in the Torah as native to Israel. Historically, bringing these to the Temple in Jerusalem was considered a great *mitzvah*—a commandment in Jewish law, often understood as a good deed.[1]

Speaking to Jews around the world, I have found that many of us ate pomegranates at Rosh Hashanah. This fruit was always significant to me on a personal level. It was a poignant indicator of my difference from those around me. Although I attended Calderwood Lodge Jewish Primary School (the only Jewish school in Scotland), I went to a non-Jewish high school. In the U.K., without a separation of church and state, our public schools were often Christian. My peers attended school assemblies in a church, and Christianity formed the foundation of the school's culture. Being Jewish, I always felt different from those around me. I knew that we observed different holidays, ate different foods, and even spoke a different language—Hebrew—in synagogue and in various classes I took. Few of them routinely ate—or would have attached any significance to—pomegranates.

All this is to say, I understood that although I was born in Scotland, that wasn't where I was rooted. The pomegranate, very much not native to Scotland, helped me understand where I could truly call home. To this day, after living in Scotland, Hong Kong, and London, the place where I feel I most belong is Israel.

I understood—even when I didn't have the language to articulate it—that my family and my people are indigenous to Israel. Though I didn't know it then, my deep emotional connection to Israel, eating the pomegranate, speaking Hebrew, observing Shabbat, facing Jerusalem when we prayed in synagogue, keeping kosher, living by the Hebrew calendar, and celebrating Jewish holidays (like Rosh Hashanah, Pesach, or Shavuot, which all began as agricultural holidays) were all manifestations of Jewish indigeneity.

The Jews are indigenous to the Land of Israel. This means we originated and are rooted there, and for thousands of years, up to this very day, we maintain a deep and emotional connection with the land itself and the cities built upon it. This perspective isn't meant to replace biblical views on Jewish identity but to support them. It is a layer of our identity that already exists; we just need to uncover it.

Today, however, Jewish indigeneity is maliciously disputed, but despite this, it accurately represents our experience and our relationship to Israel and to each other. While notions like indigeneity aren't inherently Jewish concepts, they can describe our story just as they describe that of others. When Jews speak of our connection to the Land of Israel, we call it our "homeland" or "ancestral land." We refer to it as "the promised land" and even "the land of milk and honey." But what do they represent for our relationship with Israel today, and how does it define us?

Although the Jewish people still belong to an active, evolving civilization, to truly understand Jewish identity, we must go back to the beginning of our story. One of the most powerful realizations any young Jew will have is that we are part of an unbroken chain that stretches back thousands of years. When I heard the stories of Pesach, the tribes of Israel, or the Second Temple, I knew they were the history of my people. This continuity is the essence of indigeneity. The Jewish people are at an important crossroads, and although my study began long before the horrific events of October 7, the ensuing war against Hamas, and the wave of Jew-hate that swept the Diaspora, this exploration has become more necessary than ever. As I've written before, we have a choice. We can continue allowing the non-Jewish world to define us, remain unclear about who we are, or we can explore who we were—who we have always been—so that we can define our identities and live them today.

The truth is, we are indigenous. We should recognize it. We should live it. And we should be proud of it. It is our story. Now let's tell it.

...

Since 2021 and the release of my first book in the Jewish Pride trilogy, I have defined the broad aims of Jewish Pride as to inspire, empower, and educate the Jewish people.

I hoped *Jewish Pride: Rebuilding a People* would inspire Jews to wear their Jewishness as a badge of honor and to enable them to understand the need for Jews to define Jewish identity.

Reclaiming Our Story: The Pursuit of Jewish Pride was aimed at empowering Jews to identify, reject, and heal from internalized anti-Jewishness, the plague afflicting our people.

When considering how to conclude the Jewish Pride trilogy, I knew it had to deepen Jewish understanding of our experience and identity, empowering Jews to define our identity for ourselves. It cannot be that Jews just reject non-Jewish notions of who and what we are; we must be knowledgeable and confident enough to define our own identities. We must know our story. This book, *The Jews: An Indigenous People*, aims to educate Jews on our origins, our relationship to the Land of Israel (which I define as the territory of the Israelite tribes, as well as the later Kingdoms of Israel and Judah), Judaism, our indigenous culture, and each other, as well as an understanding of how they shape our identity today. If *Reclaiming Our Story* aimed to help Jews take back control of our narrative, this book is that narrative.

INTRODUCTION

For thousands of years, the Jewish connection to and relationship with the Land of Israel was understood and acknowledged. Both to Jews and non-Jews, from a religious and a secular perspective, our roots were understood. In *Bereshit* (Genesis), the Torah states that God promised Avraham and his descendants the Land of Israel. For 2,000 years following the Jewish expulsion from Jerusalem, the Jewish connection was clear with Jews—despite many living in the Diaspora—remaining rooted and focused on Eretz Yisrael. Due to this, the primary identification of the Jews was as a people, an *Am*. And the Europeans—and Arabs—in whose midst we lived understood that the Jews were a specific people, belonging to a specific land.

Later, in selecting the Land of Israel as the site of the soon to be Jewish state, the early Zionists acknowledged that Israel was the home of the Jews. The Balfour Declaration similarly spoke in 1917 of the need for the "establishment in *Palestine* of a national home for the Jewish people [my italics]." And when declaring Britain's Mandate of Palestine in 1922, the League of Nations agreed, stating "… recognition has thereby been given to the historical connection of the Jewish people with Palestine and to the grounds for reconstituting their national home in that country."[1] The operative phrase here being "reconstituting," and as professors Ilan and Carol Troen wrote, "The 're' meant 'again.' Jews were entitled to re-turn, re-build, re-store, and re-establish themselves in their historic homeland."[2] At this point, Jewish indigeneity was not a contested political issue, it was simply a statement of fact.

However, threats to the connection between Jews and Israel began following the emancipation and the "acceptance" of Jews into many Western societies in the 19th century. This period saw the beginnings of the denial of Jewish peoplehood: The Jews came to be seen as a people defined by faith, in the Christian sense of the word. In the United States, the Reform Movement's 1896 Pittsburgh Platform specifically shed the status of Jews as a nation (and one seeking to return home), instead imposing upon them a Christianized religious identity. In 1937 this radical act of antizionism was abandoned by the Reform Movement, but the damage was already done to Jewish identity and non-Jewish perceptions of what it means to be a Jew. This attempt to deny that Jews are a nation, not simply a religious group, continued—and was greatly intensified—in postwar Soviet and Arab propaganda. And, despite the end of the Cold War, these ideas have proved an enduring and pernicious legacy of the Soviet Union—with a political impact which today has spread far beyond the realms of the far left, seeping into elements of broader left thinking, academia, popular culture, and the wider public discourse.

Particularly after the Six-Day War (June 5–10, 1967), the Soviet Union, alongside its Arab allies, embarked on a campaign to delegitimize the State of Israel. They set out to cast Israelis, and by extension all Jews, as colonizers without a prior connection to the land before the establishment of the state. The Palestinian National Charter: Resolutions of the Palestine National Council July 1–17, 1968, rebuked the Balfour Agreement, arguing: "The Balfour Declaration, the Mandate for Palestine, and everything that has been based upon them, are deemed null and void. Claims of historical or religious ties of Jews with Palestine are incompatible with the facts of history and the true conception of what constitutes statehood. Judaism, being a religion, is not an independent nationality. Nor do Jews constitute a single nation with an identity of its own; they are citizens of the states to which they belong."[3] For the Palestinian movement, it was thus not enough to assert their right to self-determination and statehood; they had to deny that the Jews were even a people worthy of a state of their own. Ultimately, as Tal Fortgang and Hannah E. Meyers argued in *Commentary*, the narrative is: "Israel is colonialist or that Jews are white Europeans"[4] because "Jews are not 'native' or 'indigenous' to the Levant." (The subregion that borders the Eastern Mediterranean Sea to the west and West Asia—or the Middle East—to the east.)

Modern Palestinian leaders have continued this trend, describing themselves as "indigenous," delegitimizing Israel, and denying the Jewish connection to the land. In 2011, for instance, Ekrima Sabri, the former Jerusalem mufti and chairman of the Supreme Islamic Council in Jerusalem, stated: "After 25 years of digging, archaeologists are unanimous that not a single stone has been found related to Jerusalem's alleged Jewish history."[5] This is an obvious lie, but it has spread around the world before the truth of Jewish indigeneity has even put on its shoes.

Despite initially languishing on the far left and the extremes of the political spectrum, these ideas have become mainstream. Look at events since the Hamas atrocities of October 7, 2023. On college campuses, in the media, on the streets of our cities, and online, Israel—and the Jews—has been delegitimized. This discourse is not focused on the establishment of a Palestinian state alongside the State of Israel, it is focused on the destruction of the Jewish state. Zionism, the Jewish indigenous rights movement aimed at restoring self-determination in our ancestral homeland, the Land of Israel, has been demonized and falsely equated with white supremacy, apartheid, colonialism, and imperialism. This is justified because, in the minds of Jew-haters, Israel is nothing but a colonial entity and the Jews no more than a European people bound only by faith. For some, this is perhaps the result of ignorance; but for most it is the propagation of a deliberate lie, one which perverts Jewish identity, and Ashkenazi identity specifically, while completely ignoring and erasing Sephardic, Mizrahi, or Beta Yisrael Jews.

Some Jews seek to combat this narrative by highlighting the fact that Israel is majority Mizrahim and Beta Yisrael. This may be understandable, but it is the wrong approach, and it is harmful as it inadvertently presents Ashkenazi Jews as European and, therefore, not indigenous. And it is why a study on Jewish indigeneity is so vital. I began researching and writing this book long before October 7, but since those horrific events, an understanding of the totality of the Jewish connection to the Land of Israel has become even more crucial.

The denial of Jewish nationhood and the mainstreaming of extreme Soviet antizionism is a direct attack on authentic Jewish experience and identity. When we assert our indigeneity, we affirm our commitment to the truth. As part of my work on Jewish Pride, I have always said that only Jews can and should define Jewish identity, and that non-Jewish definitions of what it means to be a Jew are illegitimate. I stand by this, but for Jews to define our identities, we must first understand and know our history and experience. That so many of us lack knowledge about our experience is a great tragedy for the Jewish people, and one which threatens our very survival. As Daniel J. Elazar, the Israeli academic, wrote: "We can now see throughout the Jewish world, including Israel, that it takes almost no time for a civilization to be disrupted by lack of proper education of its new generations."[6]

By providing Jews with knowledge, and an understanding of our experience and status as an indigenous people, this study will allow Jews to define our own narrative. In a post-October 7 world, this is a form of resistance. But this is important beyond October 7 and the shocking rise in antisemitism. Jews are the inheritors of a great civilization, one which has survived intact for over 3,000 years, and only because our ancestors committed themselves to its survival. And this responsibility now belongs to modern Jews.

Ultimately, I believe that Jews must reorient our understanding of what it means to be a Jew, reaffirming our connection to the Land of Israel. That is where we began. It is where we continue to be rooted. It is our home. And it is the core of who we are as a people.

Despite the continuing assault by the antizionist left, we must hold to this simple truth. As the journalist Charles Krauthammer reflected in 1998:

> "Israel is the very embodiment of Jewish continuity: It is the only nation on earth that inhabits the same land, bears the same name, speaks the same language, and worships the same God that it did 3,000 years ago. You dig the soil and you find pottery from Davidic times, coins from Bar Kokhba, and 2,000-year-old scrolls written in a script remarkably like the one that today advertises ice cream at the corner candy store."[7]

This study is an exercise in rediscovering what it means to be a Jew while reclaiming our story. Only after accomplishing that can we build lasting and multigenerational Jewish Pride. Only then can we rebuild our people.

MY AIM

This book aims to provide the definitive account of Jewish indigeneity, exploring Jewish history from an archeological and epigraphic (relating to words) perspective. Its goal is to enable all Jews to confidently say, "This is our story."

As I have always stated, Jew-hate is not a Jewish problem. It is a non-Jewish problem which impacts Jews, just as homophobia is a heterosexual issue which affects the gay community. This then means allies are crucial to defeating the scourge of antisemitism. For allies to support Jews, however, they also need to be informed of our identity and understand our experience, through our perspective, not through theirs. Particularly post-October 7, for non-Jewish people to support Jews, they must understand our connection to the Land of Israel, and why it is our home, even if many of us live in the Diaspora.

Tragically, Jewish understanding of our own history is woefully lacking, and because of this, many Jews fail to understand Jewish identity. As a minority living amongst a majority, the resulting power dynamic means we have adopted ways of thinking or identity from the majority around us that do not naturally fit our own. In recent years, we have also been influenced by American cultural colonialism, which hinders our understanding of human experience and history, shaping our identity within a racial binary of black and white. I have encountered this obstacle when explaining Jewish indigeneity to others. I felt the need to explain the lightness of my skin tone, as it often acts as a barrier to people understanding that, despite my appearance, I am indigenous to the Land of Israel. Another challenge I face is the fact that my recent ancestors were Ashkenazi Jews. Because they lived in Central and Eastern Europe in exile, people often labeled me as European. The indigeneity of Ashkenazi—their forebears' journey from the Land of Israel to exile in Europe, their experience of persecution and mass murder, and their return to the State of Israel—is often diminished, even from within our own community. It is these misconceptions that we must powerfully reject by asserting our right to define our own identities and to tell our own stories.

Zionism is often rightly described by its supporters as a decolonization movement, which saw an indigenous people reclaim sovereignty in their land 2,000 years after they were mostly expelled. Today, we must also work to free our minds and our perspectives. The Jewish people were colonized successive times and, following our expulsion from our capital, we lived in other lands under the rule of other people. Living in these worlds, their ideas, their norms, their contexts impact how we see ourselves. This is natural, but we must not lose sight of our understanding and expressions of our identities. We must free ourselves from the shackles of misunderstanding which lead us to misconstrue our own identities.

Chapters 1–4 of this book explore the origins and history of the Jewish people. Entire books are written on brief periods of Jewish history, so I am aware it is an enormous undertaking to condense roughly 1,300 years of our history into just four chapters. However, it is crucial for every Jew—and those who wish to support us—to have even a brief understanding of our history. As I explained, I am focusing my study on archeological and epigraphic evidence while exploring the historicity of the Torah. My study is not in any way designed to diminish the significance of the Torah, or the stories it contains. The Torah—as we will explore—is the Jewish constitution, containing our laws and our history. Even if there are stories that are not 100% rooted in historical fact, that does not render them unimportant. They contain historical memory; they are our founding myths and are how we—both in ancient times and today—form ourselves as a collective around specific ideas, laws, and understandings.

Following our historical study, we will explore Jewish indigeneity through an analysis of the United Nations' seven criteria for indigeneity (based on José Martínez Cobo's 1983 "Study of the Problem of Discrimination Against Indigenous Populations"[8]) as well as my own definition, which I will offer in this chapter. Despite the controversy surrounding the UN, particularly in its treatment of Jews and Israel, the UN provides the only established definition of indigeneity, making it a necessary component for our purposes. It is also gratifying to explore how an organization which excludes Jews created criteria which actually explain and demonstrate our indigeneity.

As we have done in all books in this trilogy, we will once again defer to the lived experiences of Jewish individuals. Contrary to the perception of Jews in the non-Jewish world, we are not a mere idea or a concept whose sole purpose is to play a role in the non-Jewish world for non-Jewish people. We are not the "canary in the coal mine." We are not the

"Blind Man in the Mirror," as Augustine of Hippo wrote.[9] We are real people, part of a tangible collective. And to truly grasp how these ideas impact and influence Jewish reality, we must give voice to those who experience it. Finally, in our conclusion—and the conclusion of the Jewish Pride series—we will explore in detail how Jewish indigeneity impacts our identity as well as how it fits into wider ideas of Jewish Pride.

THE PALESTINIANS

I am sure there are some who will argue, and perhaps a few will even genuinely believe, that this work is an attempt to delegitimize the Palestinian right to statehood. I support the establishment of a demilitarized Palestinian state alongside a safe and secure Israel within recognized borders; a Palestinian state that does not harbor and reward terrorists or antisemites with genocidal aspirations; that does not incite Jew-hate or deny the Jewish people their right to self-determination in our historic home; and that recognizes the importance of coexistence, compromise, and conciliation. This book is not a commentary on the Palestinian people or their aspirations for statehood. It is a book about Jewish identity, Jewish history, and the Jewish connection to the Land of Israel. All of these exist independently of the Palestinians. I am a Jew writing about Jewish identity and experience. And that is my right.

DEFINING AND DEPOLITICIZING INDIGENEITY

One of the challenges in utilizing the term "indigenous," which I hope to overcome, is that it is loaded with political connotations. Unfortunately, for many, the term does not simply denote a group of people originating in a land and maintaining a connection to it. Instead, it often implies marginalization and primitiveness. This unfortunate association has the effect of disempowering groups who self-identify, or are identified, as indigenous.

These connotations gained prominence in the 1960s and 1970s, during the era of decolonization when the world—according to the New Left—was split into oppressed or oppressor. During this period, indigeneity began to encompass not only the idea of "firstness" but also notions of a lack of development and the experience of oppression.

The notion of "firstness" (i.e. being the first in a particular place) is itself a complex criterion to insist upon when identifying indigeneity. Many indigenous groups do utilize the idea of firstness in their identity, as seen in Malaysia with the term "*bumiputera*,"[10] which refers to "sons of the soil." However, this concept becomes complicated due to the tumultuous nature of human history. There are many "first" peoples who simply no longer exist. For example, the descendants of the Canaanites live on in modern-day Jews and Lebanese, but there are no modern Canaanite identities today. Moreover, the Canaanites were actually not the first people in the Levant either. Therefore, firstness must be recognized as a complicated criterion and cannot always serve as a reliable indicator of indigeneity. We should not dismiss it entirely, however; instead, we should consider where groups, as a collective, emerged and where they have remained rooted. In this sense, indigeneity signifies a historic and continued connection.

As anthropologist Manvir Singh notes in his 2023 *New Yorker* article, "It's Time to Rethink the Idea of the Indigenous," being the first in a place does not necessarily mean you would be counted as indigenous.[11] Singh points out that even though a handful of Gaelic monks and then the Vikings were the first people to arrive in Iceland (settling there earlier than the Māori arrived in New Zealand), their descendants are rarely described as indigenous. Furthermore, the Maasai people claim to be indigenous but do not claim to be the first inhabitants. According to Maasai oral history, their ancestors arrived from an area likely in the South of Sudan only a few centuries ago.

The notion of "firstness" can also be problematic, as Singh notes, because "a politics built around indigeneity, as many [indigenous] organizers fear, can reify ethnic boundaries."[12] While indigeneity must be respected, and indigenous peoples should ideally govern their own territory, the concept should not be used to establish a hierarchy that excludes or diminishes others. It should never be used to justify racist ideas like Blood and Soil,[13] which promotes a noxious vision of ethnic purity rooted in the land. That is abhorrent, and while indigenous people do have a special relationship with their land, we must reject and condemn supremacist ideas which would harm or displace non-native peoples. Jewish indigeneity should not be used to diminish the human rights of anyone living in the State of Israel. While the Jews are indigenous to the land, non-Jewish citizens of the country, as the Declaration of Independence asserts, must be treated equally. Thankfully, modern Israel is a democracy and the rights of all its citizens are protected by law, and while it is a Jewish state, it is, importantly, not just a state for Jews.

In the case of the Jews, the claim to indigeneity doesn't rest on their being there first. We acknowledge that other people inhabited the Levant before the origins of the Jews. This fact is well documented and is acknowledged in the Torah, which describes Jews defeating the Canaanites in battle (although we will explore the historicity of this claim in the next chapter). Jews are indigenous to the Land of Israel because, while not the first inhabitants, it is where the Jewish people collectively emerged, developed, and remained rooted for thousands of years, even after many—but not all—were exiled. As indigenous activist Ryan Bellerose argued in 2017: "Indigenous status stems from the genesis of a culture, language, and traditions."[14]

The New Left claims linking indigeneity to marginalization and alleged primitiveness are less complex but more problematic and can take the form of colonial abuse. Singh describes a conversation with a teacher from the Huottüja community in Colombia regarding his thoughts on the word "indigenous." The teacher replied that it describes his people as "savage, like wild animals."[15] In this sense, the notion of indigeneity is being misused. As Joanne Barker, professor of American Indian Studies in the College of Ethnic Studies at San Francisco State University, notes in her 2001 book *Native Acts*, such intrinsic associations make it "impossible for Native peoples to narrate the historical and social complexities of cultural exchange, change, and transformation—to claim cultures and identities that are conflicted, messy, uneven, modern, technological, and mixed."[16]

There is no inherent or logical reason why indigenous people can't be modern and technologically minded. To understand the complexity of indigeneity, one must first accept that, as with all groups, there will be diversity. Indigeneity is a descriptor which applies to people stretching from the Aboriginal tribes in Australia to the Sámi people in Scandinavia, and as such there is an assortment of manifestations of this idea. This diversity is significant when considering the Jews as an indigenous people. As we will see, the political associations attached to indigeneity deter some Jews from using this term to describe Jewish identity. We must therefore have a clear idea of what it means to be indigenous and avoid falling into traps of defining indigeneity based on stereotypes of indigenous groups. This point was illuminated by the United Nations itself when creating its criteria on indigeneity. They acknowledged the difficulty in creating one definition due to the diversity of indigenous peoples, which is why they created criteria to identify rather than define indigenous people. Therefore, Jews are indigenous to the Land of Israel in the same way as the Māori are indigenous to New Zealand, even if our experiences differ.

Similarly, the notion that indigeneity inherently signifies marginalization lacks nuance. It is often the case that indigenous communities have been colonized and, as a result, lost sovereignty and their rights. That was the experience of the Jews for thousands of years. But what happens to an indigenous group if they are able to reclaim sovereignty over their land? Surely, they do not cease to be classified as indigenous. When the Jews founded the State of Israel, they were decolonizing the land. They achieved what many other indigenous peoples long to do. This should be celebrated rather than seen as the negation of indigeneity. The notion that indigenous people are inherently oppressed is deeply problematic as it strips agency from indigenous people and ignores the resilience, strength, and power that exist within these communities. This is unethical. Of course, these qualities are not meant to deny the extreme poverty rates, lack of education, or the experience of colonization seen in indigenous communities around the world. Rather, we must emphasize the complex reality—the diversity and varied historical experiences—underpinning a word so often stripped of crucial nuance.

DEFINING INDIGENEITY: THE BEGINNING OF A CONTINUING, ROOTED STORY

In coming to a definition, it is best that we start with the etymology of the word itself. The word "indigenous" stems from the Latin "*indigena*," meaning "native" or "sprung from the land."[17] I interpret this as referencing both the beginning of a people's story and their relationship with the land itself. "Sprung from the land" implies a symbiotic relationship. I will base my definition on the following questions:

1. Is this where a group's story began?
2. Is the group rooted in the land?
3. Does the group maintain its historic connections and culture in modern times?

Is this where a group's story began?

When considering this question, we have to be precise about what constitutes the start of a story—not an iteration of a story but its first chapter. Let's take the United States as an example. Excluding Native Americans, the story of most Americans can be dated from 1776 and the Declaration of Independence, or earlier when their ancestors arrived on the continent after 1491. But that is not where their collective stories began. They began elsewhere in the world. They were brought to the country as slaves from Africa, for example, or they emigrated from Europe or Asia. And although they built a country with a specific culture, when able they maintained a connection to their personal culture and their personal story. Italian Americans are an example of this. They are—by definition—both Italian and American.

We can also apply this logic to the Jewish experience. My Ashkenazi ancestors lived in Eastern Europe, but that is not where their story began. Even though Yiddish culture greatly influenced their lives, that culture was a geographically specific iteration of our indigenous Jewish culture. Yiddish was, after all, written with Hebrew letters. My ancestors prayed and spoke in Hebrew. They followed Jewish customs stemming from the Land of Israel. They were living Jewish indigeneity. Eastern Europe is not where this story began, even if important—and often tragic—chapters of the story unfolded there.

Is the group rooted in the land?

A significant part of indigenous culture, across the board and in all its diversity, is a connection to the land itself, beyond sovereignty or national borders. Without this connection, there is no such thing as indigeneity. We can obviously identify groups with a collective identity, but the specific component of indigenous identity is that they are rooted in a particular land. All indigenous groups have a unique connection to a specific land, which goes far beyond utilitarian-based land ethics. As stated by Working With Indigenous Australians, "The land is a spiritual part of the Aboriginal people and you cannot separate one from the other."[18] The land of an indigenous community constitutes a core aspect of their identity and cultural practice. This applies to the Jewish experience, even in the Diaspora. Jewish communities around the world continue to practice customs and celebrate festivals—such as Tu Bishvat (also called Rosh Hashanah La'Ilanot—literally meaning New Year of the Trees—and considered one of four Jewish new years) among many others which began life as agricultural holidays in the Land of Israel. We still live our lives via our ancient calendar and when praying, we thank God for rain (in Israel), even if we live in particularly rainy places, like Scotland. There are also specific *mitzvot* (commandments) only applicable when living in the Land of Israel. The relationship between a people and their land is crucial in defining indigeneity.

Do they maintain their historic systems, culture, and practices in modern times?

Part of what constitutes indigeneity is the continuation of a distinct historic culture and the fundamental rules of life—or "living systems" as they are technically termed—(and all that entails) into modern times. Can a group truly claim to be indigenous if their collective bears no resemblance to that of their ancestors? For this reason, indigeneity is far more complex than a matter of genetics (as we will explore). It is not the case, as we discussed previously, that a group must be "primitive" or that their culture must be completely unchanged from that of their ancestors'. Of course, cultures can evolve, but there should be a continuation of a cultural identity and a direct link—through practice, culture, and living systems—from the origins of a people's story right through to modern times. Again, take the Jews. As a collective, Jewish people still celebrate the same festivals that their ancestors did thousands of years ago. Many of us still eat according to the same dietary laws and live by the same laws that our ancestors lived by thousands of years ago, albeit in a modern setting. Indeed, regarding the State of Israel, the 1955 Israeli government yearbook said, "It is called the 'State of Israel' because it is part of the Land of Israel and not merely a Jewish State."[19] This continuity is an integral component of identifying indigeneity.

These three questions can help us define indigeneity with nuance and complexity while enabling us to recognize the diversity of this experience. Therefore, building on them, I propose the following definition of indigenous identity:

> "An indigenous people are a group whose collective identity began in one specific land, and it is in that land they remained rooted (either physically, spiritually, or culturally). This is their home and is where they originated, developed, and continued to be fixed through a connection to the environment and natural resources, living systems, culture, and practices as a people, irrespective of their sovereignty in the land."

TRIBAL MEMBERSHIP AND BLOOD QUANTUM

The connection between indigeneity and ancestry is complicated, and one with which many indigenous communities grapple. North American indigenous tribes, for instance, contend with the notion of blood quantum. Dating back to 1705 when the Colony of Virginia adopted the "Indian Blood law," which determined the percentage of one's "indigenousness" based on the percentage of your ancestry classed as having full tribal membership.[20] This was a strategy employed by American and Canadian governments in legislating indigenous identity, assessing the amount of indigenous blood an individual has and using it to create categories such as half or quarter indigenous, thus defining official tribal membership. Originally utilized during the allotment period, when indigenous individuals were granted land allotments on a reservation, the usage of blood quantum limited tribal membership and, as such, limited the amount of land owned by indigenous tribes and individuals.[21]

Despite its controversial origins imposed by colonizing forces, there are still indigenous communities such as the Navajo Nation who still use blood quantum to govern their membership, while others use it in combination with other criteria.[22] There is great diversity of opinion as to how blood quantum is perceived and utilized by indigenous nations. The Indigenous Foundation, an organization focused on raising awareness of the indigenous North American experience, has described blood quantum as "genocidal"[23] because, due to intermarriage, "indigenous blood" will be diluted, potentially leading to the extinction of indigenous tribes.

One can draw a comparison between the notion of blood quantum and the 1935 Nuremberg Laws, which the Nazis utilized to legislate Jewishness based on blood. They established categories of Jews, such as half-Jew, quarter-Jew, and eighth-Jew, extending all the way to one-sixteenth Jew (representing one Jewish great-grandparent).

Given this history, it's understandable that some Jewish individuals are wary of utilizing ideas of Jewish blood when defining Jewish identity. Like many indigenous tribes who grapple with the implications of blood quantum, Jewish communities face complex questions about ancestry, identity, and belonging that cannot be easily reduced to biological or genetic criteria, particularly as conversion is a permitted route to becoming Jewish. That said, we must also acknowledge the fact that it is possible to trace Jewishness through one's genetics. That does not in any way validate or justify the Nazis' beliefs. Rather, it is simply recognizing a basic biological reality. Furthermore, genetic ancestry does not solely determine Jewishness, but it does contribute to our understanding when investigating our history and origins.

Like other peoples, we must address this issue when discussing Jewish indigeneity, especially concerning notions of tribal membership.

We must base our understanding of ourselves not just on narratives or myths, but on demonstrable facts. Jews originated in the Middle East and, following our ethnic cleansing from Jerusalem in 136 CE, eventually spread to the four corners of the globe, while always maintaining a constant presence in the Land of Israel. During our time in Israel and then in exile,

Jews often practiced endogamy, which involves reproducing within one's own community, thus creating enough shared DNA to establish and maintain a distinct group. This, of course, was not a hard-and-fast rule. Admixture, or genetic mixing, did occur in several Jewish communities through intermarriage, conversion, and, unfortunately, rape.

It seems that, within Ashkenazi communities at least, women were more likely to have converted while men were born from Jewish ancestry. As Martin Richards, an archeogeneticist at the University of Huddersfield in England, has stated: "The simplest explanation was that it was mainly women who converted and they married with men who'd come from the Near East."[24] This is known due to studies on mitochondrial DNA, which is passed on by the mother, tracing the maternal line to Europeans, while the paternal line can be traced to the Middle East.

Study after study confirms a genetic connection between various Jewish communities, irrespective of their geographical diasporic location, and the Land of Israel. A 2010 study led by Rambam Medical Center in Haifa and the Technion (Israel Institute of Technology) confirms that "90% of Jews are genetically linked to the Levant."[25] This does not mean, of course, that 100% of the 90% is traceable to the Land of Israel. However, the fact that even a portion of Jewish ancestry can be traced back to our indigenous land 2,000 years after many of us were expelled is deeply significant.

However, due to Nazi ideology, biological racism, and concepts like blood quantum, the conversation surrounding Jewish ancestry is fraught with difficulty. We must walk a tightrope. On one hand, we must recognize it as a fact, while on the other, we must not place too much emphasis on it, especially when defining Jewish membership.

The United Nations' Declaration on the Rights of Indigenous Peoples guarantees the rights of indigenous people to define their own membership. It states: "Indigenous peoples have the right to determine their own identity or membership in accordance with their customs and traditions.

This does not impair the right of indigenous individuals to obtain citizenship of the States in which they live."[26] On this matter, Jews are no different. Membership in the Jewish people is governed through *Halacha* (Jewish law), which dictates that one is Jewish if they have a Jewish mother.[27] Liberal Judaism recognizes equilineal descent, considering those born to either a Jewish father or a Jewish mother as Jews.[28] Like other indigenous tribes, Jews also have mechanisms to banish those who are seen to have transgressed.[29] Although still present in Jewish law, this is more of a historic practice. Baruch Spinoza, for example, was famously issued a *Cherem* (exclusion) in 1655–56 for defying rabbinic authorities.

Surprisingly, the relationship of conversion to indigeneity is not as controversial as it might initially appear. Other indigenous communities also permit non-indigenous individuals to join their ranks, and Jews are no different. When one converts, they become part of Am Yisrael, the people of Israel, accepting Jewish law and adopting our customs, traditions, and practices. They make a choice to become inheritors of the great Jewish tradition alongside those born to Jewish parents and, because of this, can be counted as indigenous, regardless of their own genetic makeup.

Consider Ruth, the most famous Jewish convert, as told in *Megillat Ruth* (the Book of Ruth) in *Ketuvim* (Writings) in the Tanakh. She wasn't converting to Judaism as a religion since there is no concept of religion in the Torah, and there was no conversion process at that time (this emerged much later). Instead, she joined the Jewish people and essentially naturalized as a citizen. When reflecting on her statement "For wherever you go, I will go; wherever you lodge, I will lodge; your people shall be my people, and your God my God"[30] we must remember that YHWH—the Hebrew name for God revealed to Moses in *Shemot* (the Book of Exodus)—was a national God, a God linked to a specific people in a specific land.[31] Therefore, Ruth was essentially saying, "Your people are my people, your God is my God, and this land is my land." This is why, while we must recognize Jewish ancestry as a reality, we should not overstate its importance in defining Jewish identity and Jewish indigeneity by extension. This is why the Indigenous Foundation rightly describes indigenous membership more widely as "holistic."[32]

JEWS AGAINST JEWISH INDIGENEITY

There are some Jews who argue against Jewish indigeneity, but they are not in possession of all the facts and either misunderstand Jewish history, the meaning of the word indigenous, or both.

Take, for instance, Brooklyn-based Rabbi Andrue Kahn, who in July 2020 tweeted: "Let me say this as plainly as possible: Jews are not an indigenous people. It is appropriative to make use of this word when referring to our relationship to the Land of Israel, and it undermines the difficult work being done to fix the ongoing oppression of indigenous peoples."[33]

It seems that Kahn does not understand the complexity and nuance surrounding indigeneity and has fallen into the trap set by the New Left in the 1960s of seeing indigeneity as synonymous with oppression. As we discussed earlier, there is simply no reason why an indigenous people cannot be in positions of power and strength. To imply otherwise, and to paint indigenous groups with a broad brush, destroying our diversity, is a manifestation of the racism of low expectations. It also contradicts rhetoric from other indigenous communities, thus stripping them of their agency. This narrow definition not only erases Jewish indigeneity, it also places other indigenous peoples in boxes that may not define their experiences, while stripping them of independence and power.

This mindset was also evident in a cartoon published by the left-wing *Jewish Currents* magazine entitled "When Settler Becomes Native,"[34] which attempted to suggest that Jews claim indigeneity to legitimize Israel and delegitimize the Palestinian claims to statehood.

Similarly, in a 2021 article in *Haaretz*—"Bio-Zionism: Why Claiming Jews Are Indigenous to Israel Is So Dangerous"—journalist Abe

Silberstein argued that indigeneity is used to assert a superior Jewish claim to the land. Silberstein's argument is based on the notion that indigeneity is solely rooted in a genetic connection to a land. Some bad faith actors attempt to interpret it this way but, as we know, this is not necessarily the case. Silberstein's arguments demonstrate a misunderstanding of the wider conversation taking place with regard to indigeneity, tribal membership, and blood quantum. Silberstein also argues that Jewish indigeneity "is not just about asserting the Jewish connection to the land but asserting a superior claim"[35] to the Palestinians. We should reject this notion. The Jews are indigenous to, and have a right to self-determination in, the Land of Israel, and this has nothing to do with the Palestinians or their right to self-determination. They are not mutually exclusive.

JEWISH INDIGENEITY

Jews are indigenous to the Land of Israel. Acknowledging this fact is not intended to replace biblical ideas such as the promised land; rather, it offers us a multifaceted understanding of this relationship. The truth is that this anthropological concept can uncover layers of meaning to our identity and our perceptions of ourselves.

Throughout this Jewish Pride series, I have emphasized that Jews must define our own identity. However, many Jews remain woefully ignorant about our own history, leaving us vulnerable to outside manipulation. There are entire populations of Jews who define themselves solely as a religion or even deny or erase any Jewish connection to the Land of Israel. I have been at dinner tables where Jews describe themselves as originally Arab or Polish. This misunderstanding of the Jewish story threatens our survival and must be addressed.

The right of groups to define their own identity—with specific regard to indigeneity—is underscored by the International Labour Organization.

The first article from their Indigenous and Tribal Peoples Convention, 1989, states: "Self-identification as indigenous or tribal shall be regarded as a fundamental criterion for determining the groups to which the provisions of this Convention apply."[36] Jews are indigenous, and we have the right to define our identity and assert our indigenous status. Despite this, Jewish identity is also under attack from the wider world.

At its core, Jewishness has been distorted by external forces, reflected through what I call the "Broken Mirror of Jewish Identity." The non-Jewish world, with its power and privilege as the majority, feels entitled to dictate to us what it means to be Jewish. They impose notions of "acceptable" Jewishness onto us.

Never has this been clearer than following the October 7 massacre when Jewish identity has been repeatedly defined by the anti-Jewish Left, with Zionism presented as a genocidal cult, forcing many Jews with no choice but to reject their Zionism.

As I explained in *Reclaiming Our Story*, in the Diaspora we are a minority group and, as such, less powerful than the majority. The categories of Jewishness deemed acceptable by the wider world warp our perceptions of ourselves. Historically, we were told we should be just a religion and abandon our nationhood, so we could "integrate" as citizens. We did as the non-Jewish world commanded but this did not save us from persecution, pogroms, and genocide.

Today, with the Holocaust still in living memory, Jewish concepts such as Zionism have been bastardized once again by the non-Jewish world. But it is not too late for us to reclaim our story. The Land of Israel is our indigenous land, and thus Zionism is an indigenous rights movement. For almost 3,000 years, our land was colonized by successive empires, from the Assyrians in 721 BCE—through the Greeks, Romans, and Ottomans—to the British in 1918 CE. Despite these occupations, we never lost our connection to our land. We remained rooted in the soil, even as we were forced to scatter across the world. We retained much of what made us unique and what tied us to the Land of Israel. And throughout it all, we never stopped yearning—and working—to return home. And return we did, in 1948. The rebirth of the modern Jewish state is nothing short of a miracle. Yet, the wider world tells us it is something to be ashamed of and reject. This lie must not be tolerated.

In *Jewish Pride*, I described the relationship between Jews and the non-Jewish world as toxic and even abusive. Like any other unhealthy or abusive relationship, we must free ourselves from its grasp. We will not change ourselves or warp or diminish our identity beyond recognition to be accepted. We will not define ourselves based on non-Jewish expectations or perceptions of who we should be, how we should act, or what we should believe. Jewish action and Jewish life are not antithetical to modernity or our membership in other societies. We must define our own identity and live authentically as Jews. We must know our own story and be confident enough to tell it.

Indigeneity reminds Jews that we are a unique, distinct civilization bound to a specific land. We have a legal system, a culture, a language, traditions, and a national God. Like other indigenous peoples, we cannot be stripped from our land. We see the deep, enduring relationship that all indigenous people have with their homelands, and we are no different. As we will explore later, Jewish festivals still celebrated today—Rosh Hashanah, Sukkot, Pesach, Shavuot—were all rooted in the harvest cycle our ancestors participated in in Israel. Every Shabbat morning, we gather to hear the Torah—our legal code and history book—read aloud, a practice that has continued for 2,000 years even in the darkest of times, and one which originates in Israel. Many of our names (such as Daniel, Joshua, Ruth, Miriam, and surnames like Cohen or Levi) are the same as our ancient ancestors and we all have specific names, in Hebrew the indigenous language of the Jews. We follow the same calendar our ancestors utilized thousands of years ago. Despite our many evolutions and our diversity, we are in many ways the same people we were thousands of years ago. This is the explanation for the very survival of the Jewish people. We retained our ancient connections and carried them with us wherever we went—whatever the challenge, persecution, or hatred we faced.

Indigeneity enables us to understand this enduring relationship to each other and to our land. Ultimately, the question must be—particularly one asked in this specific book series—how this impacts our identity and our perceptions of ourselves. And it must. It must impact how we see ourselves. Jews living in Israel must recognize they are expressing their indigenous rights and are living in their indigenous land. And Jews in the Diaspora must acknowledge they can belong to multiple societies and have dual (or more) identities but should also understand they are indigenous to the Land of Israel. Understanding and activating our indigeneity also aids Jews in navigating our identities and the tensions that often arise from being diasporic. While we have an inherent connection to our indigenous land, diasporic Jews were not born in the Jewish state. And while we were born and lived in other countries with their own distinct cultures, we are still—at our roots—an indigenous people. This presents specific challenges, not least because of the immense amount of Jew-hate that exists in the Diaspora. As Ijeoma Umebinyuo, the famed Nigerian poet, wrote in "Diaspora Blues":

> So, here you are
> too foreign for home
> too foreign for here.
> never enough for both.[37]

As the original diasporic community, this is also the experience of diasporic Jews. It is one that makes integration into the Diaspora difficult, but at the same time it can make integration into modern Israeli society difficult. There is no easy solution to this issue. And this, as Umebinyuo described, is something that all diasporic communities grapple with. It is yet another challenge diasporic Jews must face. The only way to come to terms with this challenge is to accept ourselves and our indigenous identities to better make sense of our challenges.

As Jews—even if we don't realize it—we express our indigeneity all the time, from keeping kosher to visiting Israel to circumcising our sons. Our practices and customs connect us to our land and our history constantly. Acknowledging indigeneity helps us make this connection conscious and can strengthen Jewish identity. Jews are a people indigenous to the Land of Israel. We are inextricably bound to it and this bond cannot be severed. We must acknowledge this, and we must teach this to our children. We must say to each other and to the wider world with confidence: "We are Jews and we are indigenous to the Land of Israel."

Chapter 1

A HISTORY OF THE JEWS AND OUR LAND:
IN THE BEGINNING

It may have become a controversial notion in the latter half of the 20th century, but it is a historical fact that Jews originated in the southern Levant—modern-day Israel and the West Bank—specifically in the Land of Israel. Initially, they were named Israelites, and then following the destruction of the Northern Kingdom of Israel in 720 BCE, they also became known as Judahites, named after the surviving southern Israelite Kingdom of Judah.[1]

Modern Jews are a people descended from these Israelites and Judahites (whom we shall refer to collectively as ancient Israelites) who lived in the Near East (or Middle East, as it is known today) thousands of years ago. They believe in one God, and belong to a unique civilization, expressed through Judaism, their indigenous culture.

The word "Jewish" itself indicates the origins of the Jewish people. "Jew-ish" is made up of "Jew," originating from "Judah," and "ish," the old English word meaning "from the country of."[2] So, in the case of Jews, when we ask, "What's in a name?" the answer is "Everything." Even when we consider the word "Judaism," it began life not as a name for the Jewish religion and the specific worship of the Jewish God, but to indicate practices and behavior that defined Judahites, i.e. those who came from Judah. As we will explore later, it was first mentioned in the Second Book of Maccabees and was conceived in opposition to Hellenism. Rabbi and Hebraist Shaye J.D. Cohen argues: "We are tempted, of course, to translate [*Ioudaismos*] as 'Judaism,' but this translation is too narrow, because in this first occurrence of the term, *Ioudaismos* has not yet been reduced to the designation of a religion. It means rather 'the aggregate of all those characteristics that makes Judaeans Judaean (or Jews Jewish).' Among these characteristics, to be sure, are practices and beliefs that we would today call 'religious,' but these practices and beliefs are not the sole content of the term. Thus, *Ioudaismos* should be translated not as 'Judaism' but as Judaeanness."[3] It is therefore interesting that so much of the literature about the ancient Jewish people, particularly following their expulsion from Judah by Babylon in 586 BCE, focuses on Jews as a religious group, as this is a retroactive reidentification of the Jewish people. At this time, although there certainly was the worship of a deity, the Jews were a nation, and that is how they would have conceived themselves.

It is this perspective that is central to this book. I will focus on the Jewish people and their practices. In that sense, I am interested in "Judaeanness," as Rabbi Shaye J.D. Cohen calls it, or "Jewishness" in a modern sense—viewing Judaism as a culture that contains religion, rather than as a religion in itself. Acknowledging the Jews as a *people* is fundamental to understanding this work. Jews are not, nor have we ever been, merely a group who share a belief in God. We are a people, and, as a collective, we worship a national God. A national God is worshipped by a specific ethnic group in a specific land. However, due to our status as a people, secular or atheist Jews are just as Jewish as those who describe themselves as religious. For some Jews, accepting this fact requires a kind of mental recalibration.

Although we have a God, Jews really only became identified as "just" a religious group as a way to fit into the 19th-century post-emancipatory European world, which guaranteed them rights if they shed their nationhood. This conception of Jews as a "religious" group was rooted in the attempt to view the Jewish people through a Christian prism, as the concept of religion is not one which naturally occurs in Jewishness. In the period of modern nation-state building, as Stanislas Marie Adélaïde, Comte de Clermont-Tonnerre, a French nobleman, put it, "the existence of a nation within a nation would be threatening."[4] Thus, in order to be accepted into post-revolutionary France, Jews began to reject their nationhood. However, to truly understand Jewish identity—as a people and a nation with a God (or as a people with a religion)—one must view the Jewish people through a Jewish lens. This involves rejecting non-Jewish attempts to force Jewish identity into categories that fit external worldviews.

At the outset, we must acknowledge the tension between "maximalist" and "minimalist" perspectives of the Hebrew Bible. Maximalists argue that the Bible is largely true, while minimalists argue the opposite.[5] For some, these perspectives have become almost ideological approaches. This is unwise, at least from a scholarly perspective. As historian Sir Simon Schama wrote in *The Story of the Jews: Finding the Words, 1000 BC–1492 AD*, "It is already apparent that the 'minimalist' view of the Bible as wholly fictitious and unhooked from historical reality, may be as much of a mistake as the biblical literalism it sought to supersede."[6] To understand our history, we have to approach it objectively and without bias. We should not be working to prove from a preordained view whether the Tanakh—the acronym for Torah (the Five Books of Moses), *Nevi'im* (Prophets), and *Ketuvim* (Writings)—is true or not. We should instead view it as vital initial source material. If there is sufficient evidence to suggest that stories contained in the pages of the Hebrew Bible aren't rooted in historical fact, then we should accept that evidence. But this does not need to diminish its importance. It is our law, our history, and, yes, it contains our founding stories. And these stories have immense value whether or not they represent historical fact or mere memory. And, like all people, we Jews should be able to tell our own stories and mythologize our origins.

WHAT IS THE BEGINNING?

The origins of the Jews differ depending on who you ask. Those who believe the Torah's narrative argue that Abraham came to Canaan (modern-day Israel) from Ur (modern-day Iraq), and God gave his descendants the Land of Israel. *Bereshit* (Genesis) Chapter 15 documents this promise: "On the same day the Lord made a covenant with Abram, saying: "To your descendants I have given this land …"[7] Abraham then fathered Isaac, whose son, Jacob, was the father of Joseph (he of technicolor dreamcoat fame, who was one among twelve other children). Joseph was then bundled off to Egypt by his jealous brothers, where he eventually came to prominence as an advisor to Pharaoh Sesostris I. Driven out by famine in Canaan, Joseph's brothers and their families traveled to Egypt seeking refuge. Despite a period of prosperity, their descendants were eventually enslaved by the Egyptians, under the decree of Pharaoh Ramses II. According to the Torah, Moses (a young Israelite descendant of Abraham, brought up at the court of Pharaoh) heard the voice of God in a burning bush and ultimately freed his people. This is the Exodus story, and one Jews all over the world still celebrate to this day during the holiday of Pesach.

After receiving and accepting the Torah at Mount Sinai and becoming a nation, the ancient Jews—led by Moses—wandered in the desert for 40 years on their journey towards their promised land. But Moses' death meant it was to be Joshua who eventually led the Israelites back to Canaan. Under his leadership, the Israelites conquered Canaan and set up camp there. Eretz Yisrael, the Land of Israel, was then divided among the descendants of Jacob's sons, now organized into twelve tribes named for them: Reuben, Simeon, Ephraim, Judah, Issachar, Zebulun, Dan, Naphtali, Gad, Asher, Manasseh, and, last but certainly not least, Benjamin (my namesake).

These tribes were a confederation loosely overseen by a series of *Shoftim* (judges). In 1047 BCE, this period then gave way to the United Monarchy of Israel, established and first ruled by King Saul, followed by the mighty King David, and lastly by King Solomon. In 930 BCE, following King Solomon's death, the kingdom split into two: the Kingdom of Israel in the north (encompassing parts of modern-day Lebanon, Syria, Israel,

IN THE BEGINNING 31

and Jordan) and the Kingdom of Judah in the south (modern-day Israel and the West Bank).

The stories of Abraham, Isaac, and Jacob are deeply significant as a way for our people to collectively understand our origins, as is the notion that God promised Abraham the Land of Israel. This itself is a marker of our indigeneity to it. However, *proving* the events up to the establishment of the independent Kingdoms of Israel and Judah is extremely difficult due to scant archeological and epigraphic evidence outside of the Tanakh.

Israel Finkelstein, the famed Israeli archeologist, argues that the stories of the Jewish patriarchs—Abraham, Isaac, and Jacob—were really separate "local traditions"[8] from the Southern and Northern Kingdoms compiled into one story. The Jacob Cycle is told in *Bereshit* (Genesis). Finkelstein argues it evolved in Bethel, Gilead, and perhaps Shechem, in the Northern Kingdom of Israel.[9] These stories were then brought to the Kingdom of Judah (where the Torah was compiled and edited) after the Kingdom of Israel was destroyed in 720 BCE by Assyria. Given that Jacob was given the name Israel by God, Finkelstein's belief in his association with the Northern Kingdom isn't so far-fetched. Meanwhile, stories of Abraham and Isaac are said to come from the Southern Kingdom of Judah. Abraham is centered around Hebron and Mamre (in the highlands south of Jerusalem), while the stories of Isaac are rooted in Beer Sheva and Sheplah. As Finkelstein describes it, all were then compiled into the story of one family, the patriarchs of the Jewish people to speak to a singular root for all Israelites, thus reinforcing Israelite identity.

While there is much we cannot prove, what is certain (and demonstrable by archeological and epigraphic evidence) is that the Jewish people emerged during the latter parts of the Bronze Age (dated from 3300–1200 BCE). We know this to be the case because of the Merneptah Stele, an inscribed stone, discovered in 1896 by Flinders Petrie, the British Egyptologist, at Thebes, Egypt.[10] Created to celebrate the victory of Pharaoh Merneptah (son of Ramesses II, who reigned between 1213 and 1203 BCE[11]), the last three lines mention something incredibly significant, at least to the Jews. Although mostly celebrating the Egyptian victory in Ancient Libya, line 27 of 28 is said to be the first extra-biblical (beyond the Tanakh) mention of the word "Israel" in recorded history. It states: "Israel is laid waste—its seed is no more."[12]

Crucially, the hieroglyphs in the Merneptah Stele describe the Israelites as a people. While Ashkelon, Gezer, and Yanoam are given the determinative for a city—a throw stick plus three mountains—the hieroglyphic symbols used to describe Israel instead feature the throw stick and a sitting man and woman.[13] These choices indicate a difference in the fundamental characteristics of those referenced. Ashkelon, Gezer, and Yanoam are cities, while Israel at that point represented a presumably nomadic or semi-nomadic people.[14] It is also worth noting that the name "Israel" seems to derive from the Canaanite deity El (as does Azri'el, Bethel, etc.), not YHWH, who would later become the national God of the Israelites. Therefore, at this period, we can assume that the chief deity of the Israelites was not YHWH; rather, it was El, which also—as we will explore—gives us clues to the Canaanite origins of the ancient Israelites.

Although the Merneptah Stele was inscribed during the end of the Late Bronze Age (1595–1155 BCE) and beginning of the First Iron Age, dated from 1200–1000 BCE, the Jews can obviously date the origins of our story to a slightly earlier period, given we were established enough in 1208 BCE to be mentioned. In fact, recent discoveries suggest that another slab, housed in the Egyptian Museum of Berlin and predating the Merneptah Stele by 200 years, contains an even older reference to Israel (also referencing Ashkelon and Canaan, making the likelihood that this is a reference to Israel ever more possible).[15] Dating to around 1400 BCE, this seems entirely plausible because, just 200 years later, "the ancient Israelites," as suggested previously, warranted a mention in the Merneptah Stele. Whether or not this recent discovery is accurate, we know for certain that, by 1208 BCE and the inscription of the Stele (the end of the Bronze Age), a distinct people known as Israel existed in the Levant.

Up to this point, from around 1457 BCE, the Land of Canaan was ruled by Egypt. The lowlands of the southern Levant were populated by many small city-states ruling over smaller territories. However, in the highlands (north of Jerusalem) we see several larger territorial city-states (Jerusalem, Shechem, and Hazor) with relatively empty lands.[16] When discussing the Canaanites, it is worth noting that they were not homogenous; there were disparate groups of people living in the land with their own customs, gods, and administrative centers.

That we can date the first mention of the word "Israel" to 3,233 years ago (and perhaps even earlier) is truly remarkable, and one that should be significant to all Jews. It is the first time in history we—as a people—are mentioned by someone outside of our own records. It is also an inspiring symbol of Jewish continuity. Israel, the name of the people mentioned in 1208 BCE, was also the name of an independent ancient Jewish kingdom and is the name of the modern Jewish state that sits in our indigenous lands. It is also the name that we, as a Jewish collective—including those of us who still live in the Diaspora—refer to ourselves as: Am Yisrael, the People of Israel.

EXODUS FROM EGYPT?

According to the Torah, despite an inauspicious start, Joseph lived well and powerfully in Egypt, but his descendants were ultimately enslaved by the pharaohs for 430 years. After receiving his instructions from God, via the burning bush, Moses led 2 million Israelites from bondage to freedom. That story, and the eventual receiving of the Torah at Mount Sinai, are the origins of a unified Jewish nation. So, when assessing the beginning of our peoplehood, we must investigate the historicity of this founding Jewish narrative. We are not exploring whether these events happened exactly as the Torah describes. The figures alone seem to suggest that this is almost certainly not the case. Instead, we should focus on whether any ancient Israelites were enslaved in, or even by, Egypt. To argue it happened in a different way than the manner in which it was presented is not the same as arguing it did not happen at all. In a sense, that is how I approach many of the stories described in the Torah. They represent nuggets of truth, memories, or were based on fact, but then, like so much else in history, have been retold, exaggerated, and extrapolated in order to speak to a greater goal, i.e. the formation of our collective identity. Thomas Romer, professor at the College de France and the University of Lausanne, seems to share this thinking, arguing: "The Exodus is not a historical event, but it's also not totally invented by someone sitting behind a desk. These are different traditions that are brought together to construct a foundation myth, which can be, in a way, related to some historical events."[17]

Many scholars date the Exodus story to the 13th century BCE. However, at this point, Egypt was at the height of its power, and its control reached far beyond the modern borders of Egypt. Indeed, the Merneptah Stele references a people known as Israel living in Canaan in the 13th century BCE. As such, Israel Finkelstein explains, "The Exodus story in the Bible doesn't reflect the basic fact that Canaan was dominated by Egypt, it was a province with Egyptian administrators."[18] Finkelstein also argues that the Exodus story—along with the story of Jacob—is actually a tradition from the Northern Kingdom of Israel, which was later brought to the Southern Kingdom of Judah after the fall of Israel.

Discussing the Exodus story in the *Reform Judaism* magazine, Rabbi S. David Sperling labels it "fictitious."[19] This is most likely a little too strong. Nonetheless, Sperling also asserts that references to the Egyptians enslaving the Israelites are, in fact, describing the period when Egypt controlled Canaan; therefore, the ancestors of the ancient Israelites were enslaved not *in* Egypt, but *by* Egypt.[20] Israeli historian Nadav Na'aman agrees with

Sperling that the history which inspired the Exodus story actually took place in Canaan during the harsh period of Egyptian rule.

Romer suggests that the truth of the Exodus surrounds a group known as the Shasu, a nomadic Semitic-speaking tribe from the southern Levant, which was later absorbed by the Israelites. What is the connection between the Shasu and the Israelites? The Shasu worshipped YHWH, who would become the Israelite national God. On the Soleb Inscription, a temple devoted to the worship of Amun-Ra at Soleb in Nubia (modern-day northern Sudan) dated from the 15th century BCE, a pillar stands with the depiction of a prisoner with the words, "The land of the Shasu of Yahweh."[21] This seems to be the first mention of YHWH in history. Archeologist Titus Kennedy writes of the relationship between the Shasu and Israelites: "Since the only ancient people known to have worshipped a deity named Yahweh in ancient times were the Hebrews or Israelites, it also logically follows that these particular Shasu nomads associated with Yahweh could be identified with the early Israelites before they became a sedentary population in Canaan."[22] And as Romer suggests, "There may have been groups of Shasu who escaped somehow from Egyptian control and went north into the highlands to this group called Israel, bringing with them this god whom they considered had delivered them from the Egyptians."[23] This is a compelling argument given the fact both peoples worshipped YHWH.

However, while some others acknowledge that the Exodus did not occur exactly as it was written (i.e. with 603,550 men leaving Egypt[24]), they still believe these events took place in Egypt. Richard Elliott Friedman, author of *The Exodus*, argues there is clear evidence there were Western Asiatic people in Egypt during this period.[25] However, instead of a wholesale Israelite exodus from Egypt, it was only the Levites (representing the Tribe of Levi descended from Levi, the third son of Jacob and Leah, a subset of whom—the Kohanim—became the ancient Israelite priests in the temples) who left Egypt before joining up with the rest of Israel.[26]

Friedman's argument of ancient Israelites in Egypt seems to be corroborated by the fact that three Egyptian names—which are also mentioned in the Torah—fell out of use around 1085 BCE, the beginning of Egypt's Third Intermediate Period. The Egyptian names are Pi-Ramesses, Pi-Atum, and (Pa-)Tjuf, while their corresponding names from the Torah are Ramses, Pithom, and Yam Suph (Reed Sea). These three names only appear together in Egyptian texts during the Ramesside period (1292–1077 BCE), which from a chronological perspective does tally with the timing of the Exodus Story. The timing could thus mean that a group of Semitic-speaking people (the Levites, according to Friedman) were in Egypt, eventually leaving before joining the newly formed Israelite collective. It is also the case that the four-room house—common to groups living in Canaan—were also found in Egypt.[27] Furthermore, it is also possible that the ancestors of those who would become the ancient Israelites could thus have been enslaved in Egypt, and this story was passed on, and eventually became part of the Israelite narrative, as it was the experience of their ancestors, but prior to the formation of a distinct Israelite identity.

The first mention of the Exodus story in the Torah is in the *Shirat Hayam* (Song of the Sea) in *Shemot* (Exodus). Notably, this poem is written in a form of Hebrew much older than that used in the rest of the *Shemot*.[28] It is also believed to have been composed around 100 years after the supposed Exodus, when the memories were still relatively fresh, so to speak. *Shirat Hayam* mentions no numbers of freed slaves, nor that they passed through a wall of water. However, the reference to "Pharaoh's chariots and his army He has cast into the sea,"[29] suggests that a catastrophe befell the Egyptians who were pursuing them. There is no mention of Israel in this text, it only refers to "am" (people as a collective) and "People of Yahweh." This evidence suggests that the Torah recalls historical memory, the lived experience of real individuals in the 13th century BCE.[30]

But if this story is completely fiction, it is worth asking why the ancient Jews would have rooted their national origins in slavery. This does not seem a particularly inspiring or empowering origin story. If this story were completely false, then surely those putting pen to paper would have chosen something more glorious? William Dever, a professor of Near Eastern archeology and anthropology at the University of Arizona, argued the Exodus story was "produced for theological reasons: to give an origin and history to a people and distinguish them from others by claiming a divine destiny."[31] But why can't both be true? Why can't there be truth to the Exodus story *and* the fact it was an experience used to reinforce a national identity? Either way, it does seem the case that a collective closely related to the ancient Israelites were enslaved either by Egypt or in Egypt and that this story was then utilized to reinforce the emerging Israelite identity around the time of the 12th century BCE.

ENTER ISRAEL

The Torah tells us that, following the Exodus from Egypt, the Israelites invaded Eretz Yisrael and defeated the Canaanites. And with this, they established Israelite sovereignty in the Land of Israel. The Book of Joshua reports:

> "Joshua struck all the land, the hill country and the Negev and the lowland and the slopes and all their kings. He left no survivor, but he utterly destroyed all who breathed, just as the Lord, the God of Israel, had commanded ... He left nothing undone of all that the Lord had commanded Moses."[32]

Investigating the Torah's account is frustratingly difficult from an archeological or epigraphic perspective. As K. L. Noll notes in *Canaan and Israel in Antiquity: A Textbook on History and Religion*, "If the quest for the early Philistines was difficult, the search for the early Israelites is even more so."[33] The difficulties arise due to the lack of hard evidence and the fact that the events we are seeking to examine took place thousands of years ago. As a result, there are a number of competing theories regarding this element of our ancient origins.

Interestingly, there is archeological evidence which seems to contradict the Torah's perspective on how the Israelites came to control the Land of Canaan. The famed walls of Jericho—brought down by the sound of the shofar[34]—did indeed fall. But archeological findings suggest they fell 150 years earlier than the Israelite story began, around 1500 BCE.[35] However, if the ancient slab of rock in the Egyptian Museum of Berlin is true, then perhaps the Israelites did, in fact, exist in this period. It is also possible that the stories of the tumbling walls of Jericho are related to those who eventually developed into the ancient Israelites and were incorporated into the Tanakh as a result.

The Torah's reference to Joshua utterly destroying all who "breathed"[36] is also open to question as there is evidence which suggests this is not the case. Indeed, in 2020 a study found that the Canaanites were not completely destroyed by Joshua and his forces.[37] Geneticists have discovered that the DNA of ancient Canaanites lives on in modern Jews and Lebanese people in the region. In fact, they are said to "owe more than half of their DNA to Canaanites."[38] This obviously makes the destruction of the Canaanites a fictitious account of the Israelite settling of the land.

But this then begs the question as to how the Israelites came to be in, and controlling, the Levant.

Various perspectives exist. The one that seems to be the most accurate is the notion that, over a period of time, the Israelites emerged as a distinct identity, splitting from the Canaanites and migrating from the lowland city-states into the highlands above Jerusalem. Thus, instead of arriving from some other land and migrating to or conquering the land, ancient Israelites were initially part of a diverse Canaanite community. These Canaanite communities were descendants of those who populated the Levant during the Chalcolithic Era from 4500–3500 BCE. As Mark Smith noted in *The Early History of God: Yahweh and Other Deities in Ancient Israel*, "The record would suggest that the Israelite culture largely overlapped with and derived from Canaanite culture."[39] There is a degree of evidence—including archeological continuity between findings at Israelite and non-Israelite sites—to support this perspective. For example, the four-room houses (previously mentioned), so often associated with the ancient Israelites, are said to have been located in non-Israelite settlements in Canaan as well, such as in Tell Keisan.[40] It is also the case that Paleo-Hebrew—the script used to write Ancient Hebrew, which we will explore further in Chapter 6 and which dates from the 10th century BCE—developed directly from Phoenician, a Canaanite language.[41] It was only after the 6th century BCE that the Aramaic (block letters) script was gradually adopted to write Hebrew. Indeed, archeologist Mary Ellen Buck, author of *The Canaanites: Their History and Culture from Texts and Artifacts*, argues: "The Bible claims that these are distinct and mutually antagonistic groups, yet there's reason to believe that they were very closely related."[42]

However, a major difference exists between the Israelites and Canaanites: the worship of YHWH, which was likely a catalyst for the parting of the ways. We know that our ancient Israelite ancestors worshipped Canaanite deities, including El (the chief Canaanite deity and, if we interpret "Israel" correctly, the original chief God of the Israelites), Asherah (his wife), and Baal,[43] and they also, as we know, worshipped YHWH (spoken as *Adonai* in Hebrew, literally meaning "my Lord").

But the question remains: Where did the worship of YHWH originate, as he was not a Canaanite god? A theory exists—known as the Kenite hypothesis—which argues YHWH originated in Midian, a territory or a collection of tribes in what is today Saudi Arabia. Although there is no universal agreement amongst scholars, it is suggested by biblical studies researcher Nissim Amzallag that YHWH was one of the many gods worshipped in the southern Levant.[44] Karel van der Toorn agrees with this notion, arguing, "By the 14th century BC, before the cult of Yahweh had reached Israel, groups of Edomites and Midianites worshipped Yahweh as their god."[45] One specific notion is that YHWH was worshipped by the Midianite Semitic-speaking nomadic group known as the Shasu, as referenced in the previous section on the Exodus. The geographical origins of YHWH are referenced by the Tanakh in *Sefer Habakuk* (the Book of Habakkuk), one of twelve books of Minor Prophets. Discussing the power of YHWH, it states: "As a scene of havoc I behold / The tents of Cushan; / Shaken are the pavilions / Of the land of Midian!"[46] and that YHWH "came from Teman" in Edom in modern-day southern Jordan.[47]

Although the ancient Israelites didn't live as far south as Teman, they either encountered YHWH through traders or through "a long-term process"[48] of cultural exchanges which existed between people in the regions. YHWH was also spoken of as a warrior-like storm god. It was a common practice in the Near East for gods to have specific attributes, like controlling the weather. *Devarim* (Deuteronomy) suggests YHWH's Edomite origins and his weather-related power when it recalls, "O GOD, when You came forth from Seir, / Advanced from the country of Edom, / The earth trembled; / The heavens dripped, / Yea, the clouds dripped water."[9]

From 1457 BCE to around 1200 BCE, Egypt controlled Canaan, but during this period, political turmoil led to the erosion of its control. Coinciding with the Late Bronze Age collapse, the Canaanite city-state system was destroyed. The extent of this societal collapse cannot be underestimated. In *1177 B.C.: The Year Civilization Collapsed*, Eric Cline wrote, "The magnitude of the catastrophe was enormous; it was a loss such as the world would not see again until the Roman Empire collapsed more than fifteen hundred years later."[50] But this process was not just centered around 1177 BCE; it continued for at least a century. And it eventually led to the reorganization of the region and a new world order with new territorial kingdoms which were, at least for a period, independent of great empires.

Around this period, presumably in response to the upheaval,[51] the Israelites began splitting off from the rest of the Canaanite community focused around the worship of El, YHWH, Asherah, and Baal.[52] In *The Early History of God: Yahweh and the Other Deities in Ancient Israel*, Mark S. Smith argues that a process of convergence and differentiation began.[53] According to Smith, "Convergence involved the coalescence of various deities and/or some of their features into the figure of Yahweh."[54] The Israelite God was known by a number of names in the Torah, most commonly referred to as YHWH or El, or sometimes both. This fusion can be seen to be explained in the Torah, such as in *Shemot* (Exodus) where God says to Moses, "I appeared to Abraham, Isaac, and Jacob as El Shaddai, but I did not make Myself known to them by My name YHWH."[55] Meanwhile, differentiation saw Israel reject aspects of its Canaanite heritage. According to Smith, another development of Israelite monotheism focused on differentiating itself from its historic Canaanite heritage. This process is said to have begun with the rejection of Baal in the 9th century BCE. This continued in the 8th century BCE with the legal condemnation of the worship of Baal.[56]

The Mesha Stele, a Moabite inscription dated from 840 BCE, makes a clear reference to YHWH and his connection to the Kingdom of Israel (referred to via its dynasty as the "House of Omri').[57] It states: "I took from there the hear[th] altars of Yahweh."[58] Crucially, YHWH became the national God of the ancient Israelites, further underscoring our identification as a nation, people, and civilization.

It's possible that after splintering from Canaanite populations, the Israelites—as suggested by the Merneptah Stele's description of them as a people, as opposed to a city—were nomadic or semi-nomadic for a period.[59] In "The Nomadic Idea and Ideal in the Old Testament," John W. Flight notes, "unmistakable traces of that origin survive in the succeeding life of Israel. The nourishment which was furnished by this nomadic taproot has gone into the formation of certain characteristic traits which show themselves in all the later life and thought of Israel."[60] This notion of a nomadic tradition within the ancient Israelites is endorsed by the Torah itself. In *Bereshit* (Genesis), when Joseph is reunited with his brothers, he describes them as "shepherds."[61] Shepherds in Canaan (and presumably elsewhere) were nomadic, at least for part of the year, in order to source enough food and water for their livestock.[62]

The question as to why these ancient Israelites became nomadic following their split from the Canaanites remains a valid one. Perhaps, as Israel Finkelstein suggests, it was part of a pattern where different ways of life became dominant due to "economic, geopolitical, and administrative situations."[63] This implies that sometimes groups were more sedentary (though not necessarily fully sedentary), and then there were periods when they were less so. Another possibility is that a disparate collection of Canaanites who began to worship YHWH assembled, and without lingering ties to a specific city-state, they began "sojourning,"[64] as the Torah described in *Shemot* (Exodus). Alternatively, the collapse of the Canaanite city-state system may have led to a period of nomadic lifestyle among the ancient Israelites before they eventually settled in the northern highlands. It's also plausible that this nomadic lifestyle was part of the splitting-off process itself.

TRIBES, JUDGES, AND KINGS

By the time of the inscription of the Merneptah Stele, in the late 13th century (1200 BCE), the ancient Israelites had begun to settle in territory in the highlands north of Jerusalem. This settlement may have been influenced by natural patterns of sedentary living and climate change, as well as the collapse of Egyptian rule in Canaan and the Canaanite societal collapse. According to Finkelstein, there was a wave of settlement which "means that the sedentary population grew to at least four times its size."[65] At that point, according to Finkelstein and Silberman, a "social transformation" began and "in the formerly sparsely populated highlands from the Judean hills in the south to the hills of Samaria in the north, far from the Canaanite cities that were in the process of collapse and disintegration, about two-hundred fifty hilltop communities suddenly sprang up. Here were the first Israelites."[66]

According to the *Sefer Shoftim* (Book of Judges), ancient-Israelite society was organized into twelve tribes, which were the descendants of Jacob. These tribes—according to *Devarim* (Deuteronomy): Reuben, Simeon, Levi, Judah, Issachar, Zebulun, Dan, Naphtali, Gad, Asher, Benjamin, and Joseph[67]—were each allotted a specific territory in the Land of Israel. They were then arranged into a loose confederation, ruled by a Judge chosen by God, and shared an overarching Israelite identity.

This formation of ancient-Israelite society, like much else in the Torah, is rooted in historical truth. As Zachary Thomas states: "While many of the Levantine polities under Egypt's overlordship were centralized around a single settlement and ruled by a single paramount individual, there were also instances of polities allying together as a collective, under an overarching political identity but with collective decision-making."[68] Similarly, Lester L. Grabbe argues in *The Dawn of Israel*, "... everyone seems to agree that the 12-fold system is an artificial creation, but that does not mean that the tribes as such are an artificial creation."[69] Ancient Israelites had settled north of Jerusalem, living on hilltops, and their towns were, for the most part, unwalled. For protection, these communities were part of a greater network with a ruling chieftain. They appear to have been organized in what would constitute a tribe.

The notion that the tribes are named after a specific son is not necessarily accurate. Instead, they were clans, or smaller communities in a specific geographical area personified by an individual, which eventually merged to become one people—the Israelites. As Grabbe suggests, "references to tribes were usually a reference to a geography."[70] The concept of kinship and community based on geography was not unique to Israelite society but rather a common feature across many societies in the Middle East during that time. Zachary Tomas in *Israel's Political and Administrative Structures* writes, "Israel was not unique in the ancient Near East in having a segmentary structure made up of social units that were conceived as types of an extended family."[71]

The concept of the twelve tribes being direct descendants of twelve sons likely developed later as an ideological construct. However, this development holds significance for our understanding of indigeneity. It reveals that over 3,000 years ago, the ancient Israelites already had a perception of themselves as distinct and connected to a shared heritage. This process of myth-making, evident in many cultures and civilizations throughout history, plays a vital role in shaping collective identity. Consider how Jews today express their Jewishness through retelling stories that may not align perfectly with historical events but are integral to our shared identity and connection to our past. Regardless of their historical accuracy, the stories found in the Tanakh form the foundations of Jewish identity and represent a profound expression of our connection to the Land of Israel, to each other, and are ultimately symbols of our indigeneity.

As previously mentioned, the Mesha Stele also references the Tribe of Gad, indicating their long-standing presence in the region of Ataroth (an ancient town in modern-day Jordan). It describes how King Mesha took the city of Ataroth from the "people of Gad, [who] had dwelt in the region of Ataroth for a long time."[72] This aligns with the Torah's account of Gad's involvement in rebuilding Ataroth.[73] This extra-biblical source provides further support for the existence of distinct tribes within the broader Israelite community.

However, despite this tribal diversity, there appears to have been a "loose"[74] unified Israelite identity within the diversity of the tribal system. In "Israel's Political and Administrative Structures in the Pre-Monarchic and Monarchic Periods," Kyle H. Keimer and George A. Pierce make this very point. "Israel's identity and unity were rooted in its self-conception as one extended family of families, demonstrated foremost by the fact that its name is literally that of its ancestor and the father of the ancestors of the tribes that composed it."[75]

There were certainly tribes in the ancient past of the Jewish people, but, as indicated, whether there were consistently twelve of them remains unclear. If we explore the Torah, there are differing accounts of which brothers are referenced. The Blessing of Jacob in *Bereshit* (Genesis) directly references Reuben, Simeon, Levi, Judah, Zebulun, Issachar, Dan, Gad, Asher, Naphtali, Joseph, and Benjamin.[76] While the Blessing of Moses in *Devarim* (Deuteronomy) mentions Benjamin, Joseph, Zebulun, Issachar, Gad, Dan, Naphtali, Asher, Reuben, Levi, and Judah, but omits Simeon.[77] This could be down to the changing nature of which tribe was included—and in which way—in the larger Israel entity. For example, in the fifth chapter of the Book of Judges, Judah, Manasseh, Gad, Levi, and Simeon are not referenced, while the other seven traditional tribes are.[78] At the same time, the number twelve crops up several times in Jewish history. The bread in the Tabernacle consisted of twelve loaves, the high priest had twelve jewels inlaid on his breastplate and offerings to the temple were meant to be brought on twelve oxen. Similar tribal patterns can be found in the histories of other peoples in Asia Minor, Greece, and Italy,[79] suggesting a common cultural motif. Regardless of the exact number, it is evident that the tribes of Israel formed a loose confederacy, united by a shared Israelite identity and heritage.

The notion that judges ruled over Israel also seems to tally with the concept of the judges ruling over the confederation of tribes. As Lester L. Grabbe argues: "There is certain resemblance between some of the 'judges' in the book and the Canaanite kinglets known from the Amarna period. For example, Abimelech, son of Gideon, looks like the king of a Canaanite city-state."[80] Although with regard to the judges themselves, Grabbe argues that "this picture is illusionary if one assumes it reflects genuine historical memory." Grabbe then goes on to argue the Book of Judges "reflects a theological, rather than historical design."[81] In *Beyond the Texts: An Archaeological Portrait of Ancient Israel and Judah*, William Dever, contrasts it with the Book of Joshua, arguing, "The book of Judges, by contrast, has the ring of truth about it. And "several of the stories of everyday life in Judges are full of details with which any archeologist is familiar." [82]

Ultimately, regardless of the historicity of the judges, during this period, Kyle H. Keimer and George A. Pierce have argued that Israel was "a unifying political identity but one without an established succession of single leadership and with the autonomy of the individual tribes to participate in the political actions of this 'Israel.'" However, this all changed with the establishment of the United Monarchy. Or did it?

ISRAEL: A UNITED MONARCHY(?)

According to the Torah, around 1050 BCE, the Israelite tribes requested that Samuel, the prophet, appoint them a king "like all other nations."[83] Thus, the period of the Judges gave way to the United Monarchy of Israel. Tradition holds that it lasted for approximately 117 years and was ruled by Kings Saul, David, and Solomon before eventually splitting into the Kingdom of Israel in the north and the Kingdom of Judah in the south. This period holds significant importance for several reasons, including the reign of King David and the construction of the First Temple in Jerusalem by King Solomon.

However, since the early 1990s, the existence of the United Monarchy and its historical accuracy as described in the Torah has sparked intense debate. It's crucial to recognize that the Hebrew Bible provides an account of the United Monarchy and dismissing it solely based on anti-biblical bias or a minimalist perspective on the Tanakh's historicity is unjustified without thorough examination. Looking at the historical accuracy of other aspects of the Torah, such as the Northern Kingdom of Israel and the Southern Kingdom of Judah, it's clear that there is often truth in its portrayal of Jewish history. Indeed, Israel Finkelstein contends that Saul was a real historical figure who held significance in the north before the establishment of the Northern Kingdom. Like other narratives, Saul's story may have later been integrated into the southern tradition after the events of 720 BCE.[84] Lester L. Grabbe also argues that it is likely that Saul was a real person.[85] His argument is based on the fact Saul was even included in the Book of Samuel, in which the narrator's main concern lies with King David. Thus, the fact that Saul is included raises the obvious question: If Saul were purely fictional, why bother incorporating him into the narrative? After all, it is David's dynasty, not Saul's, that holds paramount importance to the Jewish people. The inclusion of Saul suggests he represents a genuine historical figure; otherwise, he would serve no narrative purpose in what would be a fabricated tale.

Importantly, there appears to be epigraphic evidence supporting the existence of King David's dynasty. The Mesha Stele provides an account of King Mesha of Moab waging war against the Israelites. This inscription is almost identical to the account of the same war in the *Sefer Melachim* (Book of Kings) from the Torah.[86] Crucially, it is said to reference *Beit David* (House of David) or "*bt dwd*." Fortunately, Ancient Moabite and Ancient Hebrew script are almost identical and only differ dialectically. The significance of extra-biblical evidence in investigating ancient Jewish history cannot be overstated. The fact that a non-Israelite source mentions *Beit David* adds considerable weight to the notion of its actual existence. Moreover, another extra-biblical source, the Tel Dan Stele, confirms battles depicted in the Book of Kings between the Kingdoms of Israel and Aram. Written in Aramaic, this stele also references *Beit David* (House of David).[87] These extra-biblical sources strongly suggest the likelihood that King David and his dynasty did indeed exist. However, questions persist regarding the extent of his power and the territories he ruled over.

Even Israel Finkelstein, who is known for his minimalist perspective, acknowledges the existence of King David and King Saul as historical figures. However, he suggests they ruled over a smaller territory, centered around the southern highlands with Jerusalem as their capital, rather than a large, centralized state. As discussed earlier, the Tel Dan Stele, in which Hazael, King of Damascus, refers to the Kingdom of Judah as the "House of David," indicates an awareness of the Davidic dynasty ruling over Judah. This recognition suggests the existence of a founder of the dynasty, namely David.

Furthermore, the narrative presented in the Hebrew Bible features real groups that did exist during that time, such as the Moabites, Ammonites, Edomites, and Philistines, whom Kings Saul and David were said to have encountered and defeated.[88]

Excavations at Gezer (west of Jerusalem) have given some credence to the notion that King Solomon was also a real historical figure. In their article "Solomon's Powerplay" in the Summer 2024 issue of *Biblical Archaeology Review*, Steven Ortiz and Samuel Wolff wrote, "It was during Solomon's reign, in the mid-tenth century, that Gezer underwent a radical change. It became a well-fortified city with a massive six-chambered gate, an adjoining casemate wall, and a large administrative building."[89]

Much of the debate surrounding the historicity of the United Monarchy revolves around the archeology of the period and whether it supports the existence of a large, powerful political entity. Like textual evidence, including the Torah, archeological evidence is subject to interpretation, and we must acknowledge the potential for bias and the presence of conjecture. As Kyle Keimer, a lecturer in the Archaeology and History of Ancient Israel, emphasizes, "the archaeological remains are unbiased data that receive meaning when interpreted by archeologists."[90]

Israel Finkelstein is skeptical of the notion of a United Monarchy and believes instead that Israel and Judah were actually two separate political entities, with Judah emerging later than the Northern Kingdom of Israel.[91] The idea of their unification, and the stories of the Kings Saul, David, and Solomon ruling a unified Israelite territory, came about retrospectively following the destruction of the Kingdom of Israel and the continuation of the Kingdom of Judah, alongside the writing of the Torah. Indeed, Finkelstein argues that, during the period of the United Monarchy, Judah was a marginal, sparsely settled polity in the southern highlands, comprising a mix of sedentary and pastoral groups and ruled from a small settlement.[92]

Finkelstein's perspective stems from findings at Megiddo, located southeast of Haifa, and led to his development of the "Low Chronology" theory. This theory involves pushing the dates of stratigraphic layers by approximately one hundred years later than previously believed.[93] Essentially, this suggests that archeological evidence discovered at these sites actually belongs to a time period later than originally thought, and therefore does not pertain to a United Monarchy at all. Instead, these findings would be attributed to the Northern Kingdom of Israel (further elaborated on in the next chapter).[94] Finkelstein employed radiocarbon testing on samples unearthed at Megiddo, which indeed yielded dates from the 9th century BCE. However, it's important to note that carbon dating, while valuable, is not without its limitations and margin of error.

However, the discovery of a "big fortified city"[95] from 2007 to 2013 at Khirbet Qeiyafa has sparked renewed debate and led to further questions about Finkelstein's theories. In their preliminary report on the findings, maximalist archeologists Yosef Garfinkel, Sa'ar Ganor, and Michael Hasel assert, "The excavations at Khirbet Qeiyafa clearly reveal an urban society that existed in Judah already in the late eleventh century BCE. It can no longer be argued that the Kingdom of Judah developed only in the late eighth century BCE or at some other later date."[96] The excavations uncovered building styles typical of the Kingdom of Judah[97] and, according to Garfinkel, are dated to the 10th century BCE, the time of King David, indicating development and expansion into the Shephelah region south-west of Jerusalem. Garfinkel also highlights findings from a dig at Khirbet al-Ra'I, which revealed "a small village,"[98] arguing that "together we have a city and a village from the time of David."[99]

Garfinkel identifies two additional sites dating back to the 10th century BCE. The first is Tell en-Nasbeh—possibly the biblical Mizpeh, where the Prophet Samuel stayed—where "a casemate city wall, which means the same urban planning" was found.[100] Garfinkel notes that this site is located in Benjamin, near the northern border of the Kingdom of Judah.

The second additional site excavated by Garfinkel is Khirbet ed-Dawwara. This site was excavated in the early 90s. It is a "small site, but there is urban planning and again you have casemate city walls and pottery just like that in Khirbet Qeiyafa."[101] Garfinkel describes Khirbet Qeiyafa as a "biblical Pompeii"[102] dating to the period of King David, as it was built and destroyed all within 20 or 30 years. As Garfinkel points out, therefore, everything found must date to the time of David. In terms of dating these finds, Garfinkel argues that, during the period of the Judges, there was no major building works, and Israelite territory was made up of small villages, but during the period of the United Monarchy, a "revolution"[103] occurred which led to the development of cities. Garfinkel argues, "we see the transition from a tribal community into a state, and we can see that it happened around 1000 BCE, the time of David."[104]

It is worth noting that Garfinkel's interpretation of his findings was met with a swift backlash. Finkelstein has questioned Garfinkel's dating, saying, "I am not so sure that all the sites that he cites date to exactly the same phase in the 10th century BCE."[105] *Haaretz*'s archeology correspondent Ariel David has also noted that "Precisely dating ancient remains is notoriously difficult, as even scientific methods like radiocarbon have significant margins of error."[106]

Much of the debate also focuses on the question of whether Jerusalem was the capital of a powerful centralized state. The general thinking is that if Jerusalem was a large city, Israel was powerful, and if it was smaller, then the state itself was less powerful. Proving this is a challenging exercise: Arab colonization led to the building of the Dome of the Rock and Al Aqsa Mosque on the mount, making excavation there impossible today. As Finkelstein notes, "the nature of the site made it difficult to peel away the layers of later centuries and the Temple Mount has always been beyond the reach of archeologists."[107]

Moreover, Finkelstein is of the opinion that "over a century of archaeological explorations in Jerusalem—the capital of the glamorous biblical United Monarchy—failed to reveal evidence for any meaningful 10th-century building activity." However, as with everything else, perspectives vary widely. Steiner argues that Jerusalem in the 10th and 9th centuries BCE was a small town with around 2,000 inhabitants.[108] Lester L. Grabbe argues it bears characteristics of a "regional administrative centre or the capital of a small, newly established state."[109] However, J. M. Cahill argued, "My own view is that the archaeological evidence demonstrates that at the time of Israel's United Monarchy, Jerusalem was fortified, served by two complex water supply systems and was populated by a socially stratified society that constructed at least two new residential quarters—one located inside and the other located outside the city's fortification walls."[110]

A potential breakthrough came in 2006, when archeologist Eilat Mazar discovered a large stone structure in Jerusalem which she claimed was part of King David's palace, as mentioned in the Hebrew Bible.[111] Writing about her findings, Mazar wrote: "The Biblical narrative, I submit, better explains the archaeology we have uncovered than any other hypothesis that has been put forward. Indeed, the archaeological remains square perfectly with the Biblical description that tells us David went down from there to the citadel. So you decide whether or not we have found King David's palace."[112]

As R. G. Fox argues in *Urban Anthropology: Cities in their Cultural Settings*, cities must be studied in their local context, as well as the larger global system.[113] And it is therefore worth considering that the way that we understand sovereignty today may not be applicable to the Near East during this period of history.

Neo-evolutionism views tribes—and the idea of kinship—as a primitive stage in societal development. However, according to Thomas, "some scholars of the ancient Near East have turned away from the preconceptions of neo-evolutionist theory and have instead placed the emic, household-based conception of socio-political structure at the core of how they understand entities like Israel as historical and archaeological subjects."[114] Through these perspectives, kingdoms in the Near East in this period can be described as "patrimonial,"[115] as conceived by Max Weber, the German sociologist. Thomas described a patrimonial kingdom as "understood by its constituents as one great household that encompassed and bound together multiple subsidiary households."[116] That is, a decentralized monarchy made up of various tribes.

Describing this notion, Keimer wrote in *Evaluating the "United Monarchy of Israel": Unity and Identity in Text and Archaeology*, "The king is not the center of a centralized political system that envelops all levels of society, but he is the head of a decentralized system built upon traditional social structures. So, while the king may establish hegemonic control that is ever evolving, his hegemony requires the buy-in of numerous people who, in effect, create and/or display their own hegemony." Considering the reality of the Israelite tribal system, this could be a representation of the relationship between the Kings of Israel and their subjects.

With regard to the transition from tribal confederacy to monarchy, Zachary Tomas, in *Israel's Political and Administrative Structures*, writes, "The adoption of kingship in Israel marks not so much a change in Israel's underlying political structure as it does a shift in where power within that structure lay and what that power would be used for. How the kings of Israel and Judah enacted their duties as defenders of their land, shepherds of their people, and servants of their patron god involved them both passively and actively in the lives and labors of their subjects."

And in the *Ancient Israelite World*, Keimer, along with George A. Pierce, described the king's position as "the father of one great household that incorporated other households, and David's appointment as king by the discretion of the people and elders of the tribes." Thus, the Israelite monarchy might not have been one of a strong centralized power, but rather a kind of confederation.

From this perspective, it is entirely possible that King David could have obtained legitimacy through a shared worship of YHWH as well as "charisma, legitimacy, and/or physical ability to levy punishment, not because they lived in a big city."[117] This would also explain arguments regarding Jerusalem being too small to represent the capital of a great power, as it has been suggested there were other ways to gain legitimacy in this period in this place.

With this in mind, perhaps the idea of a United Monarchy—where King Solomon's power stretched from the Euphrates to the border of Egypt—should not be viewed solely through a modern lens. It could simply mean he was the dominant player in the power dynamics that existed in the region. This new perception of power in the Near East "makes the archaeological articulation of political power even more of a challenge."[118] For example, as Keimer argues, within this perspective it is possible that King Solomon did embark on his extensive building project, including structures at Megiddo, Hazor, and/or Gezer. Commissioning tribal leaders to oversee the construction, obvious differences would occur with regard to their access to resources as well as their interpretation of the brief, so to speak. Within this context and this understanding of Near Eastern dynamics, the differences in the structures at Megiddo, Hazor and/or Gezer cannot be taken as evidence that King Solomon was not responsible for the construction.

Ultimately, there is clearly a wide range of competing perspectives on the historicity of the United Monarchy. It is unlikely that it existed exactly as the Hebrew Bible tells us, although it was likely rooted in an amalgamation of historic memory. The reality, however, is we just don't know. Regardless of different views on the Torah's historical accuracy, the era of the United Monarchy is that of King David and King Solomon, who reportedly built the First Temple; it thus remains a crucial moment in the evolution of the Jewish story. And its figures are still important to Jews today, as they have been for thousands of years.

Chapter 2

A HISTORY OF THE JEWS AND OUR LAND:
TWO KINGDOMS

At this early stage in our historical journey, we've already witnessed a remarkable series of developments: a transition from Canaanite separatists worshipping YHWH to ancient Israelite tribes, and then to monarchical systems of governance. And all this occurred within the first 500 years of the Jewish story.

According to the Hebrew Bible, after King Solomon's death, the United Monarchy of Israel collapsed. Solomon was punished for apostasy, abandoning his God: "In his old age," it suggests, "his wives turned away Solomon's heart after other gods, and he was not as wholeheartedly devoted to the eternal his God as his father David had been."[1] In response to this rejection, God destroyed Solomon's kingdom.

Around 926 BCE, tensions erupted between the northern and southern regions of the kingdom. The north comprised ten of the twelve tribes of Israel, while Judah and Benjamin formed the south. Like many revolts or revolutions throughout history, this one is said to have been rooted in dissatisfaction with taxation.

When Solomon's son, King Rehoboam, ascended the throne, the northern tribes, discontented with his father's policies, appealed to him. "Your father made our yoke heavy," they reportedly said. "Now lighten the harsh labor and the heavy yoke that your father laid on us, and we will serve you."[2] In an extraordinary misjudgment, instead of heeding their pleas, Rehoboam threatened to increase taxation, telling them: "My father made your yoke heavy, but I will add to your yoke; my father flogged you with whips, but I will flog you with scorpions."[3]

Unsurprisingly, led by Jeroboam (a royal guard who would later become the first king of the Northern Kingdom of Israel), the tribes of Israel rebelled against the House of David. Even after the kingdoms split, Jeroboam's assault against the north's former rulers persisted, targeting the Southern Kingdom of Judah. This hostility endured beyond Rehoboam's death into the reign of his son, King Abijam. Abijam managed to defeat the northern Israelites in the final Battle of Mount Zemaraim in 913 BCE, yet he failed to reunite the two kingdoms.

From a historical perspective, as we've already explored, there's significant debate surrounding the existence of the United Monarchy and, consequently, the origins of the two Israelite Kingdoms. Those who dispute the United Monarchy's existence (or downplay it) also tend to question the authenticity of Jeroboam's rebellion and its context, suggesting that the two kingdoms originated independently of one another. However, it's undeniable that these kingdoms were evidently connected in various ways through the worship of YHWH and other cultural practices.

Ultimately, while we can't definitively pinpoint why the two kingdoms emerged, one thing is certain—they did.

ISRAEL

It is with absolute certainty we can say the Kingdom of Israel—or the Northern Kingdom, as it is also known—existed in the southern Levant for around 200 years, from 930 BCE until 720 BCE,[4] when it was conquered and destroyed by the Assyrian Empire.[5] For most of this period, its southern neighbor was the Kingdom of Judah, the other Israelite kingdom. And although Judah survived longer (by around 200 years), of the two Israelite kingdoms, Israel was by far the larger, richer, and more powerful.[6] Indeed, Israel ruled over, according to Finkelstein and Broshi in "The Population of Palestine in Iron Age II," around three-quarters of the total population

TWO KINGDOMS

in Israel and Judah.[7] But, despite its power and reach, not a huge amount is known about the Northern Kingdom. According to Finkelstein, when Ancient Hebrew history was first written down in the 9th century BCE, much of Israel's history was already a memory.[8] Therefore, the major account of the Northern Kingdom comes from scribes from the Southern Kingdom of Judah.

Prior to the rise of Israel, Finkelstein argues, some of the northern territory was ruled by King Saul, but in different circumstances from those which are described in the Hebrew Bible. It is said that he did not rule from either of the capitals of the two Israelite kingdoms: Jerusalem and Shechem (an ancient city close to the modern-day city of Nablus in the West Bank). Instead, he ruled from the highlands, the Gibeon Bethel area, just north of Jerusalem. In this period of development, the territory was "more than city-states and less than developed states."[9] Based on the Torah, historian Diana Edelman argues, Saul's chronology cannot be firmly established: "He was associated with Israel, so any attempt to situate him in time needs to be done in relation to other Israelite kings whose existence can be verified by extrabiblical documentation ... It would seem logical to place Saul sometime during the tenth century BCE."[10]

The campaign of Egypt's King Shoshenq I (generally thought of as being referred to as Shishak in the Torah) may possibly be related to King Saul in the 10th century. *Sefer Melachim* (the Book of Kings) tells us that "In the fifth year of King Rehoboam, King Shishak of Egypt marched against Jerusalem and carried off the treasures of the House of GOD and the treasures of the royal palace. He carried off everything; he even carried off all the golden shields that Solomon had made."[11] However, Shoshenq's Bubastite Portal engravings in Karnak, Egypt, which record his exploits, make no mention of Jerusalem. Perhaps, therefore, it was not Jerusalem that attracted Shoshenq's attention but Saul's emerging polity in the Gibeon-Bethel area that caught his eye. And just as the Amarna letters 400 years previously had described Shechem's attempted expansion from a city-state into a territorial kingdom, Egypt could not stand this threatening development in its sphere of influence.[12]

After the destruction of the Saulide territories, Finkelstein argues, the city-state of Shechem (part of the territory of the tribe of Ephraim) began its expansion into the territorial Kingdom of Israel in around 930 BCE. The origins of the Kingdom of Israel begin with Jeroboam, who was viewed very negatively by the Judahite scribes who worked on compiling the Torah. Jeroboam came from Zeredah,[13] a small village, today northwest of Ramallah, and, based on his description in the Septuagint (the translation of the Tanakh into Greek), it appears he is an Apiru-like figure (a group of outlaws recorded in the Amarna letters as being a kind of bandit group). Thanks to his role in the rebellion against Rehoboam, the Tanakh and the Septuagint suggest that Jeroboam fled to Egypt. He later came back and may have been put on the throne by Pharaoh Shoshenq I and crowned at Shechem. At this time, it would appear, Shechem was an Egyptian vassal. However, when Egypt's power in the region collapsed, Israel was given an opportunity to become independent.

Following its birth, areas like the Jezreel Valley (in northern modern Israel) offer clues as to Israel's steady expansion. The *Sefer Melachim* (the Book of Kings), describe how Baasha, the third northern Israelite king who had succeeded King Jeroboam's son, Nadab, besieged Gibbethon, a small town facing Philistia. It records, "Then Baasha son of Ahijah, of the House of Issachar, conspired against him; and Baasha struck him down at Gibbethon of the Philistines, while Nadab and all Israel were laying siege to Gibbethon."[14]

Around 50 years after the Kingdom came into being, King Baasha's successor, Omri, came to the throne. Under King Omri and his descendants, the Kingdom of Israel was powerful and, according to Finkelstein, was even a "contender for hegemony over the ... Southern Levant." Archeological finds suggest the Omride dynasty of Israel were strong and big builders.[15] In the ancient city of Samaria, the new capital of the Northern

Kingdom, a palace was built that represented the power and prestige of this new Israelite dynasty and its kingdom.[16] Additionally, in Tal Jezreel there was a very elaborate compound, including a famed vineyard owned by the Omride dynasty[17] And in Jahaz and Vatroth (east of the Dead Sea) there were buildings—built by Israel—that were eventually taken over by King Mesha of the Moabites (of the Mesha Stele fame).[18]

It is also in this period, as we saw in the last chapter, that the first extra-biblical reference to YHWH appears. In the Mesha Stele, as theologian Herbert Niehr argues, "The Meša inscription (ca. 850 BCE) clearly states that YHWH was the supreme god of Israel and of the Transjordanian territory occupied by Israel under the Omrides." There were temples in Israel, but it seems that, as in Judah, organized worship of YHWH was restricted to the capital.

Whatever their origins and their relationship to the demise of the United Monarchy, both the northern and southern kingdoms were Israelite—tracing their roots to the twelve tribes—and both worshipped the same God. The Mesha Stele references Israel's worship of YHWH, while an inscription from Khirbet Beit Lei (northwest of Hebron), which has been dated from the late 6th century BCE, reads: "Yahweh [is] the God of the whole earth; the mountains of Judah belong to him, to the God of Jerusalem."[19] Inscriptions discovered at Khirbet el-Qom (in the historic territory of the Kingdom of Judah and the modern-day West Bank) talk of YHWH and his wife, Asherah, and stretch back even earlier to the 8th century BCE.[20]

Although Israelite history was written by Judahites, the Northern Kingdom was dominant over its southern neighbor. As *Sefer Melachim* records, the Northern Kingdom tried to take over Jerusalem. It is clear then why the Torah scribes hated Omri (and King Ahab, who, persuaded by his wife, the infamous Jezebel, is said to have introduced the worship of Baal over YHWH) and sought to minimize the significance of the Northern Kingdom. Despite the events taking place some 200 years previously, the memory of the Omride attack on Judah and their abandonment of YHWH must have burned brightly. This can help us understand why there can be only six references to Omri in the Torah. As Finkelstein notes, "Only six verses are given to Omri, the founder of the most celebrated dynasty of the north, the king by whose name Israel is known in Assyrian records." But, as they were building their own specific perspective of ancient Israelite history, those who wrote the Hebrew Bible viewed Israel as a competitor and illegitimate.

The earliest extra-biblical mention of the Northern Kingdom of Israel is from the Kurkh Stele—one of two Assyrian stelae circa 853 BCE—containing descriptions of the reigns of Ashurnasirpal II and his son Shalmaneser III, when "Ahab the Israelite" is referenced as well as the denominative for "land."[21] This is the first extra-biblical reference to Israel since the Merneptah Stele, 355 years earlier. Demonstrating the evolution of ancient Israelite civilization, Israel is described as a land and a king, in contrast with the Merneptah Stele which references it simply as a people. Every other reference to Israel by the Assyrians—who, as we will see, battled to control it—describes the Northern Kingdom as the "House of Omri."[22] For example, "Jehu, son of Omri" is depicted in Shalmaneser III's famed "Black Obelisk" (currently on display in the British Museum, London) paying tribute to Assyria.[23] In around 803 BCE, the Nimrud slab records King Adad-Nirari III of Assyria's adventure in the Levant, detailing how he traveled to "the Hatti and Amurru lands, Tyre, Sidon, the mat of Hu-um-ri (land of Omri), Edom, Philistia and Aram."[24] And in 722 BCE, Sargon II references "the whole house of Omri"[25] when detailing his conquest of Samaria. It is worth noting that the Assyrians never mention the Kingdom of Judah until the 8th century BCE when "Hezekiah the Judahite"[26] is referenced.

As we know, other references to the Northern Kingdom include the Tel Dan Stele (870–750 BCE).[27] This also indicates the power of the kingdom: King Hazael of Damascus describes his victory over Israel, describing how, initially, the kings of the Northern Kingdom had taken over territories of Damascus.[28] Damascus ruled Israelite territory until Hazael died and Israel fought back. Similarly, in the Moabite Mesha Stele, King Mesha describes the conquest of territories to his north by Israel's King Omri and his son. He refers to cities built by the Northern Kingdom in the north of Moab, and he celebrates his conquest over Israel.

As we have already seen, the power dynamics and geopolitical situation was constantly in flux in the Near East. It evolved from empires and city-states to territorial kingdoms. The 8th century BCE saw a new age of empire begin.[29] The first of these major new empires was the ancient Mesopotamian civilization of Assyria. From roughly 730 BCE it ruled over the southern Levant and, albeit in different ways, the ancient-Israelite kingdoms of Israel and Judah.[30] Judah became a vassal state of Assyria, while Israel was completely destroyed in 720 BCE.

Even before Israel's destruction at the hands of Assyria, it had endured a period of tumult and decline. Four out of six of its final rulers had been executed by their own people. In its latter years, the constant jostling for power created instability for the formerly great Israelite Kingdom. But the real death knell came (inadvertently) at the hands of the Southern Kingdom of Judah. During Assyria's westward expansion from around 740–732 BCE, Israel and Syria attacked Judah in an attempt to force it to join their anti-Assyrian alliance. As *Sefer Melachim* records: "Then King Rezin of Aram and King Pekah son of Remaliah of Israel advanced on Jerusalem for battle. They besieged Ahaz, but could not overcome [him]."[31] In response, King Ahaz of Judah appealed to King Tiglath-Pileser of Assyria, saying, "I am your servant and your son; come and deliver me from the hands of the king of Aram and from the hands of the king of Israel, who are attacking me."[32]

The Assyrians then discovered that in response King Hoshea of Israel had appealed to the Egyptians for help. In their fury, the Assyrians besieged Israel for four years (from 726–722 BCE), and kidnapped Hoshea before eventually conquering his kingdom. "In the ninth year of Hoshea, the king of Assyria captured Samaria," records Kings. "He deported the Israelites to Assyria and settled them in Halah, at the [River] Habor, at the River Gozan, and in the towns of Media."[33]

Judahite scribes chose to present these events as divine punishment for Israel's sins: "This happened because the Israelites sinned against the ETERNAL their God, who had freed them from the land of Egypt, from the hand of Pharaoh king of Egypt. They worshiped other gods and followed the customs of the nations that GOD had dispossessed before the Israelites and the customs that the kings of Israel had practiced."[34] But, depending on your beliefs and perspective, it is also possible that Israel simply played the game of thrones, and lost.

Following its destruction, Israel ceased to exist. The literati were deported to Assyria, foreigners settled the land, and the military was absorbed into Assyria's. This action destroyed not only the Northern Kingdom of Israel but scattered forever the remaining ten tribes of Israel: Asher, Dan, Ephraim, Gad, Issachar, Manasseh, Naphtali, Reuben, Simeon, and Zebulun. While there are those who continue the search for the ten tribes today, they are most likely lost to the pages of history, except for the Samaritans, the other contemporary group—along with Jews—directly descended from the Israelites of the Kingdom of Israel.

In the *Bible Unearthed*, Israeli authors Israel Finkelstein and Neil Asher Silberman estimate that a fifth (about 40,000 people) of the population of the Northern Kingdom of Israel were actually resettled out of the area.[35, 36] Finkelstein argues that a portion of the Israelite population fled south to their cousins in the Kingdom of Judah. Biblical studies professor William M. Schniedewind concurs. During the 9th to late 8th/early 7th centuries BCE, he argues in *How the Bible Became a Book: The Textualization of Ancient Israel*, Judah's population grew significantly, and it seems Israelites were a significant demographic within Judah. This is noted in the Book of Chronicles: "And the people of Israel and Judah who lived in the cities of Judah also brought in the tithe of cattle and sheep, and the tithe of the dedicated things that had been dedicated to the Lord their God, and laid them in heaps."[37] Archeological evidence seems to confirm the absorption of Israelite refugees into Judah. In 2017, bullate (ancient Mesopotamian clay sealings) containing names—such as "Ahiav ben [son of] Menahem"[38]—from the Kingdom of Israel were discovered in an excavation in Jerusalem, the capital of ancient Judah.

Biblical interpretation, as we will see, requires a recognition of the absorption of Israelite refugees into Judah. It allows us to explain why and how northern texts, histories—such as that of the Saulide territory—and traditions were absorbed into the Torah and later written by Judahites in Judah). In "Migration of Israelites into Judah after 720 BC." Finkelstein notes these include the absorption of ideas "competitive to the Jerusalem temple (e.g. Jacob at Bethel) and even hostile to the Davidic dynasty, into Judahite literary works. It also explains the merging of northern and southern traditions such as the Saul and David stories and the Jacob and Abraham patriarchal sagas. And it sheds light on the rise of the pan-Israelite ideology in Judah."[39]

Even though the traditions and memories of the Northern Kingdom continue to this day, it lasted only 200 years. However, it was a shining moment of ancient-Israelite strength and sovereignty in the Land of Israel, and its identity and experience are still expressed and celebrated by Jews today.

JUDAH

The Hebrew Bible tells us the Southern Kingdom of Judah existed from 930 BCE—around the same time as the Northern Kingdom of Israel—until it was destroyed by the Babylonians in around 587 BCE. It was made up of the tribes of Judah and Benjamin and was ruled by the descendants of King David (the House of David or the Davidic dynasty). Israeli archeologist Amihai Mazar underlines the profound significance of the Tel Dan Stele in suggesting its inscriptions mean that "about 140 years after the presumed end of David's reign, in the region David was well-known as founder of the dynasty that ruled a kingdom centered in Jerusalem."[40]

It is this Israelite kingdom, as we discussed in the introduction of this book, from which Jews take their name and are primarily descended. This continuity is profound. That an ancient Jewish tribe which existed 3,000 years ago gave its name to a sovereign Israelite nation in the Land of Israel, which, in turn, gave its name to its descendants, the modern Jewish people, is a remarkable fact. Moreover, the Northern Kingdom of Israel gave its name to the modern Jewish state, which sits roughly in the same territory. The contemporary Jewish links to both Israel and Judah (and their tribal ancestors) are both powerful and instructive.

There are several extra-biblical or archeological references to Judah dating to the 8th century BCE. Nadav Na'aman notes that, in an early 8th-century Assyrian wine list (a wine distribution list for courtiers in 8th-century Nimrud), "a Judahite envoy is probably mentioned alongside an Israelite envoy."[41] This would be the first extra-biblical reference to Judah in history, and demonstrates that by 780 BCE, Judah was established enough to warrant a mention alongside the Northern Kingdom of Israel and other regional kingdoms in this Assyrian wine list. Another mention comes from the Nimrud Tablet (dated around 733 BCE) which references "Jehoahaz of the land Judah."[42] Also from the 8th century BCE, although its place and date of discovery is unknown, is King Ahaz's bulla (seal), which reads "[belonging] to 'Ah. az [son of] Jehoram, king of Judah."[43] And in 2009 a bulla was discovered dating to 710 BCE that references Ahaz's son Hezekiah, reading "Belonging to Hezekiah [son of] Ahaz king of Judah."[44] I personally find the extra-biblical references to ancient Israelite history to be thrilling. We do not need validation from the outside world to confirm our history, but as is the case in any histor-

TWO KINGDOMS 67

ical investigation, the greater the evidence, the more accurate we can be in describing the events we seek to understand.

While Judah's history from the 8th century onward is more concrete, its origins are much less certain. Israel Finkelstein argues that the second half of the 9th century BCE "is the moment when one can detect the first signs of statehood in Judah."[45] This development was, according to Finkelstein, an outcome of the political and economic ambitions of the Northern Kingdom of Israel, rooted in cooperation as well as the marriage of Athaliah, King Omri's daughter to King Jehoram of Judah, the fifth king of Judah and son of Jehoshaphat.[46] This was the Israelites' way of dominating Judah and the Judahites[47] (and was perhaps the true origins of the idea of the United Monarchy, if indeed that ever existed in the way the Torah describes). Prior to this, it seems that Judah was a city-state polity, which then—with Israel's help and trade in the south—expanded into the region.

However, there are those who disagree with Finkelstein's assessment and argue that by the 10th century BCE Judah was a larger and more powerful kingdom than it is given credit for. "At the beginning of the 10th century BCE the Kingdom of Judah had a limited urban core consisting of a few small fortified cities," archeologist Yosef Garfinkel writes. But, he believes, by "the end of the 10th century BCE the Kingdom of Judah expanded into the southern Shephelah and reached the site of Lachish."[48] This assessment is based on discoveries of pottery, and also corresponds with the biblical list of cities constructed by King Rehoboam. However, as we know, there is still much to debate surrounding the meaning of archeological findings.

As was the case with debates over the United Monarchy, much of the disagreement over the development of Judah is focused on Jerusalem and its development. As we discussed in the previous chapter, the challenge of excavating Jerusalem is fraught with political difficulty today. However, evidence has been found which paints us a picture of Jerusalem's evolution. In the 14th century BCE, Jerusalem—which was centered around the Temple Mount, according to Israel Finkelstein, and not the City of David—was an important city that ruled over the southern part of the highlands.[49] A clay fragment—dated to 14th BCE—was discovered in Jerusalem containing ancient Akkadian (the lingua franca of the day).[50] It is the oldest example of writing ever found in Jerusalem. It is interesting to note that, even in this period, Jerusalem ruled over the south, while Shechem ruled over the northern part of the highlands. Even 700 years later, this is the pattern we see with regard to these centers of power and their territorial reach.

The biblical perspective on the evolution of Jerusalem suggests King David took the city from the Jebusites, thus making it the Israelite capital. But evidence that places Jerusalem in the 10th century BCE is contested. As we referenced in the last chapter, excavations done on the City of David by Eilat Mazar are said to have uncovered what was described as a palace dating back to King David in the 10th and 11th centuries BCE.[51] (These are said to have matched the biblical descriptions of King David's palace.[52]) However, in line with his Low Chronology theory, Finkelstein dates them to a century later. And it was in the 9th century BCE that Jerusalem began its process of expansion from a singular compound containing both a palace and a temple (although not in the grand way we imagine these buildings today) into a fortified city. Nadav Na'aman argues: "The capital city grew and expanded in the course of the ninth-eighth centuries B.C.E., reaching its zenith at the end of the eighth."[53]

Incredibly, a structure dated in 2024 indicates that Jerusalem actually began its westward expansion in the 9th century BCE. Initially thought to have been constructed by King Hezekiah as part of his defense of Jerusalem against King Sennacherib of Assyria, it has now been dated to his great-grandfather, King Uzziah. As Yuval Gadot of Tel Aviv University has argued, "The new research allows us to study the development of the city ... Jerusalem grew in size and spread towards Mount Zion already in the 9th century BCE ... In light of this, the new research teaches that the expansion of Jerusalem is a result of internal-Judean demographic growth and the establishment of political and economic systems."[54]

By the 8th century BCE, Judah was an established kingdom ruled from Jerusalem with a temple for worship of YHWH. Until the destruction of Israel, Judah was the weaker of the two Israelite nations. Following Israel's victory over Judah in 790 BCE, according to Nadav Na'aman, the south was essentially a vassal state of the north, with Israel blocking Judah from participating in the south Arabian trade, thus greatly impacting its economy. However, it seems that just a short time later, by the time of the Assyrian Wine List (dated in the 780s BCE[55]), relations had warmed and while Israel remained the stronger and more dominant Israelite nation, Judah was—for a period—treated more like an ally.[56]

As discussed previously, King Hazael of Damascus led successful campaigns against both Israel and Judah, relegating the Southern Kingdom again into a vassal state. This proved an unfortunate pattern for Judah. Indeed, by the time of its conquest in 587 BCE by the Babylonians, Judah had been a vassal state of Israel, Damascus, Assyria, and, then later in around 630 BCE, Egypt. It was thus obviously never as powerful as the Northern Kingdom of Israel, which was a kind of regional superpower, making its centrality in Jewish national expressions so interesting.

Ironically, Assyria's subjugation of Judah in the 730s BCE had a positive impact on the Judahite economy, which was incorporated into the southern trade network.[57] The fall of Israel, as Finkelstein argues, and the subsequent influx of Israelite refugees (who settled in Jerusalem and the surrounding areas), as well as its absorption into Assyria's sphere of influence, led to the emergence of Judah as a regional player.[58]

A bulla from the reign of King Hezekiah (715–686 BCE) is a hugely significant indicator of Judah's status in the late 8th and 7th centuries BCE. Hezekiah is a fascinating character, who appears in both the Torah and in the Sennacherib Prism (the Assyrian records). Although described in the prism by Assyria's King Sennacherib as trapped "like a bird in a cage,"[59] Hezekiah ultimately saved Jerusalem from the 701 BCE Assyrian siege by building a tunnel allowing water supplies to be brought safely into the city.[60] Analyzing the bulla, we can understand perhaps something of Hezekiah's ambition for Judah, despite Assyria's control over the region. Borrowing Egyptian iconography, and stripping it of its Egyptian significance, the winged scarab beetle became a symbol of Judahite monarchy.[61] This then came to symbolize the strength and independence of Judah, independent from Assyria.[62]

Another clue to the fact that, by this point, Judah was not a "backwater, but had a highly developed administrative system"[63] was found in the discovery of the handles of large jars stamped with LMLK seals (meaning "of the king"). In 2022, further evidence was discovered—a series of ceramic storage jars found in the remnants of the Babylonian sacking of Jerusalem—which underlines the developed nature of the Judahite elite in the 7th century. Along with olive oil, these jars contained wine with trace elements of vanilla. The presence of vanilla—likely from southern Arabian trade passing through the Negev—demonstrates a wealthy and prosperous nation, able to import it from the tropics. As researcher Ayala Amir suggests, "During the 7th century BCE, Jerusalem enjoyed unprecedented prosperity, as it grew in size, population and wealth."[64]

Sadly, despite its rise to prominence and wealth, the writing was on the wall for Judah by the late 7th century BCE. As had been the case for all of its history, the kingdom was caught between a rock and a hard place in the form of great jostling empires. Following the Babylonians' defeat of the Assyrians at the Battle of Nineveh in 612 BCE,[65] the Egyptians moved through the southern Levant to support the Kingdom of Israel's old nemesis. Their way was blocked by King Josiah of Judah.[66] As a result, Judah and Egypt met and fought at the Battle of Megiddo in 609 BCE.[67] Josiah fell in battle and was succeeded by his son, Jehoahaz. However, just three months later, Pharaoh Necho II deposed the young king and installed Jehoahaz's brother, Jehoiakim, in his place.[68]

But, four years after Megiddo, the Babylonians defeated Egypt at the Battle of Carchemish. They now set their sights on Judah and in 597 BCE laid siege to Jerusalem, which had expanded into the largest city in the southern Levant with a population of around 12,000 people.[69] With terrible timing, Jehoiakim had died the previous year and was succeeded by his 18-year-old son, Jeconiah.[70] The Nebuchadnezzar Chronicle (the only source outside of the Torah for this period of history) records what happened next: "On the second day of the month of Adar (16 March) he conquered the city and took the king (Jeconiah) prisoner. He installed in his place a king (Zedekiah) of his own choice, and after he had received rich tribute, he sent forth to Babylon."[71] Along with his loot from the Temple, King Nebuchadnezzar II carried young King Jeconiah, his court and other citizens to exile in Babylon.[72] On this epic Jewish tragedy, Jeremiah wrote, "Israel are scattered sheep, harried by lions."[73] With this forced population transfer the Babylonian exile began and, with it, the origins of the Jewish Diaspora.

Rather unwisely, given the fate of young Jeconiah, King Zedekiah revolted against Nebuchadnezzar II.[74] Unsurprisingly, the Babylonian monarch returned to Judah and once again laid siege to Jerusalem in 589 BCE. During this siege, Nebuchadnezzar was merciless. The Torah describes that the "the famine had become acute in the city; there was no food left for the common people."[75] As a response, many Judahites fled to surrounding kingdoms, such as Moab, seeking refuge.[76] In the eleventh year of King Zedekiah's reign (around 586 BCE) the city fell again and was destroyed.[77] Jerusalem was burned, the Temple pillaged, and many of the remaining Judahites were taken into captivity in Babylon.[78] This is confirmed by archeological findings which reveal "massive debris of ash, burnt wooden beams and stone collapse from the second story. A study of soil samples and fragments of a plaster-made floor from the second story, found within the collapse, shows that the floor was exposed to a temperature of at least 600°C."[79, 80]

King Zedekiah—like his predecessor, Jeconiah—was taken captive to Babylon. But not before being forced to watch the execution of his sons and then having his own eyes gouged out.[81] At this point, Nebuchadnezzar, who was clearly not in a generous mood, destroyed the Kingdom of Judah, recreating it as Yehud, a Babylonian colony.[82] Gedaliah, a grandson of the famed Judahite scribe Shaphan,[83] was made governor of the newly named Yehud province, which encouraged some of the Judahite refugees to return home.[84] However, the governor was perceived as a Babylonian stooge, and in 582/1 BCE was assassinated by a member of the Judahite royal household, Ishmael, son of Nethaniah. Fearing Nebuchadnezzar's response, many of the Judahites fled once more, this time to Egypt.[85] After around 400 years, and having outlasted its northern brother by 200 years, the Southern Kingdom of Judah had come to an end.

This was the first time in Jewish history that ancient Jews had become refugees without an Israelite state to which they could flee. What began with the Babylonian exile in 586 BCE tragically became a constant feature of the Jewish experience for almost 2,000 years, until the reestablishment of the Jewish state, the State of Israel, in 1948. It is worth considering—as we so rarely do for figures this far back in history—the trauma our ancient ancestors must have experienced in this period, particularly the descendants of those refugees who had fled from the Northern Kingdom of Israel. Just 200 years later, their ancestors' new home—Judah—had been conquered and destroyed.

However, the connection between the surviving Israelites and Judahites—as well as the contemporary Jews who evolved from them—and the Land of Israel did not diminish. During this time, the now famed Psalm 137 was written: "By the rivers of Babylon, there we sat, sat and wept, as we thought of Zion."[86] This is an ancient expression of the modern idea of Zionism: Jews living in exile, yearning to return home. The Edict of Cyrus of 539 BCE fulfilled that dream, in the same way as the founding of the State of Israel would do so more than two millennia later.[87] It was in that year, just 47 years after Jerusalem's defeat at the hands of Nebuchadnezzar, that Babylon fell to Persia and Cyrus the Great allowed the exiles to return home.[88] Under the Persian Empire, the old kingdom of Judah had become Yehud Medinata, an autonomous province, to which a number of the ancient Jews returned in order to once again govern their own affairs. And, in a miraculous turn of events, by 516 BCE, the building of the first iteration of the Second Temple was complete.[89]

CODIFYING THE TANAKH: RECORDING OUR CIVILIZATION

The Tanakh is the foundation of Jewish life, but I am not only interested in its content, I am also interested in the process of its creation, beginning in the Kingdom of Judah and continuing in exile and in the Persian and other periods. This sheds light on both the origins of the Jewish people and the prevailing ideologies of our ancient history. At the same time, it must be recognized that the contents of the Torah are vital in terms of our development as a unique collective, as it points to a distinct ethnic identity long before the Torah was composed. The stories and laws which were recorded in the Torah were circulating in ancient Israelite culture (both in Israel and in Judah) prior to its codification. This could have been in the forms of historical memory or cultural norms or the ethnic traits which already defined ancient Israelite identity, such as circumcision or refraining from eating pork, as well as the worship of YHWH (even if this was not yet an exclusive relationship on the part of all the ancient Israelites).

There are those who believe the Torah was specifically written by Moses as dictated by God at Mount Sinai. As will already be apparent from the preceding chapters, my perspective leans toward explaining our history through archeological and epigraphic evidence, alongside an exploration of the Torah as our foundational source material, rather than accepting the Torah as historical fact, without examination.

Israel Finkelstein argues that the process of compiling the written Torah began in late monarchic times (around the 8th century BCE).[90] Previously, the various stories would have been attached to specific localities: they were local traditions, for instance those related to Abraham, Isaac, and Jacob. Finkelstein thus argues that the Torah does not deal in "history" in the way we understand it today. Instead, it is more akin to memories which contain traces of historical events as well as the ideological developments of the time. This supports the notion of Jewish indigeneity because those who wrote the Torah had a perception of themselves, their shared Israelite history, the worship of YHWH, and their connection with the land itself.

In terms of when the Torah was first written, Cross and Finkelstein, among others, believe that Josiah was placed at the center of the creation of the Torah. In *Sefer Melachim*, it is recorded that in 622 BCE while renovating the Temple in Jerusalem, Hilkiah, the high priest, found "a scroll of the Teaching in the House of GOD."[91] But it is thought that instead of discovering the book of law, the scribes actually created it, and in terms of what was discovered/created, many scholars think it might have been an early version of *Devarim* (Deuteronomy). When it was read to King Josiah, he was so moved that he launched a major reform, renewing the covenant with God and eliminating idolatry from Judah. He ordered his men to "Go, inquire of GOD on my behalf, and on behalf of the people, and on behalf of all Judah, concerning the words of this scroll that has been found. For great indeed must be GOD's wrath that has been kindled against us, because our ancestors did not obey the words of this scroll to do all that has been prescribed for us."[92] *Devarim* is meant to be Moses' final speech to the Israelites, where he reviews their history, reiterates God's laws, and emphasizes the covenant and obedience as they prepare to enter the Promised Land. Being presented as Moses' work would undoubtedly have given this text legitimacy for Am Yisrael (the People of Israel).

Additionally, the centrality of Jerusalem, Judah, and the Davidic dynasty (to which Josiah belonged) has to be recognized when understanding the composition of the Torah. The scribes composed the Torahs in Judah and Jerusalem, which were ruled by the Davidic dynasty. Hence, they were made to appear dominant, despite the fact that, in reality, Israel dominated Judah.

In terms of the composition, some scholars believe that the books of *Devarim* and *Sefer Yehoshua* (Book of Joshua), *Sefer Shoftim* (Book of Judges), *Sefer Shmuel* (Book of Samuel), and *Sefer Melachim* (Book of Kings) were a single work. This was then added to and edited as Jewish history unfolded. There are, for instance, similarities in ideology, theology, and language throughout these books. In contrast, there are some striking contradictions between *Devarim* and the other books of the Torah, both in the stories it tells and in the laws it presents. For example, in *Bamidbar* (Numbers) 18:15–19, the law requires that the firstborn of every animal be given to the Kohen, but in *Devarim* 15:19–22, the law changes, directing that the firstborn be sacrificed at the Temple in Jerusalem and eaten by the animal's owner instead.

As Jewish history unfolded, other books of the Torah—*Bereshit* (Genesis), *Shemot* (Exodus), *Vayikra* (Leviticus), and *Bamidbar*—were added, and edits were made to the text to reflect the unfolding history of the Kingdom of Judah. "Much in the Bible predates the Persian period," argues academic Mary Joan Leith, "but scribal editors collected and revised preexilic texts while composing new material."[93] The Philistines are, for instance, mentioned in the stories of the Patriarchs, despite the fact that archeologists know that there were no Philistines in Canaan before the late 12th century BCE.[94] These were thus added later by the Judahite scribes responsible for compiling and codifying the Torah. Despite these discrepancies, this process was quite deliberate and designed to give a very specific account of ancient Israelite history—with a special emphasis on Judah and Jerusalem. This is why—as we discussed—the Kingdom of Israel in the north is minimized and viewed with a negative perception despite its power. As Leith writes: "The Hebrew Bible as a whole can be understood as a centuries-long curating project with one possible high point in the Persian period when the Torah/Pentateuch approached its final form."[95] Moreover, Sir Simon Schama describes the creation of the Hebrew Bible during a particularly tumultuous period in Jewish history as profoundly significant, not only for its content but also for the perspective it imparts. He writes, "A central fact, possibly *the* central fact, about the Hebrew Bible is that it is not written at a moment of apogee, but over three centuries (eighth to fifth) of trouble. That is what gives the Book its cumulative sobriety, its cautionary poetic, severity from the coarseness of triumphal self-congratulation found in imperial cultures."[96]

This centuries-long process allowed diverse experiences and perspectives to be compiled into a single, centralized narrative. As discussed, the exiles from Northern Israel brought with them their ideas, traditions, and memories, such as of King Saul.[97] These traditions were initially transmitted orally but when the Israelites came south, they were adapted, incorporated, and arranged into the written Deuteronomic history. But to legitimize rule from Jerusalem, Israel—the independent Kingdom in the north—has to be portrayed as illegitimate and sinful, ultimately being punished by God (a precursor to the Babylonian exile). Josiah, the King of Judah at the time of composition, is presented as the monarch who can unite Israel and save the day. However, as was the case in Israel, God was later said to have been angry with the people of Judah. For their alleged sins—which included idolatry, child sacrifice, and ritual prostitution—he punished them with (another) expulsion.

As discussed in the last chapter, Finkelstein argues the Patriarchs were initially local traditions which were then arranged into the Torah. Because Judah was dominant in this narrative, these stories were then woven together to make Abraham (whom Finkelstein argues is associated with the southern states and Mamre, in the highlands south of Jerusalem, more specifically) *the* patriarch of the people of Israel, even though Jacob and Isaac are also supremely important.[98] Finkelstein argues that, to ensure the creation of a pan-Israelite identity, the patriarchs were described as visiting areas beyond their immediate localities. Abraham—who was from the south—thus visits territory in the Northern Kingdom, while Jacob—from the north—visits areas in the south.[99]

The wrath of God is invoked to explain the failures of the Hebrew kingdoms and the destruction and conquest which overwhelmed them. The second writer of the Torah has to explain why the hopes of Josiah—who died in battle at Megiddo against the Egyptians in 609 BCE less than 20 years before Jerusalem was destroyed—were entirely unsuccessful. Finkelstein argues that, along with adding to the Torah, the second composer went back and edited points in the first section in order to offer an explanation of these later events. Although King Manasseh was a successful monarch, making decisions that positively impacted Judah, he is thus shown to be so awful that even Josiah's piety couldn't counteract the wrath of God. *Divrei Hayamim* (which is referred to as the Book of Chronicles in English) II 33 is solely focused on how terrible he is, suggesting: "Manasseh led Judah and the inhabitants of Jerusalem astray into evil greater than that done by the nations that the LORD had destroyed before the Israelites."[100]

When considering how the Torah was composed, while it is important to identify what is ideology and what is "real" history, this does not undermine any aspect of the Torah. It is a powerful example of identity-building and demonstrates our ancient ancestors' self-perception. It is also true that there are stories from the Torah that have been verified by modern archeologists. This is why, while the Torah should not be rejected as a historical document, it must be placed in its proper historical context and understood from that perspective.

The process of adding to and editing of the Torah continued until a set of texts was created, although there is (rather unsurprisingly) a debate as to when this occurred. During the Second Temple period (516 BCE–70 CE), there were various groups (Sadducees, Pharisees, and Essenes) each with their own interpretation of Jewish law and ideas of which books were to be included in the Hebrew Canon. There was, therefore, no authoritative canon in the Second Temple period.[101] Certain books, such as the Maccabees, which we will explore soon, were not included in the Canonical Tanakh. In *Against Apion*, written in the early 2nd century CE, Flavius Josephus (whose work we shall further explore and whom we shall henceforth refer to as Josephus) said there were 22 books in the Tanakh; however, the Tanakh has 24 books, suggesting two additional books were added to the canon after the early 2nd century CE.[102] All of this points to the fact that the earliest the canon was completed was in the 2nd century CE. This is likely to have been, in part, a response to the emergence of Christianity, and a desire to set Jewishness in stone, so that it would not be confused with Christianity.

The Torah is said to have been canonized during Persian rule and, following this, the other collections of writing which make up the Tanakh were also canonized: the *Nevi'im* (Prophets) in 200 BCE and *Ketuvim* (Writings) by 200 CE. The process which led to the compilation and the codifying of the Tanakh began around 800 BCE. That was around 2,700 years ago. And around 500 years after the origins of the ancient Israelites. This document—or rather, series of documents—is the Jewish history book, legal code, and constitution, and, as we will discover, is one of the key components of Jewish continuity which enabled us to survive for 2,000 years in exile.

DIASPORA/EXILE

The Jewish people became mostly diasporic (although *always* maintaining a physical presence in the Land of Israel) after the Roman expulsion from Jerusalem in around 135 CE. However, the origins of the Jewish Diaspora began with the Babylonian exile around 700 years earlier in 597 BCE.

It is always important to bear in mind that although ancient Jews—like modern Jews—managed to build meaningful lives in the Diaspora, some even choosing not to return to Judah following the Edict of Cyrus, this experience was imposed upon us. It was not a choice, freely made. It is why some Jews speak not of the Diaspora, but instead of Galut, or exile.

The exile in Babylon began the process of the Israelite evolution into modern Jews. Without their land, without a temple, these ancient Israelites had to evolve in order to survive as a collective. "The exile is the watershed," biblical scholar Yehezkel Kaufmann writes. "With the exile, the religion of Israel comes to an end and Judaism begins."[103] Jewish historian and theologian Michael L. Satlow describes this experience as "religious trauma."[104] However, while there was an evolution of Israelite identity—and there certainly *was* trauma—understanding these ancient Israelites through the prism of religion is to apply a modern concept to ancient people. They would not have seen a separation between their societal structure and their worship of YHWH. The trauma they experienced in exile was all-encompassing and reached every aspect of their culture; it was rooted in their very self-conception. How would these Israelites maintain their identity when stripped from the Land of Israel? That is the challenge with which they were faced.

These events took place 2,500 years ago, but in them we find the roots for modern Jewish expression and identity. This evolution is arguably what allowed Jewishness to thrive in exile. Previously, YHWH was strictly a national god worshipped by the priestly classes in the Temple in Jerusalem. However, at this point there had to be a shift in focus to allow

Jewish identity to continue in exile. It became the methods—such as the *brit milah* (circumcision)—through which we demonstrated our specific heritage, beliefs, and roots even in exile.[105]

Although it played a pivotal role in the development of Jewish identity, Professor Angelika Berlejung from the University of Leipzig suggests "that the biblical presentation, the 'history,' which had come to a standstill in the Babylonian period, resumed only in 539 BCE with the Books of Ezra and Nehemiah."[106] We know scant details about the ancient Jews' initial time in exile, to which only the Books of Jeremiah, Ezekiel, and Ezra refer. However, despite its forced nature, extra-biblical sources tell a story of opportunity and integration for many of the exiled Judahites in Babylon.

These indicate that Judahites were able to work and make a living in Babylonian society. "Communities of ordinary Judeans in exile were able to purchase, lease and inherit moveable and immovable goods and slaves, to marry, to participate in economic enterprises and to exercise their trades and religion without any restrictions," suggests Berlejung.[107] A cuneiform from 498 BCE reveals the ancient Jews to have been living in the Babylonian settlement of Al-Yahū-du—Judahtown. In these settlements, the Judahites were mostly farmers, working the land granted to them and, in return, paying their taxes and serving in the military.[108]

While some clearly yearned for their home, the exiled Judahites were treated well by the Babylonians. King Jehoiachin and his five sons lived amongst other exiled Levantine monarchs and officials and were given rations of grain and oil.[109] It is thought that the non-royal Judahite exiles were able to achieve prosperity. The Judahites appear as witnesses in the Murašû Archive—a collection of cuneiform tablets describing the business dealings of one family—implying they were peers of the Murašû family.[110] These date to the mid-5th century BCE—decades after the return of Judahite exiles to Judah. These Judahites thus chose to remain in Babylon, demonstrating that at least some of the exiles believed there were benefits to doing so, rather than returning to, and having to rebuild, Judah.[111]

Archeologist Laurie E. Pearce has also pointed to the fact that Judahites served in the royal court in Susa (known as Shushan, the setting of the story of Purim in the Torah),[112] while also pointing to the fact that, at Sappir, there were even Judahites with the moniker "royal merchants."[113] Despite the nature of their exile, Berlejung believes the Judahites in Babylon lived "economically and legally in a situation that was not uncomfortable or life-threatening."

None of this detracts from the resilience demonstrated by these ancient Jews. They experienced the trauma of exile, losing much of the wealth they had in Judah, but many of them refused to give up their identities—either returning to their homeland when allowed to do so or maintaining their commitment to Jewish life in the Diaspora. In short, they rallied. It takes a huge amount of strength and will to withstand a catastrophe like the exile and to rebuild lives and maintain identities. Indeed, around 1,000 years later, the descendants of the exiled Judahites who chose to stay in Babylon wrote the Babylonian Talmud. Compiled by Rav Ashi (president of the Sura Academy from 375 to 427 CE) and then Ravina II, the famed Babylonian rabbi, it is made up of the Mishnah (a written collection of the oral tradition) and the Babylonian Gemara (hundreds of years of rabbinic debate over the biblical interpretation). It is a striking example of Jewish continuity, that even in exile, we never stopped developing our civilization nor severed our connection to our indigenous land. Written in Babylon, it was nonetheless still preoccupied with the Land of Israel and all the laws and customs which flowed from it.

We have an understanding of the events following Judah's fall and the return of (some of) the exiles thanks to the Books of Ezra, Nehemiah, and Chronicles (not found in the Torah—the Five Books of Moses—but in the *Ketuvim* (Writings) section of the Tanakh). In *Divrei HaYamim*, Ezra offers an explanation for the fall of Judah, blaming Jews who sinned so God punished them by allowing Babylon and Nebuchadnezzar to destroy them and Jerusalem.[114] This theme would follow in the Book of Eicha which states: "Her enemies are now the masters, / Her foes are at ease, / Because the LORD has afflicted her / For her many transgressions; / Her infants have gone into captivity / Before the enemy."[115]

This notion of exile as a punishment is both a coping mechanism and an ideological tool for a devastated and confused group of people. The loss of the Temple, and the implications for the power of YHWH, would have left the Judahites in a kind of "psychic limbo."[116] So, they were trying both to explain their circumstances and promoting what they saw as proper worship of YHWH as a form of identity reinforcement. "Embracing a narrative of divine punishment, purification, and redemption as articulated by prophets like Jeremiah and Ezekiel," Mary Joan Leith argues, "the Golah community developed new modes of piety and worship as they went about curating their heritage—their cultural traditions and memories—whether in oral or written form."[117]

Although our ancestors were able to return to the Land of Israel just 47 years following the exile, this period of Jewish history was fundamental to the development of modern Jewish identity. It taught us crucial lessons—and posed fundamental questions—on how to maintain our Jewish identities while living in a state of exile. Lessons and questions with which we are still engaging today.

Chapter 3

A HISTORY OF THE JEWS AND OUR LAND:
POST-EXILIC ISRAEL

RETURN TO ZION: COMING HOME

Following the Edict of Cyrus in 539 BCE, a number of the Israelites gradually returned home from Babylon to Judah, now known as Yehud Medinata.[1] However, it was not a "mass return," as described in the Book of Ezra; instead, a small group of Judahites returned home over a period of time.[2] And while the land itself was not emptied following the exile, it was scarcely inhabited.

The Torah says that God was responsible for Cyrus' policy.[3] However, this was a form of ideological propaganda. A 539 BCE cuneiform, known as the Cyrus Cylinder, paints a different story: "I am Cyrus, king of the world … from as far as the settlements on the other side of the Tigris, where their temples have long lain in ruin, I returned the gods who lived therein to their places and provided them with permanent temples. I gathered all their inhabitants and returned them to their homes. Daily, may all the gods whom I have brought back to their holy sites speak on my behalf for long life and plead my favor before Bel and Nebo."[4]

Although now much smaller in size than the Kingdom of Judah,[5] Yehud was an autonomous region within the Achaemenid Persian Empire.[6] As the Cyrus Cylinder suggests, this was common throughout the Persian Empire, where the policy of allowing autonomy, worship, and national expression was widespread. There is a view that the continued involvement of the Davidic dynasty in the governance of Yehud, through Sheshbazzar, "the Prince of Judah," and later his nephew, Zerubbabel, suggests that, rather than simply being an autonomous region, Judah continued as a client kingdom of Persia.[7] The influence of the Davidic dynasty continued until Darius I (520–515 BCE), when a civil war was fought and won by the Priests of Jerusalem.[8] For the elite, who remained in Babylon, the conquest of Persia over Babylon did not materially change their situation. As Satlow wrote, "they would simply have given their taxes to somebody else."[9]

Little is known about the post-exilic period, and there is little extra-biblical evidence to inform our understanding, with exception of the Elephantine papyri and ostraca (documents from the Egyptian border fortresses of Elephantine and Aswan), which detailed an Israelite collective worshipping at a temple there in Egypt.[10] However, two seals—used to close jars—which were found in Jerusalem in 2020, provide an impression of the rebuilding of Jerusalem which occurred during the Persian period. "The imprint bears the image of a person sitting on a large chair with one or two columns in front of him," the Israeli Antiquities Authority suggests. "The character is probably a king …"[11] During this period, Jerusalem, which had been destroyed by the Babylonians, was rebuilt as a center for administration and worship. Following the period of Jerusalem's destruction, Mizpah, in the territory of Benjamin, likely became the largest population center and Bethel the major center of worship.[12] It took Jerusalem until 445 BCE to replace Mizpah as the capital of the Israelite territory in Judah.[13]

One of the significant developments in this period were the attempts to define Israelite identity, and the issue of intermarriage. Both Ezra and Nehemiah described this "intermarriage crisis." Ezra 10 suggests, "Then Shecaniah son of Jehiel of the family of Elam spoke up and said to Ezra, 'We have trespassed against our God by bringing into our homes foreign women from the peoples of the land; but there is still hope for Israel despite this. Now then, let us make a covenant with our God to expel all these women and those who have been born to them, in accordance with the bidding of the Lord and of all who are concerned over the commandment of our God, and let the Teaching be obeyed.'"[14] It is likely that in the devastation that emerged as a result of the exile, Ezra was focused on consolidating the Jewish people, and their presence in the Land of Israel, as they were now spread over several territories and without sovereignty.

Despite the developments that took place in this period regarding expressions of Jewishness and worship, we would not yet describe this practice as Judaism. That was a word that was not used until Maccabees II in the 2nd century BCE. In this period, the word "Jew" had no religious connotations as we would understand it today. That would only emerge much later. "A 'Jew' in the Persian period was someone living in, or with acknowledged roots in, Judah/Yehud," believes Leith.[15] Comments made in Ezra and Nehemiah regarding intermarriage—or the intermarriage crisis—have to be considered from that perspective, not a religious one.[16]

Megillat Ruth (the Book of Ruth) was also written in the Persian period and takes a different account of intermarriage and conversion. In Ruth, Chapter 1, she is reported to have said, "Do not urge me to leave you, to turn back and not follow you. For wherever you go, I will go; wherever you lodge, I will lodge; your people shall be my people, and your God my God."[17] The centrality of Ruth to Jewish history cannot be ignored and informs the notion of conversion and how a "foreigner" can become a Jew, through accepting the Jewish people and our God. Her story was included in the Biblical Canon and she is described as being King David's great-grandmother.[18]

Among other things, the Book of Nehemiah details the reconstruction of the walls of Jerusalem.[19] However, there is no archeological evidence that a city wall was constructed in the Persian period. Minimalist Hillel Geva describes its population during this period as "minute,"[20] while Israel Finkelstein believes the lack of evidence—both in terms of buildings but also material culture, like pottery—indicates that, following the 586 BCE destruction, Jerusalem had been reduced back to its pre-8th century BCE position and was once again centered on the Temple Mount.[21]

Despite its diminished size and population following the exile, Jerusalem remained central to ancient Jewish identity. It was in this period, in around 516 BCE, that construction of the first iteration of the Second Temple was completed.[22] This version of the Temple was modest and, as noted in Ezra, did not compare with the First Temple. "Many of the priests and Levites and the chiefs of the clans, the old men who had seen the first house, wept loudly at the sight of the founding of this house,"[23] Ezra 3 records. One of the few archeological discoveries from this period is the Yehud Coinage, believed by some to be connected to paying fees at the Temple. These are related to the minting of coins in Jerusalem in the middle of the 4th century BCE.[24] This implies that Jerusalem, even in this greatly reduced state, and its new, modest temple, were still places of pilgrimage to Judahites in the surrounding areas.

The events of Purim, the Jewish holiday, are also believed to have occurred in this period. It is said to commemorate the attempted genocide, and ultimate saving of the Jews in Persia by Queen Esther and her uncle Mordechai. Although recorded by Josephus in Antiquities of the Jews,[25] this is most likely not rooted in any historical fact. Rather, there is a—contested—theory suggesting Purim was an adaptation of the Persian New Year, Nowruz. Regardless of its origins, it is unsurprising, given its rule over the Jewish people, that Persia would feature in one of our holidays. It is also not—as we know—a Yom-Tov (literally translating as "Good Day," but a holiday governed by the same laws as Shabbat in the Torah) holiday, but a national holiday.

In all, the Persians ruled Judah for around 207 years, until 330 BCE when they were defeated by the Greeks.[26] From that point until 140 BCE, and the founding of the Hasmonean dynasty, the Greeks ruled or controlled Yehud, which was now renamed Judea. The treatment of Jews in this period mostly mimicked the Persians, apart from in the reign of Antiochus IV, which we will explore in the rest of this chapter.

FROM GREEKS TO HASMONEANS: FROM COLONY TO SOVEREIGNTY

The period of Greek rule in Judah lasted from 330 BCE to 140 BCE. This period is referred to as the Hellenistic age (meaning Greek-like), as it was known for the export and imposition of Greek culture. We usually split Greek control over the Land of Israel into two different periods: Early and Late Hellenistic. Alexander the Great and the Ptolemaics fall under the early period, while the Seleucids and the Jewish Hasmoneans, who reclaimed Jewish sovereignty, in the later period.

Alexander the Great arrived in the Land of Israel in around 329 BCE (just four years prior to his death).[27] In a series of stunning victories, he defeated the Persians, just as they had defeated the Babylonians. The status quo established during Persian rule was maintained by Alexander: Jewishness was respected, and Jews were given freedom and autonomy to express their identity as they saw fit within the wider Empire structure.[28] Of course, this was still a period where the Jewish indigenous land was ruled by a foreign power, but this situation is favorable in comparison with what came later.

As we will see, during his brief rule, Alexander established Alexandria in Egypt, which became home to a thriving and important Jewish community. Despite, or maybe because of, his achievements, Alexander died in 323 BCE, at the age of 32, leaving no heirs.[29] His empire was then divided between his generals. Ptolemy I Soter, who founded the Ptolemaic dynasty, ruled over Egypt,[30] while Seleucus I Nicator, who established the Seleucid Empire, ruled from Damascus over Mesopotamia (and much of the modern Middle East).[31] The Land of Israel lay directly between these competing empires, so it is unsurprising that it came to be included in both their spheres of influence.

Much of the scant knowledge we have of the Land of Israel under Ptolemaic rule comes from the Zenon papyri, dating to the 3rd century BCE. Zenon was a Greek living in Ptolemaic Egypt who traveled on trade missions to the Land of Israel as secretary to an important Egyptian official.[32] But even this does not give us a huge amount of information. However, archeology reveals that, until the later Hellenistic period and the Hasmoneans, Judea was very modest and small (both in terms of settlements and demographics)[33] and had not yet been fully rebuilt after its destruction by the Babylonians.

What we can understand from this period was the evolution of Hellenized Jews. The rise of Hellenized Jews is both particularly relevant to the experience as Jews today grappling with our identities, as well as to the origins of the Chanukah story and the eventual return of Jewish sovereignty in the land. Perspectives on the Hellenized Jews vary: Some view them as evolving their Jewishness, others as abandoning it. Both seem to be true, depending on the time and place in discussion, although Hellenized Jewishness was not inherently bad. Some manifestations of it were clearly an attempt to fuse the duality of Greekness and Jewishness for Jews living in the Hellenized world, not unlike the efforts made by later Jews in the Diaspora. The Jerusalem Talmud records that practices such as Roman-style haircuts and teaching Greek to their sons were "permitted the family of the Rebbi."[34]

The Hellenistic period also evolved the role of the Torah. Prior to this, Michael LeFebvre argues, the Torah was conceptualized as a set of laws, but it was "a preeminent description of Yahwistic ideals as practiced by Moses."[35] The Greek idea that prescriptive law was a necessary hallmark of a civilization influenced the Jews, who also wanted to be seen as civilized by their rulers. Thus, the Jews living in the Hellenized world created the Torah as prescriptive law for the masses for the first time. "The Hebrew Bible underwent great dissemination in the Hellenistic period, prompting other literary productions in the process," biblical scholar and historian of ancient Judaism, Reinhard Kratz, argues.[36]

Living in a specific Jewish quarter, the Alexandrian Jews were, at their height, part of the largest and most important Jewish community in the world (even larger than that in Jerusalem).[37] Deeply integrated, they were the first to translate the Torah into a foreign language, from Hebrew to Koine Greek.[38] This translation, known as the Septuagint, was completed in the 3rd century BCE.[39] Despite becoming the basis for the Christian Old Testament, the Septuagint was translated in a clear attempt to maintain Jewish traditions and law and understand Jewish history in Alexandria. The Letter of Aristeas, a 2nd-century document presented as being an account of the creation of the Septuagint,[40] tells how the king (presumably Ptolemy II) ordered it to add to the translation of the "law of the Jews" in his library.[41] Alexandrian Jews also built the Alexandria Basilica Synagogue—an enormous structure—believed by some to be the first ever synagogue in history (synagogue itself is a Greek word).[42] Sadly, despite their prominence, the Jews of Alexandria were not able to escape a recurring theme of Jewish history: Facing hate and prejudice, they are said to have experienced one of the first pogroms in history in 38 CE.[43]

By 201 BCE, the Seleucids, under Antiochus III, had successfully conquered the Land of Israel from the Ptolemaics.[44] They ruled until the Maccabean revolt and the establishment of the Hasmonean dynasty in 134 BCE.[45] Initially, their treatment of the Jews was akin to that of the Ptolemaics. Antiochus III (223–187 BCE) respected the autonomy of the Jews and rewarded them for assisting him in the wars against the Ptolemaics, even supplying "wine, oil, incense, wheat, wood, salt, etc., that were needed for sacrificial use at the king's expense."[46, 47]

All this changed when Antiochus' son, King Antiochus IV Epiphanes, took the throne in 175 BCE. Antiochus IV's policy aimed at eradicating "Judaism altogether from the Holy Land"[48] stood opposed to previous Greek attitudes toward the Jews. As Erich S. Gruen writes, "Early Greek attitudes toward the Jews, insofar as they can be discerned, were more often favorable than unfavorable. The Jews, in turn, became increasingly familiar with and adaptive to Hellenism."[49] Gruen's comments regarding the Jewish adaptivity toward Hellenism as a result of the Greeks' attitudes toward the Jews are fascinating, foreshadowing a trend we have seen several times in the Diaspora. The favorable treatment of Jews by Antiochus III set the stage for the further development of Hellenized Jewishness. If the Seleucids had been confrontational from the start, then it is unlikely we would have seen such an adoption of Greek culture. However, as is so often the case, despite initial apparent respect, the Seleucids eventually turned against the Jews, leaving them fighting for survival—both culturally and literally.

Much of our knowledge of the Maccabean revolt against the Seleucids comes from just a few sources. Most significant are the first and second book of Maccabees and Josephus' work, written in the first century CE. The two Maccabean accounts offer different perspectives on similar events. They are not sequels but are two versions of the same story. Their differences lie in a number of details, including the original language of their composition and the dates they cover. Maccabees I was written in Hebrew (but only a Greek translation remains) and covers the period of roughly 175–134 BCE (the entire Chanukah revolt until the establishment of the Hasmonean dynasty).[50] Maccabees II was originally written in Greek, composed somewhere in the Diaspora, and only tells the first part of the story, from 175–161 BCE, ending when Judah HaMaccabee was killed.[51] Maccabees I was written only slightly later than the events it records, during the reign of John Hyrcanus (the grandson of Mattityahu ben Yohanan, who sparked the Maccabean revolt) and was composed to legitimize the Hasmonean dynasty.[52, 53]

Significantly, Maccabees II sees the word "Judaism" used for the first time in history. As it was written in Greek, the word used is "*Ioudaismos.*" This was not in reference to a religion but used to denote "to side with or imitate the Jews,"[54] ultimately meaning Jewishness. It was used in opposition to "*hellenismos,*"[55] meaning Greekness.

From Maccabees II, we know that the period prior to the Chanukah uprising was one of great civil strife. During this period prior to the accession of Antiochus IV, the position of high priest of the Temple was, as it had been previously, held by the Oniad family. The various Oniad high priests balanced the need to respect their Greek overlord, Antiochus III, while also honoring and preserving Jewish tradition.[56] This fine balance was hard to maintain. Tragically, what brought this period of peace to a dramatic end was an internal conflict rooted in differing approaches to how the Jews interacted with the Greeks. Due to individual ambitions and family rivalries, the High Priest Onias III (who opposed the Hellenization of Judea) and Shimon (Simon), a Hellenizer and the financial manager of the Temple, fought over Shimon's plan to allow the Seleucids to plunder the Temple. According to Erich S. Gruen, Shimon "sought to extend his responsibilities to regulation of the market, thereby prompting appeal to the king's representatives and a suggestion that the funds contained in the Temple treasury be made available to the Seleucid regime."[57] Although Antiochus III did not take funds from the Temple, the civil conflict continued and the murder of one of Onias III's supporters led him to request aid from the Seleucids.[58]

According to Josephus, after Onias III was forced to abdicate, his brother Jason (formerly known as Joshua)[59] took his place. Not only did Jason attempt to ingratiate himself by raising taxes to increase revenue for the cash-strapped new monarch, Antiochus IV, but he also intensified the Hellenization of Jerusalem. He built a gymnasium[60] and an ephebate (a place for training young men) and, although the true meaning of his intentions are debated, it seems as if he was suggesting a Greek-style polis be created in Jerusalem.[61] Gruen argues the tangible implications were not the creation of the polis, but rather—through the gymnasium and an ephebate—the dissemination of Greek culture, and its supposed superiority over Jewish.[62] At this point, the Hellenization of the Jews clearly became immensely problematic and nefarious. As Maccabees II says,

"Jason, also did away with our Jewish customs and introduced new customs that were contrary to our Law."[63]

However, after three years as high priest, Jason sent Menelaus (the brother of Shimon who had previously quarreled with Onias III) as an envoy with funds for Antiochus IV. But Menelaus played Jason at his own game and bribed the king to be made high priest himself.[64] Menelaus' appointment meant the traditional Jewish practice of the Onias family supplying the high priest was broken for the first time in 200 years.[65] Menelaus had Onias III assassinated. This act was received very badly by the Jerusalemite population.[66] They petitioned Antiochus IV to punish the assassin, as well as Menelaus' brother, Lysimachus, who had plundered the Temple coffers. Antiochus IV intervened, ordering the accused assassin, Andronicus, to be executed. Nonetheless, Menelaus was cleared of all charges and retained his position.[67]

Having now been given his loot by Menelaus, Antiochus IV was once again focused on Egypt, but this left a vacuum for power in Jerusalem and civil war erupted between the Jews.[68] After a failed invasion, Jason, who had previously been outmaneuvered by Menelaus, was forced to retreat to Transjordan, leaving the high priest in control of the war-torn city.[69] At the same time, Antiochus IV was, once again, retreating from Egypt. Upon hearing of the violence which occurred in his absence, Antiochus unleashed a massacre in Jerusalem, which, according to Maccabees II, resulted in the murder of 40,000 Jews with a similar number sold into slavery.[70] With this event, the king's power and authority were firmly established. As Gruen reports, "the king installed officials, presumably with garrisons, to keep the Jews under heel: Philip in Jerusalem and Andronicus at Mount Gerizim in Samaria. They would also provide a bulwark for the regime of Menelaus."[71]

However, Antiochus IV was not satisfied and began a policy of cultural genocide—attempting to erase Jewishness in the Land of Israel.[72] At this point, Antiochus also defiled the Temple, erected idols, banned sacrifices in the Temple, and burnt the Torah. Maccabees II tells us the Temple was rededicated to Zeus Olympios and the sanctuary at Mount Gerizim to Zeus Xenios.[73] He also banned circumcision.[74] Josephus, described how:

> "Antiochus was not satisfied either with his unexpected taking the city, or with its pillage, or with the great slaughter he had made there; but being overcome with his violent passions, and remembering what he had suffered during the siege, he compelled the Jews to dissolve the laws of their country, and to keep their infants uncircumcised, and to sacrifice swine's flesh upon the altar."[75]

This policy was a direct attack on the expression of Jewishness as our connection to God. In *Bereshit* (Genesis), this connection is explained: "Any uncircumcised male who is not circumcised on the flesh of his foreskin shall be cut off from his people; he has broken my covenant."[76] Disobedience of these new diktats came with the death penalty.

At this point, in Modi'in, Mattityahu ben Yohanan began the Maccabean revolt. Mattityahu had been a minor priest in the Temple in Jerusalem.[77] However, in response to the increasing Hellenization, he—being a Zealot—moved his family to Modi'in. Maccabees I tells how, after killing a Greek official, Mattityahu ignited the revolt, shouting, "Whosoever is zealous of the law, and maintaineth the covenant, let him follow me."[78] Fleeing to the hills, along with his followers he was pursued by the Greeks who waged war on Shabbat. Refusing to fight, 1,000 Judean Zealots were killed.[79]

Maccabees I records that after Mattityahu's own death he was succeeded by Judah HaMaccabee (Judah the Hammer).[80] Judah's guerrilla warfare soon escalated into a wholesale revolt in 167 BCE. At that very moment, King Mithridates I of Parthia launched an attack on the Seleucid Empire from the east, seizing the city of Herat in what is now Afghanistan. As a result, Antiochus IV had to shift his army eastward, leaving a smaller force behind to confront the uprising in Judea. This shift proved crucial to the Maccabees' success. That same year, 167 BCE, the Judeans engaged in their first battle against the Greeks: the Battle of the Ascent of Lebonah,[81] and then in 166 BCE they fought the Battle of Beth Horon, winning both.[82] Following other victories at the Battle of Emmaus (165 BCE)[83] and at the Battle of Bethsura (164 BCE),[84] the Maccabees entered Jerusalem and rededicated the Temple. And thus, the Chanukah story was born.[85] Despite this success, Judah HaMaccabee was later killed in around 160 BCE, during the Battle of Elasa, and the war ultimately lasted—on and off—for another thirty years, until 134 BCE, when the Hasmoneans took control of the Land of Israel, placing it back in Jewish hands.[86] That a group of Jewish Zealots defeated the mighty Seleucid army is an astonishing feat. No wonder we commemorate it to this day.

There is no consensus as to why Antiochus IV broke with previous Seleucid policy and began persecuting the Jews. Some argue it stemmed from a desire to homogenize all people under his control and make them Greek. More modern scholars have argued it was more a response to the infighting between the Hellenized and more traditional Jews. Both Elias Bickermann and Victor Tcherikover, two scholars of the Maccabean revolt, blame the actions of Jewish leaders for the uprising. Bickermann argues the Hellenized Jews were trying to reform Jewish practice and encouraged Antiochus IV to institute legal reforms.[87] Tcherikover argues the revolt was one against the elite by the peasants. Others, such as Rabbi James Ponnet, suggest the revolt started life as a civil war: "The Hanukkah story is really about a revolt against the Hellenized Jews who had fallen madly in love with the sophisticated, globalizing superculture of their day."[88] Joseph P. Schultz supports this notion, stating, "the Maccabean revolt less as an uprising against foreign oppression than as a civil war between the orthodox and reformist parties in the Jewish camp."[89]

Either way, the context should not be forgotten. Judah was a colony—and had been for hundreds of years by this point. The Seleucids were in control. Their culture was dominant. At times, they very overtly looked down on aspects of Jewish culture. It is no surprise therefore that Jews trying to win favor with their overlords would actively promote Greek culture. As I explored in *Reclaiming Our Story*, it is also likely they internalized Greek views on its supremacy over Jewish culture, such as their views on circumcision as a form of mutilation which led some Jewish men to engage in epispasm, the reversal of circumcision.[90] It is true they could also have enjoyed aspects of Greek culture, but the existing power dynamics cannot be disregarded. We know that Antiochus IV placed increasing constraints on Jewish action and, ultimately, descended to cultural genocide. Is it really fair to say that the Maccabean revolt was a civil war, or indeed is it fair to blame those earlier Hellenized Jews who tried to "Greekify" Jewishness, when there was a much larger, more powerful actor involved?

Regardless of what sparked the rebellion, it culminated in a miraculous Jewish victory, restoring Jewish sovereignty to the Land of Israel for the first time since 586 BCE.

THE HASMONEANS: SOVEREIGNTY

The Hasmoneans ruled the Land of Israel, from 140 BCE to 37 BCE.[91] This was the last period in which Jews had true sovereignty in our indigenous land until 1948 and the rebirth of the Jewish state. Like the Chanukah story which led to its founding, the main sources we have for this period of Jewish history are Maccabees I & II, along with *The Wars of the Jews* and *Antiquities of the Jews* by Josephus.

As Maccabees I records, the dynasty emerged after Shimon HaTarsi (Simon Thassi), the last of the Maccabee brothers, became High Priest of Jerusalem.[92] He was the son of Mattityahu haKohen Ben Yonatan and brother of Judah HaMaccabee. In 139 BCE, Rome, now the dominant player in the region, recognized the Hasmonean dynasty as a state.[93]

However, in comparison to the Kingdom of Judah, Judea was, as we have seen, a greatly reduced territory, not at all comparable with the Southern Kingdom hundreds of years earlier. The Hasmoneans, however, greatly expanded their territory, Shimon began this trend by conquering Beth-Tsur and Yafo and building the fortress of Adida (Moshav Hadid).[94] During this period, Jerusalem once again emerged as a large city.[95] For the first time in 400 years, since the Babylonians destroyed it in 586 BCE, Jerusalem was finally comparable with the pre-exile city.[96]

As author Yonatan Adler suggests, during the Hasmonean period, Judaism, as the widespread adherence of the laws of the Torah, first emerged. Adler's work in *The Origins of Judaism: An Archaeological-Historical Reappraisal* is focused not on when Judaism as a system of belief emerged, but rather when it emerged as a practice adhered to by the masses. Focusing on archeological and epigraphic evidence, he believes the Hasmonean use of the Torah as a unifying and legitimizing force for their new dynasty was pivotal. He writes: "In adopting the Pentateuch as the legal foundation of the newly emergent Judean state, the Hasmonean rulers provided a rallying point around which the people of Judea might unite. With this, Judaism itself would have been born."[97] John Collins agrees with Adler's thesis, noting that, for the Hasmoneans, the Torah was a political tool. In the middle of the 2nd century BCE, he believes, we can identify a rise in literature that was "intensely concerned with *Halacha*" (Jewish law).[98] Ironically, the Hasmoneans, despite their family history of fighting the Greeks, were exceptionally Hellenized. But, because of its unifying power, they recognized Judaism—as the widespread and practical expression of Jewishness—was a powerful glue for their new state. Of course, the traditions did not emerge with the Hasmoneans. They are much older than that. However, Adler's point is that this is when Judaism became adhered to by the masses as "authoritative law."[99] Prior to this, Kratz argues, following the Torah was only for a small group of "educated elite and thus a negligible—if not marginal—circle."[100]

However, in a sign of the family infighting that would eventually lead to the destruction of the dynasty, Shimon was assassinated by his son-in-law, Ptolemy.[101] He was then succeeded by his third son, Yohannan/John Hyrcanus in 134 BCE.[102] In occupying both the position of high priest and king, the Hasmoneans diverted from the traditional Jewish practice, where these roles had been separated.[103]

In around 135/134 BCE, the Seleucid emperor, Antiochus VII, commenced a siege of Jerusalem which lasted for several years. As part of the eventual peace settlement arranged by John Hyrcanus, the Judean king, he had to assist the Seleucids in their war against the Parthian Empire.[104] However, in 129 BCE, during the Battle of Ecbatana in modern-day Iran, Antiochus VII was killed.[105] By 113 BCE, and truly independent from Seleucid interference, John Hyrcanus continued the process of enlarging his kingdom (begun by Shimon, his father).[106]

It was also John who is said to have forcibly converted people, such as the Idumean people, to Judaism. This is the first and only period in Jewish history this practice was policy.[107] Based on this scenario whereby we have, for the time, a mass of non-Jews converting to Jewishness, Adler argued that it is here, rather than during the Babylonian exile, that Jewishness also took on a religious identity.[108] With the conversion, the Torah was spread as law. And thus, Jewishness also became rooted in how one behaves, rather than simply what one is. Adler suggests that, in this period, Judean identity changed from an ethno-geographic term to an ethno-religious identity.[109] However, the central focus on the Land of Israel never receded, suggesting this notion may lack the necessary nuance. Clearly, in our history and evolution, Judaism took on a religious identity, but it was always one that remained rooted in the Land of Israel, with an emphasis on peoplehood. However, with a focus on practice there also came a focus on right and wrong ways to practice. This was thus also the time when Jewish sectarianism developed. During this Hasmonean period, we see Sadducees, Pharisees, and Essenes emerge. In terms of their differences, the Sadducees, made up of the priestly class, the aristocracy, and the upper classes,[110] only accepted the Torah (the Five Books of Moses).[111] The Pharisees, who were the everyday Jews,[112] believed in the oral tradition—the traditions developed over generations in Israel and Judah which were passed down through cultural transmission, including orally, later written in the Mishnah, compiled by Judah ha-Nasi in around 200–220 CE, which, along with the Gemara, the commentaries and debates on the Mishnah, make up the Talmud—as well as the Torah.[113] And there were also the Essenes, who were particularly pious and rejected both the Sadducees and the Pharisees[114] and are believed by some scholars to be those who wrote the Dead Sea Scrolls when they left Jerusalem to reside at Khirbet Qumran.[115] They began fighting with one another over the "correct" way to practice and express Jewishness in this new era. As Dan Shapira writes in *Tablet*, "in 96 BCE, the Sadducee Hasmonean king Alexander Yannai opened a bloody eight-year-long civil war against his more pietist Pharisee opponents, while using Greek mercenaries."[116] The Pharisees ultimately won this Jewish sectarian battle and their ideas eventually led to the evolution of Rabbinic Judaism. This became the mainstream, prioritizing rabbis as authority figures and the synagogue as a replacement for the destroyed Temple, given that pilgrimage to the Temple in Jerusalem was no longer possible after 70 CE.[117]

Sadly, the monarchs who followed John were consumed with a thirst for power and often engaged in barbaric feuding. John's son, Aristobulus, the high priest, had his own mother (the reigning queen) starved to death and imprisoned his own three brothers.[118] Despite his short reign, Aristobulus also expanded the kingdom to include the Galilee and the Golan.[119]

On his death, King Aristobulus' wife, Salome Alexandra, freed his brothers from prison and appointed Alexander Jannaeus king.[120] Under King Alexander, Judea expanded even further to include Acre, and then Gaza in 94 BCE.[121] But while they were expanding Judean territory at a rapid rate, the Hasmoneans remained Hellenized[122] and were deeply unpopular within the Judean population. In 67 BCE Queen Salome's son, Hyrcanus II, came to power on her death, but ruled for just three months.[123] His short reign was the beginning of the end of true Jewish sovereignty in the Land of Israel for just under 2,000 years. In yet more family infighting, Hyrcanus II was overthrown by his brother, Aristobulus II.[124] Aligning himself with the Arab king, Aretas III, Hyrcanus attempted to retake Jerusalem by siege.[125] However, Aristobulus requested assistance from the Romans—newly in charge of the former Seleucid Empire—via a bribe which caused the Nabateans to retreat (although Aristobulus still pursued them, killing 600 men[126]). Continuing to quarrel over the throne, both Hyrcanus and Aristobulus visited Pompey (the Roman general) following his arrival in Damascus in 63 BCE, hoping to resolve the issue.[127] Not waiting for a response, Aristobulus journeyed to Alexandrium (between Scythopolis and Jerusalem).[128] As a result, Pompey marched into Judea, causing Aristobulus to surrender.[129] Despite this, Pompey's troops were blocked from entering the city by Aristobulus' supporters.[130] This was a disastrous miscalculation which resulted in Aristobulus' arrest and a siege of Jerusalem.[131] Hyrcanus II—whose supporters had led Pompey's troops in—was then returned to the throne.[132] However, he was now a puppet king with the real power in the hands of Antipater the Idumaean, governor of Idumaea, whose son, Herod the Great, would become the founder of the Herodian dynasty.[133]

After periods of unrest and resistance, in 40 BCE, Antigonus II Mattathias (Aristobulus' son) was installed as King of Judea by the Parthians (who, through a series of wars, ultimately destroyed the Seleucid Empire and ruled as the dominant empire in the Near East from 247 BCE to 224 CE)[134] while Hyrcanus was physically mutilated, making him unfit to serve as high priest, and was exiled to Babylon.[135] However, the Romans quickly defeated Antigonus and, as we will explore in the next chapter, installed Herod, who took Mariamne, Antigonus II Mattathias' niece, as his second wife, thus continuing the Hasmonean dynasty, at least for a short while.

The two men continued fighting one another until Antigonus was defeated and executed in 37 BCE[136] (by crucifixion, according to the Roman historian Cassius Dio[137]). Antigonus II Mattathias was the last Hasmonean king of Judea. As we will learn, paranoid Herod eventually wiped out the last of the male line Hasmoneans,[138] but the Hasmoneans lived on in the children born to Mariamne and Herod (until, according to Josephus, he had them both murdered[139]). Ultimately, though, the actions and incompetence of the Hasmonean rulers resulted in the end of the dynasty and Jewish sovereignty over our indigenous land for 2,000 years. It was not until 1948 that we would reclaim it with the establishment of the State of Israel.

Chapter 4

A HISTORY OF THE JEWS AND OUR LAND:
THE END OF JEWISH SOVEREIGNTY

UNDER ROME: FROM CLIENT KINGDOM TO COLONY TO EXPULSION

Born in 72 BCE, King Herod, while raised a Jew, was not of Judean heritage.[1] He was the son of Antipater, an Edomite who converted to Judaism, and Cyprus, a Nabatean Arab princess from Petra.[2] Antipater was wealthy and powerful, and to secure his own position as governor of Idumaea, he successfully encouraged the weak Hyrcanus II to assert his claim to the throne after being usurped by his brother, Aristobulus II—who Antipater feared would strip him of his own power. After supplying him with troops in the Roman civil war, Julius Caesar made Antipater chief minister of Judea[3]—even after Hyrcanus II had been stripped of his power by Rome. His sons, Phasaelus and Herod, were then appointed governors of Jerusalem and Galilee respectively.[4] Herod soon demonstrated a desire to align himself with Rome,[5] executing a band of anti-Roman Zealots rather than allowing the Sanhedrin (council of Jewish elders) to exercise their right to try them for their crimes. His actions angered the Sanhedrin and pleased Rome, a trait which he would display throughout his governorship and eventual reign.

Herod's dependence on Rome was evident in 40 BCE, when, for a brief moment, the Hasmoneans reclaimed the throne under the hapless Antigonus.[6] In response, Herod rushed to Rome, presumably to seek assistance against Antigonus. The Roman Senate responded by appointing Herod as King of Judea.[7] But his reward was some time coming. For three years a civil war raged between Herod and Antigonus until, in 37 BCE, Herod laid siege to and eventually retook Jerusalem, with the assistance of a large Roman army.[8] At this point, Herod dispensed with his first wife, Doris, the mother of his first child, Antipater, and married the Hasmonean princess Mariamne. It was a politically savvy move—connecting his monarchy to that of the Hasmoneans granted legitimacy to the ambitious king's rule.[9]

When Herod came to the throne, he began an extraordinary wave of killings designed to assert his dominance and to see off any rivals, which left them powerless against him. He executed the Sanhedrin—with whom he had quarreled previously—and those who had supported Antigonus, as well as Hyrcanus II.[10] Relations with his own family were not much better: he had his own wife, Mariamne, and uncle executed.[11] Fearing that his brother-in-law, Aristobulus, a popular and handsome Hasmonean who had been appointed high priest, might emerge as a rival,[12] Herod had him drowned in a bath.[13]

The Jewish state, as so often the case throughout its various iterations, was frequently caught amongst the fighting and machinations of foreign powers. During the 32 BCE Roman civil war[14] Herod's protector,[15] Mark Anthony (alongside his lover, the famed Cleopatra), was defeated by Octavian. However, at the last minute, Herod switched his allegiance to Octavian,[16] who in turn confirmed his support for Herod[17] and even increased his territory to reclaim Judea and Samaria.[18]

During his time in power, Herod can be credited with building Judea. Despite the common perception of him as a tyrant, forcing Jews to make his vision a reality through forced labor, many of the most important sites within modern Israel, such as Masada or the Kotel, were constructed thanks to Herod. Unlike so many of his royal predecessors, the archeological legacy left by Herod is truly extraordinary: He rebuilt the ancient Israelite capital of Samaria (renamed Sebaste to honor Octavian); the incredible port of Caesarea was built, also named in honor of Octavian; and Jerusalem was developed as well, including his renovation of the Second Temple—the Western Wall of which is known by Jews today as the Kotel. Herod doubled the size of the Temple Mount,[19] with Josephus writing:

> "Now the outward face of the temple in its front wanted nothing that was likely to surprise either men's minds, or their eyes. For it was covered all over with plates of gold, of great weight: and at the first rising of the sun reflected back a very fiery splendor, and made those who forced themselves to look upon it, to turn their eyes away: just as they would have done at the sun's own rays. But this temple appeared to strangers, when they were coming to it at a distance, like a mountain covered with snow. For as to those parts of it that were not gilt, they were exceeding white."[20]

But despite his building works, Herod was deeply unpopular with his Jewish subjects, who felt he was Hellenizing Judea and insulting traditional Jewish law by bringing in foreign customs such as gladiatorial battles.[21] In 4 BCE, after years of corruption, excess, extravagant building works, oppression of the Judeans, and a propensity toward executing his family members, Herod died at Jericho.[22] As he instructed, Judea was divided between Herod's three sons, Herod Archelaus, Herod Antipas, and Philip and his sister, Salome I. This would set the stage for the complete erasure of any semblance of Jewish sovereignty and lead us down the path to direct rule from Rome. This period of rule is known as the Herodian Tetrarchy.[23] It did not last long: Soon after Herod's death in 4 BCE, according to Josephus in *The Jewish War*, a revolt erupted due to Archelaus' incompetence.[24] This was brutally suppressed by the Romans, under the control of the governor of Syria, Publius Quinctilius Varus, and, along with Jerusalem being occupied, 2,000 Jews were crucified.[25] In 6 CE, Archelaus' territory was recreated as a Roman province[26] and Archelaus was dead by 18 CE, when he was just 41 years old.

DIRECT RULE FROM ROME (MOSTLY)

This new Roman province was now renamed Judaea, with its capital moved from Jerusalem to Caesarea Maritima.[27] But even though from 586 BCE the Land of Israel was mostly ruled by foreign powers, colonization was not able to snuff out its Jewish connection. Judaea, like Judea and Yehud—the Roman, Greek, and Persian names for the territory—were all derived from the Judah, the ancient Jewish tribe and kingdom. It is also worth noting that, during these periods, Jewish distinctiveness was nearly always respected (with the exception of Antiochus IV, of course), with Jews often given degrees of autonomy.

Unsurprisingly, the period of direct rule from Rome—overseen by the governor of Syria—provoked unrest and rebellion, with Jews fighting their colonial overlords. Following the imposition of direct rule, a census was created by Quirinius, the governor of Syria, in order to raise taxes to be sent to Rome.[28] Josephus claimed this led to an uprising by Jewish Zealots under Judas of Galilee (not to be confused with Judas Iscariot, who betrayed Jesus).[29]

The root of the Jewish outrage at this census lay in the laws of the Torah, which, for some reason, said it was illegal to count the number of Jews, as well as the fact it would lead to taxation paid using coins that bore the figure of the Emperor Caesar.[30] According to Josephus' *Antiquities of the Jews*, Judas, along with Zadok the Pharisee, founded the Zealots during this rebellion.[31] This group was known as the "fourth sect" of the Jews in this period (the other three being the Sadducees, the Pharisees, and the Essenes) and was vehemently opposed to Roman rule of the Land of Israel, and opposed all who cooperated with Rome, including other Jews.[32]

The Romans had divided Judaea into five administrative districts with centers in Jerusalem, Gadara, Amathus, Jericho, and Sepphoris.[33] But despite being merely a province, ruled directly from Rome, until 28 CE, a degree of Jewish autonomy, particularly with regard to legal matters, was maintained. There was, however, an underlying tension between the Jews' right to worship and the imperial cult of Rome, which worshiped the Emperor. This rose to the surface between 39 and 40 CE, when a crisis under Caligula occurred.[34] In an act that desecrated Jewish law, which prohibits idol worship, and assaulted Jewish monotheism, Emperor Caligula sought to erect a statue of himself in the Temple in Jerusalem.

Around the same period, following a pogrom in Alexandria, Philo, the famed Jewish philosopher, traveled to Rome to meet Emperor Caligula. Requesting that the rights of Jews in Alexandria, previously confirmed by Emperor Augustus, be upheld, Philo pledged the loyalty of the Jewish community, offering "prayers, preparation of votive offerings and quantity of sacrifices, not only at general festivals but also on a daily basis."[35]

But, for Caligula, this wasn't enough, and he still wanted to assert his dominance over the Jews and our worship. When Caligula ordered Petronius, the governor of the Roman province of Syria (which now included Judaea), to erect the statue in the Temple, the Jews protested in their thousands, not just in Judaea, but in Alexandria, Thessaloniki, Antioch, and the Galilee.[36] Sensibly, Petronius was slow to carry out his order, giving Caligula time to change his mind and retract it. Agrippa I (Herod Agrippa's grandson) then called in the favor and the order was canceled, and for a period, Jewish worship was left untainted by non-Jewish ideas.

In 41 CE, in a miraculous turn of events, a form of Jewish sovereignty was returned to the Land of Israel,[37] when Emperor Claudius (who succeeded Caligula in 41 CE, following his assassination) gave the title of King of the Jews to Herod Agrippa (grandson of King Herod the Great and Mariamne the Hasmonean).[38] Having spent his youth in Rome, Herod Agrippa had struck up a friendship with a young Claudius, likely explaining his appointment. With his territory enlarged by his friend, Herod Agrippa ruled over a land as large as that of his grandfather, Herod the Great. Given his upbringing in Rome, and his heritage as both a

Hasmonean and a member of the Herodian dynasty, the new king was able to bridge the gap between the Jews and the Romans and gave hope to the Jews that their restored sovereignty could be preserved. Herod was an active participant in Jewish worship—and publicly read the Torah to his subjects—clearly valuing his Jewishness.[39] His friendship with Claudius guaranteed the rights of Alexandrian Jews, which were then extended over the Jewish Diaspora across the Roman Empire.[40]

But tragedy struck in 44 CE when Herod died suddenly.[41] With his death, Judaea returned to direct rule from Rome, and, once again, the hopes of Jewish independence were dashed.[42]

THE FIRST JEWISH–ROMAN WAR

There were three major Jewish revolts against Rome in the first century or so after the imposition of direct rule from Rome. The First Jewish–Roman War lasted for eight years, from 66–74 CE, and witnessed major events such as the siege of Masada and the destruction of the Second Temple, the latter altering Jewish expression forever.

Much of our understanding of this war comes from Josephus, an eyewitness to these events whom we have mentioned and cited earlier. His personal history reflects the broader struggles of the Jewish people during this time. Born Yosef bar Mattathyahu in Jerusalem, he was part of the Jewish aristocracy and priestly class.[43] Before becoming a historian, he was a military general, commanding the Jewish forces in Galilee, and fighting against the Romans. However, in 67 CE he surrendered to Vespasian following the siege of Yodfat[44] and was enslaved as a prisoner of war. During this time, Josephus had a prophecy of Vespasian becoming emperor. When this came true and Vespasian was crowned emperor two years later, he granted Josephus freedom and bestowed on him his family name—Flavius.[45] As a result, Josephus defected to the Romans and was even granted Roman citizenship. Despite being a Jew, he was kept as a translator to Titus (the emperor's son) during the siege of Jerusalem, which resulted in the destruction of the Second Temple.

Josephus subsequently wrote *The Jewish War* in around 75 CE and *Antiquities of the Jews* in 94 CE. Despite transferring his loyalties to the Romans, he wrote these works to advance the perspectives of Judeans. As Steve Mason, the Kirby Laing Chair of New Testament Exegesis in the school of Divinity, History and Philosophy at the University of Aberdeen, suggests, in Josephus' eyes "the Judeans are peace-loving and civil; in other books (*Antiquities of the Jews, Contra Apion*), ... they have the highest form of culture in the world."[46] Perhaps Josephus was trying to make amends for past betrayals or maybe he was defending his people at a time when the Jewish were facing a great struggle for survival and sovereignty over their land.

In his writing, Josephus presented the aforementioned Zealots as a continuous movement which eventually led to the First Jewish–Roman War of 66–73 CE (which we will explore later), although many scholars now believe that Josephus exaggerated the role of "fourth sect" in the First Jewish–Roman War to minimize the involvement of the Sadducees, the priestly aristocrats, of which he was a part.[47] However, as historian Martin Goodman argues, it is unlikely it could have begun without support from the priestly aristocracy.[48] Josephus was, at this point, still balancing his identities as a Jew and as a Roman and would want to diminish his own role—or the role of his class—in this major rebellion against one facet of his identity.

In *For the Freedom of Zion: The Great Revolt of Jews against Romans, 66–74 CE*, Guy MacLean Rogers lays the blame for the conflict at Rome's door[49] and notes there had always been tension between the Jews and their colonizers. But the financial needs of Rome, and the resulting heavy taxation on the Jews (and other colonized people), had exacerbated the situation with Nero's order that Gessius Florus, the governor, seize treasure from the Temple, igniting the spark. While the war was started by Nero, it was concluded by Emperor Vespasian, who sought to use it to legitimize his new Flavian dynasty and perhaps sought to exploit Rome's victory to distract from the devastation of the civil war at home that brought him to power. It is also possible that the emperor viewed the destruction of the Temple as a means to do away with a competitive cultic practice that threatened the dominance of Rome.

Some modern scholars claim the war is not as significant as was previously thought. However, MacLean Rogers believes that the huge resources and effort deployed by Rome to quell the rebellion indicate it was a hugely significant event, not just in the history of the Jews, but also of Rome.[50] One of the most important events in the war was, of course, the destruction of Jerusalem, with the infamous siege beginning in 70 CE. Led by Titus and assisted by an Alexandrian Jew, Tiberius Julius Alexander, the siege began just before Pesach and lasted for five months.[51] The first two walls of the city were quickly destroyed by the Romans but, as was the case throughout our history, the Jews fought back: Outmanned and outgunned, they prevented the Romans from reaching the third wall.

During this period, as would later be the case with the Bar Kokhba revolt, coins were minted celebrating the Jewish rebellion. They were dated from the year the fight began, with coins inscribed with "Year two for the freedom of Zion" discovered in 2022 excavations.[52] During the siege, however, the impact on the Jews in Jerusalem was devastating. According to Josephus, Jews inside the city walls—including many who had fled to Jerusalem—were forced to endure famine, disease, and even turned to cannibalism.[53] Josephus' story of Mary of Bethezuba, who, driven mad by hunger, killed and ate her own infant son,[54] was just one example of the horrors that befell the Jews during the siege of Jerusalem. As a result of the dire situation, temple sacrifice was suspended on August 6,[55] and by August 30, on 9th Av, according to the Hebrew calendar, after the Romans had breached the walls, the Temple was burned to the ground on Titus' orders.[56] According to Josephus, the

THE END OF JEWISH SOVEREIGNTY

trauma of seeing their temple burned was paralyzing for the Jews. He wrote, "Upon the Jews seeing this fire all about them, their spirits sunk, together with their bodies: and they were under such astonishment, that not one of them made any haste, either to defend himself, or to quench the fire: but they stood as mute spectators of it only." After a rampage of murder following the Roman victory, Jewish men were enslaved, forced into gladiatorial competitions,[57] and endured forced labor in Egyptian mines[58] as well as in building Roman structures such as the Colosseum.[59]

Even at this point in our history, just under 2,000 years ago, the history of Jews is remarkable. But, as Josephus argues, neither its age nor its riches could prevent Jerusalem from being destroyed. With a blunt finality that comes with a profound sense of loss, Josephus wrote, "Yet hath not its great antiquity; nor its vast riches; nor the diffusion of its nation over all the habitable earth; nor the greatness of the veneration paid to it on a religious account, been sufficient to preserve it from being destroyed. And thus ended the siege of Jerusalem."[60]

The Arch of Titus in Rome commemorates the looting of the Temple by the Romans. Depicted on the arch is a relief of Roman soldiers carrying items stolen from Jerusalem, including the famed Menorah from the Temple. As the arch shows, the Menorah was carried through the streets of Rome in the summer of 71 CE as part of a victory parade. It was then housed in Rome's ironically named Temple of Peace. However, the Temple was destroyed by fire in around 192 CE, and many presume the Menorah was lost in the flames. However, there was one reference to the Menorah in the 2nd century CE by Rabbi Simeon Ben Yohai, who claimed to have seen it in Rome.[61] Byzantine historian Procopius of Caesarea wrote that in 455 CE the Vandals raided Rome and carried away its treasures.[62] It is then possible these treasures—including those stolen from Jerusalem in 70 CE—were taken to Constantinople by general Belisarius when he raided the Vandal kingdom in 534 CE.[63] Specifically, he references "... the treasures of the Jews, which Titus, the son of Vespasian, together with certain others, had brought to Rome after the capture of Jerusalem."[64] After this, there are theories that the Menorah was, in fact, returned to Jerusalem and placed in the House of the Menorot.[65] But, as far we know, the Menorah has been lost to history.

Despite the fact that Jerusalem was destroyed, the war continued until 74 CE. Jewish strongholds at Herodium and Machaerus were destroyed within two years, while three years after the destruction of the Temple, Masada (Herod the Great's former palace) was destroyed. The siege at Masada is said to be the last stand in this first Jewish–Roman War and, according to Josephus, 967 of those inside Masada committed mass suicide rather than submit to the Romans.[66] On entering Masada, up to which they had built a ramp, the Romans found "a citadel of death."[67] Mason argues that Masada was not a military base for Judaean rebels, as had been recorded, but rather it was a refugee camp. He writes, "Masada's wartime Judaean inhabitants [were] family men seeking the security of the former royal refuge for their women and children. Fearing the bloody factionalism in Jerusalem ... they remove themselves from the fray to this remote, fortified site ... [hoping to] ride out the storm in security."[68] Ronny Reich, from the University of Haifa, shares this thinking: "From 66 until the final siege, Masada was 'a camp of displaced persons.' It was not a 'Zealot' stronghold but rather a place for different kinds of refugees."[69]

While Josephus claimed that, when they reached the summit of Masada, the Romans found only death and destruction, more recent scholarship has questioned this contemporaneous and partial account. There are theories, promoted by those such as Shay Cohen, professor of Hebrew Literature and Philosophy at Harvard University, that the Romans killed the Jews they discovered hiding on Masada.[70] This would explain the discovery of a small number of skeletal remains. Whatever the truth, the siege at Masada ended the First Jewish–Roman War.

While Josephus' claim that 1.1 million Jews were killed during the war is unlikely, it is certain the Jewish population had been greatly diminished due to murder, famine, and enslavement. Israeli historian Moshe David Herr estimates that one-third of the Jewish population in Judaea was killed during the First Jewish–Roman War[71] (with, according to historian Seth Schwartz, 97,000 Jews displaced[72]). These stark figures inevitably bring to mind other times in our history when the Jewish population has been decimated. Although, during this war, we were not being targeted as Jews, as we would be on other subsequent occasions, this pattern of death and destruction dominates our history. But so does our survival. And miraculously, even after our sovereignty was stripped and our land stolen from us, we maintained our Jewish identities and our practice, even if we had to evolve to fit our new circumstances.

The destruction of the Temple and what this came to mean for Jewish worship for the rest of our history was significant. Following its destruction, the Temple could no longer be the focal point of Jewish worship. In response to this cataclysmic shift, Jewishness shifted its focus to the study of Torah, and our law, as opposed to worship at a specific altar. Even though the Jewish Diaspora was well established by this point, a portion of their focus had also been on the Temple, to which they undertook pilgrimages.

The move toward the synagogue, Torah study, and leadership by the rabbis allowed Jewishness to continue. The focus on Torah study was particularly significant in ensuring that Jews in the Diaspora developed a literacy in Jewish law. This was a key component of the continuity of the Jewish people, which enables us to claim indigeneity. The laws which emerged in the land, that governed the lives of our ancient ancestors, continue to be relevant for us today, because of this development. Following Jerusalem's destruction, the central Israeli city of Yavne became an important centre of Rabbinic Judaism. Under the leadership of Rabbi Yohanan ben Zakkai, who is said to have escaped Jerusalem prior to its destruction, the rabbis created systems which would allow Jewishness to adapt to the new post-temple world.[73] This new situation established rabbis as the central Jewish authority, leading to the development of Rabbinic Judaism, which, as mentioned in the previous chapter, remains the dominant form of Jewish expression today. It also resulted in the creation of the Mishnah and, later, the Talmud as the definitive sources of Jewish law and thought.

However, we should not mistake this shift for an abandonment of the Jewish aspiration for statehood and a connection to the Land of Israel. Our indigeneity continued to be a central binding factor and expression of our Jewishness until 1948. We always yearned to return. We see this idea continued during the Bar Kokhba revolt, which we will explore shortly, when Rabbi Akiva, already living in the Diaspora, gave support to this war in the hopes that it would lead to a Jewish return to the land. The Talmud even encouraged Jews to live in the land, regardless of who was in charge.[74] With reference to the continued holiness of the land, the Mishnah is also recorded as stating: "… Eretz Yisrael is more kadosh than all the lands. What is its kedusha? The [produce for] Omer, Bikurim and Shtei Halechem are brought from its land as opposed to all other lands."[75] We also, as we will explore in the coming chapters, continued our practices that evolved in the land. We continued to refer to ourselves as Am Yisrael—the people of Israel. We understood that, despite the fact our sovereignty was stripped and our land colonized, we were still a nation belonging to a specific land.

BAR KOKHBA REVOLT

Unlike the First and final Jewish–Roman Wars, where the fighting took place in Judaea, the Kitos War, which took place from 115–117 CE, was largely fought in the Diaspora.[76, 77] Also known as the War of Quietus—after Lusius Quietus, the Roman general who eventually crushed the rebellion—this second Jewish–Roman War is more accurately viewed as a series of revolts, rather than a single conflict. Prior to their outbreak, tensions between Jews and non-Jews had been high for many years; in Alexandria, for instance, non-Jews committed pogroms against their Jewish neighbors. While the Romans were distracted fighting the Parthian War, the Jews in Cyrenaica, Egypt, Cyprus, and Mesopotamia—as well as in Judaea itself—took their chance and attacked Roman soldiers. Not a huge amount is known about the Kitos War; however, we do know it ended with the expulsion of Jews from Cyrene, while Jews in the other regions were pacified by force.

However, the Jews of Judaea were not quiescent for long. Following a long period of unrest as they unsuccessfully sought to reclaim their land, in 132 CE the Jews of Judaea rose up once again under the leadership of Shimon Ben Koseva (who was later renamed Bar Kokhba).[78] This marked the outbreak of the final Jewish–Roman War, which lasted until 135 or early 136 CE.[79] During this period, as had been the case previously, Rome was in a state of decline, facing rebellions in Britain, Gaul, and Spain. But another trigger for the revolt lay closer to home with the renaming of Jerusalem as Aelia Capitolina in 129/130 CE and the construction of a pagan city on its ruins.[80] Eusebius' writings suggest that the renaming of Jerusalem was a punishment for the Bar Kokhba revolt and an attempt to erase the Jewish connection to the land. However, this does not seem to have been the case, as evidence suggests the renaming of Jerusalem preceded the outbreak of the conflict.[81] As the historian Miriam Ben Zeev Hofman argues, the finding of coins over the past half-century settles the issue. "A number of hoards have been found in refuge caves in different places around Judea in the last fifty years, which display coins of Bar Kokhba along with coins representing the founding of Aelia Capitolina—which means that the Roman mint started to operate before or during but not after the Bar Kokhba War," she suggests.[82] In short, the attempt to turn Jerusalem into a Roman, pagan city was a catalyst, rather than a punishment, for the revolt.

Unlike the First Jewish–Roman War, this conflict was centered only in Judaea, with neither Samaria nor Galilee participating. However, Bar Kokhba was a brilliant military strategist and was initially successful, leading to the establishment of an independent state that encompassed much of Judaea.[83] Archeological discoveries—most recently, in 2024, the discovery of a coin in the Judaean Desert engraved with "Eleazar the Priest" in Ancient Hebrew[84] and also bearing the inscription "Year One of the Redemption of Israel"—indicate this success. In 1960 and 1961, letters written by Bar Kokhba himself were discovered in caves at Nahal Hever near Ein Gedi, by the Dead Sea,[85] along with papyri with the words "Shimon Bar Kosebah hannasi al Yisrael" (Shimon Bar Kosebah, Prince over Israel) indicated the success of the revolt.[86] The letters contain orders to harvest a field (and threats of punishment if instructions weren't followed), suggesting the rebels were clearly in control of an area with fields to harvest at that point. The letter thus tells us definitively that En-Gedi was an important territory for Bar Kokhba's forces.

Once again, Jewish sovereignty in the land had been reclaimed. Although not everyone shared his high regard for the rebel leader, Bar Kokhba was hailed as the "messiah" by Rabbi Akiva in Yavne,[87] who gave him the name "Bar Kokhba," or "Son of the Star,"[88] said to be a reference to the Star Prophecy verse in the *Bamidbar* (Numbers) 24:17: "A star rises from Jacob."[89]

However, as the Romans adopted a scorched earth policy, the fortunes of the Jewish fighters turned. The revolt ultimately came to an end in 135 CE, when Bar Kokhba was killed by Roman troops at the fortress of Betar.[90] After his death, the Romans conducted a campaign of annihilation and the Jews who remained were enslaved and murdered—including Rabbi Akiva. The early 1960s Nahal Hever discoveries—later referred to as the Cave of Horrors—shed some light on the terrible last days of the Bar Kokhba revolt, with baskets filled with human skulls and the remains of 40 women's and children's bones uncovered. Fighters and their families, it appears, had fled to the caves as defeat became a certainty.

Following the destruction of the Bar Kokhba revolt, the practice of dating coins starting from the year of the rebellion ended. Instead, a practice began to date from the year of destruction. A 2nd-century CE coin, found in a Judean Desert cave, is dated in its first line to "Year 4 of the Destruction of the House of Israel," a reference to the end of the Bar Kokhba revolt.[91] In 132 CE, the province of Judaea was merged with Galilee into an enlarged province named Syria Palaestina. Hadrian built a temple to Jupiter on the Temple Mount, burning the Torah scrolls and erecting statues of himself and the Roman god. What followed was the ultimate punishment for Jews: Expulsion from Jerusalem. According to Eusebius, Hadrian declared that the "whole nation should be absolutely prevented from entering the district round Jerusalem, so that not even from a distance could it see its ancestral home."[92] And with this, for the first time in a millennium, after 1,000 years of continuous Jewish presence, Jerusalem was tragically made Jew-free.

TWO THOUSAND YEARS OF EXILE: CONTINUITY AND EVOLUTION

Following our expulsion from Jerusalem, it would take another 2,000 years before a Jewish state was reborn in 1948. For another 200 years—until 313 CE[93]—the Roman occupation continued, which was followed by over three centuries of Byzantine rule from 313–636 CE.[94, 95] In 636, Muslim Arabs conquered the land and ruled until 1099 CE.[96] The Crusader Period lasted from 1099–1291 CE,[97] then the Mamluks ruled from 1291–1516 CE.[98] The Ottoman Empire then conquered the Land of Israel in 1516 CE,[99] holding sway until 1917 CE, when, following their defeat in the First World War, the British Mandate of Palestine was established.[100]

However, despite the loss of our sovereignty over the land, the Jewish people and their civilization survived and evolved, both in the Land of Israel and beyond. As we have already seen, communities emerged in Babylon (597 BCE) and Alexandria (332 BCE). And, as early as 161 BCE, Jews voluntarily moved to Rome, following the establishment of the Hasmonean dynasty.[101] The Diaspora, however, took on a new dimension and dynamic once the Romans expelled us from Jerusalem in 136 CE.

The first four chapters of this book give a brief overview of the first 1,300 years of Jewish life. Our epic journey took us from a separatist Canaanite community through a collection of tribes to a monarchical system, colonization and exile, the reclamation of sovereignty and then exile once again. For the next 2,000 years, wherever Jews settled we put down roots and many of us, as we had first done in Babylon, worked to preserve our Jewishness. In time, Jewish communities all over the world emerged. From the oldest in Babylon to Rome and then to more modern communities in China. Of course, Jewish identity also evolved. Sub-ethnic identities emerged and geographical iterations of our indigenous culture sprang up. Sephardic was Iberian flavored, Ashkenazi bore the mark of central and Eastern European, while Mizrahi had a North African and Middle Eastern hue, and Beta Yisrael contained Ethiopian traits. But despite these evolutions (and their important and specific customs and identities), our connection to our indigenous land and culture remained strong and central to our identities as Jews.

But what preserved Jews and Jewishness? Yes, we were bound by our belief in one God and we adhered to the laws and customs set out by the Torah, but we were also connected to and rooted in the Land of Israel. Crucially, we retained our sense of being a people and maintained our national identity. We were Jews, bound to the Land of Israel, hoping, praying, and trying to reclaim it. Even though we put down roots in the Diaspora, as Nancy E. Berg states in *Exile from Exile: Israeli Writers from Iraq*, we were "neither assimilated nor annihilated."[102] The modern Zionist movement presented those in the Diaspora as weak. In a speech at the Second Zionist Congress held in Basel on August 28, 1898, Max Nordau coined the term "Muscular Judaism" (*Muskeljudentum*). He spoke of the new Jew, the Zionist Jew, replacing the old diasporic Jew.[103] It is true that modern-day Zionism is our indigenous rights movement which eventually reunited us with our native land, but we cannot disregard and diminish the achievements of the community in the Diaspora in preserving Jewishness and our connection to Israel.

While there were always Jews living in our land, and while Jews always returned home, we should value the efforts of our ancestors in exile. They were the ones who, despite being cut off from the life source that was the Land of Israel, kept this tiny collective alive. It is their commitment to Jewish life, Jewishness, and the Land of Israel that made modern Zionism possible. Were it not for their commitment, work, and effort, there would not have been a people to return home. We would have ceased to exist. Zionism and its achievement—the State of Israel—stands upon their shoulders.

The rebirth of the Jewish state in 1948 was a modern-day miracle. It was then the Jews did something truly extraordinary: For the first time in over 2,000 years, the Jewish people were sovereign over our indigenous land. We decolonized our land and, while a strong and important Diaspora remained, Jews from literally all over the world returned home—and continue to do so: In 2022, 70,000 Jews made *Aliyah* to Israel.[104] And so our story continues to evolve.

It is this history which Jewish schools, institutions, and organizations *must* teach along with literacy in understanding the Tanakh and Talmud. All Jews should be taught our history. They should be given an opportunity to understand their story. Because that is what this is. The history described in these chapters is the origins of *all* Jewish people. This is our story. And it's time we reclaimed it.

Chapter 5

A STUDY ON JEWISH INDIGENEITY

THE UNITED NATIONS

On September 13, 2007, the United Nations adopted the Declaration on the Rights of Indigenous Peoples, consisting of 46 articles designed to protect the rights of indigenous people worldwide. The first line reads: "Affirming that indigenous peoples are equal to all other peoples, while recognizing the right of all peoples to be different, to consider themselves different, and to be respected as such."[1] It is this which Jews must see in themselves and that others must see in us. We are a distinct people indigenous to Eretz Yisrael, emerging in the Land thousands of years ago and there we remained rooted, physically, culturally, and spiritually.

However, according to the United Nations, the Arabs—despite being a colonizing power—are considered indigenous to the Land of Israel.[2] Despite the UN's racist attempt to deny Jewish indigeneity, its own criteria, as I will demonstrate in the next two chapters, apply to Jews and prove that Jews are indigenous to Israel. The first four criteria are discussed and analyzed in this chapter, with the remaining three the subject of Chapter 6.

At the outset, we should recall the context in which the UN set its criteria: the Leftist notion that indigenous people are inherently oppressed. According to indigenous scholar, Sheryl Lightfoot, underlying the UN's seven criteria are these three ideas: "1) a pre-colonial presence in a particular territory; 2) a continuous cultural, linguistic, and/or social distinctiveness from the surrounding population; and 3) a self-identification as 'Indigenous' and/or a recognition by other Indigenous groups as 'Indigenous.'"³ The first two criteria are clearly rooted in the notion that people have to have been colonized to be considered indigenous. It is obvious that many—even most—indigenous people have been colonized, the Jews included, but basing the criteria to identify indigeneity on this notion is deeply troubling. The third point is equally problematic. Why should the perspective of *other* indigenous communities, who may know nothing about a group—or even be prejudiced against them—matter? Don't all groups have a right to self-identify and tell their own story? This is especially troublesome when it comes to Jews, as the progressive world—which includes many (though thankfully not all, as seen in the founding of an Indigenous Embassy in Jerusalem)—is largely anti-Zionist. In this ideological context, the very idea that Jews are indigenous to Israel is often summarily dismissed.

Despite its current ideas about indigenous groups, the UN initially followed the example of its predecessor, the interwar League of Nations, in favoring the nation state over indigenous people.⁴ However, with the onset of the decolonization movement from the 1960s, its perspective shifted.⁵ It then evolved to embrace the wider Leftist politics of that period, which sought to establish a binary divide of colonized or colonizer and oppressed and oppressor.⁶

However, this shift did not initially benefit indigenous communities. We can identify a significant contradiction within UN General Assembly Resolution 1514 (1960). Its first article states: "The subjection of peoples to alien subjugation, domination and exploitation constitutes a denial of fundamental human rights, is contrary to the Charter of the United Nations."⁷ But, at the same time, Article six states: "Any attempt aimed at the partial or total disruption of the national unity and the territorial integrity of a country is incompatible with the purposes and principles of the Charter of the United Nations." This inherent contradiction explains why Chickasaw legal scholar James (Sa'ke'j) Youngblood

Henderson described indigenous people as "the unfinished business of decolonisation."[8]

As the century progressed, indigenous people and their issues gained influence at the United Nations. In 2007, the United Nations Declaration on the Rights of Indigenous Peoples was adopted by the UN General Assembly. However, rather than simply focusing on the preservation of indigenous communities "as distinct peoples," this too has a focus on human rights and the notion that they are inherently oppressed.[9] As writer Phil Henderson has suggested, the "UNDRIP must be seen primarily as a tool for further stabilizing the state-centric international order, while providing minimal protection for indigenous individuals, ignoring indigenous peoples."

As we will see, it is possible to demonstrate that—even using the UN's underdeveloped and binary understanding of indigeneity—Jews are indigenous to the Land of Israel. However, because parts of the UN definition are so flawed, we shall also reference the definition of indigeneity I outlined in Chapter 1 to determine Jewish indigeneity:

> "An indigenous people are a group whose collective identity began in one specific land, and it is in that land they remained rooted (either physically, spiritually, or culturally). This is their home and is where they originated, developed, and continued to be fixed through a connection to the environment and natural resources, living systems, culture, and practices as a people, irrespective of their sovereignty in the land."

This definition is both depoliticized and seeks to understand the relationships that exist between indigenous groups and their respective lands. Unlike the UN criteria—and much of its rhetoric surrounding indigeneity—this does not presuppose oppression as an inherent part of the indigenous experience. Instead, its focus is on the role that indigenous lands play in the formation and maintenance of indigenous identity. It is important to acknowledge that indigenous people are not monolithic, and we have a multitude of experiences. The Jewish people, like any other indigenous people, must be free to define their own experience and identity without being forced to base our notion of indigeneity on the experience and identity of other communities. For instance, the idea of conversion is sometimes raised to deny the right of Jews to identify as indigenous. I have been told: "You cannot convert into other indigenous tribes, so Jews cannot be indigenous." Not only does this misunderstand the role of initiation into non-Jewish indigenous tribes, but it casts all indigenous people as the same. This is a reductive and exclusionary perspective. Indigeneity does not—and should not be understood to—connote a set of people whose experiences, identities, and self-expression can be put neatly into a single box. There is no sensible or logical reason why Jews—or any other indigenous people—should not be able to maintain both our indigenous identities and the features of our identity which make us unique. These chapters will demonstrate, definitively, that Jews are indigenous to the Land of Israel and must be recognized as such. They will enable us, as modern Jews, to add another layer of understanding to our relationship with the Land of Israel, the modern State of Israel, and countless generations of Jews who came before us and will ultimately follow us. Each generation of Jews is part of an unbroken chain of living culture, tradition, practice, and belief. We are all, each of us, deeply connected to the land from which we sprang thousands of years ago, even if that relationship isn't clear or understood.

This conversation took on an even greater significance following the genocide committed by Hamas against Israel on October 7, 2023. Following this massacre in Israel, Jews in the Diaspora and in Israel were met with a deluge of hate which sought to present Israel as a settler colonial project and its people as colonizers. It has rarely been more important for Jews to understand our own story. We must be able to reject the racist lies told against Israel and the Jewish people. It is impossible to sever the Jews from our land, and we must understand why. Our history is real and tangible. And the cultural practices which began in the land, which are drawn from the land itself, continue on in the lives of modern Jews today.

Ultimately, the notion of indigeneity enables Jews to conceptualize our identities more clearly. Understanding the status of Jews as an indigenous people must impact our perceptions of ourselves and our Jewishness at large. We are an indigenous people and should be recognized as such.

"SELF-IDENTIFICATION AS INDIGENOUS PEOPLES AT THE INDIVIDUAL LEVEL AND ACCEPTED BY THE COMMUNITY AS THEIR MEMBER."

Historically, Jews have not used the classification of indigeneity to describe our relationship with the Land of Israel or with one another. However, we understand Israel as the place where our roots lie, and, as we will explore, it remains a place to which many Jews feel deeply connected today. It is through this lens that we will analyze the relevance of this first criterion to the Jewish people. Of course, there are Jews who actively reject their relationship with the Land of Israel. In *Reclaiming Our Story*, I explained that these Jews have internalized non-Jewish notions of Jews and Jewishness and have allowed the non-Jewish world to define their narrative. This is tragic, but these Jews currently still represent a minority outlook.

Despite being born in the Diaspora, many Jews outside of Israel feel a closer connection to Israel than they do to the countries of their birth. A 2023 study by the Institute for Jewish Policy Research revealed that 52% of Jews in Spain, 49% in France, and 33% of Jews in Britain feel more closely related to Israel than the countries in which they live.[10] Of course, this also means that 48% of Jews in Spain, 51% in France, and 67% in the U.K. feel more closely connected to those countries than Israel. But that does not mean they don't feel as connected (or even connected to an extent) to

Israel. Identity is not necessarily a binary "either/or." In the U.K., a 2015 City University study found that 93% of Jews say Israel plays a part in their Jewish identity.[11] These statistics represent Jewish indigeneity and the profound connection that exists between individual Jews from the Diaspora and Israel. The notion that Jews feel more connected to Israel than their own countries is not a manifestation of the anti-Jewish canard of dual loyalty. These Jews may feel more connected to Israel, but in no way pose a risk to the countries of their birth or wish it harm in any way. In fact, they may feel connected to their home country as well, just to a lesser extent. Personally, although I do feel British, I am more connected to Israel than the U.K. I am proud of being British and I choose to live in the U.K., for the moment, while also understanding that Israel is where I would consider to be my home. These are not mutually exclusive.

A 2010 study, "Committed, concerned and conciliatory: The attitudes of Jews in Britain towards Israel" by the Institute for Jewish Policy Research (IJPR) found that 95% of British Jews have visited Israel at some point in the past.[12] The IJPR used this (along with the number of British Jews making *Aliyah*) as an indication of the attachment of British Jews to Israel. And more recently in 2023, The Campaign Against Antisemitism found that 97% of British Jews felt personally connected to events happening in Israel.[13] It is clear that Israel holds deep significance for the Jewish people, regardless of how we prioritize our individual identities. This connection exists because Israel, as the indigenous land of the Jews, is an integral part of Jewish identity, representing a deep, powerful, and enduring emotional bond. This is why, even though many Jews may not yet identify as indigenous, the strong emotional connection between Jews and Israel serves as evidence of this first criterion.

Regarding the second part of this criterion, being accepted "by the community as their member,"[14] Jews have important laws (*Halacha*) that govern Jewish membership. Individual Jews are thus officially recognized as Jewish through various Jewish streams.

While individuals can adopt customs and even beliefs, without going through an official conversion process, in a post-Rabbinic Judaism context, they would not be considered as Jewish. As we discussed in the Introduction, to be Jewish, you can either be born to Jewish parents[15, 16] or it is also possible through either Orthodox or Reform Judaism, and other streams of Judaism, to convert. This process will look different and last different lengths of times depending on the denomination governing the process.

But regardless of the stream, all Jews have laws that dictate membership, meaning the Jewish collective has a general agreement on how one becomes Jewish—being born or converting. Obviously, within that agreement there is disagreement—for instance, which conversion process is recognized by whom—but this diversity of thought or practice does not in any way undermine the idea that the collective accepts an individual as part of the community. Indigenous people—even within individual tribes—do not need to be monolithic. Jews certainly have never been, and for thousands of years different Jewish groups have argued about the best or most authentic way to express our Jewishness.

The idea that an indigenous people must maintain a closed practice with laws governing membership and acceptance of individuals is important. It isn't rooted in a sense of superiority, but rather it is a mechanism to safeguard the survival, and continuity, of our civilizations. Indigenous communities are expressed through unique cultures, and to preserve the cohesive fabric of a tribe there must be established rules dictating membership. Similarly, it cannot be right that any individual can declare their membership of a tribe or community with which they have no prior connection without first undergoing an initiation process, such as conversion. This process ensures that newcomers understand and respect the traditions, values, and history of the community they seek to join, thereby maintaining the integrity and coherence of the indigenous group.

Ultimately, it matters not that most Jews would not yet utilize indigenous as a descriptor for their connection to Israel. This is an evolving conversation; one this book will contribute to. However, it is clear when analyzing the core ideas within these criteria it fits the Jewish experience. The powerful emotional connection many Jews feel towards Israel, coupled with the well-defined criteria for Jewish membership, clearly aligns with the United Nations' standard for indigeneity.

"HISTORICAL CONTINUITY WITH PRE-COLONIAL AND/OR PRE-SETTLER SOCIETIES"

As we have already explored, a significant problem with this part of the criteria is its assumption that colonization is an inherent part of the indigenous experience. There is no good reason why this must be the case. Of course, we are aware that colonization is often—perhaps even more often than not—the experience of indigenous people and it certainly was regarding the Jewish experience. However, to argue it is inherently so, is problematic. It strips indigenous people of their agency and their power and imposes a victim identity on them.

However, the emphasis on the continuity of culture and civilization contained within this criterion is correct. Continuity is fundamental to the indigenous experience. This concept is echoed in my definition of indigeneity, where I reference the importance of "continuous culture." This is key when establishing criteria for defining indigeneity. Indigeneity inherently suggests an unbroken bond with a land, and the continuity of culture and systems of living. Therefore, for any community to be recognized as indigenous, this ongoing connection must remain. Indigenous groups today are the custodians of great and specific ideas, traditions, values, and beliefs. In our case, Jews today have inherited the great Jewish law, traditions and the deep bond with the Land of Israel that originated over 3,000 years ago.

There has also been a continuous Jewish presence in the land for our entire existence as a people—an important factor when considering the notion of a connection with ancient societies. This is significant in countering the myth that, after our expulsion by the Romans, the Land of Israel was free of Jews until we began returning in the 19th century. This piece of misinformation is propagated by non-Jews as well as Jews. In 2020, author David Mevorach Seidenberg suggested that "It was the Roman Empire's conquest that caused the Jewish people's separation from the land."[17] However, while many Jews were indeed expelled from Jerusalem, our spiritual and physical connection with the land was never broken. As historian, Simon Sebag Montefiore wrote in *Jerusalem: The Biography*, "To be in Jerusalem [today] is to stand at the crossroads of time, to witness the unfolding drama of history, to feel the pulse of eternity beating in the heart of the city."[18]

Following the Bar Kokhba revolt, and the expulsion of Jews from Jerusalem, Galilee became the main center of Jewish life in the Land of Israel, although there were also Jews living in Beit She'an, Caesarea, the Golan Heights, and along the edges of Judea.[19] During the late Roman period, the Land of Israel continued to see significant developments in Jewish thought and Jewish law. In around 200 CE, Judah ha-Nasi (Judah the Prince) compiled the discussions of the *tannaim* (rabbinic sages) and *amoraim* (Jewish scholars who taught the Oral Torah) into the Mishna. And in 450 CE the Jerusalem Talmud was finalized.[20]

It is thought that Jews continued to make up the majority of the population in the land until after Constantine converted the Roman Empire to Christianity in the 4th century.[21] During this period of colonization when Jews were living in Eretz Yisrael but without sovereignty, the fortune of the Jewish community in the Land of Israel depended on who was in power.

Israeli academic Sylvia Schein has underlined the significance in Acre (Akko). "By the 1250s, Acre, ... the city in which the largest Jewish community in Palestine was located, became one of the most important centers of Jewish studies in the Middle East,"[22] she suggests. Likewise, medieval rabbi, halakhist, and Talmudist R. Solomon Adret (Rashba) wrote in 1280: "It is a custom among the sages of the Holy Land and of Babylon, that if a question should be asked, nobody answers but says, 'Let us be guided by the sages of Acre.'"[23]

The title of archeologist Dan Bahat's 1976 book, *Twenty Centuries of Jewish Life in the Holy Land: The Forgotten Generations*, highlights the continued Jewish presence in the Land of Israel. "Even if a majority were forced from one exile to another, many Jews stayed on, reinforced from time to time by returning exiles," he suggested.[24] For 2,000 years Jews yearned for, attempted to reach, and successfully returned to, the Land of Israel. Moreover, the 19th-century First *Aliyah* was not in fact the first. Jews had been successfully resettling in Eretz Yisrael for millennia. In 1211, 300 rabbis made *Aliyah* mainly from France, England, and Provence. The Jewish poet Yehuda al-Harizi records that while in Jerusalem in 1216, he met several learned French Jews, mentioning "men of great piety who came from the land of France to dwell in Zion."[25] In his *Milchamot Hashem*, written in 1235, Rabbi Avraham, the son of Rambam, also references a group of French scholars who made *Aliyah* and passed first through Egypt, where he lived.[26] Tsfat, one of the four Holy cities of the Land of Israel,[27] has had a continuous Jewish presence since the time of the Maccabees. And during the Spanish and Portuguese Inquisition, some Sephardic Jews returned to their homeland after being expelled from the Iberian Peninsula. In the 19th century, even before the First *Aliyah*, Jews from Yemen made *Aliyah*, and Ethiopian Jews attempted to do the same. Since the re-establishment of Israel in 1948, over 3 million Jews have made *Aliyah*, returning to live in the same lands as their ancient ancestors.[28]

The idea of historical continuity with pre-colonial or ancient societies also applies to the Jewish relationship with the land. The Land of Israel was colonized by successive empires, but the Jewish connection remained unchanged. Jerusalem, for instance, has endured as the capital of the Jewish nation for thousands of years. In *Devarim* (Deuteronomy),

Chapter 3, verse 12, it is noted that Jacob was told of Jerusalem that it was "... the site that the Lord your God will choose from among all your tribes, as a place established in His name. It is there that you shall go to seek His presence."[29] Jerusalem is said to be the administrative and spiritual center of the United Monarchy, and it was the capital of the Kingdom of Judah and the Hasmonean dynasty. Psalm 122 is attributed to King David, writing: "Pray for the peace of Jerusalem and for the welfare of all its inhabitants. They shall prosper that love thee."[30] Even at that relatively early stage in our history, Jerusalem was the central focus, and beating heart, of the Jewish people. Following its destruction and the exile of the Judean elites to Babylon, Psalm 137 was written. It states: "If I forget thee, O Jerusalem, let my right hand wither. Let my tongue cleave to the roof of my mouth, if I remember thee not; if I set not Jerusalem above my chiefest joy."[31]

Later, in 70 CE, the Bar Kokhba revolt broke out after the Emperor Hadrian erected a shrine to Jupiter on Jerusalem's Temple Mount, the site of the Second Temple. Despite being expelled following the revolt, Emperor Julian nonetheless allowed Jews to once again settle in Jerusalem.[32] Jews continued to live in Jerusalem over the subsequent centuries. In the late 19th century, contemporaneous records show they constituted almost 50% of the population.[33] Unsurprisingly, in 1948, Jerusalem was declared the capital of the modern Jewish state, Israel. As the State of Israel's first Prime Minister, David Ben-Gurion, correctly argued: "The State of Israel has, and will have, only one capital, Eternal Jerusalem. So it was 3,000 years ago and so it will be, as we believe, for eternity."

Our people's enduring connection to Israel and Jerusalem is recognized by Jews in the Diaspora. Our synagogues are built to face Jerusalem. When we pray, we turn toward Jerusalem. And during the Pesach Seder we declare: "*l'shana haba'ah b'yerushalayim*" (next year in Jerusalem). Indeed, during the British Mandate of Palestine, the name "Eretz Yisrael" or the "Land of Israel" was part of the territory's official

Hebrew name. This connection represents a clear line of continuity between contemporary Jews and our ancestors who populated the land thousands of years ago.

The Jewish people today can rightly claim an unbroken lineage stretching back to our ancient societies and civilizations. Our connection to the land endures, just as it has throughout history. Their land remains our land, and their capital remains our capital. Both physically and spiritually, we are deeply rooted in the land and the communities that have inhabited it for generations.

"STRONG LINK TO TERRITORIES AND SURROUNDING NATURAL RESOURCES"

This is perhaps one of the most significant indicators of indigeneity—the criterion that reveals a profound relationship between a people and the land itself. This connection is crucial when considering the notion of indigeneity. It is reiterated in the 25th Article of the UN declaration, which suggests:

> "Indigenous peoples have the right to maintain and strengthen their distinctive spiritual relationship with their traditionally owned or otherwise occupied and used lands, territories, waters and coastal seas and other resources and to uphold their responsibilities to future generations in this regard."[34]

As my definition also highlights, this underscores the deep relationship between a people and their land. Indigeneity is not merely the notion of being the first in a place; rather, it is the special and enduring connection that exists between people and the land from which they emerged. In terms of the Jewish experience, our connection to the soil in the Land of Israel could not be more clear. Jews disembarking from planes at Ben

Gurion Airport in Tel Aviv, including Ethiopian Jews coming home to Israel in 2020, famously kissed the ground, honoring the holiness of the Land of Israel and the emotional connection which exists between it and the Jewish people.[35] However, like most customs in Jewish culture, this was not a new practice. Maimonides (Rambam) noted that "Great sages would kiss the borders of Eretz Yisrael, kiss its stones, and roll in its dust."[36] Even earlier, the Talmud suggests that "Rabbi Abba would demonstrate his great love for the Land of Israel by kissing the rocks of Acre as he returned to the Land."[37] This remarkable connection between the Jews and their land is enduring and ever present in the core of Jewish identity and expression.

The Jewish calendar is replete with key Jewish holidays, nearly all of which originate from the connection Jews have to the territories and natural resources of Eretz Yisrael. Rosh Hashanah, Sukkot, Pesach, and Shavuot all began as agricultural holidays.

Pesach is said to be the festival most observed by Jews around the world. It honors the Exodus from Egypt and the origins of our story as a nation, but it also marks our connection with the Land of Israel itself. Historians agree that before Pesach became a story about the Exodus from Egypt, it started life as two separate festivals: One harvest festival (for settled farmers) and one rooted in animal sacrifice (carried out by nomadic shepherds). The harvest festival was based on the barley harvest and was rooted in sanctifying the first crops. The animal sacrifice was carried out by the nomadic Israelites (or by their ancestors) and was designed to "ward off evil" and to ensure their families and flocks were protected as they journeyed on.[38] Some historians believe that these festivals were then fused with the Exodus story to create Pesach as we know it today. As Tamara Prosic wrote in *The Development and Symbolism of Passover*: "The combined feast became a commemorative celebration through which the people relived the events on which the existence as an independent nation was based."[39]

At this point, during the reign of King Josiah, who, as we have seen, is said to have built the First Temple and reigned when the Torah was written, Pesach evolved from being a practice carried out by individual families or communities to a national observance centered on the Temple in Jerusalem. In *Devarim* (Deuteronomy), it is stated: "You are not permitted to slaughter the Passover sacrifice in any of the settlements that your God but at the place where your God will choose to establish the divine name, there alone shall you slaughter the Passover sacrifice, in the evening, at sundown, the time of day when you departed from Egypt."[40]

Many years later, as they have done for centuries, Jews all over the world, in vastly different places with different seasons, join together to honor the agricultural year of the Land of Israel. Whether or not this is at the forefront of their minds—most Jews at Pesach will be thinking of the Exodus from Egypt, itself a symbol of Jewish continuity and indigeneity—is irrelevant. The roots of this practice remain whether we are aware of it or not, and the agricultural rotation in the Land of Israel still dictates the annual cycle of Jews living all over the world.

Sukkot, Pesach, and Shavuot specifically were the *Shalosh Regalim*—the three pilgrimage festivals—during which ancient Jews made pilgrimages to the Temple in Jerusalem. This commandment is stated in *Devarim* (Deuteronomy), Chapter 16, verse 16: "Three times a year shall all your men appear before the Lord your God in the place that God will choose [presumably referring to the Temple in Jerusalem], on the festivals of *Pesach* (Passover), *Shavuot* (the Feast of Weeks), and *Sukkot* (the Festival of Booths). They shall not appear empty-handed. Each shall bring his own gift, appropriate to the blessing which the Lord your God has given you." This commandment was fulfilled by Jews in the Land of Israel, where this practice took on a new social meaning. It became a way for Jews to meet and gather, uniting from their various villages and towns all over the Mediterranean region to celebrate their identity. Since the destruction of the Second Temple in 70 CE, these festivals, along with others, have been celebrated through synagogue attendance and other customs, such as the Pesach Seder. These, as we know, are still celebrated to this day. Though the customs evolved, sometimes out of necessity or cultural development, the core remains constant.

Another Jewish holiday directly connected to the Land of Israel is *Tu BiShvat*. Referenced in the Mishnah as one of the four Jewish new years, it marks the beginning of the agricultural cycle for the purpose of biblical tithes. This calculation was used for Orlah, the biblical prohibition on eating fruit produced by a tree during the first three years after its planting.[41] The practice of Orlah is still observed by Orthodox Jews today. *Tu BiShvat* is widely celebrated by millions of Jews around the world. It is marked by eating fruit and dairy and is considered the modern Israeli Arbor Day, a day dedicated to planting trees.

An additional practice which signifies the Jewish relationship with the land in Israel is the practice of *Shmita* (Sabbatical Year), a Jewish law which dictated that every seven years, the land must be allowed to rest. In *Shemot* (Exodus), it states: "Plant your land and gather its produce for six years. But on the seventh let it lie fallow and it will rest …"[42] This is a kind of agricultural Shabbat, and just as people rest after six days of work, the land must be given an opportunity to rest after six years of work. This law, still maintained in some capacity both symbolically and practically in the modern State of Israel, underscores the symbiotic relationship which exists between people and nature, and specifically the Jews and the Land of Israel.

Yet another indicator of the remarkable connection between Jews and the Land of Israel was the centrality of the Land in Jewish thought, prayer, and civilization. This focus remained ever constant, even during times of exile. Reading these thoughts and prayers on Jews and Israel is a stunning signifier of our indigeneity. The connection that exists between the Jewish people and the Land of Israel is supremely strong and emotional.

In *Bereshit* (Genesis), God says to Abraham: "On that day, the Lord formed a covenant with Abram, saying, 'To your seed I have given this land, from the river of Egypt until the great river, the Euphrates river.'"[43] And in the Amidah, the central Jewish prayer, it says: "Sound the great shofar for our liberty, and raise a banner to gather our exiles, and gather us together quickly from the four corners of the earth, into our Land. Blessed are You, G-d Gatherer of the dispersed of His people Israel."[44] This eternal yearning, as we have already dissected, was expressed in Psalm 137 when the exiles in Babylon yearned to return to Zion. In Psalm 126, during *Birkat Hamazon* (Grace After Meals), it states: "When the LORD restores the fortunes of Zion—we see it as in a dream."[45] Rabbi Yehuda Halevi (1075–1141), before making *Aliyah* and eventually dying in Jerusalem, bemoaned living in exile in Spain, declaring:

> "My heart is in the east, and I in the uttermost west—How can I find savor in food? How shall it be sweet to me? How shall I render my vows and my bonds, while yet Zion lieth beneath the fetter of Edom, and I in Arab chains? A light thing would it seem to me to leave all the good things of Spain, seeing how precious in mine eyes to behold the dust of the desolate sanctuary."[46]

In the middle of the 20th century, those who crafted the State of Israel's Declaration of Independence placed this historic connection between the Jewish people and the Land of Israel front and center:

> "The Land of Israel was the birthplace of the Jewish people. Here their spiritual, religious, and political identity was shaped. Here they first attained statehood, created cultural values of national and universal significance, and gave to the world the eternal Book of Books. After being forcibly exiled from their land, the people kept faith with it throughout their Dispersion and never ceased to pray and hope for their return to it and for the restoration in it of their political freedom. Impelled by this historic and traditional attachment, Jews strove in

every successive generation to re-establish themselves in their ancient homeland. In recent decades they returned in their masses. Pioneers, defiant returnees, and defenders, they made deserts bloom, revived the Hebrew language, built villages and towns, and created a thriving community controlling its own economy and culture, loving peace but knowing how to defend itself, bringing the blessings of progress to all the country's inhabitants, and aspiring towards independent nationhood…"[47]

A beautiful example of the link between Jews and the Land of Israel is the prayer for rain. Included in the Amidah from Shemini Atzeret (the 8th day of the Sukkot holiday) to Pesach, we utter the words, "*Masheev ha'ruach u'moreed hagashem*." (Who causes the wind to blow and the rain to fall.)[48] That Jews all over the Diaspora, including countries like Scotland, where I grew up, still pray for rain in Israel is a remarkable and powerful indicator of our indigeneity to this land.

Perhaps most moving, is that many Jews choose to be buried in Israel (10,000 between 2007 and 2017[49]), even if they pass away in the Diaspora. Equally powerful is the fact that some Jews are laid to rest with soil specifically brought in for this purpose from Israel.[50] A 1950 *JTA* article described how "Ten thousand small sacks of soil from Mt. Zion have been dispatched to the United States to Jewish burial societies for the graves of Orthodox Jews to whom this soil is sacred."[51] Whether they are buried in Israel or with soil from Israel, in their final journey, these Jews, from all over the world, are reunited with their home, their land. The connection between the Jewish people and the territories and surrounding natural resources of the Land of Israel is clear, and it is expressed in a myriad of ways. All of which demonstrate our indigeneity.

"DISTINCT SOCIAL, ECONOMIC, OR POLITICAL SYSTEMS"

Like any other civilization, Jews have distinct systems that govern our society. In "The Beginnings of Jewishness," Shaye J. D. Cohen noted that "Yehudim had their own language, customs, institutions, dress, cuisine, religion, and so on."[52] Although Cohen differentiates Yehudim from Jews, considering them to be our ancient ancestors, many of the systems still governing Jewish life developed in the Land of Israel during the period of Jewish sovereignty. The UN includes the presence of such systems as part of its criteria indicating indigeneity. In the definition of indigeneity that I propose, I discuss the development of a people as a collective in a specific place and the continuation of the systems, cultural practices, and traditions that emerged in that land. It is the continuation of these systems or cultural practices that would define a modern people as indigenous to a specific place.

SOCIETY

When we discuss society, we have to remember that when Jews were first living together in our indigenous land (whether they had sovereignty or not), they had clear systems which ruled their societies. These governed slavery, family, gender, ideas of the state, and so much more. Of course, while there are very practical and tangible threads that connect us to our ancient predecessors, these systems originated over 3,000 years ago. People—including indigenous people—evolve and progress over time, and some systems naturally fall by the wayside. Nor should we forget that Jewish history was interrupted through our displacement. Even though there was a continuous Jewish presence in the land, Jews spread all over the world after the Romans expelled us from Jerusalem. Many of us were then living in new countries with new laws and new systems which obviously had an impact on how we lived. Unfortunately, the UN fails to consider or recognize the notion and impact of expulsion when outlining its criteria for identifying indigenous people. Their focus on colonization ignores the fact that expulsion or ethnic cleansing can also be a part of that experience. This, in turn, has an effect on how a group expresses its identity.

Despite our experience as a dispersed people, there are Jewish social systems which continue to this day. The concept of *Kehilla* (community) rests on the belief in a community which is bound together by a sense of shared peoplehood, and all that encompasses. Our community, in other words, is connected by much more than a shared belief system and, as Jews, it is our responsibility to support one another. We are a family, and we are responsible for taking care of all our members' physical and spiritual needs.

The significance of communal life was recognized in the Talmud's debate between ancient Jewish scholars on whether someone engaged in community life should stop and pray. It was ruled that "… one who is occupied with one mitzvah is exempt from other mitzvot."[53] The debate, which raged among earlier Talmud scholars, was ended by Mishnah Berurah (Rabbi Israel Meir Ha-Kohen, 1839–1933), who declared: "Most later authorities have ruled [that one does not need to stop to pray]."[54] This exemption serves as an indication of the significance of community. The importance of communal life, and what it must include, was laid out in another portion of the Talmud: "A talmid haham (Torah scholar) is not allowed to live in a city that does not have these 10 things: a beit din (law court) that metes out punishments; a tzedakah fund that is collected by two people and distributed by three; a synagogue; a bath house (mikveh); a bathroom; a doctor; a craftsperson; a blood-letter; (some versions add: a butcher); and a teacher of children."[55]

These ideas continue today, albeit under altered circumstances. The concept of a Jewish community—and its resources—is crucial at key moments in the lives of Jews, regardless of their level of religious observance. Jews reach out to a mohel for the circumcision of their sons, to synagogues for assistance with b'nai mitzvah, to rabbis for officiating weddings, and to burial societies for Jewish burial rites. Many Jews also volunteer their services to help the Kehilla run effectively. The Chevra Kadisha, which literally means "Holy Society," is a moving example of this and is present in every Jewish community in the Diaspora, caring for the deceased and preparing them for burial.

Due in part to our exclusion from the wider world, as well as the importance we place on community, Jewish versions of nearly all kinds of communal life exist. There are organizations that deal with all aspects of our lives from childcare, education, emotional support, and even financial support. It is a racist canard that all Jews are wealthy. As I explored in *Jewish Pride: Rebuilding a People*, poverty and social needs are huge issues in the Jewish community.

Jewish Care is an organization which exists to support Jews, one with which my family and I have had personal experience. Descended from the Jewish Board of Guardians, established in London in 1859, Jewish Care was officially founded in 1990 following the merger of the Jewish Welfare Board and Jewish Blind Society. The Jewish Care website says its purpose is to "provide care that is Jewish at heart for older people. And we support their family members every step of the way. Every week, we touch the lives of 10,000 people."[56] Speaking in retirement about her Jewish constituents, Margaret Thatcher, the former British Prime Minister, pointedly remarked on Kehilla: "My, they were good citizens." She had never, she suggested, had a Jew come to one of her constituency advice surgeries in "poverty and desperation. They had always been looked after by their own community."[57] The prevalence of the Jewish communal support, and the role this plays in creating and fermenting Jewish society, is profound.

In 1997, political scientist Daniel J. Elazar identified five different forms of Jewish community structure: Very small communities organized around one organization or congregation; integrated communities whereby several congregations or organizations exist but are united by a single community; government-recognized communities which serve as official representatives of the Jewish community; several larger organizations who create a kind of monopoly of Jewish communal needs; and, finally, large communities where organizations compete with one another.[58] Elazar also charts five different functions for organizations within the structure of the Jewish community: religious/congregational, educational/cultural, external relations/defense, communal-welfare, and Israel/World Jewry.[59] These different categories of Jewish organization would encompass the entirety of an individual or community's needs.

Each of Elazar's structures is formed based on the specific needs of the community. The Jewish community in Britain works differently to that in America, based on sheer scale alone. But the defining feature of all these organizational structures is its voluntary basis. Jews are able to exclude themselves if they so wish. However, if a Jew wishes to engage in an iota of Jewish life, they will require an element of interaction with the Jewish community. Kehilla is an essential part of Jewish life in a Jewish community. These values have their roots in ancient Jewish ideas of Kehilla and the significance of Am Yisrael, the People of Israel, and the idea of "*Kol Yisrael arevim zeh ba'zeh*" (all of Israel are responsible for each other).[60] This idea is lived in a very real and tangible way in Jewish communities all over the world.

ECONOMY

Although the Jews lost sovereignty and many were expelled from our land, our ancient economic practices, such as the giving of Tzedakah (meaning charity, but directly translating to righteousness), have continued in the lives of modern Jews. For Jews, the idea of giving is a mitzvah. Mitzvot, the plural of mitzvah, are generally thought of and referred to as a good deed, but they are technically of the 613 commandments that Jews are required to observe. They are Jewish laws.

Like so much else in the Jewish civilization, the laws of Tzedakah[61] can be traced back to our relationship with the agrarian society that existed in the ancient Land of Israel. The laws of *pe'ah* and gleanings were laid out in the books of *Devarim* (Deuteronomy) and *Vayikra* (Leviticus) and were specifically written to ensure philanthropy and support for those in need. *Vayikra* states: "When you reap the harvest of your land, you shall not reap to the very edges of your field, nor gather the gleanings of your harvest."[62] *Pe'ah* was thus the instruction to leave the edges of fields unharvested, while gleanings were rules regarding not picking up crops that were dropped during the harvest. Farmers were also instructed to leave any part of their crop they missed during the harvest if the majority had been dealt with. These laws show the importance of community and shared responsibility stretch back to the ancient Jewish world. As referenced previously, the ancient Jewish law of *Shmita*, also saw debts forgiven and as the land was allowed to rest, all produce grown was able to be picked by anyone. Importantly, these economic practices are also still obeyed both symbolically and practically in modern Israel. The first *Shmita* in modern Israel was in 5712 (1951)[63] and the next will be in 5789 (2028).[64]

As history progressed and the economy diversified, funds were created to support the needy. However, long after Jewish sovereignty over our land ended and our economy evolved, these ancient laws continued to be relevant and were debated by Jews living in the Diaspora. The 13th-century Spanish rabbi Jacob Asher (also known as the Baal haTurim), wrote a commentary on the use of singular "you" and plural "you" with regard to the laws of *Pe'ah*.[65] In the 16th century, Rabbi Moses Alshich discussed the idea of ownership with regard to *Pe'ah*. In *Torat Moshe*, he writes as if God were speaking: "You shouldn't think that you are giving to the poor person from your own property, or that I have despised him by not giving bread to him as I have given to you. For he is also my child, just as you are, but his portion is in your produce."[66]

Although not explicitly referenced in the Torah, supporting those less fortunate was a significant aspect of the ancient Jewish economic system. In *Devarim* (Deuteronomy) 16 it states, "*Tzedek, tzedek tirdof*" ("Justice, justice thou shalt pursue").[67] The repetition underscoring its significance to Jewish practice. The use of the word Tzedakah emerged in a post-temple world when it became an even more significant concept than it had previously been. Following the destruction of the Second Temple, the late Lord Rabbi Jonathan Sacks suggested that Jews "found three major substitutes for sacrifice ... prayer, charity, and hospitality. When you invited the stranger into your house, he or she had a meal at your table, and in Hebrew the words for 'altar' and 'table' are very similar. The Rabbis said that when the altar was destroyed, the table became the altar."[68] Thus, charity took on even greater importance in Jewish culture and the notion of Tzedakah was born.

This Jewish focus on charity was deepened in the Talmud, and later by Maimonides. In his Mishneh Torah ("Laws of Charity"), the great Sephardic sage included "the Eight Levels of Giving." The highest level of Tzedakah, he argued, was to teach a person to fish, as the old proverb suggests. "The greatest level, above which there is no greater, is to support a fellow Jew by endowing him with a gift or loan, or entering into a partnership with him, or finding employment for him, in order to strengthen his hand so that he will not need to be dependent upon others."[69] The impact of Maimonides' writings and thoughts can't be underestimated. The Mishneh Torah as a whole, including the Laws of Charity, is still studied today. The Daily Rambam Study, an annual study cycle which includes the study of Mishneh Torah, indicates that these laws and the systems they speak to are still very much part of Jewish thought and action today.

While individuals may not always recognize that this practice is rooted in ancient Jewish customs and systems, the high rates of Jews who give to charity indicate that the cultural norm of Tzedakah is alive and well. In 2020, for instance, the *Jewish Chronicle* reported that a 2019 poll found that 93% of British Jews give to charity, compared with just 57% of the wider population.[70] A 2017 Pew report found that American Jews are more generous, in terms of giving, than their non-Jewish counterparts. Pew found that "60 percent of Jewish households earning less than US$50,000 a year donate, compared with 46 percent of non-Jewish households in that income bracket."[71] The outsized role that American and British Jewish people play in their respective countries' philanthropy informs our understanding of the endurance of the concept of Tzedakah in the lives of Jews. What makes this all the more remarkable is that the roots of this cultural practice lie in the systems and ideas that sprung up in the Land of Israel thousands of years ago. It is yet another example of the incredible continuity of the Jewish people and our connection to our ancient customs—specifically with regard to economic practices—and traditions.

POLITICS

Politics can be defined as "the study of the ways in which a country is governed."[72] The governance of ancient Israel, as well as that of modern Jews, was rooted in the Torah. And beyond being a document given by God, the Torah can be viewed, according to Yonatan Adler, as a kind of Jewish constitution.[73] He notes that in the Septuagint, the earliest translation of the Torah from its original Hebrew to Greek, Torah is translated as "*nomos*," the Greek word for law.[74] It thus played a significant role for those who governed ancient Jewish society.[75] As is the case today, with the ongoing Jewish debate over *Halacha* and the validity of specific laws, this was a major point of conflict between Pharisees, Sadducees, and Essenes, who were fighting over whether interpretations were to be treated as authoritative.

We can see the significance of these laws to Jews and our culture in 1st-century texts, which tell us that there were public readings of the Torah in synagogue settings. Later rabbinic texts also discuss the public reading of the Torah. This practice continues today. Many Jews gather in a synagogue—as our ancient ancestors would have done—to hear the public reading of the parsha (a specific Torah portion). The adherence to these laws—whether it's circumcision, *kashrut* (dietary laws), or celebration of festivals—still plays a role in governing Jewish society to this day, even in the Diaspora.

The question of when Jewish law came to be obeyed by the masses, marking the emergence of Judaism as a practice, set apart from the Jews as a people, has long been debated.[76] By the 1st century CE, E.P. Sanders suggests in "Judaism: Practice & Belief," Judeans everywhere shared "a common set of practices and beliefs centered on Mosaic Torah and the remainder of what were jointly regarded by this time as hallowed scriptures."[77] Sanders terms this "Common Judaism": "a system of practices and beliefs shared by practically all Judeans living during the first century of CE." Thus, by this period, Jewish society was governed by a specific and clear set of laws, as laid out in the Torah.

And, as Professor Joshua Berman argues: "The Torah is a political document as much as it is a religious document."[78] Berman believes that its conception of equality means that ancient Jewish, rather than Greek, civilization was the very first form of democratic thought. "The theology of covenant in the Pentateuch set the stage, metaphysically speaking, for Israel to conceive of itself as a society devoid of inherent and cosmically legitimated hierarchy found elsewhere," he suggests.[79] Given the historical context—religion encompassed the relationship between people and between people and the earth—this suggests they were discussing all aspects of society, not just the relationship with God. In ideas which were not seen again until the Enlightenment, the Torah deals with the issue of political power and places the monarch under God. Unlike the European monarchs who emerged later, and were seen as God's representative on earth, the Israelite monarchs were subservient to God. This is consistent with the radical notions surrounding the economy and our responsibility for those less fortunate, which, as we have seen, the Torah, despite being 2,700 years old, contains. As Berman argues, unlike in Ancient Greece, when democracy was not seen as requiring equality, in ancient Judah even the man on the street benefited from the egalitarian ideas found in the Torah. Given the period in which the Torah was first composed, this is both extraordinary and another facet of the profound civilization created by ancient Israelites and carried on by modern Jews today.

Thanks to the Torah, Jewish law has been characterized by an extraordinary level of continuity. Its precision and detail mean it can, if we choose, allow it to guide our lives as it did for those who lived not just decades but centuries before us.

In this chapter, we have already discussed the significance of many aspects of Jewish society and culture that have continued directly to this day. Indeed, the final criterion, as set out by the United Nations, is a "resolve to maintain and reproduce their ancestral environments and systems as distinctive peoples and communities."[80] This would have been impossible without the systems in place that governed our lives.

While the development of our civilization was interrupted, many systems which governed Jewish life are still very much in place today as they were thousands of years ago. Shabbat is one such system, which has governed Jewish life for thousands of years. *Bereshit* (Genesis) and *Shemot* (Exodus), two of the five books of the Torah completed 2,500 years ago, establish the commandment for Jews to rest on the seventh day, honoring God's rest after creating the world. The Torah itself is not explicitly specific about what constitutes labor in the context of resting. It references field labor (*Shemot* (Exodus) 34:21;[81] *Bamidbar* (Numbers) 15:32–36[82]) and kindling fire (*Shemot* 35:2–3[83]) as examples of forbidden labor. However, great Jewish thinkers have provided commentary on the Torah throughout history, adding detail to the laws of Shabbat. In essays on Shabbat in the longest chapters of the Mishna, 39 *Melachot* (categories of labor that are forbidden on Shabbat) are discussed. This tractate lays down comprehensively the specifics of the Shabbat laws. They include *Zore'ah* (planting), *Meraked* (sifting), and *Bishul/Ofeh* (cooking/baking).[84] This detail in and of itself is an indicator of a developed system used to govern a territory. The language used in ancient Jewish writings refers to the Shabbat restrictions as "illegal,"[85] as Josephus did when describing the right to travel on Shabbat. Additionally, Judean author Aristobulus refers to Shabbat as "legislation"[86] and as "legally binding." The earliest non-Judean writer who spoke of Judeans and Shabbat was Agatharchides of Cnidus, who wrote in the middle of the 2nd century: "The people known as Judeans … have a custom of abstaining from work every 7th day."[87]

And by the 1st century CE, Shabbat prohibitions had become a "hallmark of the Judean way of life"[88] around the Mediterranean. Similarly, today, Jews all around the world perceive Shabbat as legally binding and adhere to the laws set out in the Torah that govern the observance of Shabbat. Although these laws have evolved with time, their roots can be traced to the Torah. Today, Jews who observe Shabbat (Shomer Shabbat) will refrain from driving or riding in cars or other vehicles, observing a modern iteration of the laws referenced by Josephus. Josephus also notes a legal dispute between Essenes and other Judeans, stating, "The Essenes are stricter than all Judeans in abstaining from work on the seventh day, for not only do they prepare their food the day before to avoid kindling a fire on that day, but they do not venture to remove any vessel or even go to stool."[89] Today, Jews mark Shabbat by avoiding cooking, baking, or kindling a fire, and will prepare food beforehand, just as our ancient ancestors did. That not all Jews observe the Shabbat laws is irrelevant. These are still Jewish laws (whether we obey them or not), they still characterize Jewish life, and they are still carried out by many Jews today. According to Julian D.M. Lew in "Jewish Law—Its Development and its Coexistence in the Non-Jewish World," the Torah is the "oldest living system of law"[90] in the world. As Lew says, it is a living law, and the obeyance of these laws is a direct reflection of our indigeneity. The Torah was written, in part, to govern Jewish life, specifically Jewish life in our land. However, the power of this law continues to govern the lives of modern Jews, whether we live in the land or elsewhere, and in many ways, the modern Jewish state—just as it did for our ancient ancestors thousands of years ago.

Chapter 6

A STUDY ON JEWISH INDIGENEITY CONTINUED

DISTINCT LANGUAGE, CULTURE, AND BELIEFS

The UN's fourth criterion for assessing indigeneity—that a people should have a distinct language, culture, and belief system—is a reasonable expectation. The notion of Jewish difference is something some modern Jews struggle with. It is seen as being at odds with modern universalism and integration and, due to the long history of Jew-hate, is perceived as a threat to our personal security and survival. But the reality is that, like all people, we *are* distinct, and we *must* accept it. Our language, culture, and beliefs are evidence of this.

In my definition of indigeneity, I argue that to be considered indigenous, a people must have "living systems, culture, and practice" rooted in a specific land and ingrained in a particular place. This idea of continuity is thus crucial when identifying an indigenous people. In our case, we have a language, cultural practices, and a belief system that emerged in Israel thousands of years ago—but one that continues to guide Jewish life today whether Jews are living in Israel or the Diaspora.

LANGUAGE

There are several Jewish languages: the various Judeo-Arabic languages, Ladino, and Yiddish. All of these are significant expressions of Jewish diasporic life and should be treated with the utmost respect. These languages developed in different parts of the world because of our expulsion from our indigenous land. Despite originating in various diasporic locations, they were tied to one another by their connections to our indigeneity; after all, they are all written with Hebrew letters.[1] However, in spite of their importance to their respective diasporic communities and Jewish culture as a whole, these languages are not our native language. Regardless of the script they utilize, they are not the singular Jewish language that connects all Jews in all places at all times. Our native tongue—the language that represents Jewish indigeneity and all Jewish people—is Hebrew.

The significance of Hebrew to the Jews cannot be overstated. It is referred to as *Leshon Hakodesh*—"the Holy tongue"[2]—and it is the language of our ancestors and our liturgy. "I hold that this is the same reason why our Rabbis call the language of the Torah 'the Sacred Language,' because the words of the Torah, and the prophecies, and all words of holiness were all expressed in that language," Moses ben Nachman (also known as the Ramban) argued.[3] This ancient language is still spoken in synagogues and in prayer all over the Jewish world today. Modern Hebrew, rooted in this ancient tongue, is the official language of the State of Israel and is also spoken, to some degree, by many Jews in the Diaspora. Yiddish, the language of Ashkenazi Jews which emerged in 9th-century central Europe, was considered as the language of the new Jewish state because it was spoken by the vast majority of Jews at the time. However, in the end, Hebrew was chosen specifically because of its historic ties to our land. As linguist Max Weinreich wrote in *History of the Yiddish Language*, Volume 1, the "very making of Hebrew into a spoken language derives from the will to separate from the Diaspora."[4] This was about returning home, in more ways than one.

This fact alone reveals an indigenous relationship. Hebrew emerged in the Land of Israel, where the people historically spoke it, and it continues to be spoken today in modern-day Israel and in the Diaspora by their descendants. However, the holiness of Hebrew specifically attaches to Ancient Hebrew, not to the modern Hebrew spoken on the streets of Tel

Aviv. Nonetheless, this nuance should not lead to a misunderstanding of modern Hebrew and its connection to the Land of Israel—not just the State of Israel. The *shoresh* (roots) of modern Hebrew are largely derived from its ancient ancestor. Modern Hebrew is simply a contemporary iteration of the ancient versions of Hebrew that preceded it. Its evolution does not negate its significance. Indigenous peoples can evolve while still maintaining their ancient connections. That a language, which began and was spoken thousands of years ago in the Levant, is still spoken by the same people thousands of years later is remarkable, especially given our diasporic nature.

I attended a Jewish elementary school in Scotland, where I studied Hebrew in both its ancient and modern forms. This continuity is just one profound example of the endurance of the Jewish people. When, as a 13-year-old Jew wearing a kilt and speaking with a Scottish accent, I read my parsha (Torah portion) at my Bar-Mitzvah in 2000, I was reading in the language of my ancestors. At the time, I was not aware that I was expressing and honoring Jewish indigeneity. But, like the thousands of young Jewish people who celebrate their Bar- or Bat-Mitzvah every year, that's precisely what I was doing. Despite my Scottishness, I was reading from the same book, in the same language—a language emerged from our indigenous land—that countless generations of Jews had done before me.

THE ORIGINS OF HEBREW

Modern Hebrew began life thousands of years ago as Paleo-Hebrew and was one of three Canaanite dialects (Aramaic and Amorite being the others), a subgroup of the Northwest Semitic language, and is the only Canaanite language still spoken today.[5] Although the language existed in spoken form long before it was written, its ancient script derived from and was identical to the Phoenicians, a Canaanite group. This reinforces the notion that the ancient Israelites split off from the Canaanites at some point. The oldest known examples of Ancient Hebrew writing is said by some to lie in the Qeiyafa Ostracon dating to around 1000 BCE (although this is contested by those who take a more minimalist view of ancient Jewish history), which is also interpreted by some to be the earliest ever mention of Saul and the Kingdom of Israel.[6,7] The Zayit Stone (discovered in 2005 and dating from 1000 BCE) consists of the earliest example of the full Paleo-Hebrew alphabet.[8] This indicates that in the 10th century BCE, the ancient Israelites likely had a strong political and social structure with scribal schools, which eventually led to the standardized script and the Hebrew language which came to be used in the 8th and 7th centuries BCE.[9] However, some scholars, such as Hebrew language historian Seth L. Sanders, argues the Zayit Stone reflects a branch of script development that ceased to exist before Hebrew emerged in the late 9th century BCE. These ancient scripts emerged prior to the creation of independent nations—such as Israel or Edom—but, as they emerged, they developed their own distinct national variations of the Northwest Semitic language and quickly adopted national forms of the new alphabetic script.[10]

Ancient Hebrew script and language continued to develop and in around the 6th century BCE,[11] Jewish scribes in Babylon began to depart from the Paleo-Hebrew script and use the Aramaic script. The use of this regional lingua franca of the day,[12] created *Ktav Ashuri* (Hebrew written in Aramaic script).[13] Because the Aramaic alphabet was identical to the Paleo-Hebrew one,[14] this change only had an impact on written Hebrew, not its spoken form. At this point, we can thus see the Torah being rewritten in this "modern" Hebrew script. However, the process of modernizing Hebrew was not complete and the script with which Hebrew letters were written continued to evolve until the 1st century CE. For example, the Hebrew letter "samekh" developed its circular form only in the middle Hasmonean period, around 100 BCE, and this became the standard form at the beginning of the Herodian dynasty in the 1st century CE.[15] There are nonetheless several examples of Paleo-Hebrew being used long after the return from the Babylonian exile. Examples of it have been found, for instance, in the Dead Sea Scrolls, dated to the 2nd to 1st centuries BCE. But, following the Jewish expulsion from Jerusalem and the end of the Jewish–Roman War, the Paleo-Hebrew alphabet fell completely out of use among Jews after 135 CE.[16]

As the Diaspora spread around the world, Jews began to learn and speak the languages of the countries in which they now lived. Over time, they also began to develop their own distinct diasporic Jewish languages: Yiddish in the 10th century[17] and Ladino in the 15th century, following the Edict of Expulsion.[18] However, Hebrew was still spoken in synagogues and was learned for the teaching of Talmud and Torah. Moreover, the notion that Hebrew was a dead language prior to its revival in the 19th century is false. Since the Middle Ages, diasporic Jews used Hebrew to communicate between the communities in different lands.[19]

From the latter part of the 18th century, Jews in the Diaspora began working on modern Hebrew dictionaries. Given its dominance in that part of the world, German Jews were mostly focused on Yiddish, but one German Hebrew dictionary—Isaac Satanow's three-part *Sefer ha-Shorashim* (Book of the Roots)—was published in 1787.[20] During the same period, several dictionaries were produced in London. The most prominent was by David Levi, titled *Lingua Sacra,* published between 1785 and 1788.[21] In the 19th century, more dictionaries appeared, and in 1837, Abigail Lindo, a British Sephardic woman related to Benjamin Disraeli and the Montefiore family, created another English to Hebrew dictionary, *A Hebrew-English and English-Hebrew Dictionary.*[22] Other Jews in other regions, such as Judah Leib Ben-Ze'ev, born in the Polish-Lithuanian Commonwealth, also worked to create Hebrew dictionaries.[23]

Ben-Ze'ev's work on Hebrew grammar in *Talmud lashon 'Ivri* was the main Eastern European source for Hebrew study for a century.[24] These efforts by Jewish lexicographers are a powerful statement of the significance of Hebrew to these 18th- and 19th-century Jews. And despite speaking Yiddish or German or English, they saw the value in Jews—wherever they lived—speaking Hebrew, the indigenous language of the Jews. A sentiment still shared by many Jews today.

These efforts continued until modern Hebrew truly took off in 1881, when Eliezer Ben-Yehuda and his friends agreed to exclusively speak Hebrew in their conversations.[25] Ben-Yehuda had learned Ancient Hebrew as a child when studying Torah and eventually understood that reviving Hebrew as the spoken language of the Jews was vital for the success of a Jewish nation and Jewish national rights. However, at least fifty years prior to Ben-Yehuda, Jews from around the world who had made *Aliyah* spoke Hebrew to each other—as they had done for centuries previously.[26]

Eventually, modern Hebrew became the official language of the modern Jewish state. In this context, Hebrew serves as a powerful symbol of the continuity of the Jewish people at large. We are rooted in our ancient lands and culture, but we evolve. The Academy of the Hebrew Language is tasked with "preserving its Hebraic nature according to its deep, historical origins while catering for the natural development and evolution of the language in the modern era."[27] Even with the advent of new vocabulary, the continuity of indigenous Jewishness remains ever strong. It is no exaggeration to say that, in its modern or ancient forms, nearly all Jews around the world are familiar with Hebrew in some context. Whether speaking it on a day-today basis or reciting it during Shabbat prayers, we all continue to hear, speak or listen to the indigenous languages of the Jews.

This connection binds us to one another, regardless of where we were born. It also allows us to engage with our civilization directly. Our texts are written in Hebrew; so for Jews, particularly those of us in the Diaspora, to deepen our connection to, and analyses of, these texts we must learn Hebrew. Reading translations is insufficient. Similarly, just like Jews in the Middle Ages, speaking Hebrew allows Jews today to communicate with, and feel connected to, one another irrespective of our first languages. Beyond this, Hebrew tethers Jews to our land. That we continue to speak—in some form or another—the native language spoken by our ancient ancestors who lived in the Land of Israel, is a profound manifestation of Jewish indigeneity.

CULTURE

Culture is an exceptionally broad term. Anthropologist Edward Burnett Tylor defined it as "that complex whole which includes knowledge, belief, art, morals, law, custom, and any other capabilities and habits acquired by man as a member of society."[28] Given our 3,000-year history, Jewish culture is extensive, and this is one of our greatest strengths. The width and breadth of Jewish culture encompasses such a wide range that every Jew can find something within it with which to connect.

The practical expressions of Jewish culture—the customs and traditions that enable us to express our Jewishness as a distinct and indigenous people—are the elements that make us who we are. While some aspects of Jewish culture evolved over time in the Diaspora, many continue to be rooted in our ancient customs and the Land of Israel.

Like all indigenous peoples, we Jews today inherit a rich cultural tradition, passing it on to future generations and thereby continuing the cycle of Jewish life. The significance of expressing Jewish culture goes beyond keeping specific traditions alive for thousands of years; it keeps us alive as a distinct group of people. As Ahad Ha'am, the great Zionist thinker and founder of cultural Zionism, wrote: "More than Jews have kept Shabbat, Shabbat has kept the Jews."[29]

Jews are not monolithic; despite the ties that bind us, we never have been. When we talk about ideas, practices, or values from the past, we are not assuming they relate to every single Jew today or in the past, including those who lived in the Land before our expulsion. And while Jewishness has a distinct definition, individuals rightly have the freedom to express their Jewishness in ways that feel appropriate to them. We know, for example, that Jews are instructed to keep kosher, observe the festivals, and adhere to a plethora of other commandments as laid out in the Torah. These remain Jewish practices and customs, even though there are Jews who choose not to observe them. Individual choice does not negate the idea that we, as Jews, as a collective, are the inheritors of specific traditions and values.

Shabbat traditions and laws are part of our religious life. But they are also, along with a host of other Jewish traditions and laws, an expression of our Jewishness and our Jewish indigeneity, whether we are religious or atheist. As the late Gary Tobin, founder of the Institute for Jewish & Community Research, put it: "The dichotomy between religion and culture doesn't really exist ... Every religious attribute is filled with culture; every cultural act filled with religiosity. Synagogues themselves are great centers of Jewish culture." As an agnostic Jew, I find it incredibly important that all Jews feel a connection to Jewish cultural practices, including those laid out in the Torah or the Talmud. These are how we express our Jewishness; without them, what do we have?

BRIT MILAH (CIRCUMCISION)

There are countless expressions of Jewish culture, from our food and songs to our family values, the high regard we hold for education, our love of debate, and even symbolic acts like the smashing of the glass at Jewish weddings. However, due in part to its universality for Jewish men, the first aspect of Jewish cultural life we will explore is the *brit milah* (circumcision). Jewish baby boys are circumcised when they are eight days old, as instructed in the Torah. In *Bereshit* (Genesis) 17:11, it is written: "You shall circumcise the flesh of your foreskin, and that shall be the sign of the covenant between Me and you."[30]

Beyond the Torah, we are not aware of why the practice of circumcision began. Yonatan Adler describes it as "an early cultural practice whose origins are lost in the mists of time."[31] It seems that, like other cultural practices such as abstaining from eating pork, it was carried out by our ancient ancestors and later codified by the Torah. Although a marker of ancient Jewish identity and a symbol of indigeneity, the brit is much more than that; it was a law, referred to by Philo as a "commandment of the law."[32]

We know that, historically, circumcision was widely adhered to and seen as a significant symbol of Jewishness. Antiochus IV banned circumcision with the death penalty prescribed for mothers whose sons were circumcised. Hellenized Jewish men engaged in epispasm (reverse circumcision, as discussed in *Reclaiming Our Story: The Pursuit of Jewish Pride*). By contrast, following their victory, the Maccabees forcibly circumcised all uncircumcised boys in Israel. In the writings of 1st-century CE writers, circumcision is used to indicate a Judean male.[33] This became one of the methods by which Paul sought to distinguish and separate early Christians from Jews. In Galatians he declared: "Listen! I, Paul, am telling you that if you let yourselves be circumcised, Christ will be of no benefit to you."[34] By using it as a way of differentiating Jews from Christians, Paul highlighted the significance of circumcision to Jews.

It is clear, then, that not only was this a tradition deemed significant to Jews, it was also a marker of ancient Jewish identity. As Fred Rosner writes in the *Encyclopedia of Jewish Medical Ethics*:

> "Several eras in subsequent Jewish history were associated with forced conversions and with prohibitions against ritual circumcision ... Jews endangered their lives during such times and exerted strenuous efforts to nullify such edicts. When they succeeded, they celebrated by declaring a holiday. Throughout most of history, Jews never doubted their obligation to observe circumcision ... [those who attempted to

reverse it or failed to perform the ritual were called] voiders of the covenant of Abraham our father, and they have no portion in the World to Come."[35]

We do not know whether devotion to this practice was rooted in the covenant with God or was simply an undying expression of Jewish specificity and identity. But we do know that this cultural act remains one of the most important expressions of Jewishness. A 2016 study found that 91.7% of men in Israel were circumcised (given there are also Christian as well as Muslim Israelis, for whom circumcision is encouraged, but not enforced, this would mean almost all the Jewish men are circumcised).[36] Even in the Diaspora, the overwhelming majority of Jewish boys are circumcised at eight days old (if their health allows). Another 2016 study found that 98.7% of Jewish men in the U.K. were circumcised, indicating the continued prevalence of this practice in Jewish expression.[37] While a small movement of Jews chooses not to circumcise their sons, this practice remains one of the primary ethnic markers of Jewish identity, regardless of whether the child's family is secular or religious, or whether they live in Israel or the Diaspora. It holds significance beyond even the Bar-Mitzvah or other widespread Jewish practices. The significance of this act is such that men who join the Jewish people also undergo a *brit milah* if they are not already circumcised, and if they are, they undergo *hatafat dam*—where a mohel draws a symbolic drop of blood from the penis at the point where the foreskin would have been or was attached—as a symbol of this fundamental Jewish act.

Although other cultures in the region and beyond also circumcise their sons, that does not diminish its significance in defining Jewish identity. It is why Jewish communities (among others) fear laws which aim to ban circumcision, such as that proposed in Iceland in 2018.[38] Obviously, there must be regulations to ensure its safe practice, but to ban circumcision for Jews is to deny us a significant expression of our indigeneity (and our right to make a covenant with our God), which is itself protected by the UN Declaration on the Rights of Indigenous Peoples. This is yet another reason why it is imperative that Jews are recognized as indigenous, because, in theory, this recognition affords us an additional layer of protection ensuring the practice of our ancient customs. Banning Jewish customs such as circumcision could be interpreted as going against the eight criteria in the United Nations Declaration on the Rights of Indigenous Peoples, which, in Article Eight, guarantees that "Indigenous peoples and individuals have the right not to be subjected to forced assimilation or destruction of their culture."[39] Banning our ability to practice our customs, even if not intended, is a form of forced assimilation.

The enduring significance of this practice is evident in the fact that nearly all Jewish men, regardless of their geographical location, continue to undergo circumcision to this day, more than 3,000 years since it emerged as a practice in the Land of Israel. This tradition serves as a profound expression of Jewish indigeneity and the unbroken continuity of Jewish culture.

THE MIKVEH

Another Jewish practice legislated in the Torah, practiced by ancient Jews and still maintained by Jews today, is the mikveh, a plunge pool used for ritual immersion. The Torah, specifically in *Vayikra* (Leviticus), instructs Jews to "bathe their flesh in water"[40] in "a spring, or a cistern, a gathering (mikveh) of water."[41] The mikveh is considered so important that Yisrael Meir Kagan (Chofetz Chaim), the famed 20th-century rabbi responsible for writings including the *Orach Chayim*, the book on Jewish ritual, argued that its construction must take place prior to the building of a synagogue or even buying a Torah scroll.[42] Even in the Mishnah, four chapters are devoted to the building of the mikveh.[43]

While important for the entire family, it is particularly significant for women, as its usage was not prescribed in law for men in the same way as it was for women. Connected to the concept of *Taharat haMishpacha* (family purity) and the laws of *Niddah* (a woman's purity during menstruation), the mikveh is also referenced in *Vayikra* for this purpose.[44] According to these laws, seven days following the last menstruation, a Jewish woman is instructed to immerse herself in a mikveh. These laws have played an active and important role in shaping the lives of Jewish women and continue to do so today.

Beyond the dictates of the law, the use of the mikveh in ancient Israel was widespread. As Yonatan Adler in *Origins of Judaism* revealed, over 1,000 ancient immersion pools have been found in the former territories of Judea, Galilee, and Perea.[45] The majority of these pools date from the early Roman period (the middle of the 1st century BCE to the Bar Kokhba revolt in 132 CE). Moreover, 36 immersion pools from the Hasmonean period have been discovered in locations such as Jerusalem, Keren Naftali, and Gamla.[46] These pools have been uncovered in all areas inhabited by ancient Judeans, not just in Jerusalem. This indicates that they were used as part of everyday life, not solely before entering the Temple. Considering the laws surrounding Jewish ritual purity, the lack of archeological evidence of mikveh prior to the Hasmonean period suggests that ancient Jews may have washed in springs.

This cultural practice continued even as most Jews spread all over the world, becoming part of the Diaspora. The oldest artifact in the former Jewish Museum of London is a 13th-century mikveh discovered in the remnants of the Crespin family home in London in 2001.[47] This was a cellar mikveh, presumably used only by the Crespin family, similar to the ones used in ancient Judea, rather than the communal mikvehs you see today.

Although still incredibly common among Orthodox Jews, other Jewish streams, such as Reform, also still use the mikveh. Academic Jack Wertheimer notes that a number of non-Orthodox Jews are embracing the mikveh for non-traditional uses.[48] Rejecting the necessity of the mikveh for *Niddah*, it is also being used for other life cycles or expressions of Jewishness, such as prior to a Bar- or Bat-Mitzvah or even following a divorce.[49] In 2001, writer Anita Diamant founded Mayyim Hayyim (Living Waters), "a 21st-century creation, a mikveh rooted in ancient tradition, reinvented to serve the Jewish community of today."[50] To ensure it is open and welcoming to all Jews, Mayyim Hayyim operates under Orthodox rabbinic supervision, and according to their website, provides over 1,600 immersions annually. In 2012, ImmerseNYC, another modern mikveh, was founded by Rabbi Sara Luria as part of the Marlene Meyerson JCC Manhattan. The ImmerseNYC website features a series of testimonials from Jewish individuals regarding their immersion experience at the ImmerseNYC mikveh. One woman writes, "What I loved most about my daughter and myself immersing to mark her Bat-Mitzvah wasn't just the way she got so comfortable, wasn't just the way she witnessed me, wasn't just the way our mikveh guide enhanced our experience … What I loved most was the way we shared a Jewish sacred moment together."[51]

Many Jews, and in particular Jewish women, still engage in the mikveh ritual, as our ancestors did thousands of years ago, and the mikveh remains an important expression of their cultural heritage. This practice exemplifies both the permanence and fluidity of Jewish culture. While maintaining an understanding and adherence to Jewish law, it is also being adapted. As Carrie Bornstein, Mayyim Hayyim's former director, suggested, "Part of what it means for us to be welcoming is providing gender-reassignment ceremonies, so it was about looking at the Jewish legal system to figure out what we needed to do to fulfill the letter of the law, but also to see what's open for interpretation."[52]

The ongoing practice of the mikveh stands as a remarkable testament to Jewish cultural continuity and indigeneity, with virtually every Jewish community worldwide having at least one mikveh for communal use. Just like numerous other traditions, this contemporary Jewish practice traces its roots back to the Land of Israel, where our ancient ancestors observed it in accordance with the Laws of Torah.

BELIEFS

"*Shema Yisrael Adonai Eloheinu Adonai Eh.ad*" ("Hear, O Israel: The Lord is our God, the Lord is One").[53] These words, the first uttered in the Shema prayer, declare the belief system of the Jews: the worship of one God, and only one God. For thousands of years, Jews throughout history have inherited this notion, which, in turn, has defined our culture.

According to the instructions given in the subsequent paragraph of the Shema, this declaration of belief is physically manifested by the use of tefillin on foreheads and by affixing mezuzot on doorposts and gates.[54] These timeless practices are upheld by Jews today, just as they were adhered to by Jews thousands of years ago. There exists undeniable evidence, supported by various sources, that tefillin, specifically, was observed by Jews in the 1st century CE including discoveries in caves within the Judean Desert.[55] These acts serve as declarations of Jewish monotheism, representing the defining feature of Jewish belief. The religious beliefs found in Jewish culture are so embedded even atheist or agnostic Jews such as me acknowledge the concept of Jewish monotheism. Even if God is not central to our Jewish identity, we still recognize the fundamental Jewish idea of one God.

As discussed in earlier chapters, the evolution of the Jewish people is intricately linked to the worship of our national God, YHWH. A national God is a deity specifically revered by a particular group in a distinct land. While YHWH is not the sole example of a national God—Marduk for the Babylonians serves as another[56]—YHWH remains the national God of the ancient Israelites and continues to be worshiped by Jews today. This enduring continuity serves as a significant and powerful symbol of Jewish indigeneity, particularly as the worship of a national God establishes a lasting connection between a people, a specific land, and a particular deity. And that enduring relationship persists to this day: one people, one land, one God.

Our ancestors' devotion to YHWH played a pivotal role in the emergence of the ancient Israelites as a distinct entity, a people who separated from the broader Canaanite community to focus their worship on this deity. Although YHWH was not initially the sole god venerated by our ancient forebears, the Jewish belief in, and worship of, one God evolved over several centuries. By the 9th century BCE, through the teachings of the prophet Elijah, YHWH became recognized as the principal God to whom "one owed the powers of blessing the land."[57] In this ancient teaching, the connection between the Jewish God and the Land is perfectly clear. As we know, YHWH is said to have promised the Land of Israel to Abraham. Indeed, the Torah begins with the creation story to demonstrate that God created the world and gave the Land of Israel to the Jewish people. YHWH is also responsible for looking after the Land of Israel,[58] as *Devarim* (Deuteronomy) states: "The eyes of the Lord ... are always upon it, from the beginning of the year to the end of the year."[59]

While Jews are referred to as a monotheistic people, our ancient ancestors recognized the existence of—and, as we know, at some stage even worshiped—other gods. They were thus actually monolatristic: Believing that many gods exist but worshipping one specific deity. It is also true that because the Israelites emerged from the Canaanites, their worship included worship of Canaanite gods. As we have seen, these included El (from whom Israel is said to have taken its name and presumably the root of the Hebrew word Elohim, meaning God), Asherah (considered to be El's wife[60]), and Baal. In an earlier draft of *Devarim* (Deuteronomy), YHWH is described as one of the sons of El.[61]

The ending of the Iron Age (1200–550 BCE) saw the rise of ancient nation states associated with particular national gods.[62] During the period from the Judges to the first half of the United Monarchy, Mark Smith suggests in *The Early History of God: YHWH and the Other Deities in Ancient Israel*, we see the convergence of various gods (El, Asherah, and Baal) into representations of YHWH.[63] Specific features of the worship of these other gods—specifically El—were absorbed into the Israelite worship of YHWH. In *Bereshit* (Genesis), God is referred to as El Shaddai, and in the Torah, there are many times God is referred to as El followed by another name. Other examples of this include El Kana in *Bereshit* 14 and El Elyon in *Bereshit* 21.

As we explored in Chapter 3, it was during the reign of King Josiah major reforms were implemented, which were important steps toward Israelite monotheism. While specific features of the worship of these other gods were absorbed into the Israelite worship of YHWH, polemics were also written against them. During King Josiah's reign (640–609 BCE), the statues of Asherah and Baal, which had been built in the First Temple,[64] were torn down. "Then the king ordered the high priest Hilkiah, the priests of the second rank, and the guards of the threshold to bring out of the Temple of GOD all the objects made for Baal and Asherah and all the host of heaven," *Sefer Melachim* (Book of Kings) records. "He burned them outside Jerusalem in the fields of Kidron, and he removed the ashes to Bethel."[65] Nonetheless, even as we moved toward monotheism, it is clear that we weren't quite there yet—an acknowledgment of other gods remained, even if we were to reject them. A quote from *Shemot* (Exodus) demonstrates this situation: "I am your God who brought you out of the land of Egypt, the house of bondage: You shall have no other gods besides Me."[66]

This process continued, and by the end of the post-exilic period, YHWH became *the* national God of the Jewish people. Features of the older Canaanite heritage, such as Baal, were not only seen as non-Yahwistic, but due to his role as a national God, as non-Israelite too. Interestingly, as we have seen, YHWH was the God of both the Kingdom of Israelites and the Kingdom of Judah. Both kingdoms were ancient Israelite and provide examples of Jewish sovereignty in the land.

Following the Babylonian exile and later, the expulsion of the Jews by the Romans, we carried YHWH with us wherever our journeys in the

Diaspora led. Even as a six-year-old attending Glasgow's Calderwood Lodge Jewish Primary School, we recited the Shema every day before class, declaring that as Jews we worship the God of Israel, and only the God of Israel. This daily recitation of the Shema symbolized our commitment to this central Jewish belief. Regardless of whether Jews reside in the Land of Israel or in the Diaspora, we remain the People of Israel, steadfast in our collective devotion to the God of Israel, our national deity. This epitomizes the essence of Jewish indigeneity concerning belief. A distinct Jewish identity evolved around the worship of YHWH (among other gods), and a unique Israelite identity coalesced around the veneration of YHWH as the national God of the Israelites in the Land of Israel. This tradition endures to this day. And even though Jews now live all over the world, this concept of worshipping one specific God continues to define and unite the Jewish people across borders and generations.

THE LAND AND GOD

Another central and continuous Jewish belief is that God promised the Jewish people the Land of Israel.

Bereshit (Genesis) tells us that after sending Avraham from Ur (modern-day Iraq) to Canaan, God tells him: "To your offspring I assign this land."[67] According to the Torah, this promise is the source of the relationship between the Jews and the Land of Israel. But more than just the land promised to the Jews, Israel is itself divine. As *Devarim* (Deuteronomy) tells us: "It is a land which your God looks after, on which your God always keeps an eye, from year's beginning to year's end."[68] As we will explore in Rabbi Isaac Choua's interview, there are mitzvot (Jewish laws) only applicable to the Land of Israel. These beliefs are the root of the Jewish connection to the Land of Israel. It is why, as we have already referenced, Jews kiss the ground upon arrival or are buried with bags of soil from the land.

This belief is not separate from our indigeneity; it is another manifestation of it. It helps us understand why Jews remained committed to this land for 2,000 years in exile. For Jews, the land is holy, it was promised by God, and it is our home. As we have explored, this connection is deep and multifaceted. However, from a biblical perspective, the Jewish bond with Eretz Yisrael can be explained by God's promise to us. Many secular Jews would balk at my inclusion of this belief in a study on indigeneity, but as a core Jewish tenet and explanation of how the Land of Israel came to be Jewish it cannot be dismissed. However, the belief that the Land of Israel was given to the Jews by God should not dictate modern political borders, as religious Zionism might argue today. Instead, acknowledging this central Jewish idea is simply uncovering another layer of connection between Jews and Israel that already exists.

This traditional Jewish belief is particularly important for modern Jews. Jews today often misunderstand or mischaracterize Jewishness, perceiving it through a Western and Christian lens where religion can be compartmentalized and separated from other aspects of life. This is not the case with Judaism. Judaism is the indigenous culture of the Jews, originating in the Near East through the cultic worship of YHWH. In this context, God cannot be separated from action, society, culture, government, or land. They are interconnected in a holistic relationship. However, through the absorption of the Western idea of religion, many Jews—especially in seeking to promote Zionism—diminish the significance of the Jewish belief that God promised us the Land of Israel. It is true that modern political Zionism began as a movement rooted in secular nationalism. While religious Zionism, rooted in the idea that God promised the Jewish people the Land of Israel, was always present, it only became a significant movement later. These early Zionist thinkers were undoubtedly influenced by emancipation and the contemporary secularization of Europe; Theodor Herzl (the founder of modern political Zionism) himself was an atheist and envisioned a secular Jewish state. There is nothing wrong with this, but it is worth acknowledging that these ideas were created in response to Christianity, and as we know, Judaism is not the same as Christianity.

The reality is that Judaism—the indigenous culture of the Jews—cannot be separated from Jewishness—one's expression of one's Jewish identity. They are one and the same. Many of the expressions of Jewish culture we have explored in these chapters began as laws laid out in the Torah. This does not diminish their significance or our indigeneity to the land. Rather, the fact that Jewish scripture claims the land was promised by God only adds to the evidence of the depth of the Jewish relationship to the Land of Israel. We must also ask ourselves: How would we treat ideas of God in other indigenous peoples? Would we respect them and understand the significance of traditional stories and myths, or would we diminish them, arguing they are irrelevant to their connection to their respective lands? As Assistant Chief Wayne Adkins of the Chickahominy Tribe stated regarding their reclamation of the sovereignty in 944 acres of their ancestral land, "That's where we came from. That's where we were when the settlers came … It was meant to be. It was divine intervention that it came up the way it did. It was one of the places where John Smith mapped. It's historically important to us."[69] Ultimately, a secular perspective rooted in peoplehood or a religious perspective rooted in God are not in fact mutually exclusive. They each represent layers of understanding and meaning in our identity; all Jews should embrace both and see them as important bricks that make up the structure of Jewish identity.

The belief that God promised the Land of Israel to the Jewish people is a core Jewish tenet. Perhaps, alongside the Shema, it is *the* Jewish belief. It has existed for thousands of years and bound the Jewish people to the land even in exile. It is therefore supremely important, and a symbol of Jewish indigeneity whether you believe it is true or not.

FORM NON-DOMINANT GROUPS OF SOCIETY

As we saw previously, "indigenous" comes from the Latin *indigena*, meaning "native" or "sprung from the land." However, during the colonial period, it served to define the distinction between Europeans and those they had colonized, thus providing the meaning with a particular undertone. It took on an even more specific nuance in the 1960s and 1970s with New Left's focus on decolonization and liberation. This thinking ultimately split the world into oppressed and oppressor, fixing each into a binary category from which there was no escape. It is these developments which make the sixth criterion laid out by the United Nations so problematic.

Asserting that an indigenous people must "form non-dominant groups of society" strips them of their agency and is an affront to the very principles of decolonization. Arguing that an indigenous group must remain a minority in their own land hinders their ability to regain or maintain self-determination while preserving their connection to the land and thus their status as indigenous. This is not a zero-sum game. When a group, such as the Jews or the Armenians, reclaims sovereignty over their indigenous land, this does nothing to weaken the claims of indigenous tribes in Canada. Are the Inuits, the indigenous people of Greenland, who make up 88% of the country's population, no longer indigenous as they constitute the majority?[70]

Despite being part of the Jewish experience for over 2,000 years, Zionism emerged in the 19th century as a response to the never-ending cycle of Jew-hate to which Jews were subjected—and, tragically, still are—in the Diaspora. It is this cycle that Zionism sought to break by establishing Jewish sovereignty in a specific territory. After a brief debate, it was decided that the land must be the Land of Israel. And thus, the fight for Jewish sovereignty began in earnest. Despite the fact that this notion was unheard of in the 19th century, the Zionist movement was a decolonization—and indigenous rights—movement. It sought to re-establish Jewish sovereignty in the land from whence they came. The rebirth of Israel, the Jewish state, in 1948 should have served as an inspiration to all displaced indigenous people and those from whom their sovereignty was stolen. It is a modern-day miracle that a Jewish state exists in the Land of Israel. But Jew-hatred, combined with Leftist trends of the latter half of the 20th century, have sullied perceptions of this achievement.

Denying indigenous peoples the opportunity to decolonize and reclaim their homes—which the UN criterion effectively does—is a form of paternalistic racist abuse. Indigenous people should be supported in regaining their sovereignty. They should be encouraged to develop and evolve while retaining that which makes them unique. The Jewish experience—like that of the Armenians—does not fit this pernicious criterion. We should not pretend it does. Instead, we should reject and condemn it. What Jews achieved in Israel in 1948 and in the ensuing seven decades is a shining example of decolonization and the ability of an indigenous people to regain their land. And we should celebrate it as such—both for ourselves and indigenous people the world over.

RESOLVE TO MAINTAIN AND REPRODUCE THEIR ANCESTRAL ENVIRONMENTS AND SYSTEMS AS DISTINCTIVE PEOPLES AND COMMUNITIES

The final UN criterion for identifying indigeneity—the "resolve to maintain and reproduce their ancestral environments and systems as distinctive peoples and communities"[71]—aligns with my definition of indigeneity, in which I state: "This is their home and is where they originated, developed, and continued to be fixed through a connection to the environment and natural resources, living systems, culture, and practices as a people, irrespective of their sovereignty in the land." As we have seen, one of the most extraordinary features of Jewish history is our continuity. Given how long ago Jews emerged in the Levant, it is truly an astounding feat, and it is particularly impressive given the diasporic nature of our experience following our expulsion from Jerusalem.

Since that moment we have seen the continuation of a living Jewish civilization; all the more so after we reclaimed our home in 1948. Wherever we lived in the world, Jews maintained our connection to our land, our laws, and each other. This was achieved through maintaining and reproducing our ancestral environments and systems as distinctive peoples and communities. We describe ourselves as Am Yisrael (The People of Israel). We continue to celebrate the ancient Jewish festivals, many of which were rooted in the Land of Israel. We continue to circumcise our boys, giving us a physical representation of our Jewishness. Many Jewish women continue to obey the laws regarding ritual purity and the use of the mikveh. And we continue to eat the same food. As I recalled in the Prologue, I remember my mother instructing my father to buy pomegranate for Rosh Hashanah. Pomegranate is one of the *Shivat Haminim* (seven species of fruit native to the Land of Israel as mentioned in the Torah). We were Jews from Glasgow, Scotland—where pomegranate is very much not native—but still we honored our indigeneity by consuming it.

However, one of the major ways in which Jews maintained and replicated our ancient systems was through our adherence to the Laws of Torah. And one fascinating way Jews preserved these legal systems was through the synagogue.

As Yonatan Adler remarks, historically "Synagogue was the principal vehicle for the dissemination of the Torah."[72] It remains so today. What is a more effective replication of ancient systems than ensuring a people's legal code is widely known? This is how the synagogue began life. Known in Hebrew as the *beyt knesset* (house of assembly), it was initially an institution where people assembled to hear the Torah read aloud. This was widespread in ancient Judea. Philo attributes weekly public readings of the law to Moses. "He considered that they should not only be capable of both action and inaction in other matters but also should have expert knowledge of their ancestral laws and customs. What then did he do? He required them to assemble in the same place on these seventh days, and sitting together in a respectful and orderly manner [to] hear the laws read so that none should be ignorant of them."[73] Philo describes synagogues as a common feature in Judean communities everywhere. Josephus also writes that ordinary Judeans gathered to hear the Torah, to hear the law and to learn it in detail. This, according to Josephus, was effective: "Were anyone of us to be asked about the laws, he would recount them more easily than his own name. So, learning them thoroughly from the very first moment of consciousness, we have them, as it were, engraved in our souls."[74] The Theodotus inscription (found in 1913 in the City of David in Jerusalem) is a hugely important ancient reference to a synagogue.[75] It was found in a water cistern in the southeastern spur of Jerusalem during excavations by Raymond Weill and states: "Theodotus, son of Vettenus, priest and archisynágōgos, son of an archisynágōgos, grandson of a archisynágōgos, built the synagogue for the reading of the law and the teaching of the commandments…"[76]

The first building to be identified as a synagogue was found on Masada, where a *Devarim* (Deuteronomy) scroll and *Ezekiel* scroll were also found. However, this practice of assembling to hear the law of Torah was not specific to Jews in Judea; Jews in the Diaspora also kept this practice. Philo claimed that, in the period of Emperor Augustus, there were several synagogues in Rome where Judeans would gather—particularly on Shabbat. In this context, prayer was not the primary aim of these ancient structures—instead it was to hear the laws and discuss them. Most historical accounts don't mention prayer, and it is possible that prayer was meant for the temples when sacrifices were made.

Although prayer is now a central component of the synagogue, it is still a place where Jews gather to hear our law, the Torah. It is wonderful that every single synagogue in the world is reading the same parsha (Torah portion) at the same time. There are 54 parashot (plural of Torah portion), one for each week of the year, so that in the course of a year, we read the entire Torah from start to finish. This is a remarkable example of Jewish unity and continuity. All Jews, no matter where they are in the world, are hearing the same portion of Jewish law and history, which has been heard by their ancestors in the same synagogue setting for 2,000 years. And today, the synagogue is still a central part of Jewish life. In the U.K., a 2016 census suggests there were 454 synagogues across the country.[77] In the U.S., a 2001 census indicated there were 3,727 in the United States.[78] And apparently there are 1,000 in Jerusalem alone.[79] A 2021 Pew report suggests that "One-in-five U.S. Jews say they attend services at a synagogue, temple, minyan, or havurah at least once or twice a month, including 12% who go weekly or more often. One-quarter (27%) say they attend a few times a year, such as for High Holidays."[80] As we have discussed, it does not matter whether every Jew does or does not attend synagogue for it to remain a Jewish practice, in which Jews still participate today—in the way in which our ancestors did for thousands of years. The continuation of the synagogue, whether in the Diaspora or in modern Israel, are exceptional examples of the Jewish maintenance and reproduction of our ancient civilization and our continuity as a living culture.

Another striking example is the Hebrew calendar. This is a (mostly) lunar calendar, and like all other calendars in the Near East, it was linked to the agricultural cycle. This is another demonstration of Jewish indigeneity to the Land of Israel. The calendar, which is still utilized today, was born out of the land itself. It was not simply created *in* the land, but *from* the land. Although the calendar is considered lunar, it is in fact solilunar, because, although the festivals were linked to the moon, some are also linked to agriculture, which are in turn connected to the solar calendar, the annual cycle of the seasons.

It is the practice of the Southern Kingdom of Judah, which began its year on the 1st of Tishrei, which Jews continue today. However, it was not until the time of Hillel II (Nasi [prince] of the Sanhedrin 320–385 CE) that the calendar we use today was fixed.[81] Before that, for many hundreds of years, the calendar was based on observation and new months were indicated by the sighting of a crescent moon, with two eyewitnesses required to testify to the *Sanhedrin* for it to be approved.[82]

Initially, the new Jewish month was signaled to the communities inside Israel and outside by lighting fires on mountaintops. However, the Samaritans purposely lit fires on the wrong days to confuse the Jews,[83] so messengers had to be sent to inform the communities of the new month. The inability of the messengers to reach communities in time led communities outside of Israel to celebrate festivals for two days rather than one.[84] This practice is still carried out by Jews in the Diaspora today. Between the years 70 and 1178 CE, this observation-based calendar was replaced by a modern, mathematically calculated one.[85]

Today, the Hebrew calendar is one of the official calendars of the modern Jewish state, the State of Israel. Contemporary holidays created after 1948 were fixed to the Jewish calendar, not the Gregorian. For example, *Yom Ha'atzmaut* (Israeli Independence Day) falls on 5th Iyar[86] every year and *Yom Hashoah* (Jewish Holocaust Commemoration Day) on 27th Nisan.[87]

The Hebrew calendar is also how Jews commemorate their dead. And, in 2024, it was decided that from 2025 onward the memorial for the October 7 massacre would fall on the 24th of Tishrei in line with the Hebrew calendar.[88] On an individual level, the anniversary of a loved one's passing is also marked by the Hebrew calendar and every year we say *Kaddish* and light the Yahrzeit candle—just as I do for my late father, Malcolm, on the 8th *Shevat* every year. Bar and Bat Mitzvot are also dated by the Hebrew calendar. My Bar-Mitzvah was on January 8, 2000, because my Hebrew birthday (27th *Tevet*) fell on January 5, even though, according to the Gregorian calendar, I was still only 12. The festivals that Jews continue to celebrate, from Rosh Hashanah to Chanukah to Shavuot are also dated in line with the Hebrew calendar, thus the Gregorian dates change every year. This calendar still shapes Jewish life to this very day. Even the most atheist Jew will still use it to chart aspects of their Jewish life.

During periods when Jews were persecuted, they continued to honor who they were and reproduce their historic environments. Holocaust historian Avraham Rosen noticed that when gathering testimony of those who survived the Shoah, they referenced the Hebrew calendar. He remembered being told by one survivor that "our deportation took place before Shavuot."[89] Rosen also remarked that because the Jewish calendar is a lunar calendar, with every month beginning with a new moon and a full moon marking the middle of the month, even in Auschwitz Jews were able to roughly mark the point at which they were at in a Jewish month. We have also heard testimony that Jews fasted on Yom Kippur. They did this even though the principles of *Pikuach nefesh* (saving a life) meant they did not have to fast, given their dire and life-threatening circumstances. Their decision to mark Jewish festivals itself is a reproduction of ancestral environments, as the Torah legislates a "a sabbath of complete rest for you"[90] to be observed on the 10th day of 7th month. It forbids work and legislates some form of self-torment, saying "you shall practice self-denial."[91] It also states that if one doesn't mark this day he shall be "cut off from his people."[92] By the first centuries of the new millennium it was customary to fast as the form of self-infliction. Josephus described the vestments worn by the high priest on Yom Kippur and said the holiday was the "day on which it was the universal custom to keep fast to God."[93] Beyond this, the fact that some Jews chose to fast on Yom Kippur in Auschwitz meant they were aware of the Hebrew date and continued to see it as a relevant component of contemporary Jewish life. Even in the darkest of times, Jews resisted Jew-hate by being actively Jewish.

It is clear from these two chapters that according to the (six, mostly non-problematic) United Nations Criteria and their Declaration on the Rights of Indigenous Peoples, as well as my own definition, Jews are indigenous to the Land of Israel. The challenge was not finding information to support these claims but choosing the most compelling evidence from a vast mountain of tradition and practice. I am confident you could have considered different examples that would also demonstrate Jewish indigeneity according to these criteria and definitions. And you would be right to do so. That is the weight of evidence that exists for Jewish indigeneity.

* * *

At this point in our exploration, we will shift from scholarly analysis to the lived experiences of Jewish individuals. This is a crucial part of any study on Jewish identity. We are not merely a theory and must not be treated as such. As with *Jewish Pride: Rebuilding a People* and *Reclaiming Our Story: The Pursuit of Jewish Pride*, I have interviewed Jews from around the world, representing various aspects of Jewish diversity. In the following five chapters, you will read the stories and perspectives of five Jews, enriching our understanding of Jewish indigeneity from a lived perspective. Each interview represents a different facet of Jewish indigeneity:

Rabbi Isaac Choua—A Sephardic Jew whose family lived in Lebanon.

Yaffa Tegegne—An Ethiopian and Ashkenazi Jew, and daughter of Baruch Tegegne, the community leader credited with initiating the *Aliyah* of Ethiopian Jewry to Israel.

Vlad Khaykin—A Jew whose family is from the former Soviet Union.

Dr. Efrat Sopher—A Jew whose family lived in Persia and whose grandfather was sent by Ben-Gurion to establish diplomatic relations with the Shah of Persia.

Dr. Winston Pickett—A Jew who converted (and my personal mentor).

Chapter 7

AN INTERVIEW WITH RABBI ISAAC CHOUA

Rabbi Isaac Choua may hail from Brooklyn, NYC, but his parents and their families were born and lived for many generations in Lebanon. The family did not want to leave Lebanon, but the outbreak of the country's brutal civil war in the 1970s—which was ignited by the Palestine Liberation Organization—forced their hand. Like many Jews, Isaac suggests, they had a deep attachment to their diasporic home. Isaac's family history can be traced back to Spain. While many Sephardic Jews moved north to Amsterdam when they were expelled from Spain and Portugal in the 15th century, others, like Isaac's ancestors, made their way east, resettling in North Africa, the Levant and Land of Israel, Turkey, or other countries in the Near East.

For Isaac, his family living in southern Lebanon, so close to their ancestral home in Israel, was in some senses immaterial. Both regions are part of the southern Levant, and as such there was always a close relationship between them. There were also significant cultural similarities: Jews in southern Lebanon even observed only one day of Yom Tov (a Jewish High Holy Day), a practice usually reserved for those living in Israel. While the rest of the Diaspora instituted an additional second day of Yom Tov to ensure they were precise in their holiday celebrations, Lebanon was part of the same territory as Eretz Yisrael, allowing Jews there to maintain the original tradition of marking Jewish holidays with only one day.

The connection between the two parts of the southern Levant stretches back thousands of years and includes the historical ties between the Phoenicians and the Israelites. In *Sefer Melachim* (the Book of Kings), the

Phoenician king, Hiram of Tyre, is said to have been a loyal friend to both King David and Solomon,[1] providing materials and craftsmen to the former and maintaining a covenant of friendship with the latter. Their royal houses were also related; Ahab, King of Northern Israel, married Jezebel, the daughter of the King of Tyre (1 Kings 16:31), likely due to the practice of intermarriage to secure alliances. The Phoenicians and Israelites never went to war with one another, a sharp contrast with the relationships between the Israelite kingdom and its other neighbors. In the Babylonian Talmud, the Hebrew script (as opposed to the Aramean script we use today) is the same as the Libona script (Phoenician script).[2]

Isaac's family story, along with his recognition of Jewish indigeneity, reinforces his sense of being Levantine. In a way, Isaac is fortunate. His family lived outside of Israel, but their proximity to it—and their home in the southern Levant—dramatically reduced what Isaac describes as "the mental colonization" often experienced by Jews in the Diaspora. This topic arises frequently in our conversation. Isaac explains that when people think of the Levant, they immediately associate it with Arabs. However, Arabs only came to dominate the region through colonization, and it encompasses many more groups, including the Jews.

Jews are a Levantine people, and this is highly significant. The central point of indigeneity is a collective's connection to the land, the environment, and natural resources. The Land of Israel—and everything it encompasses—is situated in the southern Levant, the Near East. This naturally features in our relationship with the land. The *Shivat Haminim*, the seven species of produce native to Israel, thrive there because of its climate. Israel is Levantine, and as Jews we should embrace this fact. Those of us who live in the Diaspora should understand ourselves as a Levantine diasporic people. Our indigenous culture, which shares many elements with other cultures in the Levant and the wider Mediterranean, is rooted in that region, and this influences how we express it today. Hebrew, for instance, was initially a Canaanite dialect that was later written in an

Aramaic script (Aramaic itself being a Semitic language, alongside Hebrew, Amharic, Arabic, Tigrinya, and Tigre). As Isaac argues, when Jews speak Hebrew today, we are expressing our indigeneity and our Levantine roots. This is something we must never forget.

Isaac recalls a significant teaching from Maimonides' Mishneh Torah,[3] in which we are instructed: "As soon as a child begins to speak, one should teach them [the verse] Moshe charged us with the Torah, as the inheritance of the congregation of Jacob[4] and [the verse] 'Hear, O Yisrael: The Lord our God, the Lord is one.'"[5] Notably, Maimonides emphasizes the teaching of the verse about Moshe and the Torah before the Shema, a verse many consider the foundational declaration of Jewish belief. This order offers a deep insight into Jewish identity. Before a Jew can wholeheartedly declare their commitment to the Oneness of God, they must first understand their unique heritage and the commandments which form their identity—the inheritance from Jacob. Recognizing oneself as a descendant of Jacob, also known as Bené Yisrael, is not just an acknowledgment of lineage, it's an affirmation of a deep-rooted connection to a rich history and legacy. This recognition cements one's place in a continuum upon which the rest of one's Jewish identity rests. This foundational pillar binds individuals to the stories, struggles, and triumphs of their ancestors.

The notion of the Torah being an "inheritance" underscores its enduring significance to every generation of Jews. An inheritance is not merely a gift; it's a cherished possession passed down, bearing the weight of history, values, and identity. In this light, the Torah isn't just a set of laws or teachings; it represents the DNA of the Jewish people, a roadmap that has guided them through millennia. By receiving it as an "inheritance," Jews are reminded of their duty to preserve, study, and live by its teachings, ensuring its continuity for future generations.

Israel is often described as a Western country, sometimes for nefarious reasons. While it is Westernized in some ways, such as being a parliamentary democracy, it is not Western. Israel is situated in the southern Levant and is the sovereign nation of its indigenous people, the Jews. Western perspectives, particularly from America, often present Ashkenazi Jews as the archetypal Jew and depict us as European. This not only diminishes us, but it is also not our reality. Ashkenazi Jews lived and developed their cultures in Europe, but these were geographical iterations of our indigenous culture. Yiddish, for example, was written with Hebrew letters, and many Yiddish words have Hebrew roots. Labeling Ashkenazi Jews as European ignores the Levantine nature of the Jewish people.

When Jews themselves accept this idea, according to Isaac, it is a form of mental colonization. This is a conversation we Jews must take seriously. Many of us were expelled from our indigenous land, and the rest were deprived of sovereignty for thousands of years. In both situations, we were ruled by foreign powers, making us a colonized people—perhaps the original colonized people, given the length of our exile. Any relationship between a majority and a minority involves a power imbalance, especially when one group is a tiny, colonized minority. Isaac points out that even the proudest Jews and Zionists express this idea of Jews as a colonized people. He references a speech by David Ben-Gurion, Israel's first Prime Minister and a Zionist forefather, which Isaac believes demonstrates a colonized mindset. Ben-Gurion said: "We do not want Israelis to become Arabs. We are duty-bound to fight against the spirit of the Levant, which corrupts individuals and societies, and preserve the authentic Jewish values as they crystallized in the Diaspora."[6] Ben-Gurion is undoubtedly a great Jewish hero, but no one is above reproach. It is shocking to hear Jewish values in the Diaspora described as authentic, while those from the Levant are dismissed. This is clearly not the case. The values developed in the Diaspora are not inauthentic, but they are not our indigenous culture. Instead, they are geographical iterations of it. Attempting to separate Jewish culture in this way is impossible. Isaac believes that when we fight against the spirit of the Levant, we are fighting against where we are from. As an indigenous people, this is impossible. How can we fight against where we are from? A land makes a people, and a people make a land.

Isaac and I discuss Jews who have embraced our indigeneity, but, he argues, this should mean a lifelong process of learning and studying to deepen our understanding and connection.

Of course, this does not mean that we should reject the countries where we live or where we were born. As Dr. Efrat Sopher, a Persian Jew, argues in her interview in Chapter 10, integration is entirely possible. But to successfully integrate, we must have a very clear understanding of who we are to avoid being swept along by the tide of assimilation. Adopting Christian or Western ideas that do not fit our civilization leads to assimilation, even if one retains a strong Jewish identity and Jewish Pride. The non-Jewish majority often reflects back palatable versions of Jewish identity through the "Broken Mirror of Jewish Identity." Accepting these versions is not compatible with Jewish Pride. This is not because their ideas are necessarily wrong; it is simply that we should not take our cues on our identity from a world that does not understand or accurately reflect our civilization.

I have been very open throughout this book that God does not play a role in my Jewishness. However, discussing these issues with Isaac, a rabbi, has helped me understand that Jewish perceptions of God are a key part of our indigenous connection to the Land of Israel.

The worship of the Jewish God is inherently tied to the Land of Israel and constitutes a significant aspect of our indigenous connection to the land. The Torah clearly outlines the relationship between Jews and the Land of Israel, and explaining it through the covenant made to Abraham and reaffirmed with the generations after that by God does not diminish this connection. Indeed, it is our right as an indigenous people to express our cultural ideas authentically. As Article 12 of the United Nations Declaration on the Rights of Indigenous Peoples states:

> "Indigenous peoples have the right to manifest, practice, develop, and teach their spiritual and religious traditions, customs and ceremonies; the right to maintain, protect, and have access in privacy to their religious and cultural sites; the right to the use and control of their ceremonial objects; and the right to the repatriation of their human remains."[7]

Similarly, Jews, like all people, are allowed to create myths surrounding their origins. Isaac explains that myths are often perceived negatively, but that does not necessarily mean they are made up and therefore not part of our story. Whether these myths are historically accurate or not is irrelevant. What is relevant is that a nation believes it. We cannot and do not need to dismiss them; they are a part of our indigeneity. We can contextualize them, but, regardless of their historicity, myths represent layers of meaning in the relationship between Jews and the Land of Israel. They serve as descriptions of our relationship, providing a deeper understanding of our bond to the land. As Isaac explains, this connection is reinforced by the existence of mitzvot that can only be carried out in Israel. This is how a Jew achieves their best self, Isaac suggests. It is impossible to manifest our true selves outside of Israel in the Diaspora.

Even as a rabbi, Isaac believes he can't fulfill his full potential because he is not living in Israel. There are laws that are only relevant in the land and, if we're not there, we cannot engage with them physically or intellectually. Isaac speaks of Jerusalem as the beating heart of the Jewish people. Despite the fact that the Diaspora existed long before the exile of Jews from Jerusalem by the Romans, the city has always been central to Jewish identity. All Jews face Jerusalem when we pray, symbolizing the unity of the Jewish people and our connection to Israel. Isaac emphasizes that this connection has always been more than symbolic. It is living. Jews have continuously sought to return to Israel, and many did so throughout history, not just in modern times. Isaac feels that living in the Diaspora limits his ability to fully express his culture and fulfill his potential, underscoring the deep, intrinsic bond between Jewish identity and the Land of Israel.

That's why some describe the Diaspora as the "Galut" (exile). According to Isaac, Jews outside of Israel have been cut off from our home. While Isaac still lives in New York, and while we are always at liberty to live where we choose, we cannot deny the special place Israel holds for us. Living—or being born—in the Diaspora does not in any way diminish our indigeneity to Israel. It is our home. As Isaac notes, one historical way this connection was expressed was through Halukka, the organized collection of funds for distribution among the Jews in the Holy Land and for aiding those who chose to make *Aliyah*. The act of Jews in the Diaspora maintaining Jewish life in Israel during periods of colonization is a profound example of both Jewish unity and our connection to Israel. It wasn't just seen as a personal decision to move to Israel; it was the responsibility of the entire Jewish community to support those who did so. This practice stretched back to the earliest period in Rabbinic Judaism and continues, in some form, to this day. Even before the advent of Halukka itself, Jews in the Diaspora sent funds to Israel. Alexander the Alabarch, a wealthy Alexandrian Jew, paid for nine gates at the Second Temple in Jerusalem to be "overlaid with massive plates of silver and gold."[8] Thousands of years later, in the aftermath of the October 7 massacre, hundreds of millions of dollars were sent by Jews in the Diaspora to Israel.

Ultimately, what Isaac reminds us of is an active Jewishness rooted in authentic practice and learning. He emphasizes that while each person has the right to define their relationship with their Jewishness, this personal definition does not change the intrinsic nature of Jewishness itself. Today, some Jews correlate Tikkun Olam with social justice movement activism. "Not only is the modern definition incorrect—since in a legal framework like the Torah, concepts have specific legal definitions—but it has also been used to reshape Jewishness to align with ideas of universalism that are foreign to traditional Jewish thought," he argues. "This is entirely contradictory to Jewish values." What is paramount is for Jews to achieve literacy in Jewish laws, history, and tradition.[9] This is also recognized by the United Nations in its 13th article, which argues: "Indigenous peoples have the right to revitalize, use, develop, and transmit to future generations their histories, languages, oral traditions, philosophies, writing systems, and literatures, and to designate and retain their own names for communities, places, and persons."[10] As we have seen throughout this book, Jews are a civilization, and to truly interact with it, we need knowledge and action. It is not merely an idea or "faith"; it is a way of living life with meaning and purpose. It is how we connect with our Jewish past and our Jewish future. This oneness defines us, and we must not run away from it or reject it. As a Jew living in America, Isaac draws a comparison to the U.S. pledge of allegiance, which reads, "One Nation under God, indivisible."[11] That also applies to the Jews. Our monotheism is not just rooted in our relationship with one God; it describes our peoplehood, unity, and connection to one Land, the Land of Israel. Even though God is not central to my Jewishness, I, along with all other atheist or agnostic Jews, must at least recognize that the concept of one God is a central Jewish belief. It is, along with Israel and Torah, how we have sustained ourselves for over 3,000 years, and it is how we will survive and grow in the future. This does not mean we cannot evolve and change, but as Isaac argues, "we have to grow together." And oneness does not itself necessarily imply homogeneity; we are a diverse group of people. We always have been. Let's not forget that we began life as different tribes. But even then, there was an overarching Israelite identity. And so today, Isaac says, while we must embrace our diversity, it is through dialogue, tradition, Torah, God, and Israel that we must be unified by our Jewishness.

This idea is exemplified by Isaac's writing on Jewish Pride and on Jewish connection:

"To declare our Jewish Pride in the Nation while neglecting Jewish practice is to stand on a foundation of sand—ever-shifting and without strength. Our ancestors fought too hard and suffered too greatly for us to reduce our heritage to mere words devoid of action. Jewish Pride must be deeply rooted in Jewish practice, for it is through our rituals, our observances, and our steadfast commitment to our covenant and traditions that we honor our past and forge our future. We must embrace our practices with the same fervor and dedication our ancestors showed, for only through such commitment can we ensure our pride is not just felt but lived. Our pride must be a living, breathing part of who we are, demonstrated through our actions, our faith, and our unwavering dedication to our heritage. Only then can we claim a pride that is profound, unshakeable, and true."[12]

I couldn't agree more.

Chapter 8

AN INTERVIEW WITH YAFFA TEGEGNE

Forty-three-year-old Yaffa Tegegne was born in Montreal, Canada. While her mother's family were Ashkenazi, her father was the legendary Ethiopian rights activist, Baruch Tegegne, who campaigned for the return of Ethiopian Jews to Israel from the 1970s to the 1990s.

Growing up in Montreal, with its mix of Jews from all over the world—including Israel, Iraq, Morocco, and Russia—Yaffa had both an implicit understanding of the diversity of the Jewish peoplehood and our connection to our indigenous land. They were bound together by being part of the immigrant Jewish experience and their inherent connection to one another as fellow Jews. Growing up four decades after the rebirth of the Jewish state, Israel was a central part of their identity. Most of the children in Yaffa's school, including Yaffa herself, had family in Israel. Their relationship to Israel was very much a living connection. It was, as Yaffa says, "very natural," and, although she was born in Montreal, she always felt as if Israel was also home. Hers is the living embodiment of an indigenous connection. We can belong to numerous countries and societies, and Yaffa has a strong connection to Canada, but she also belongs to Israel.

Like countless other Jews around the world, Yaffa's indigeneity is evident in Jewish practice and culture. It is—whether we realize it or not—a remarkable expression of our connection to our land. As we have seen, the vast majority of Jewish practice originated in the land. Through our festivals and our language, Hebrew, we honor our connection with Eretz Yisrael itself. And we live by laws written in the Kingdom of Judah during periods of our sovereignty. Jewish expression—not simply our beliefs—was how Jews were defined. Yes, we developed into a monotheistic people, but we differed from the other nations in the region through our actions and our practices. And growing up, Yaffa's family—particularly her father's family—were no different. They celebrated Shabbat each week. Yaffa learned Hebrew at school, and Israel remained a central focus for her family, and with it a deep sense of home.

Growing up as a Jew with a mixed ethnic background, Yaffa faced questions about her heritage. Ignorance sometimes led to her Jewishness being questioned and, even from a young age, she found herself in the role of educator. She understood she had to educate other Jews, as well as non-Jews, about the Ethiopian experience and story.

At law school, Yaffa chose to take a course in Talmudic Law. This enriched her understanding of Jewish civilization, helped her grasp the incredible legal system created in the Torah and Talmud, and left her with tremendous respect for the body of knowledge within Jewish texts and the elaborate legal system which it reflects. As we have already explored, the Torah is, at its core, humanitarian. The notion of the sanctity of life is a legal concept created in Jewish texts. We take this for granted because these Jewish texts became the basis for Western ideas of law. But, at the time, this was not the case in every society and that remains the case today. Her Talmudic legal study leads Yaffa to emphasize that every Jew should be literate. "We are a truly longstanding civilization. We have law, jurisprudence, debate, education, and tremendous intellectual pursuits for thousands of years. If only people knew how much we had behind us," she suggests.

Her father's work also led Yaffa to recognize and understand the power and centrality to Jews of Zionism. For the Ethiopian Jewish community, Zionism is not rooted in Herzl's 19th-century political movement. Theirs was, in a sense, the fulfillment of their destiny—to return home to Jerusalem. They prayed three times a day, facing Jerusalem, and their entire

Jewish life was centered on the Land of Israel. Israel was everything, and they were just biding their time until they could return home. "It was just a matter of fact that this is where they belonged," Yaffa says of her father's Zionist beliefs. Ethiopian Jews' traditional name, Beta Yisrael (the House of Israel), exemplifies this powerful connection. But Baruch's work isn't simply a guiding beacon for Yaffa and the Ethiopian Jewish community, but for all Jews. The deep and unending yearning to return home to Israel. Because that is what it is for us. It is our home.

Long periods of isolation meant Ethiopian Jewry believed they were the last Jews. Quite naturally, they believed they were responsible for safeguarding and maintaining Jewishness. Theirs was also, in a sense, the purest form of Jewish expression as they only followed the Tanakh, and did not have access to the Talmud or rabbinic teachings. And, as Yaffa tells me, their Jewishness was arguably most alike to that of the ancient Jews that existed in the world.

This had an impact on the laws they followed. For example, chicken—in the Torah—is excluded from the laws of *kashrut* regarding milk and meat. Its inclusion is a later addition by the rabbis. They also did not celebrate Chanukah or Purim, as those stories are not included in the Biblical Canon. The Ethiopian community, unburdened by Western ideas of identity, understood their Jewishness to be all-encompassing: Life, society, law, God, and land were all wrapped into one. They did not face the challenges experienced by Jews living in Europe: The demand they adopt a Westernized view of religion to be accepted by wider non-Jewish society.

Baruch was born in Wozaba, a hilltop village in the region of Gondar, where most of the Jews of Ethiopia lived. Close in age to another sibling, he was given to his grandparents so they could take care of him. From a very young age, his brilliance shone through. Baruch's grandfather was a very learned community leader. Together, they memorized the Torah and he showed Baruch the way to Jerusalem.

Jacques Faitlovitch, one of the first Ashkenazi Jews to make contact with them, played a crucial role in bridging the gap between the Ethiopian Jews and the wider Jewish world. A French-Polish Jew, Faitlovitch's efforts to educate and empower Ethiopian Jews reflected a deep commitment to the idea of Jewish unity and solidarity. Through Faitlovitch's work, Baruch and others were given the opportunity to receive a formal education in Hebrew and agriculture, skills that would not only enable them to serve as teachers in their own community but also to connect more deeply with their Jewish heritage and identity. For Baruch, this experience was transformative, opening up new possibilities and horizons beyond the confines of his village.

Even though Ethiopian Jews were not yet recognized as Jews by the State of Israel, and as a result were denied the right of return, in 1956, separated from his parents and family, 12-year-old Baruch was one of 20 pioneering Ethiopian Jewish students selected for a historic journey to the newly established State of Israel. Settling in Kfar Batya, an orphanage that housed Jewish children from around the world, including young Holocaust survivors, his experience foreshadowed Yaffa's upbringing in a diverse Jewish community. The idea of this group of disparate young Jews finding their home together in Israel is moving and powerful.

Baruch remained in Kfar Batya until he was around 18 or 19, when he faced the difficult choice of either returning to Ethiopia or remaining in Israel without citizenship. Upon his return to Ethiopia, he was deeply troubled by the living conditions he encountered. While the tribes of Ethiopia carried themselves with pride, isolation, poverty, and anti-Jewish sentiment had taken a toll on the Jewish community. Baruch was determined to ensure that Ethiopian Jews could stand proudly and embarked upon a mission to bring them to Israel to participate in the unfolding Jewish experiment. Seeing Jews from around the world migrating to Israel, he questioned why Ethiopian Jews couldn't do the same. This was two decades before Operation Moses, the Israeli government's initiative to bring Ethiopian Jews home to Israel.

Working for an Israeli agriculture company in Ethiopia, Baruch used his connections to acquire land and establish a kibbutz on the border with Sudan. He relocated his Jewish community and established a thriving farm with several hundred residents. However, their efforts were met with opposition when the border territory became contested. The Sudanese, influenced by Soviet antizionist propaganda, accused them of establishing a Zionist military base. Tragically, the farm was destroyed in a fire, resulting in the loss of everything the Jews had built. This serves as a stark reminder of the far-reaching and pernicious impact of Soviet antizionism.

In 1974, the position of Jews in Ethiopia worsened with the overthrow of Emperor Haile Selassie in a communist revolution. As in the Soviet Union, this period saw increased persecution of various groups. However, as Yaffa reflects, the situation was especially dire "for the bottom tier." Faced with escalating danger, Baruch made the difficult decision to flee to Sudan. To evade detection, he adopted the guise of a Muslim and feigned muteness, forced to conceal his Jewish identity due to the severe risks involved.

Showing remarkable resilience, Baruch crossed the Sahara Desert and found himself in Nigeria, where, lacking documentation, he was arrested and imprisoned. After enduring unimaginable hardship, he eventually managed to escape from captivity. From there, he secured passage on a Greek ship eventually bound for Israel. His arduous journey demonstrates the profound connection between Jews and Israel: It is our homeland, and we will bear any hardship to return to it. Baruch's odyssey wasn't unique: In later years, such as during Operations Moses, Joshua, and Solomon, Ethiopian Jews endured huge adversity and danger to escape to Israel. "The desperation to leave Ethiopia wasn't solely due to the conditions there. Life in Ethiopia was always challenging," Yaffa explains. "The desire to leave stemmed from the fact that they believed Israel was their true home. That's why they went to such lengths to leave."

In 1976, Baruch returned to Israel, where he embarked on advocacy efforts for the remaining members of his community. At that time, only about 50 Ethiopian Jews lived in Israel, facing considerable challenges, including prejudice within the Jewish community and severe disadvantages. Despite these obstacles, the Ethiopian community in Israel remained determined to bring their people home. Organizing gatherings to plan their strategies, Baruch and other community leaders took part in activism and protests. He even arranged a meeting with Elie Wiesel to raise awareness of their plight and orchestrated protests at the Knesset, rallying non-Ethiopian Jews to join their cause. They tirelessly lobbied the government to facilitate the return of their brethren, navigating complex geopolitical considerations, including the Cold War climate. But Baruch was undeterred. Drawing upon the experience of his own journey, he was the first person to submit a comprehensive plan to Mossad and the government outlining a route for the Jews to escape Ethiopia via Sudan—a plan that would eventually be executed.

He also decided to take his campaign to North America, leaving Israel—in part due to the resistance he faced from the government—and moving to Canada. His lobbying effort proved remarkably successful, leading to the establishment of a solidarity movement akin to that which advocated for Soviet Jewry. Thanks to Baruch's relentless advocacy, Jews worldwide contributed funds to facilitate the rescue of Ethiopian Jews and their relocation to Israel: Holocaust survivors donated; individuals gave their Bar-Mitzvah money; and even members of the non-Jewish Black community contributed. Yaffa recounts how a German Jew who owned an airline that flew planes to Mecca offered them for use by the Ethiopian Jews. The grassroots solidarity movement, sparked by Baruch, exemplified the power of collective action.

What's truly remarkable, as Yaffa emphasizes, is that there was no strategic advantage to bringing these Jews to Israel. The operations were undertaken simply because they were Jews with a right to return home. This principle guided Jews from diverse backgrounds, whether in America, Canada, or Germany, to support people they had never met and likely never would. But they were all part of the same Jewish people.

Together with the renowned Ethiopian Jewish activist Ferede Aklum, Baruch organized the initial unofficial missions to bring Ethiopian Jews home via Sudan. These efforts laid the groundwork for Operations Moses, Joshua, and Solomon, spanning the period 1984–1991, which allowed the majority of the Ethiopian Jewish community to be resettled in Israel. Despite his monumental contributions, Baruch found himself ostracized by the Israeli State and banned from re-entering the country. This rejection must have been deeply painful for Baruch, who had dedicated his life to bringing his people home to Israel. Ultimately, it took the intervention of his North American friends to overturn the ban and allow Baruch to return. As Yaffa reflects, the Ethiopian Jewish story encapsulates both the best and worst of Jewish and Israeli society. It is a testament to resilience and solidarity in the face of racism and doubt, culminating in the successful rescue and resettlement of Ethiopian Jews in their ancestral homeland.

Baruch settled in Montreal, where he married Yaffa's mother and continued his efforts to assist Ethiopian Jews, this time by working to bring them to Canada. However, the trauma and challenges he faced strained the family, ultimately leading to their divorce. Baruch later returned to Israel to live, focusing on the absorption process of Ethiopian Jews into Israeli society following the rescue operations. Spending more time in Israel with Baruch allowed Yaffa to delve deeper into his story and better understand his remarkable journey. Baruch passed away when Yaffa was 29, and his funeral became a pivotal moment in her appreciation of his work in bringing Ethiopian Jewry home.

The funeral drew a massive crowd, with 1,000 people in attendance, traveling from far and wide to pay their respects to this Jewish hero.

Yaffa has a profound sense of belonging to Israel. She feels that, in a sense, being born in Canada was a mistake and she should have been born an Israeli. She believes Israel is where everything feels right, where Jews can breathe freely without constantly worrying about how the non-Jewish world will treat them. For Yaffa, Israel is not just a place to live; it is home, a natural and inherent part of Jewish identity.

Today, she sees herself continuing her father's legacy and carving her own path as a Jewish leader, representing the story of Ethiopian Jews. As a mother, Yaffa is committed to instilling Jewish Pride and awareness of the connection to Israel in her children. Together with her husband, who comes from a Persian Jewish background, they are creating intergenerational pride and a strong sense of Jewish identity. In so doing, Yaffa embodies her father's vision for Ethiopian Jews and for all Jews—to stand tall and proud, honoring their connection to their indigenous land.

The story of the Ethiopian Jews serves as a powerful testament to Jewish indigeneity. Despite being isolated from the broader Jewish world, this community maintained a deep connection to its indigenous land over millennia. Their journey from Ethiopia to Israel, often under harrowing circumstances, highlights the enduring bond between the Jewish people and our home. If this isn't a testament to Jewish indigeneity, then I don't know what is.

Chapter 9

AN INTERVIEW WITH VLAD KHAYKIN

Vlad Khaykin was born in Gomel, Belarus, in 1983. Once home to a flourishing Jewish community, Gomel was situated within the historic Pale of Settlement, the designated area within the Russian Empire where Jews were permitted to reside.[1]

Vlad's paternal grandfather experienced firsthand the horrors both the Nazis and Stalin visited on Gomel. Just days after the Nazis invaded Belarus in August 1941, 16-year-old Natan returned from vocational school in Ukraine to find his hometown and its surrounding areas devoid of Jews due to the mass extermination of the Shoah.[2] Natan was initially sheltered in a basement by a non-Jewish neighbor, but he was eventually betrayed and captured by the Nazis, who rewarded those who informed on Jews and harshly punished those who sheltered them. While he was being transported to a death camp on the back of a truck, there was an Allied bombing raid, prompting his captors to abandon the vehicles for safety. Natan took his chance, escaped, and found refuge in the forest.

After surviving in the forest for a period (the details of how long have been lost), he encountered the Red Army and pleaded to join their ranks. Despite his youth, they accepted him. As a young soldier, Natan fought alongside the Russian army, participating in the liberation of numerous European capitals from fascism; and was just 6 miles from the Reichstag in Berlin when Russian forces famously raised the Soviet flag aloft. Returning home as a military veteran and hero, Natan was dismayed to discover that Stalin's regime—which had initially supported the establishment of the State of Israel—soon began to vilify Jews as "Zionist Fascists."

Natan found this slur unfathomable to him, considering his experience fighting against fascism and seeing its evils up close. Yet this was how the Soviet regime treated its Jewish citizens—including those who had fought to free their homeland from the Nazis.

Vlad's maternal grandfather, Eduard, was a formidable figure—a wrestler, sailor, and all-round "bad-ass," complete with an anchor tattoo. He was also a talented musician, who played at weddings throughout his hometown. Even decades later, after emigrating from the former U.S.S.R. and settling in San Francisco, people would recognize him on the street from his wedding performances. But Eduard also related to his grandson a darker side to his life in the Soviet Union. While playing at weddings, anti-Jewish abuse was common. If he was asked to play a Jewish song, someone would invariably harass him with racist remarks such as: "Why are you playing this kike music?" Eduard, though, refused to tolerate such abuse and would fight back. This resilience and determination to stand up against antisemitism left a lasting impression on Vlad, shaping his own desire to combat Jew-hate. In some ways, he tells me, "fighting antisemitism was the family business."

There was plenty of antisemitism to fight in the Soviet Union. Jews were relegated to second-, even third-class, citizenship. The Soviets persecuted numerous minorities within their empire, including the indigenous peoples of the region, but Jews faced a specific level of distrust and discrimination.[3] While the regime attempted to forcibly assimilate other groups, Jews were perceived as a particular threat to the socialist order. Legally classified as a nation, Jews were subjected to a spiritual and cultural genocide. All connections linking Jews to the global Jewish people and their ancestral land were criminalized. Rooted in Jewish indigeneity, nationalism, and the Zionist movement, Hebrew was regarded as especially dangerous, and banned.

Despite the risks involved, Jews in the Soviet Union demonstrated a staunch and unwavering commitment to their heritage and civilization, secretly forming underground groups to study Hebrew. The bravery of these individuals, who risked their lives to keep the flame of their indigenous language alive, cannot be overstated. These clandestine gatherings were put under close surveillance by the KGB, and participants were often subjected to arrest and imprisonment in Gulags; some were never seen again.[4]

In our conversation, Vlad draws a parallel between the treatment of Jews in the Soviet Union and the experiences of indigenous peoples around the world. Although there were differences—the communist regime hadn't occupied or colonized Russia, unlike other parts of the Soviet Union and elsewhere in Eastern Europe—Jewish culture came under a colonial-like assault. Vlad links this plight to that of indigenous peoples in North America, where the government perpetrated cultural genocide by eradicating indigenous cultures and languages through forced assimilation. The significance of language for indigenous peoples cannot be overstated. It is underlined by Article 13 of the UN Declaration on the Rights of Indigenous Peoples, which asserts the right of indigenous peoples to revitalize, use, develop, and transmit their languages to future generations.[5] Language is vital for the continuity of an indigenous culture. This is why, as we know, it was Hebrew, not Yiddish, which was chosen as the official language of the newly established State of Israel. Hebrew is our language. While the various Jewish diasporic languages are important and deserving of respect, they are not our indigenous language. Hebrew serves as the linguistic thread that bound and continues to bind all Jews together, regardless of when and where we live. It is integral to our status as a distinct and indigenous people and is fundamental to our understanding and expression of this unique identity.

For Vlad, the Soviet assault on Hebrew continues to resonate—in his very name. Every time he hears it, he's reminded that his parents opted for a Slavic, rather than a traditional Hebrew name, out of fear. Vlad likens giving a child a Jewish name in the Soviet Union to a scarlet letter, one designating your lowly status, a symbol of shame, turning one into a feared and suspected social pariah and reviled subaltern. What's remarkable is that Vlad's parents were forced to make this decision just two years before Mikhail Gorbachev came to power and less than a decade before the Soviet Union collapsed.

When I ask if Vlad has ever considered changing his name, he reveals that he has contemplated doing so. At one point, he even adopted the Hebrew name, Judah. Vlad's younger brother, Yonatan, who was born in the United States after the family fled the Soviet Union, was given a Hebrew name. This represented the family's newfound freedom to reclaim their Jewish identity and their connection to Israel.

Expressions of Jewishness were severely restricted by the Soviet state. Hebrew publishers were shut down, leading to a scarcity of siddurim (prayer books). Synagogues were closed, and Jewish communities were prohibited from recruiting rabbis to serve them. Yeshivot, institutions for the study of Hebrew text, met the same fate. As Vlad explains, there was a "dearth of Jewish life for Jews in the U.S.S.R." Religion, in general, was not viewed favorably by the Soviets. Marx famously referred to it as "the opium of the people" in 1843.[6] However, the persecution of Jewish life was rooted in more than just a disdain for its perceived religion. Vlad notes that various religious groups were treated differently; for example, Muslims were allowed contact with other Muslim communities, and their prayer books were permitted. In contrast, Jews were barred from contacting outside communities and Israel. This discrimination against Jewish religious expression was fueled by both conspiratorial antisemitism and a broader campaign against Jewish difference and indigeneity. All forms of Jewish expression were targeted because they represented Jewish specificity.[7]

Despite being permitted, Yiddish was also subject to restrictions in the Soviet Union. Vlad highlights the contrast between the number of publications allowed in Yiddish compared to those in other indigenous languages, despite Yiddish having a larger number of speakers. Even though Yiddish evolved as a geographically specific expression of historic Jewish culture, it was regarded with deep suspicion. Yiddish, written with Hebrew letters and retaining Hebrew roots in many, albeit Germanified, words faced further challenges with the introduction of the orthographic reform in 1920 in the Soviet Union. This reform aimed to naturalize the spelling of words and forms derived from Hebrew and represented a significant assault on Jewish specificity and indigeneity. The attack was enforced through violence; as Vlad points out, "indigenous culture doesn't die; it is killed." This was precisely what happened to the culture of Jews in the Soviet Union. In Chapter 5, we discussed circumcision as a potent physical manifestation of Jewish indigeneity. Unsurprisingly, like the Hebrew language, this practice faced significant obstacles in the Soviet Union. Vlad himself was circumcised at the age of seven, only after his family was finally permitted to leave the USSR for the United States.

The suppression of Jewishness under the Soviet regime made it extremely difficult for Jews to express their identity. They were deprived of opportunities to engage with Jewish law, literature, and civilization. In 1962, for instance, the baking and sale of matzah was outlawed. Soviet authorities would smash ovens used for making matzah before Pesach; highlighting, as Vlad notes, how the Soviet Empire was threatened by something as seemingly innocuous as a cracker. But, of course, the Soviet authorities felt particularly threatened by Pesach with its theme of liberation and its potent reminder of Jewish difference and connection to another land.

Vlad's most poignant memories concern the Jewish community's efforts to preserve their identity despite the odds. Whenever possible, they would gather to observe holidays, although these celebrations often lacked Jewish content. Jews simply did not know how to "do Jewish." Vlad recalls. But these gatherings were acts of profound resistance, with arrest at the hands of the ever-watchful KGB a constant threat. Yet, despite the peril involved, Jews understood the importance of coming together to commemorate their heritage. Highlighting the significance of such gatherings in honoring Jewishness and our distinctiveness, Vlad recalls the Hebrew song, *"Hineh Ma Tov."* Its lyrics resonate: *"Hineh ma tov uma na'im Shevet achim gam yachad."* ("How good and pleasant it is for brothers and sisters to sit together.")[8] Despite enduring huge hardships, the Jews of the former Soviet Union worked to maintain a sense of their Jewish identity. It may have been clandestine, imperfect, and dangerous, but many clung to it, much like countless generations of Jews throughout history who held fast to their Jewishness in whatever ways they could manage.

Soviet Jews were forced to exist in a society that actively rejected them, instilling a profound sense of shame associated with being Jewish. They were depicted as backward and archaic, racialized, and portrayed as unattractive, defined solely by their physical characteristics. Consequently, many Jews felt compelled to conceal their Jewishness, yet they often found themselves outed, bullied, and ostracized from society.

After the Six-Day War (June 5–10, 1967), antisemitism in the Soviet Union escalated, prompting many Jews to seek refuge in Israel. However, departing the country was not straightforward; individuals had to secure exit visas, the issuance of which was subject to Soviet policies that frequently prohibited Jews from leaving. Boris Kochubievsky, one of those seeking to emigrate, spoke for many others in a letter to Leonid Brezhnev, the Soviet leader. "I am a Jew," he wrote. "I want to live in the Jewish state. That is my right, just as it is the right of a Ukrainian to live in Ukraine, the right of a Russian to live in Russia, the right of a Georgian to live in Georgia. I want to live in Israel. That is my dream, the goal not only of my life but also of the lives of hundreds of generations that preceded me, of my ancestors who were expelled from their land. I want my children to study in the Hebrew language. I want to read Jewish newspapers, attend a Jewish theater. What is wrong with that? What is my crime …?" Despite his plea, Kochubievsky was arrested and confined to a mental institution in Kiev; a common way to dispense with undesirables and justified by asserting those wanting to abandon the Soviet motherland—the world's first socialist country and the best nation in the world—must be "insane."

Many Jews, like Vlad's uncle Yuri, attempted to leave the Soviet Union, only to be refused exit visas. This is where the term "refusenik" originated. However, being refused meant being trapped in the very society they sought to escape. Branded as traitors, reactionaries, and enemies of the state and society, refuseniks faced ostracism in every aspect of their lives. They lost their jobs, their friends, and everything they had worked for. Individuals with PhDs were forced into menial or manual work. Some were sent to Siberia or imprisoned in labor camps. They were treated, Vlad suggests, as "human refuse."

But despite the risks, individuals like Kochubievsky—fueled by both a desire to flee the horrors of the Soviet Union and a strong Jewish sense of identity—persisted in their attempts to emigrate. That their connection to Israel remained steadfast is all the more impressive given that Jews in the Soviet Union lived without easy access to Jewish history or texts. Many Jews in the Soviet Union rejected the notion that they were "merely Russian" and recognized their heritage as part of a distinct ethnic minority. Vlad recalls the story of his mother realizing for the first time that Jews had a state of their own. Turning to her mother, she said: "Let's go there, where we can be the majority. Where we can be free."

The Campaign for Soviet Jews, led by Jews both within the Soviet Union and in the Diaspora, and supported by many non-Jewish allies, stands as one of the most successful solidarity movements in history, yet it is often overlooked in contemporary Jewish discourse. However, for Soviet Jews, it served as a lifeline. By feeling connected to the global Jewish peoplehood, they gained a tremendous sense of strength. They understood that they were not alone; they were part of a global collective that cared for them because they were Jews, not despite it.

While the external campaign to free them gained momentum, Jews within the Soviet Union engaged in what Vlad describes as "auto-emancipation." As has been the case throughout Jewish history, they resisted in every possible way. As communication with the outside world became easier after the 1950s, they smuggled Jewish texts, tefillin, and Judaica into the U.S.S.R.—an act of indigenous resistance that affirmed their origins, belonging, and specificity. Underground publications called samizdat ("self-published") were produced to keep Jewish culture and thought alive, fostering a deep understanding of Jewish identity. And the mere act of identifying with Israel as the Jewish homeland and celebrating Jewish holidays were important acts of resistance.

Physical resistance also occurred, exemplified by the Dymshits–Kuznetsov aircraft hijacking in 1970. Although ultimately unsuccessful, the attempt by the group of 14 refuseniks, 12 of whom were Jewish, to hijack a plane and fly it to Israel via Sweden, stands as a significant act of resistance.

When Vlad was six years old, his family received permission to leave the Soviet Union. Fearing that the authorities might reverse their decision, as they had previously done, the family wasted no time in leaving. For Vlad, this experience mirrored the Pesach story: When the opportunity to gain freedom arises, one must depart swiftly, carrying only the essentials. Despite being limited to $90 and a single suitcase per person, they were grateful to embark on their journey to freedom. That journey began in Ukraine, from where they traveled to Vienna and then on to Ladispoli, a transition town outside of Rome where many Soviet Jewish refugees awaited visas. After a wait of nearly five months, they were finally granted permission to travel to America.

Settled by the Hebrew Immigrant Aid Society (HIAS) in Buffalo, New York, Vlad's family enjoyed the support of various communities as they began to integrate. The local Jewish community in Buffalo played a crucial role, helping them find their first apartment and ensuring there was food in the refrigerator on their arrival. Vlad is deeply moved by the assistance provided by Jews and our allies, particularly individuals like the Black civil rights leader and steadfast Zionist, Bayard Rustin, who campaigned tirelessly on behalf of Soviet Jews. While half of Vlad's family chose to emigrate to Israel, his father's love for America led them to the United States. In their new home, Vlad's family embarked on a journey to reclaim their Jewish identity and indigeneity. For the first time, they openly and proudly celebrated Shabbat every week, taking part in traditions that have been practiced by Jews for thousands of years. Lighting candles, eating challah, and reciting prayers became central to their lives as they embraced their Jewish heritage. Reflecting on Jewish history, they understood that action was at the core of Jewish identity—it was imperative to live as Jews in every aspect of their lives.

In response to the banning of Hebrew in the U.S.S.R., Vlad felt compelled as an adult to study the language. He saw it as a way to reintroduce that knowledge and connection back into his family. Recognizing that his ancestors were deprived of the opportunity to learn and speak Hebrew, Vlad saw it as his duty to do so. He wanted to ensure that his children would hear their ancestral language spoken by their parents and experience the connection that Hebrew fosters among Jews, as well as to their land. Vlad also pursued an MA program in Near Eastern and Judaic Studies, driven by his desire to end his family's enforced Jewish illiteracy.

Due to his family's experiences, Vlad has dedicated his life to defending and promoting Jewish life, culture, and Hebrew, viewing them as fundamentally important not only to the Jewish people, but to humanity as a whole. He believes that the diversity of the human family is beautiful, and Jews are an integral part of that diversity. Vlad condemns efforts to homogenize Jewish families, emphasizing that Jewishness is an expression of humanity and cultural richness that should be preserved. He argues that just as UNESCO is tasked with protecting physical sites and intangible human heritage, there should be equal attention given to preserving languages, cultures, religions, ideas, and practices. He urges everyone to resist attempts to diminish human expression, arguing that it is unacceptable for anyone to try to erase Jewish identity and humanity.

In reclaiming his Jewishness, Vlad reclaimed his indigeneity. He had always been indigenous, but it wasn't until his family was allowed to leave the Soviet Union that Vlad could fully express and embrace this crucial aspect of his identity. He emphasizes that all Jews must recognize the privilege of being able to express their identity in today's world, and urges them to do so. As our conversation comes to an end, Vlad passionately declares that we have the power to shape the next chapter of our people's story. Despite the Soviet Union's attempt to silence us, we refused to let them dictate our identity. We are not relics of history but vibrant and evolving human communities. Our cultures are dynamic and significant, and we refuse to conform to society's expectations of indigenous peoples. We will write—and tell—our own story.

Moved by his words, I responded with a simple Hebrew word, "Amen."

Chapter 10

AN INTERVIEW WITH DR. EFRAT SOPHER

Born in Jerusalem in 1977, Dr. Efrat Sopher is our only Sabra interviewee. Those born in Israel are named after the Sabra fruit; with its spiky exterior and soft interior it symbolizes the stereotypical Israeli personality. Following Miriam, her grandmother, and Avigail, her mother, Efrat was the third generation of women born in Israel, a testament to the enduring significance of this land in shaping her Jewish identity and life experience.

Even before the rebirth of Israel in 1948, her great-grandparents—Miriam's parents—made the decision to leave their lives in Aleppo and relocate to British-ruled Mandatory Palestine. Despite being born in Syria, their bond with the Land of Israel was their priority, and they made frequent visits before ultimately making *Aliyah*.

Zionism and an enduring connection to the Land of Israel also run deep on the other side of Efrat's mother's family. Her maternal grandfather, Meir, was born in Isfahan, Iran. He made *Aliyah* in the early 1950s to help build the fledgling Jewish state. Even before leaving Iran, the family was passionately engaged in the Zionist movement, maintaining regular correspondence with David Ben-Gurion (who later became Israel's first Prime Minister). What is remarkable about her family's journey—and the *Aliyah* of countless other Jews—is that it was driven more by positive than negative factors. Despite the fashionable lie that Israel is some form of Western-backed, white colonial project, these families experienced their return to Israel as a homecoming. Their attachment to their indigenous land led them to leave behind comfortable lives in their countries of birth. Before their departure, Meir's family was firmly entrenched in the establishment and integrated into Iranian society. He was a legal scholar and Zionist advocate, and his father held a position as an officer in the army. Despite all this, Meir still made the choice to make *Aliyah*.

But while they returned home to Israel, Efrat's family maintained its connections to Iran, thus carving out a dual identity. In the fall of 1957, Meir was approached by Ben-Gurion to establish diplomatic relations with His Imperial Majesty Mohammad Reza Pahlavi, Shah of Iran. Efrat's enduring connection to Iran persists to this day and she has met the Shah's son, His Royal Highness Reza Pahlavi, Crown Prince of Iran, on multiple occasions. She has discussed their family connection with him, and he has expressed his view that the relationship between Iran and the Jews can be traced back to the era of Cyrus the Great, as we explored in Chapter 3.

Making the journey from Israel back to Iran on his secret mission, Meir used the fact that he was the editor of the publication *Star of the East* to establish a cover story that he was working as a journalist. However, after a period, his activities were noticed, and he was summoned for interrogation by the head of Iran's military intelligence and chair of the Supreme National Security Council, General Ali Kia. Having now reappeared in Iran after leaving for Israel, Meir was viewed with suspicion. However, in the meeting, he was honest to General Kia about his work and intentions, and tensions eased. As Meir explained to the Shah himself when asked whom he loved more, Israel or Iran, "Iran is my mother, and Israel is my father, and it is impossible to love one parent more than another." In 1958, Meir was appointed as ambassador to Iran and stayed in his post until 1973.

This is a clear example of the duality faced—and struggled with—by Jews in the Diaspora. Meir was a Jew and an Israeli, and he was also raised in Iran; and this naturally formed part of his identity. This duality is to be expected; it is the demand often made on Jews by the wider world to make us choose between our identities which is problematic and damaging. As I have argued throughout the Jewish Pride series, we do not have to choose. Recognizing this can free Jews of the neurosis which often plagues us, particularly in the West. We are allowed to be Jews—acknowledging this connects us to Israel as our indigenous land—while also having a diasporic identity, which has also formed part of our worldview and how we see ourselves. Of course, as with other communities, being part of a diaspora comes with tensions, as referenced in Ijeoma Umebinyuo's poem *Diaspora Blues* from the Introduction. However, if we acknowledge these tensions and embrace the experience of duality, we can work toward achieving a sense of peace in our identities. Being an Israeli, Efrat adds a special dimension to these five interviews. Thus far, each participant has detailed their connection to Israel and how they and their families were able to express and interact with Jewish indigeneity while living in the Diaspora. Efrat, on the other hand, was born in Israel. She regards this as a privilege. Being born—and growing up—in Jerusalem itself always felt special to her. Jerusalem is the capital of the modern State of Israel and was, as we have seen, the capital of the Kingdom of Judah and central to Jewish life for 3,000 years. Following the destruction of the Northern Kingdom of Israel, it was in Jerusalem that Jewish worship was centered and where generations of Jewish kings administered their kingdoms. And even after we lost sovereignty, and the territory of Judah shrank, Jerusalem remained a constant focus of the Jewish people. Growing up there, Efrat says, "You could feel the connection. You could feel the history. You could really feel it."

When learning Jewish history at school, and the history of Jerusalem in particular, there was none of the sense of distance experienced by Jews in the Diaspora. Efrat learned the history of the Land of Israel living in the Land of Israel. She learned the history of Jerusalem in Jerusalem. After school, she could see the sites described by her teachers in class. As Efrat repeatedly suggests in our discussion, she has always felt very much a part of a living, thriving civilization.

Efrat's family was also aware of the power of Jewish action. She recalls understanding as a child that these practices connect us to Jews throughout time. This connection and continuity are, as we know, a crucial part of indigeneity as a category. It is remarkable that Jews all over the world observe the same calendar, holidays, and traditions that have been used and expressed by Jews for thousands of years, the vast majority of which emerged in the Land of Israel. In her home, Shabbat was—and still is—celebrated every week. She was always actively encouraged to take part in Jewish traditions, and literacy in Jewishness was always praised. This, in a sense, is a model Jewish upbringing. We must encourage our children to be active participants in Jewish life. The traditions and customs are theirs to claim too and can enrich their lives in innumerable ways. At the same time, our children must know what it means to be Jewish. They must be literate in Jewish history. If not, they will either not connect with it, or, worse, they will internalize what it means to be a Jew from the outside world.

Efrat's childhood in Israel offers valuable lessons for us today. Each of us bears a responsibility to embrace our indigeneity and express it through both knowledge and action. This connects us to the unbroken thread of Jewish life. Regardless of where we live in the world—whether within the land or outside it—we must be literate in our narrative and actively express our Jewish identity. Among atheist or agnostic Jews, there has been a trend toward the belief that Jewish action is solely an expression of Judaism, as a religion, and thus not relevant to Jewish cultural life. However, as this study makes clear, Jews are a people and have consistently expressed our distinctiveness through action. Jewish expression isn't exclusive to any particular group of Jews. All Jews have the right to express their Jewish identity as they see fit—and the duty to do so. This is how we ensure the continuity that has been a defining aspect of Jewish experience for over 3,200 years.

Due to her father's work, Efrat's family eventually relocated to the U.K., where, for the first time in her life, she found herself as a Jewish minority among a non-Jewish majority. This experience added another dimension to Efrat's identity. Initially, she attended a Jewish elementary school, which she credits with helping her transition into the Diaspora. However, having been raised in the Jewish state, in the Jewish capital, where the only festivals she witnessed were Jewish, she found it an adjustment to be surrounded by Christian holidays and traditions. In contrast, Jewish ones, at least publicly, were scarcely visible. This could have weakened Efrat's identity—and indeed, it did cause some complications—but through the constant reinforcement of her Jewishness and indigeneity at home, Efrat always maintained a solid foundation. She always possessed an understanding of who she was and where she came from. Like her grandfather and great-grandparents before her, she integrated into diasporic society, yet never lost sight of the fact that, regardless of where she resided in the world, no matter how deeply she integrated into diasporic society, her roots would always lie in Israel. She also always felt distinct as a Jew. She never felt superior—or inferior—to her peers. However, she recognized that Jews constitute a unique group of people with ties to Israel. Having lived in Scotland, Hong Kong, and London myself, this sentiment deeply resonates with me. Wherever I have resided in the world, Israel remains my home.

However, living in the Diaspora presented its own set of challenges for Efrat. She recalls being focused on gaining a place at the quintessentially British City of London School for Girls. After much effort, Efrat was elated to be admitted to this top private high school. However, starting at school marked the beginning of the most significant challenge to her identity she has experienced. What's truly empowering and inspiring about Efrat is that, while adapting to her new context, who she was never fundamentally changed. At the City of London School, she began to experience the dance that Jews—and other diasporic individuals—often find themselves performing when living outside their homeland. However, what sets Efrat's experience apart is that she didn't internalize it. Instead, she intellectually examined the experience, extracting the best from British society and integrating it into her evolving identity. Like anyone else, she wanted to fit in and be accepted, and she did adopt certain distinctive British characteristics. When speaking English, for instance, she sounds like a native of England. But when speaking Hebrew, she retains her Israeli roots. And therein lies the essence. Efrat refused to choose between her identities. While living in the U.K. and interacting with British people left its mark on her, she remained steadfast in her refusal to reject, distort, or diminish her Jewishness, her distinctiveness, and her connection to Israel.

Efrat argues that the real danger lies in failing to acknowledge these challenges. They exist and are real. And other groups experience them, too. This isn't a problem. Yet, as a response to the trauma of millennia of persecution, Jews sometimes respond by downplaying their differences, and consequently, their Jewishness. This fear leads many Jews to avoid actively engaging in a dialog about their identities. However, this dance isn't inherently problematic. Identity is fluid, and different facets of it can be emphasized at different times, depending on the circumstances. While always proud of her Jewish identity, Efrat acknowledges that sometimes her Iranian connection feels more prominent, while at other times, her Britishness takes precedence. When she moved to Los Angeles to study, for instance, her Britishness became more apparent. This is natural to the human experience. Importantly, it does not diminish Efrat's Jewishness or her indigeneity. It is an integral part of her sense of self and therefore always present. Reflecting on her grandfather Meir's experience of being both Israeli and Iranian, she describes him as "an insider and an outsider at the same time." This, she believes, perfectly encapsulates the Jewish experience in the Diaspora. We are Jews, belonging to a unique land-based civilization, yet born—or living—outside of that land. This doesn't mean we don't belong to the U.K.; it simply means we also belong elsewhere simultaneously. Ultimately, as Vlad remarked in his interview, humanity is a mosaic formed through the diversity inherent in the human experience. We must recognize what makes us different, distinct, and unique so that we can contribute to this beautiful kaleidoscope of humanity.

Like me, Efrat says that when growing up she wouldn't have articulated in a precise or developed manner her sense of indigeneity to Israel. Nonetheless, she consistently regarded Israel as her home, even after relocating to the U.K. Moreover, she didn't think of Israel merely in terms of being the country in which she lived but something bigger and more profound: The home of the Jewish people, and she was determined to embody that in all aspects of her life. Visiting Efrat's home, you see the connection to the Land of Israel. Judaica is everywhere, with paintings featuring Jewish themes set in Israel on the walls and bowls of ceramic pomegranates symbolizing the *Shivat Haminim*. For Efrat, integrating Jewish symbols and those associated with the land and its history is an essential expression of her Jewish identity. "It's alive," she comments. It has always been an active part of her life. Referring back to the definition of indigeneity proposed in the Introduction, Efrat emphasizes that indigeneity must find expression through living symbols and cultures. It's not a relic frozen in time; it's dynamic, evolving while remaining deeply rooted in the land. For Efrat, indigeneity embodies "truth. It cannot be denied."

Today, Efrat is instilling an awakened sense of our indigeneity in her two sons. She leads by example, she says, emphasizing that if she wants her sons to actively engage with their indigeneity, she and her husband Daniel "must walk the walk." This concept is firmly rooted in the notion of a living civilization. She believes it's crucial to view Jewishness as a dynamic culture that evolves continuously, emphasizing our connection to Israel, irrespective of location, and the importance of understanding our history and narrative comprehensively. "Our indigeneity is an undeniable reality," Efrat argues. "However, we must actively embrace it within ourselves and others. We cannot assume that the next generation will inherently sense it and engage with it if we do not guide them in claiming their heritage as an indigenous people. We must lead by example and demonstrate our commitment. They must witness it in action, and they must be educated about it. It is essential for the continuity of the Jewish People."

It is Efrat's approach which has sustained Jewishness for over 3,200 years and, thankfully, it will continue to do so for millennia to come.

Chapter 11

AN INTERVIEW WITH DR. WINSTON PICKETT

Dr. Winston Pickett is the most passionate Jew I have ever met. He is my mentor. And 51 years ago, he converted and joined the Jewish people.

Born in New York State in 1952, Winston grew up in a suburban neighborhood in Connecticut. For a man who eventually devoted his life to Jewishness, his early years could not have been more different. His "very bucolic" rural Connecticut upbringing was among the "WASPs"—White Anglo-Saxon Protestants—who used to dominate the politics, culture, and society of East Coast America.

But Winston's family were only partially in this camp. His father and eldest sister were Episcopalian, while his mother and other sister were Catholic. Although he found himself gravitating more toward Episcopalian practices, he attended both services growing up. As the third child, he was given a choice. The two of us laugh at the thought of his parents never expecting him to choose to become Jewish. One of the reasons he felt more attuned to Episcopalianism was because it was in English, whereas Catholic masses at that time were still in Latin. For Winston, most likely aware of anti-Catholic prejudice which presented Catholics and their religion as alien, Catholicism felt "too foreign." It is fascinating that his life would eventually lead him toward becoming part of a people which is indigenous to the Land of Israel situated in the southern Levant.

Growing up, he always felt there was a God. He described saying the Lord's Prayer before bed each night. Kneeling down to pray, he had a strong sense of the divine. This belief and practice continued well into his teenage years when, at his Episcopalian prep school, he would occasionally get up to attend morning prayers before breakfast. It was his time at boarding school that precipitated—and in many ways led to—his first encounter with Jewishness. His roommate was a lapsed Catholic, who Winston describes as "angry at the world." Set against the backdrop of the Vietnam War and the upheavals of the late 1960s, this was hardly uncommon. The two teenagers argued and debated constantly, with his roommate unfairly labeling Winston, who was still working out his identity, "a phony." Although discomforting, these discussions made Winston begin to think about and explore his identity.

Instead of pursuing law at an Ivy League university after he graduated high school, Winston instead chose to attend Kenyon College in rural Ohio. There, he encountered a mentor who would change the course of his life. At the time, students were granted a deferment from the draft. But Winston already recognized he was a pacifist and did not want to fight in Vietnam when he graduated college, and his deferment ended. Intellectual and moral curiosity led him to take a class on religion. At the end of his first year, Winston chose to write a paper comparing the works on religion of Paul Tillich and Martin Buber. Buber's *I and Thou* took a Jewish approach, while Tillich's *Dynamics of Faith* was rooted in Christianity. His paper was an expression of a scholarly contest between Buber and Tillich, and, for Winston, Buber won. This opened up his philosophical awareness that there was another way to engage with God beyond the Christian context of his upbringing.

Around the same time, Winston learned that Professor Eugen Kullmann[1] was teaching a course on Hermann Hesse, whose works, like *Siddhartha*, Winston had voraciously consumed as a teen. Winston jumped at the chance to join Kullmann's class. Over the course of the seminar, Winston found himself enthralled as Kullmann spoke about the history of Western civilization and thought, presenting a kaleidoscope of ideas which ranged from Hesse to Plato and Aristotle to Maimonides.

Although he was awarded an A+ on his paper comparing Buber and Tillich, Winston was dismayed that there was no commentary or feedback. What he truly sought was debate that would expand his mind and heart. He thus sought out Kullmann to discuss his paper further. From this moment, the path to Winston's academic career—and indeed his future life—began to open up. Kullmann, Winston suggests, was a "*Moreh Derech*," a guide and mentor, who believed in his intellectual and emotional ability and made the world seem full of exciting, dynamic, and endless possibilities.

Always eager to learn more, Winston ended up taking every single one of Kullmann's classes over his four-year college degree. In fact, he holds the record for taking the most classes with Kullmann ever. He describes his time studying with Kullmann as his "grand tour of the greats of Jewish intellectual thought." And, with each step along this intellectual journey, he felt closer and closer to Jews and Jewishness. But, ever the romantic, what he learned was not simply contained in his head; it entered his heart, too. He incorporated what he learned into his sense of who he wanted to be. He began studying Ancient Hebrew so he could engage with the texts directly, as opposed to through mere translation. For Jews to truly interact with their civilization, for ancient Jewish scriptures to become living texts, Winston believes, they must learn Hebrew.

This attitude, in many ways, continues to shape Winston today. Even though his first foray into Jewish civilization was rooted in study and intellectualism, it was also always about much more than that. Even in our discussions about my work, I have never met someone as passionate about Jewish history and texts as Winston. His engagement goes far beyond simple intellectual curiosity.

At graduate school, Winston chose to pursue a PhD program at Hebrew Union College—Jewish Institute of Religion in Cincinnati, Ohio.[2] This experience proved something of a surprise. Previously, his interaction had been largely with Jewish civilization and texts. But now, for the first time, he was among contemporary Jews who lived and actively expressed their Jewishness. Jews were no longer just part of an intellectual tradition; they were a living, breathing people. As he got to know them, he found that all of his cohort had just returned from studying in Israel and were incredibly excited about their time in the Jewish land. Winston knew Israel was the ancient homeland of the Jews and the core of their civilization, but, beyond that, he was obviously not as connected as his Jewish peers. Internally, he questioned these ties. He asked himself what it was based on and came to understand that this Jewishness is rooted in Israel; a "living, breathing Judaism, which was even more dynamic," as he puts it, than he had previously thought. This is the essence of indigeneity.

During his time at graduate school, Winston experienced what he described as "a eureka moment." At Kenyon, he'd actively participated in Jewish practices with Kullmann. But now he found himself somewhat isolated. While his peers in rabbinical college were assigned to different communities to serve during the High Holy Days, Winston was left alone. It was during this time that Winston felt a strong desire to engage with Jewishness not just intellectually but in a more personal and practical manner. At one point, he was invited to High Holy Day services held in his professors' homes, creating a wonderfully warm and intimate environment. It was in these gatherings that Winston began to dip his toes, so to speak, into the practice of Judaism, and began crafting sermons.

Having met and fallen in love with a Jewish woman, Winston decided to convert before their marriage. He initially chose to join the Jewish people through Reform Judaism (with Orthodox conversion following 20 years later). His initial conversion process was overseen by his professors, serving as the Beth Din (Jewish court). Due to his dedication and deep understanding of Judaism, the process was relatively swift. They recognized that Winston's love for Jewishness ran deep, extending beyond his desire to marry a Jew. Although, like most American boys, Winston had already been circumcised, as part of his later Orthodox conversion, he underwent *hatafat dam* to symbolize the covenant with God, as prescribed by the Brit.

While working on his doctorate, Winston began leading a small Jewish community in northern Kentucky and working as a journalist, writing for the *American Israelite* in Cincinnati, Ohio. While working with the *American Israelite* paper, his relationship with the State of Israel began to develop. Given his academic background, Winston always viewed Israel as the indigenous land of the Jewish people. But it was only in 1985, when Winston received an invitation to the Jewish Agency's inaugural conference for the Jewish press in Jerusalem, that he was able to visit the Jewish state. For someone who had never set foot in Israel, but had devoted years to studying, discussing, and writing about the Jewish relationship with the Land of Israel, this was a momentous occasion. Arriving in Jerusalem, he felt at "the very center of the Jewish world" and Jewish history. And he was.

During the trip, he woke up early one morning and decided to visit the Haas Promenade. There, by himself, he experienced something truly remarkable. For the first time, he watched the sun slowly rise over Jerusalem, the epicenter of Jewish life for 3,000 years. As the golden rays illuminated the Jerusalem stone, it felt as though the entire city was aglow. In that moment, it hit him—he was finally home, and everything fell into place. It was a profound realization of belonging and purpose. Like many Jews worldwide, who often describe visiting Israel as "going home," he felt a deep connection to Israel.

Since his encounter with Kullmann at Kenyon College, Winston had been on a journey—a journey of intellectual understanding and self-discovery. Winston's journey was marked by unexpected surprises, despite his decision to embark on it. His experience in Jerusalem in 1985 was no exception. While he recognized his Jewish connection to Israel, he was taken aback by the depth of his emotional response and the impact of his overwhelming sense of homecoming. Finally, he was among his people, in his land. He was a Jew, in the land of the Jews, and he couldn't help but weep tears of joy. Upon returning home, Winston experienced a newfound sense of tranquility in his relationship with Jewishness. Without even realizing it, his deep connection to modern (and ancient) Israel had been the missing piece of the puzzle. Now he felt complete.

Winston's marriage ended in divorce. Tragically, when Winston later remarried, his new wife, Rabbi Charisse Kranes, was diagnosed with cancer soon after his return from Israel. Assigned to work at a Reform Synagogue in Seattle, she fought bravely, but Winston couldn't shake a nagging thought: If she doesn't make it, I am moving to Israel. In May 1989, Charisse passed away. Winston moved to Israel the following month. While he immersed himself in an Ulpan to learn Modern Hebrew, ironically, he was soon appointed as the New York correspondent for the *Jerusalem Report* and was sent back to the United States.

In New York City, Winston met his remarkable future wife, Fiona Sharpe, a British Jewish woman also based in the city. Fiona is an extraordinary individual in her own right, having fought valiantly against Jeremy Corbyn and serving as a spokesperson for the group Labour Against Antisemitism. After helping thwart the threat posed by Corbyn, Fiona remains dedicated to advocating for the Jewish people. Together, they form an awe-inspiring couple. During their first date, Winston and Fiona delved into deep conversations about family, their childhoods, and their shared dream of making *Aliyah*. And so, they embarked on this journey together.

Shortly after Fiona and Winston made *Aliyah* together in the early 1990s, the assassination of Yitzhak Rabin shook Israel to its core. The country was convulsed with grief and turmoil. Winston felt it all. He experienced the essence of Jewish indigeneity firsthand. As an Israeli and a Jew, he realized that his own story in the Land of Israel was unfolding amidst the collective story of his people.

Winston's experience as an Israeli was shaped by the intricate interplay of history, geography, and politics. In this context, he felt a connection not only to his fellow Israelis but also to Jews worldwide. This sense of belonging is one of the many reasons why Jews, and indeed others, are incredibly fortunate, although it's a privilege that can sometimes be taken for granted. Regardless of where they come from, all people are searching for belonging. As Jews, we are privileged to have it. We have a community to which we belong, and a land in which we belong. Despite the internal strife within our community and disagreements over membership rules, the global Jewish response following October 7 demonstrated the diverse yet unified nature of our people. In this unity, we find a profound sense of belonging.

Many ignorant individuals mistakenly believe that the ability to convert to Judaism negates the classification of Jews as indigenous people. This notion is deeply offensive. Winston's extraordinary journey exemplifies the truth. By joining the Jewish people, he embraced all that it represents, including developing an indigenous connection to the Land of Israel. Winston's story emphasizes the power of learning for all Jews. Jewish Pride is work, and Winston has dedicated decades to this endeavor. He engaged in learning, questioning, exploration, deep thought, and discussion, all of which led to a transformative experience of becoming Jewish.

Winston serves as a role model for all Jews, whether they converted or were born Jewish. His example teaches us to fully embrace Judaism in every aspect of our lives: to do Jewish, be Jewish, read Jewish, live Jewish, and think Jewish. Winston's journey highlights the importance of a continuing dedication to understanding and connecting with Judaism. Nearly all my interviewees have emphasized that indigeneity exists, but it must be actively claimed and embraced, regardless of the route one takes to become Jewish. Those born Jewish must also commit to this work. While it may give some of us a head start, it alone is not sufficient. As Winston beautifully demonstrates, this work can lead to a profound understanding of oneself and one's heritage. We are reflected in the pages of the Tanakh, the Talmud and the entire corpus of Judaic literature—they constitute our heritage and birthright.

The learning, exploration, and a literacy that connects us to every Jewish person alive and to the Land—and State—of Israel roots us in the garden of Jewish life, where we can truly flourish. It's so much more than simply tracing one's past to the physicality of the land. While that connection does exist and holds significance, it alone is not sufficient. It's about the collective identity of the Jewish people and their connection to the land. It was a community of individuals who made the land their home, who built a civilization. By choosing Judaism, Winston did the same. He embraced this collective identity and the Land of Israel. It belongs to you, and you belong to it. We are of the Land, and the Land is of us.

And as the late Lord Rabbi Sacks wrote: "To be a Jew is to join the journey of our people, the story of Pesach and the long walk across centuries and continents from exile to homecoming."[3] Each of us should be on that journey. I couldn't be prouder to have Winston, side by side, man by man, Jew by Jew, on our journey.

Chapter 12

THE JEWS: AN INDIGENOUS PEOPLE

The Jews are indigenous to the Land of Israel. By now, this truth should be undeniable. It is not a claim but a fact carved into the history and experience of our people and this land.

Throughout this book, we've explored not just the ancient history of Jews in Eretz Yisrael, but the ongoing traditions and practices still rooted in the land today. There's a direct, unbroken line that connects Jews, wherever we live, to our ancestors who lived in the southern Levant thousands of years ago. This is a deeply emotional bond that has survived across time and distance, a testament to our people's enduring relationship with our indigenous homeland.

However, the crucial question still remains: How does this impact us as Jews today? For most other indigenous people who were, or are still, denied sovereignty in their lands, the issue of indigeneity is often focused on the distribution of resources or property. But Jews regained sovereignty in our homeland in 1948, so this issue is no longer relevant to us. Instead, this question is rooted in our perceptions and understanding of ourselves. To truly feel and express Jewish Pride, we must have a clear understanding of who we are, where we came from, and of what we are proud. This is vital for all people, but particularly for Jews, whose identity is so often defined by the world around us. It's vital, too, when we see the relentless vilification of Israel as a colonial entity and the Jewish connection to Israel being diminished or denied.

However, reclaiming our identity as Jews can never, and should never, be simply a response to the hate we face, nor is it solely a form of resistance (even though it can function in this way). Jews have to know who we are at all times. We are the heirs to a great civilization, and without our commitment to it, and our commitment to passing on our laws and our practices, it will die. This is a simple fact. Each of us must remember that Jewishness does not belong to us. We are its caretakers for future generations, and it is our responsibility to ensure we pass on something whole and healthy, not broken and warped. And to guarantee this, we must do the work.

We must understand exactly what it means to be a Jew—from a Jewish perspective. It's time to free ourselves from the negative external influences that cloud our identity and reject non-Jewish definitions that distort our reality. We must know our story. And we must tell it—to ourselves and to the world—declaring, "We are Jews, and we are indigenous to the Land of Israel."

ZIONISM: AN INDIGENOUS RIGHTS MOVEMENT

Ever since the Soviet Union launched its war against Zionism in the second half of the 20th century, the definition and meaning of our movement has been stolen and bastardized by the wider world. The demise of the Soviet Union over three decades ago and the collapse of Soviet-backed regimes elsewhere in the world has had no impact on this assault; if anything, it has gone from strength to strength—a pernicious, living legacy of Stalinism. Zionism has been framed, never more so than since October 7, as a form of colonialism, white supremacy, and imperialism. The greatest irony of all this is that it was the Soviet Union—not Israel—which operated a form of colonialism and imperialism throughout Eastern Europe, Africa, and Latin America—a pattern of behavior which lives on in Putin's Russia today. The Soviets thus perpetrated a lie about Israel which actually described their own politics and society. These are anti-Jewish lies which are rooted in thousands of years of anti-Jewish tropes, centered on the blood libel and conspiracy fantasy.

Indigeneity is the conceptual framework through which we can understand Jewish identity and our relationship with the Land of Israel. Thus, to understand Zionism, we must conceptually reframe it to acknowledge it as the indigenous rights movement of the Jewish people. Whatever its different strains and the disputes within the movement, Zionism had one simple and overriding goal: to allow the Jewish people to exercise their right to self-determination in their indigenous home: the Land of Israel. This goal correlates precisely with Article 3 of the UN Declaration on the Rights of Indigenous Peoples. "Indigenous peoples have the right to self-determination," it states. "By virtue of that right they freely determine their political status and freely pursue their economic, social, and cultural development."[1]

Zionism is an ideology created by Jews for Jews and it is one which is rooted in thousands of years of Jewish history. Founded by Theodor Herzl, modern political Zionism emerged in the 19th century as a response to the enlightenment, post-emancipatory Jew-hate, and the rise of the nation state.[2] However, throughout 2,000 years of exile, a return to Israel has been a central Jewish focus. In the very first sentence of *Der Judenstaat* (*The Jewish State*), the pamphlet written by Theodor Herzl in 1896 in which he advocated for a Jewish state, Herzl himself acknowledges the ancient roots of his modern political aspirations. "The idea which I have developed in this pamphlet is a very old one: it is the restoration of the Jewish State,"[3] he writes. Herzl was not wrong: Maccabees I, written 2,000 years ago, affirms the ancient Jewish desire to return to *our* home: "We have neither taken other men's land, nor holden that which appertaineth to others, but the inheritance of our fathers, which our enemies had wrongfully in possession a certain time. Wherefore we, having opportunity, hold the inheritance of our fathers."[4]

Likewise, the most important Jewish prayer, the Amidah, contains the "Ingathering of the Exiles," which is itself a yearning for the Jews to return home to Zion: "Sound the great shofar for our freedom, raise high the banner to gather our exiles, and gather us together from the four quarters of the earth. Blessed are You, Lord, who gathers the dispersed of His people Israel."[5]

As the late Chief Rabbi, Lord Sacks, argued:

> "Israel remained the focus of Jewish hopes. Wherever Jews were, they built synagogues, each of which was a symbolic fragment of the Temple in Jerusalem. Wherever they were, they prayed about Jerusalem, facing Jerusalem. They remembered it and wept for it, as the psalm had said, at every time of joy. They never relinquished their claim to the land, and there were places, especially in the north, from which they never left. The Jewish people was the circumference of a circle at whose centre was the Holy Land and Jerusalem the holy city."[6]

Thus, the fashionable assertion that Jews either spontaneously or randomly decided to return to Israel in the 19th century, or today have no connection to the ancient Israelites, is false. Genetically, as well as, of course, culturally, we are related to the ancient Israelites, and our focus on Israel—and desire to return home—throughout our exile was clear.

The continuous nature of Jewish civilization and its roots in, and focus on, the Land of Israel is key to Jewish indigeneity. For any serious scholar of history or anthropology, the connection between the Jews and the Land of Israel is clear for all to see. However, as has been graphically demonstrated by the response to October 7, too many people seek to continue the work of the former Soviet Union: To deny Jewish indigeneity, portray Jews as a colonial people with no connection to the Land of Israel, and present Zionism as a white, imperialist project. This is the essence of antizionism—a movement which has made huge inroads into academia, the media, and, tragically, the wider public consciousness—and it is nothing less than the racist delegitimization of the Jewish people's right to self-determination and to sovereignty. Israel is neither a colonial state nor a white-supremacist state. It is neither a symbol nor bastion of Western imperialism. These are anti-Jewish lies told about Israel to demonize it and to bring about its destruction. Islamists and the "progressive Left" treat Israel as the Collective Jew, or the Jew among Nations. And as historian Vernon Bogdanor writes, "The older antisemitism insisted that Jews had no place in the national community. The new antisemitism insists that Israel has no place in the international community."[7]

Antizionism is antithetical to Jewishness. As I examined in *Reclaiming Our Story*, the second part of the Jewish Pride trilogy, Jews have internalized Jew-hate for thousands of years. Antizionism exemplifies this process in action in our times. It is perhaps the ultimate expression of internalized Jew-hate. It also illustrates one of the key manifestations of internalized anti-Jewishness: deployment. In the 15th and 16th centuries, some Jews converted to Christianity and then spent their lives demonizing Jews. Today, antizionist Jews aren't content to simply reject Israel. Instead, they deploy their Jewishness as a weapon to provide a sheen of respectability and legitimacy to Jew-hate focused on Israel. In other words, they kosher antizionism. Antizionism is an illogical position for Jews to take. After all, who are Jews without Israel? Who are *any* indigenous people without their native lands? It is impossible to separate the Jews from Israel. We must be clear to those Jews who are so warped by Jew-hate that they shed this connection. They have strayed too far, and unless they make amends, they have no place among us. We may be diverse in our practices and beliefs, but antizionism is simply not a legitimate expression of Jewish identity.

And just as we must deepen our understanding of our identity as Jews, we must also deepen our understanding of Israel and our connection to it. Understanding Zionism as the indigenous rights movement is crucial—

both for ourselves and the wider world. We have to accurately describe our experiences, our history, and our relationships. The United Nations' position on the right to self-determination is rooted in the notion that an indigenous people have the right to define their own destiny and to create a society in their image. To be masters of their own destiny. This is what the Jewish people have done in Israel since 1948. It is an act of decolonization unprecedented in world history. Never before has an indigenous people been colonized and exiled from their land and then able to reclaim their sovereignty 2,000 years later.

"Indigenous peoples have the right to the lands, territories, and resources which they have traditionally owned, occupied, or otherwise used or acquired," Article 26 of the UN Declaration on the Rights of Indigenous Peoples declares.[8] The Australian scholar Julie Cassidy terms this notion "reversion." "The sovereignty of the dispossessed peoples continues, awaiting reversion, despite the loss of territory and even total illegal annexation," she argues. "[W]here people have been forcibly subjugated, their sovereign title continues in abeyance and can later be restored. Even a state which has been totally extinguished can resume its sovereignty when the resurrected "new" state and the old pre-colonization state are identical."[9] This was the goal of Zionism and its campaign to reclaim sovereignty in the Jewish indigenous land. It is also key to understanding our legal rights to the Land of Israel. Jews never ceded or relinquished sovereignty. We did not voluntarily abandon the land. Instead, the land was conquered and, as such, stolen from us. Of course, the Roman Empire, which was responsible for taking the land, no longer exists, and, before the Jews were finally able to reclaim it, our homeland changed hands on multiple occasions. However, none of this changes the fact that the land was stolen and the claim to indigeneity does not simply expire over time.

Scholar Jeremy Waldron cites the Jewish right to the Land of Israel as an example of this reversion, stating: "It is also believed the steps taken by the United Nations towards the establishment of the State of Israel only reinforced the legitimate claims of the Jews to their historical rights. Prior to Israel's re-entry into these territories, it has been suggested the occupants (i.e. Arabian and Jordanian States) were unlawful belligerents, who therefore acquired no legal title to the country, despite its annexation. In line with this suggestion, many in the international community saw Israel's return to be a legitimate assertion of the State's right to exercise full sovereignty over its kindred lands."[10]

In creating modern Zionism and re-establishing Jewish sovereignty in the Land of Israel, the Jews reclaimed what is ours and what was stolen from us thousands of years ago. As we saw previously, in the same manner that the early Zionists bought land in Eretz Yisrael from Turkish landowners, in 2022, the Chickahominy Tribe purchased 944 acres of their ancestral lands using a $3.5 million state grant, regaining sovereignty for the first time since the 17th century. On this momentous occasion, Virginia Governor Ralph Northam stated: "Returning this historically significant parcel of land to the Chickahominy is one way to recognize tribal sovereignty, honor their rich history, and ensure that the tribal nation has a place where they can continue their sacred traditions and share their stories."[11] Similarly, Assistant Chief Wayne Adkins argued: "This is a repatriation of the historically significant land and rich culture of our people, and pays respect to a history that for too long has been held hostage … This gives us a presence back on the river that we came from. We're coming back. It opens a new era for the tribe to share our history."[12] As both Northam and Adkins' words underline, the relationship which exists between an indigenous people and our land is unique and rich, and it is only with sovereignty in that land that we can fully manifest our specific identities. Like the Chickahominy in their lands, the Jews are not a colonizing force who took over vast swathes of land to which we had no claim or connection. We did not seek to homogenize foreign peoples, imposing our culture and our values on them. Supported by the international community who recognized our connection to Israel, we simply took back what was stolen from us. No more, no less. Our aim was encapsulated by Herzl in *Der Judenstaat*: "We shall live at last as free men on our own soil, and in our own homes peacefully die."[13] And in 1948, thanks to Zionism, the indigenous rights movement of the Jews, this became our reality for the first time in 2,000 years.

JUDAISM: OUR INDIGENOUS CULTURE

To fully embrace Jewish indigeneity and reject the non-Jewish world's attempt to impose its thinking upon us, the Jewish people must re-examine how we define our Jewish identity. There is no aspect of this process more vital than the notion of Judaism as a religion. This perspective is so deeply embedded in our collective psyche that it seems almost like a natural truth. Overcoming it will be extraordinarily difficult and will require significant effort on both individual and collective levels. However, despite being so embedded, this concept is actually a relatively modern phenomenon. The Jewish people were always self-described as an *Am* (people). There is no word for religion in the Tanakh. And while the Modern Hebrew word for religion is *Dat*, historically, it first appeared in *Megillat Esther* (the Scroll of Esther), where it was first used to reference law.[14]

The redefinition of Judaism began in earnest between the 16th and 18th centuries when Judaism started being referred to specifically as the Jewish religion, in response to the Christian discourses that dominated at the time. Prior to the Reformation, "*religio*"[15] was used only in reference to Christianity, but after this point it came to be used in a broader sense, meaning a set of theological beliefs; in other words, what we define today as a "religion." Crucially, this definition was applied to Jews by Christian scholars. Richard Baxter, in his "The Reasons of the Christian Religion." for instance, wrote in 1667:

"Four sorts of Religions I find only considerable upon earth: The meer Naturalists, called commonly Heathens and Idolaters; the Jews; the Mohametans; and the Christians. The Heathens by their Oracles, Augures and Auspices, confess necessity of some supernatural light; and the very Religion of all the rest consisteth of it."[16]

Given its dominance in the Western world, this Christian thinking soon began to influence Jewish scholars, such as Moshe Chaim Luzzatto. The renowned scholar Abraham Melamed believes that Luzzatto was the first Jew to use the phrase "The Jewish religion" (*religione hebrea*).[17] The process accelerated in the 19th century, following the Haskalah (Jewish Enlightenment), when new definitions of Judaism were created in order to assimilate Jews and Jewishness into Europe. By this process, Jews were "remade" in the likeness of the new post-Enlightenment world. In 1836, Joshua van Oven, a Jewish community leader in London, defined Judaism as "an inward feeling of awe and veneration, induced by the knowledge of the existence of an omnipotent and eternal God, the creator, preserver, and regulator of the universal, whom we strongly feel bound to worship and adore."[18] This could be a description of Christianity.

As Melamed suggested, "The very fact that they found it useful to make such new definitions is clear proof of the need they found to redefine Judaism, under the pressure of their new circumstances."[19] This redefinition of Judaism was inauthentic. While it is possible, as we have already explored, for indigenous people to evolve, the notion of Jews as simply a religious group, like Christians or Muslims, is not an accurate representation of our identity. Unlike the "Jewification" of the Greek Symposium, which created the Pesach Seder, this was not a case of cultural evolution but rather an attempt to remake Jews in the likeness of the Christian majority.

For Jews, even those of us who do not believe in God, He cannot be separated from our daily lives or actions. Some Jews infuse their Jewish actions with God; others do not. Nonetheless, the actions undertaken by both are the same. When I say *Kaddish* for my late father, Malcolm, on his Yahrzeit every year, for instance, I light the Yahrzeit candle and recite the mourner's prayer, which is solely focused on exalting God's name. But when I say *Kaddish*, I am not thinking of God; I am thinking of my father and our connection with the Jews who have commemorated their dead in this way for thousands of years.

Given its definition as "the service and worship of God or the supernatural,"[20] it is possible to argue that the Jewish belief in, and worship of, Hashem constitutes a religion. However, we should investigate our identity through our own lens, not through the lens of Christianity, which is the conceptual framework many of us have for religion. Thus, even if Jews do have a religion in line with that definition, I would argue it is fundamentally different—as we have seen—from that of Christianity. Given its historical context, "Judaism" would still be the incorrect term to describe it; rather, it should be understood as our indigenous culture.

Another definition of Judaism which requires further investigation is the notion it is a faith. If we accept that Judaism is not a religion (in the Christian context), then we should reject the idea of faith as it is understood by Christians. But what about the issue of faith within Judaism? It is true that Jews have the concept of emuna—a Hebrew term often translated into English as "faith," but more accurately meaning "reliability, trustworthiness, dependability, steadiness."[21] But this concept differs from the Christian notion of faith. In terms of the difference between emuna and faith (or pistis as the Greeks originally called it), we can turn briefly to *Zwei Glaubensweisen* ("Two Types of Faith") by Martin Buber.[22] This was a work written in German, but translated into English, and is another indication of the weakness of translation and the nuance and clarity we lose by not being able to interact with these important works in their original language. In *Zwei Glaubensweisen*, Martin Buber explores the differences in Christian and Jewish belief. In English, the book is translated into "Two Types of Faith," but that is not a direct translation; rather, it would be "Two Beliefs." And though they are used synonymously, as Oxford Professor of Philosophy Mark Wrathall stated, "It's commonplace to treat belief and faith as synonyms ... but there are important differences."[23] Emuna is rooted in a dynamic relationship with God, emphasizing trust, loyalty, and a profound personal connection with the Divine, hence the Jewish propensity to wrestle with God. It's less about adhering to doctrines or creeds and more about engaging in a lived relationship with God, thriving on ongoing dialog and encounters where the individual actively participates in their covenant with the Divine. In contrast, Pistis tends to focus more on believing in specific truths or doctrines. On emuna and pistis, Buber states in the English translation of his work, "The faith of Judaism and the faith of Christendom are by nature different in kind."[24]

This Jewish relationship with Judaism is exemplified in *Pirkei Avot* (Chapters of the Fathers), which states: "*Hafoch ba hafoch ba, de'kula ba*" (Turn it over, and [again] turn it over, for all is therein)."[25] We are meant to forensically examine Judaism and intellectualize it so that we can grapple with it. This is what the Talmud is—an examination. Judaism does not ask you to park rational or critical thinking at the door. This discussion highlights the challenges we face when investigating or understanding Jewishness through translations and a non-Jewish lens. It clearly demonstrates that to explore our own civilization, we must do so in the language in which it was written: Hebrew. Alongside that, we must perceive Judaism through a Jewish lens. If we don't, we end up using English words to define our concepts and then applying a Christian context to understand them.

Another key reason why faith, in the Christian context, is not an accurate way of describing Jewish belief is that Judaism is not based on a formal creed or dogma. For example, Christianity has the Apostles' Creed, which summarizes Christian beliefs. But, as Rabbis Kaufmann Kohler and Emil

G. Hirsch, have argued: "Many attempts have indeed been made at systematizing and reducing to a fixed phraseology and sequence the contents of the Jewish religion. But these have always lacked the one essential element: authoritative sanction on the part of a supreme ecclesiastical body."[26]

In debates about faith and Judaism, Maimonides' *Shloshah Asar Ikkarim* (translated as the Thirteen Principles of Faith) is often cited as evidence. It's understandable why this might cause confusion—after all, the title itself includes the word "faith."[27] It is also true that these principles, while influential and perhaps more akin to a guide, do not constitute a creed. They represent Maimonides' view on what Jewish beliefs might encompass but are not universally accepted. Other prominent rabbis, known as Anti-Maimonideans, have offered alternative perspectives on what should be considered the core tenets of Judaism. Thus, as Rabbis Kaufmann Kohler and Emil G. Hirsch also argued: "In the same sense as Christianity or Islam, Judaism cannot be credited with the possession of Articles of Faith."[28] And rooted in the difference between emuna and pistis, the distinction between Jewish and Christian belief is clear.

Another redefinition of Judaism—this time as a "world religion"—was to take the Christianizing of Judaism a step further. Scholars of religion Christopher R. Cotter and David G. Robertson define the idea of world religions as "a particular way of thinking about religions which organizes them into a set of discrete traditions with a supposedly 'global' import."[29] World religions are also said to include Christianity, Islam, Buddhism, and Hinduism. They are usually described as being large, spread internationally, and having influenced the development of Western society. For a multitude of reasons (not least that Judaism is not a religion in the Western understanding of the word), it is a mischaracterization to include Judaism in this category. Judaism is not large; there are only 15.7 million Jews (as of 2023) in the world. We do not seek to convert those who are not Jews. And while Judaism did play a foundational role in Western society, this is because Judaism was exported around the world—not by Jews, but by Christians.

The notion of "world religions" is a paradigm pioneered by the 20th-century Scottish writer and academic Ninian Smart. It is a Western-colonial view of Judaism and Eastern religions, and it does not accurately define or describe Judaism and its connection to the Jews and the Land of Israel. Nor does it fit into the Western and Christian idea of religion and identity. Ironically, the idea of "world religions" was meant to make Christianity less central in the study of religion; Smart himself established the first religious studies department in the U.K. in the late 1960s, having previously been a professor of theology. But, of course, the concept of "world religions" was based on a Christian model of understanding religion. "While the World Religions paradigm was brought in to allow the inclusion of non-Christian religions in education, it has instead remodelled them according to liberal Western Protestant Christian values (akin to what the Church of England promotes), emphasizing theological categories," argues Religious Studies academic Suzanne Owen.[30]

While rejecting Judaism as a "World Religion," a potentially more accurate definition of Judaism could be "Indigenous Religion." Kenneth H. Lokensgard and Alejandro V. Gonzalez define "indigenous religions" as "the ancestral religions of peoples who are native to particular landscapes. Their religions help them achieve the goal of living successfully in those places. Thus, indigenous religions vary, just as the places their practitioners inhabit vary. Yet, the many religions practiced by indigenous peoples share common themes. These themes include emphasis upon relationship and place."[31] This definition certainly fits the Jewish experience and relationship with the land, but Lokensgard and Gonzalez are more accurately outlining indigenous culture rather than just describing indigenous religion. For Jews, as with other indigenous peoples, such as Inca people who worship Pachamama, the Earth Mother goddess, God cannot be separated from the daily culture and practices of the people. Therefore, it seems that even when identifying indigenous religions and attempting to understand the diversity of belief which exists, Lokensgard and Gonzalez continue to use a Christian view of the world, where ideas of God can be delineated from other aspects of culture. For Jews and other indigenous peoples, culture encompasses religion (in the narrowest sense) but isn't confined to it. Religion is a component of culture rather than a defining characteristic on its own.

A crucial part of reclaiming our identity as Jews is reframing our understanding of Judaism. While it includes a belief in God, it is not a religion in the Christian sense of the word; it is the indigenous culture of the Jewish people, which contains God. The process of reframing will not be easy, but it is essential for living our lives as Jews authentically. To achieve this, we must understand our civilization through a Jewish lens. In terms of God, individual Jews can indeed live without believing in Hashem. However, the fact remains that God cannot be separated from Jewishness because He is so intertwined with Jewish expression.

As we explored in Chapter 6, it may also seem that notions such as God promising us Eretz Yisrael are at odds with more modern ideas like indigeneity. However, this misunderstands the very concept of indigeneity. It is a framework that explains a people's emotional, physical, and spiritual relationship with a land, which can include the belief in a deity or deities. The belief that the land was promised to us by God doesn't weaken our indigeneity; it strengthens it. Our ancient ancestors believed that the land they lived in was given by God and, therefore, was special to them.

Viewing Judaism through a Christian lens distorts and dilutes its true essence as our indigenous culture. For hundreds of years, Jewish identity has been shaped by outside influences, defined by the majority around us. This has led to the adoption of definitions and concepts that do not reflect our authentic experiences. To rebuild our people and reclaim our story, we need to reject these external definitions and constraints and embrace an identity that honors our indigeneity. Judaism should be seen not as a religion but as a rich culture and civilization deeply intertwined with our land, God, and peoplehood. This shift is crucial for maintaining the integrity of our identity and ensuring it accurately reflects our unique experiences and historic truth.

JEWISH INTEGRATION AND THE RIGHT TO BE DIFFERENT

One of the greatest challenges faced by Jews in the Diaspora is the challenge of integrating into the non-Jewish societies in which we live while retaining what makes us a distinct people. This is not necessarily an inherent challenge but it is still one which has an impact on many Jews due to Jew-hatred, which forces us to choose between our identities. Through the notion of the "Broken Mirror of Jewish Identity," which reflects palatable versions of Jewishness to Jews from the non-Jewish world, Jews are presented with models of the "Good Jew" and the "Bad Jew."[32] In order to survive and navigate a hostile world, many Jews work to become "Good Jews." This is not their fault; they are dealing with the often crushing pressure of antisemitism. However, the choice with which Jews are faced is an assault on Jewish authenticity and uniqueness.

Instead of being forced to make these pernicious choices, the best way to successfully integrate into the non-Jewish world is by being authentically Jewish. We should wear our indigeneity as a badge of pride. Like any other indigenous people, we deserve to be seen as who we are. We should not be expected to change ourselves, or hide a part of our identity, to be accepted. We should not be faced with the accusation of dual loyalty. We have a dual connection, not a dual loyalty. Honoring this is possible.

This issue most frequently arises when we are forced to deny who we are in order to be accepted. Often when faced with the accusation of dual loyalty, I see Jews diminish their connection to Israel. On April 21, 2024, Michael White, the former political editor of *The Guardian*, posted on social media platform X, "Of course I know how Jewish Brits feel about 7/10 and aftermath, though most such I know are ashamed of their own disreputable Netanyahu government."[33] White was accusing British Jews of having dual loyalty, a trope rooted in conspiracy fantasy that frames diasporic Jews as being more loyal to Israel or Jews than to the countries of their birth. In response to White, I wrote: "Jews have dual identities, not dual loyalty: Jews naturally have a connection to Israel, as our indigenous land, but almost half of us don't live there and have other citizenships."[34] I am not going to allow White's accusation to force me to diminish my connection to Israel. I am British and I am a Jew, and therefore indigenous to Eretz Yisrael. They are not mutually exclusive.

However, due to Jew-hate, balancing our identities in the Diaspora is challenging. As Ijeoma Umebinyuo's "Diaspora Blues" poem[35] illuminates, this is not just a challenge for diasporic Jews; it is something all diasporic people experience, and it is something Jews must acknowledge. We are grappling with the challenge of integration as many other people are. But we often fail to acknowledge it. And we must, even if it makes us uncomfortable. We must recognize this facet of our experience so we can more easily navigate it. Acknowledging our indigeneity is a vital part of this process as it makes clear our identity and our connection to Israel. I am a British Jew. I vote in British elections. I was raised in the U.K., and this has undoubtedly had an impact on how I live my life. However, because of my Jewishness, I am indigenous to the Land of Israel and am therefore deeply and emotionally connected to the modern State of Israel. It is my home. And I have to recognize this duality. Efrat's testimony is a powerful representation of how we accept this duality and embody various identities, while still being able to nurture and respect Jewishness. It is also the case, as she so rightly suggested, that the only way to integrate is to simultaneously honor your Jewishness. Otherwise, you are not respecting all the various aspects of your identity; this is a distinctly damaging and unhealthy way to live. Everyone will rank their identities according to their own ideas, experiences, and circumstances. My primary identity is Jewish and my primary connection is to Israel. However, that does not mean I am not connected to my British culture or the U.K. at the same time. One does not preclude the other. But we cannot grapple with these issues unless we are being honest with ourselves about our connections and identities. Acknowledging and embracing our authentic indigenous identity is to assert our right to be different to—not better or worse than—those around us.

As Vlad recalls, the Soviet Union offers an extreme example of the choices the non-Jewish world often forces Jews to make. The very real threat emanating from the government forced Jews to try to forge papers so they could legally pass as non-Jews. This is what Jew-hate does to us: It forces us to choose, or worse, to hide. In the West, for hundreds of years, Jews have been coerced into hiding and forced to shed those very things which make us distinct and different. American Jews are no different (nor were the German Jews in the 19th century). To make it means being accepted into non-Jewish society, but on its terms. We obviously have to recognize the inherent power dynamic which exists between the majority and minority in the Diaspora, but that does not mean we should erase our differences and deny our indigeneity.

Instead, we should embrace them. This is not as challenging as the world around us may make us believe. It is entirely possible to authentically express your Jewish identity—in all that encompasses—and your other identities at the same time. My own experience suggests that in order to do this successfully, the most important thing is to find a kind of inner peace with regard to who you are. For years I struggled with my sexual orientation, and even when I worked toward LGBTQ+ Pride, I saw that part of my identity as being separate from my Jewish identity. Now, years later, I realize they are not different, because they are both a part of me. I am a gay Jew, and I feel comfortable being both. This inner comfort ultimately makes my expressions of my identity much more fluid and comfortable because I feel able to be authentically me.

However, I only developed this peace by grappling with my identities, by engaging in introspection into how I really feel about these parts of myself. This is especially the case if Jews in the Diaspora are to feel able to integrate without making the enormous sacrifices often expected of Jews. Israelis often cannot fully relate to the neurosis that exists in the Diaspora. This makes perfect sense. They are in our indigenous land. They are the majority. We, on the other hand, are navigating very hostile worlds which are always forcing us to choose.

Ultimately, if we are to continue making our homes in the Diaspora, we must refuse to choose. We must embrace what makes us different. Once we feel peace in our identities, if we feel physically safe, we should be able to express them. In May 2023, I watched His Majesty King Charles III's coronation. I waved my British flag, and I wore my kippah because I was not willing to minimize my Jewishness—and all that means—in order to participate in a historic British event. This is the beauty of our indigeneity: Almost everything Jewish we do throughout the week is an expression of our deep and emotional connection with the Land of Israel. We just need to acknowledge it and wear it as a badge of honor and pride.

I am proud to be a Jew. I am proud to be indigenous. I am proud that my people, despite the horrors we have faced, have maintained our peoplehood, maintained our connection to our indigenous land, and maintained our sense of self. And this strong, proud Jewish identity does not preclude me, in any way, from participating in British civic life. And we must not believe anyone who says otherwise.

INDIGENEITY AND JEWISH PRIDE

Jewish Pride gives Jews permission. It gives us permission to be different, to own our identities, to assert ourselves, and to engage in self-reflection, both as individuals and as a community. It is not simply the act of Jews feeling good about themselves; it is not even just about Jews feeling pride in their Jewishness, although it is an obvious component. That is the end of the process, not the beginning. It is something we must work toward. Ultimately, Jewish Pride is a movement which provides each of us, as part of the collective and as individuals, with the skills, tools, and confidence to do the work. To embark on a journey of introspection, of working to understand one's identity deeply without shame and with a sense of empathy. It is a process, possibly without an end.

One of the fundamental tenets of Jewish Pride is that Jews are the only ones who can and should define Jewish identity. And Jews must understand what it means to be a Jew, from a Jewish perspective, in order that they can feel pride. Along with our own illiteracy, Jews also receive constant messages from the wider world regarding our identity. Some of it is overtly harmful, such as the accusation that Israel is a colonial entity, while other ideas, like the notion that Jews are simply a religious group with a "faith" (in the Christian context), are simply inaccurate descriptions used by the world so it can understand us through its own lens. To reject these ideas and to pursue Jewish Pride, Jews must understand Jewish identity and be literate in Jewish history and experience. And recognizing Jewish indigeneity provides a crucial conceptual framework which explains the very core of Jewish identity. It explains the full complexity of Jewish identity, our relationship to each other, and, most importantly, our relationship to the Land of Israel. It enables Jews to understand the emotional connection we have to the land, and to the modern state which sits upon it. Every Jew I have spoken with since October 7 felt real grief after that awful day. Although many found it hard to articulate why. Indigeneity provides the answer.

But it is important to recognize that we do not develop, and work toward, Jewish Pride solely as an act of resistance. Nor do we assert our indigeneity solely in response to the wider world's delegitimization of the Jewish connection to the Land of Israel. For while we must reject non-Jewish definitions of Jewish identity, we can only do so with an understanding of who we are and where we come from. And this is how we develop Jewish Pride. Conversely, Jew-hate—and the damage it causes to how we see ourselves, how we act, and what we do in order to be accepted—threatens Jewish Pride.

Following the genocide committed against Israel by Hamas on October 7, we saw a huge swell of Jewish Pride from all over the world, but we also witnessed an increasingly vocal Jewish minority stand against Israel, their indigenous land, and with Palestinians. It is, of course, not inherently problematic for Jews to stand with the Palestinians, but for them to attack and denigrate Israel is illogical and contrary to their own identities as Jews. As I explained in detail in *Reclaiming Our Story*, this is an expression of internalized antisemitism and understanding Jewishness through the lens of the non-Jewish world. Jews from Europe, the United States, and beyond protested against Israel, accepted the lie that it is a colonial state, and stood beside those who support Hamas and are bent on our homeland's destruction. Those Jews may be a minority, but we cannot underestimate the danger they pose to our civilization. They will foster future generations of Jews with internalized antisemitism in the form of antizionism and they will legitimize Jew-hate.

This is why so many young, progressive Jews are not able to withstand the intellectual, political, and cultural onslaught of antizionism. For the most part, they are ignorant of Jewish identity, in the way we have explored in this work. They do not understand what it means to be a Jew. They do not understand our history, and they certainly do not understand that we are indigenous to the Land of Israel. They think it's just a culture or a religion (in the Christian context). And they do not have the framework of indigeneity to understand their Jewish identity and to be part of an ancient civilization and people. This is the danger we face when we do not recognize, understand, and embrace our experience and identity. And this is why Jewish indigeneity is a crucial concept for Jews. It solidifies our understanding of ourselves, our experience, and our history. It is the ultimate explanation of Jewish identity in all its facets.

In order to further Jewish Pride across the generations, I created the head, hands, and heart model. And each is deeply intertwined with Jewish indigeneity. The Head represents knowledge. We must know Jewish history. We must be able to tell our own story. The Hands represent Jewish action. And Jewishness must be lived. As we know, it is not a faith. It is not an idea. It is a way of life. For generations, Jews were defined by the things we did. These actions separated us from those around us and acted as profound symbols of Jewish difference. By living our Jewishness, we are expressing the fact that we are indigenous to the Land of Israel. The Heart component is the feeling of Jewish Pride. The feeling of belonging to the Land of Israel and to the Jewish people. And both are cultivated—and intensified—through the notion of indigeneity.

A DECOLONIZED JEW

Recognizing and embracing our indigeneity and authentically expressing our Jewishness is our right and our responsibility as Jews. As perhaps the most repeatedly persecuted minority group in the history of the world, it's also an act of resistance. For millennia, both physically and mentally we have been colonized. Our sovereignty was stolen. Most of us were stripped of our land. We were told who and what we are, coerced—or actively forced—into twisting ourselves to be accepted by our non-Jewish overlords. But despite all of this, we've managed to hold on to our core. We have maintained our connection to the Land of Israel, in myriad ways. This connection lies at the heart of Jewishness. It exists whether we acknowledge it or not, but to live in harmony with ourselves and each other, we must recognize and cherish it.

Our traditions and customs span thousands of years; they originated in the Land of Israel over three millennia ago and they live within us today. As a collective, we abide by many of the same laws and, despite it evolving in important ways, continue to express Jewishness much like our ancestors did. This continuity is a profound expression of our uniqueness and our indigeneity. We are a distinct people and a distinct civilization. And we must acknowledge it. We are not a Western or European people. We are a people with roots in the southern Levant, in the Near East. And it is crucial for Jews to understand and confidently express this identity.

Jewish literacy in Jewishness became especially significant after October 7 and Israel's subsequent war of self-defense, but it's always relevant. We must immerse ourselves in the Jewish world to understand ourselves, and the wider world, through our own lens. We must acknowledge the ideas of the wider world, but we must understand that we are a civilization unto ourselves. We have a distinct set of ideas, actions, and beliefs. The Five Books of Moses are not the Old Testament. They are the Torah. Even though the West dates its calendar from the birth of Jesus, even Jews living in Western or Western-influenced societies do not live in Anno Domini (the Year of Our Lord), as Jesus is not our Lord. We exist in the Common Era.

The time has come for us to reclaim our story. We refuse to be dictated to. We refuse to be told what it means to be Jewish. And we will not allow ourselves to be diminished for acceptance nor allow our connection to our indigenous land to be erased. It's time to stand up and be counted, defending ourselves, as generations of Jews who came before us defended Jewishness themselves.

Indigeneity gives us language to name and therefore understand our experiences. As I wrote in the Introduction, indigeneity uncovers layers of meaning that already exist. But we have to uncover them. We have to name them because that is how we fully realize ourselves.

Many Jews will make *Aliyah* and return home, but we can proudly live as an indigenous people in the Diaspora. Healthy integration, honoring both aspects of our identities, is possible, and is a commitment we must make anew. Wherever we reside, we must dedicate ourselves to our Jewishness and prioritize it alongside our other identities. It is not an incidental part of who we are. We are part of an ancient civilization, and we must honor it. All Jews must reclaim their right to Jewish action. These aren't just "religious" acts, and they belong to all Jews, regardless of how we interact with the spiritual or the Divine; they are expressions of Jewish civilization, fundamental to our identity as a distinct people. And Israel, whether we live there or not, is our home. We can have multiple homes, but Israel is our home. And how lucky we are. We are part of an unbroken lineage which has maintained its bond with our indigenous land for over 3,000 years. And now it is our turn to claim it, so we can pass on this awakened sense of Jewish identity to the next generation, thus ensuring the healthy and proud continuation of the Jewish people.

My Jewish Pride trilogy began in Hong Kong on October 4, 2019, when I first put pen to paper. Since that beginning, Jews all over the world have embraced its message and begun the journey of reclaiming their stories and identities. This work is the finale of my Jewish Pride trilogy, and I hope that you, my reader, understand—and feel connected to—your Jewish identity even more deeply than you did before. But this is not the end. In some ways, it is just the beginning. The work to build our Jewish Pride movement must continue for generations to come. Let us go forth and proudly proclaim our Jewishness and our enduring love for, and connection to, the Land of Israel.

We know who we are. We know where we are from. And we will tell the world.

Am Yisrael Chai.

The People of Israel Live.

Proudly.

ISAAC	YAFFA	VLAD

EFRAT  WINSTON

THE AUTHOR

NOTES

Prologue

1   The pomegranate is also said to represent wisdom, as it is meant to have 613 seeds, the same number as the mitzvot in the Torah. Although the seeds of the pomegranate do not actually number 613, this slight deviation from truth does not undermine its significance to the Jewish people.

Introduction

1   The Palestine Mandate, 1922. The Palestine Mandate. Available at: https://avalon.law.yale.edu/20th_century/palmanda.asp
2   Troen, I. and Troen, C. (2019) "Indigeneity," *Israel Studies*, 24 (2). Available at: https://doi.org/10.2979/israelstudies.24.2.02
3   The Palestinian National Charter: Resolutions of the Palestine National Council July 1–17, 1968. Available at: https://avalon.law.yale.edu/20th_century/plocov.asp
4   Fortgang, T. and Meyers, H.E. (2022) "A new legal approach to Jew-hatred: Using anti-Semitic indigeneity arguments against anti-Semites," *Commentary*, December. Available at: https://tikvah.org/wp-content/uploads/2022/12/A-New-Legal-Approach-to-Jew-Hatred-Tal-Fortgang-and-Hannah-E.-Meyers-Commentary-Magazine.pdf
5   Joffe, A.H. (2012) "The Rhetoric of Nonsense: Fabricating Palestinian History," *Middle East Quarterly*, Summer, pp. 15–22. Available at: https://www.meforum.org/middle-east-quarterly/palestinian-history-nonsense
6   Elazar, D.J. (n.d.) "Jewish Religious and Ethnic Identity," Jerusalem Center for Public Affairs. Available at: https://dje.jcpa.org/articles2/jewreleth.htm
7   Krauthammer, C. (1998) "At last, Zion," *Washington Examiner*, May 11. Available at: https://www.washingtonexaminer.com/weekly-standard/at-last-zion
8   Martínez Cobo, J. (1987) *Study of the Problem of Discrimination Against Indigenous Populations: Final Report*. Available at: https://digitallibrary.un.org/record/133666?ln=en&v=pdf
9   Augustine of Hippo (430) "Commentary on Psalms 57:3," Catena Bible & Commentaries, Psalms 57. Available at: https://catenabible.com/com/5851ccc09ac03ecd-4b8e6af1?utm_source=chatgpt.com
10 Law Insider (n.d.) "Bumiputera." Available at: https://www.lawinsider.com/dictionary/bumiputera
11 Singh, M. (2023) "It's time to rethink the idea of the indigenous," *The New Yorker*, February 20. Available at: https://www.newyorker.com/magazine/2023/02/27/its-time-to-rethink-the-idea-of-the-indigenous
12 Ibid.
13 United States Holocaust Memorial Museum (n.d.) "Origins of Neo-Nazi and White Supremacist Terms and Symbols." Available at: https://www.ushmm.org/antisemitism/what-is-antisemitism/origins-of-neo-nazi-and-white-supremacist-terms-and-symbols
14 Bellerose, R. (2017) "Are Jews Indigenous to the Land of Israel?", *Tablet Magazine*, February 9. Available at: https://www.tabletmag.com/sections/israel-middle-east/articles/bellerose-aboriginal-people

15 Singh, M. (2023) "It's time to rethink the idea of the indigenous," *The New Yorker*, February 20. Available at: https://www.newyorker.com/magazine/2023/02/27/its-time-to-rethink-the-idea-of-the-indigenous

16 Barker, J. (2011) *Native Acts: Law, Recognition, and Cultural Authenticity*. University of North Carolina Press

17 Singh, M. (2023) "It's time to rethink the idea of the indigenous," *The New Yorker*, February 20. Available at: https://www.newyorker.com/magazine/2023/02/27/its-time-to-rethink-the-idea-of-the-indigenous

18 Working with Indigenous Australians (n.d.) *The Land*. Available at: www.workingwithindigenousaustralians.info/content/Culture_3_The_Land.html

19 State of Israel (1955) Government Year-book 5716. Government Printer

20 Forbes, J. (n.d.) *Blood Quantum II*. University of California, Davis. Available at: https://web.archive.org/web/20100610050121/http://nas.ucdavis.edu/Forbes/Blood_Quantum_II.html

21 Ibid.

22 Navajo Nation Office of Vital Records and Identification (n.d.) FAQs. Available at: https://novri.navajo-nsn.gov/Faqs

23 The Indigenous Foundation (n.d.) "Blood Quantum." Available at: https://www.theindigenousfoundation.org/articles/bloodquantum

24 Ghose, T. (2013) "Most Ashkenazi Jews are genetically Europeans, surprising study finds", *NBC News*, October 8. Available at: https://www.nbcnews.com/sciencemain/most-ashkenazi-jews-are-genetically-europeans-surprising-study-finds-8c11358210

25 Shtull-Trauring, A. (2010) "Landmark study proves 90% of Jews are genetically linked to the Levant", *Haaretz*, June 10. Available at: 06-10/ty-article/landmark-study-proves-90-of-jews-are-genetically-linked-to-thelevant/0000017f-e0bb-df7c-a5ff-e2fba5950000

26 United Nations (2018) "United Nations Declaration on the Rights of Indigenous Peoples". Available at: content/uploads/sites/19/2018/11/UNDRIP_E_web.pdf

27 Sefaria (n.d.) Kiddushin 66b:16. Available at: https://www.sefaria.org/Kiddushin.66b.16?lang=bi

28 Liberal Judaism (n.d.) "Jewish Status FAQ." Available at: https://www.liberaljudaism.org/jewish-status-faq/

29 Kunesh, P.H. (2007) "Banishment as cultural justice in contemporary tribal legal systems," *New Mexico Law Review*, Winter

30 Sefaria (n.d.) Ruth 1:16. Available at: https://www.sefaria.org/Ruth.1.16?lang=bi

31 YHWH (pronounced Yud, Heh, Vav, Heh) also known as the Tetragrammaton, is a four-letter Hebrew name for the Jewish national God in the Torah.

32 The Indigenous Foundation (n.d.) "Blood Quantum." Available at: www.theindigenousfoundation.org/articles/bloodquantum

33 Kahn, R.A. (2020) X.com, July 7. Available at: https://x.com/rabbiandruekahn/status/1280482583898476544?ref_src=twsrc%5Etfw%7Ctwcamp%5Etweetembed%7Ctwterm%5E1280482583898476544%7Ctwgr%5Ef4a81c8ec253ede02045915b8504ee91d4f8b378%7Ctwcon%5Es1_&ref_url=https%3A%2F%2Fwww.jpost.com%2Fisrael-news%2Fjews-are-indigenous-to-israel-and-a-rabbi-should-know-it-scholarsays-634817

34 Brager, S. (2021) "Comic / When Settler Becomes Native," *Jewish Currents*, October 13. Available at: https://jewishcurrents.org/when-settler-becomes-native

35 Silberstein, A. (2021) "Bio-Zionism: Why Claiming Jews Are Indigenous to Israel Is so Dangerous," *Haaretz*, December 21. Available at: https://www.haaretz.com/israel-news/2021-12-21/ty-article-opinion/.highlight/bio-zionism-why-claimingjews-are-indigenous-to-israel-is-so-dangerous/0000017f-df8b-d3a5-af7f-ffaf5b7a0000A

36 International Labour Organization (ILO) (1989) "C169—Indigenous and Tribal Peoples Convention, 1989 (No. 169)," NORMLEX. Available at: https://normlex.ilo.org/dyn/normlex/en/f?p=NORMLEXPUB:12100:0::NO::P12100_ILO_CODE:C169
37 Umebinyuo, I. (n.d.) "Diaspora Blues," *The Ijeoma Project*. Available at: https://www.scribd.com/document/533473946/462846398-OceanofPDF-Com-Questions-for-Ada-Ijeoma-Umebinyuo-PDF

Chapter 1

1 In terms of the word we use for Jews, their evolution goes as follows: Judah (the tribe and later Kingdom) was Yehuda in Hebrew, which then was renamed Judea by the Greeks. They described the people from Judea as *Ioudaioi*, which then became *Juieu* in Old French before developing into *Iuw*, and then finally in the 18th century, Jew.
2 Babbel Magazine, July 27, 2023, "What Does the Suffix "-ish" Mean?", *Babbel*. Available at: https://www.babbel.com/en/magazine/ish-meaning
3 Cohen, S.J.D. (1999) *The Beginnings of Jewishness: Boundaries, Varieties, Uncertainties*. University of California Press
4 Clermont-Tonnerre, December 23, 1789, "Speech on Religious Minorities and Questionable Professions." Available at: https://revolution.chnm.org/d/284/
5 Lendering, J. (n.d.) "Maximalists and Minimalists," Livius.org. Available at: https://www.livius.org/articles/theory/maximalists-and-minimalists/
6 Schama, S. (2014) *The Story of the Jews: Finding the Words (1000 BCE–1492 CE)*. London: Vintage
7 Sefaria (n.d.) Genesis 15:18. Available at: https://www.sefaria.org/Genesis.15.18?lang=bi&with=all&lang2=en
8 Albright Live (2024) *Episode Nineteen: The Patriarchs: The Jacob Cycle*. Available at: https://www.youtube.com/watch?v=0BDBrAmdOYQ
9 Ibid.
10 Reinsch, W. (2018) "122: Merneptah Stele Proving Israel's 3,200 Year Existence." Available at: https://armstronginstitute.org/122-merneptah-stele-proving-israels3200-year-existence
11 Encyclopædia Britannica (n.d.) "Merneptah." Available at: https://www.britannica.com/biography/Merneptah
12 Hasel, M. (2008) "Merenptah's reference to Israel: critical issues for the origin of Israel." In: Hess, R.S., Klingbeil, G.A. and Ray, P.J. (eds.) *Critical Issues in Early Israelite History*. Grand Rapids: William B. Eerdmans Publishing Company
13 Spiegelberg, W. (2016) "Der Siegeshymnus des Merneptah auf der Flinders Petrie-Stele," Zeitschrift für Ägyptische Sprache und Altertumskunde, 34 (1). Available at: https://doi.org/10.1524/zaes.1896.34.jg.1
14 Biblical Historical Context (n.d.) "Israelite Origins: The Merneptah Stele." Available at: https://biblicalhistoricalcontext.com/israelite-origins/israelite-origins-the-merneptah-stele/
15 Shanks, H. (2012) "When Did Ancient Israel Begin?," *Biblical Archaeology Review*, January/February. Biblical Archaeology Society. Available at: https://library.biblicalarchaeology.org/collections/where-did-early-israelites-come
16 It is interesting that Jerusalem and Shechem would later become the capitals of the ancient Israelite Kingdoms (Israel with Shechem and Judah with Jerusalem).
17 David, A. (2019) "For You Were Not Slaves in Egypt: The Memories Behind the Exodus Myth," *Haaretz*, April 19. Available at: https://www.haaretz.com/archaeology/2019-04-19/ty-article-magazine/.premium/for-you-were-not-slaves-in-egypt-thememories-behind-the-exodus-myth/0000017f-f246-da6f-a77f-fa4ef8220000

18   Ibid.
19   Sperling, S.D. (n.d.) "Were Jews Slaves in Egypt?," *Reform Judaism*. Available at: https://www.reformjudaism.org/were-jews-slaves-egypt
20   Ibid.
21   Windle, B. (2019) "Three Egyptian Inscriptions about Israel," *Bible Archaeology Report*, March 8. Available at: https://biblearchaeologyreport.com/2019/03/08/three-egyptian-inscriptions-about-israel/
22   Flurry, J. (2022) "The Soleb Inscription: Earliest-Discovered Use of the Name "Yahweh" and Evidence for the Much-Debated Era of the Exodus," Armstrong Institute, October 10. Available at: https://armstronginstitute.org/768-the-soleb-inscriptionearliest-discovered-use-of-the-name-yahweh
23   David, A. (2019) "For You Were Not Slaves in Egypt: The Memories Behind the Exodus Myth," *Haaretz*, April 19. Available at: https://www.haaretz.com/archaeology/2019-04-19/ty-article-magazine/.premium/for-you-were-not-slaves-in-egypt-thememories-behind-the-exodus-myth/0000017f-f246-da6f-a77f-fa4ef8220000
24   Sefaria (n.d.) Exodus 38:22. Available at: https://www.sefaria.org/Exodus.38.22?lang=bi&aliyot=0
25   Friedman, R.E. (2018) *Exodus*. San Francisco
26   Friedman discusses the authorship of the Torah (the Five Books of Moses), describing four main texts, known as J, E, P, and D. He argues that E, P, and D were all authored by Levite priests. These texts are the ones which tell of Moses, Pharaoh, and the plagues, while J, which does not seem to have been written by Levites, fails to mention the plagues at all. Friedman also argues that the Levites—and only the Levites—had Egyptian names, such as Moses, Phinehas, Hophni, and Hur. Egyptian influences are clear in other aspects of Israelite material culture, but only among the Levites. According to Professor Michael Homan in *To Your Tents, O Israel*, there is great similarity between the battle tent of Pharaoh Ramses II and the Tabernacle and its surrounding courtyard.
27   Bunimovitz, S. and Faust, A. (2002) "Ideology in stone: Understanding the four-room house," *Biblical Archaeology Review*, 28 (4). Available at: www.academia.edu/1481656/Bunimovitz_S_and_Faust_A_2002_Ideology_in_Stone_ Understanding_the_Four_Room_House_Biblical_Archaeology_Review_ 28_4_32_41_59_60
28   Russell, S.C. (2009) *Images of Egypt in Early Biblical Literature*. Berlin: Walter de Gruyter
29   Sefaria (n.d.) Song of the Sea. Available at: https://www.sefaria.org/topics/song-of-the-sea?sort=Relevance&tab=notable-sources
30   Biblical Archaeology Society (2024) "Exodus: Fact or Fiction?" Available at: https://www.biblicalarchaeology.org/daily/biblical-topics/exodus/exodus-fact-or-fiction/
31   Watanabe, T. (2001) "Doubting the Story of Exodus" *Los Angeles Times*, April 13. Available at: https://www.latimes.com/archives/la-xpm-2001-apr-13-mn-50481-story.html
32   Sefaria (n.d.) Joshua 10:41. Available at: https://www.sefaria.org/Joshua.10.41?lang=bi
33   Dever, W.G. (2003) *Canaan and Israel in Antiquity: A Textbook on History and Religion*. Sheffield: Sheffield Academic Press
34   Sefaria (n.d.) Joshua 6:5. Available at: https://www.sefaria.org/Joshua.6.6?lang=bi
35   van der Plicht, J. and Bruins, H.J. (2001) "Tell es-Sultan (Jericho): Radiocarbon results of short-lived cereal and multi-year charcoal samples from the end of the Middle Bronze Age," *Antiquity*, 75 (287), pp. 666–673. Available at: https://www.cambridge.org/core/journals/radiocarbon/article/tell-essultan-jericho-radiocarbon-results-of-shortlived-cereal-and-multiyear-charcoal-samples-from-the-end-of-the-middle-bronze-age/49BF732173E7890A2B0EC1B21CB6A817

36 Sefaria (n.d.) Joshua 10. Available at: https://www.sefaria.org/Joshua.10?lang=bi
37 Agranat-Tamir, L., Waldman, S., Martin, M.A.S., Gokhman, D., and others (2020) "The genomic history of the Bronze Age Southern Levant," *Cell*, 181 (5). Available at: https://www.cell.com/cell/fulltext/S0092-8674(20)30487-6
38 National Geographic (2020) "DNA from the Bible's Canaanites lives on in modern Arabs and Jews," *National Geographic UK*. Available at: https://www.nationalgeographic.com/premium/article/dna-from-biblical-canaanites-lives-modern-arabs-jews
39 Smith, M.S. (2002) *The Early History of God: Yahweh and the Other Deities in Ancient Israel*. Grand Rapids: William B. Eerdmans Publishing Co.
40 Zevit, Z. (ed.) (2001) *The Religions of Ancient Israel: A Synthesis of Parallactic Approaches*. London: Continuum
41 Biblical Archaeology Society (2023) "The Oldest Hebrew Script and Language," *Biblical Archaeology*. Available at: https://www.biblicalarchaeology.org/daily/biblical-artifacts/inscriptions/the-oldest-hebrew-script-and-language/
42 Buck, M.E. (2019) *The Canaanites: Their History and Culture from Texts and Artifacts*. Series: Cascade Companions. Eugene: Cascade Books
43 Smith, M.S. (2002) *The Early History of God: Yahweh and the Other Deities in Ancient Israel*. Grand Rapids: William B. Eerdmans Publishing Co.
44 Amzallag, N. (2023) "Yahweh and the Origins of Ancient Israel," in *Yahweh and the Origins of Ancient Israel: Insights from the Archaeological Record*. Cambridge: Cambridge University Press
45 Van der Toorn, K. (1996) *Family Religion in Babylonia, Ugarit and Israel: Continuity and Changes in the Forms of Religious Life*. Brill
46 Sefaria (n.d.) Habakkuk 3:7. Available at: https://www.sefaria.org/Habakkuk.3.7?lang=bi&with=all&lang2=en
47 Sefaria (n.d.) Habakkuk 3:3. Available at: https://www.sefaria.org/Habakkuk.3.3?lang=bi
48 Tebes, J.M. (2021) "The Archaeology of Cult of Ancient Israel's Southern Neighbors and the Midianite-Kenite Hypothesis," *Erscheinungsraum*, 12 (2). Available at: https://er.ceres.rub.de/index.php/ER/article/view/8847/8453
49 Sefaria (n.d.) Judges 5:5. Available at: https://www.sefaria.org/Judges.5.5?lang=bi
50 Cline, E.H. (2014) *1177 B.C.: The Year Civilization Collapsed*. Princeton: Princeton University Press
51 Bellows, A. (n.d.) "Mi Chamocha? Who is like you, God?: A look at El, Ba'al and Asherah in Ancient Israel," *Revue Biblique*, Sefaria. Available at: https://www.sefaria.org/sheets/86030?lang=bi
52 Finkelstein, I. and Silberman, N.A. (2001) *The Bible Unearthed: Archaeology's New Vision of Ancient Israel and the Origin of Its Stories*. 1st Touchstone ed. New York: Simon & Schuster
53 Smith, M.S. (2002) *The Early History of God: Yahweh and the Other Deities in Ancient Israel*. Grand Rapids: William B. Eerdmans Publishing Co.
54 Ibid.
55 Sefaria (2024) Exodus 6:3. Available at: https://www.sefaria.org/Exodus.6.3?lang=bi&aliyot=0
56 Smith, M.S. (2002) *The Early History of God: Yahweh and the Other Deities in Ancient Israel*. Grand Rapids: William B. Eerdmans Publishing Co.
57 Edelman, D.V. (ed.) (1995) *The Triumph of Elohim: From Yahwisms to Judaisms*: v.13 (Contributions to Biblical Exegesis & Theology). Kok Pharos Publishing
58 Lemaire, A. (2022) "What Does the Mesha Stele Say?" Available at: https://www.biblicalarchaeology.org/daily/biblical-%20artifacts/inscriptions/what-does-the-mesha-stele-say/

59 Flight, J.W. (1923) "The Nomadic Idea and Ideal in the Old Testament," *Journal of Biblical Literature*, 42 (3/4). [Online] Available at: https://www.jstor.org/stable/3259089?seq=2
60 Ibid.
61 Sefaria (2006) Genesis 46:32 (The Contemporary Torah, Jewish Publication Society). Available at: https://www.sefaria.org/Genesis.46.32?ven=The_Contemporary_Torah,_Jewish_Publication_Society,_2006&lang=bi&with=all&lang2=en
62 Penn Museum (n.d.) "Animals in Canaanite Culture." Available at: www.penn.museum/sites/canaan/Animals.html
63 Kedem (2023) *The Rise and Fall of Ancient Israel—Prof. Israel Finkelstein. Ep4: Rise in the Highlands*. Available at: https://www.youtube.com/watch?v=coIvz4R2Rq4
64 Sefaria (2009) Exodus 6:4 (Metsudah Chumash, Metsudah Publications). Available at: https://www.sefaria.org/Exodus.6.4?lang=bi&with=METSUDAH%20CHUMASH,%20METSUDAH%20PUBLICATIONS,%202009&lang2=en
65 Finkelstein, I. (2013) *The Forgotten Kingdom: The Archaeology and History of Northern Israel*. Atlanta: Society of Biblical Literature
66 Finkelstein, I. and Silberman, N.A. (2001) *The Bible Unearthed: Archaeology's New Vision of Ancient Israel and the Origin of Its Stories*. 1st Touchstone ed. New York: Simon & Schuster
67 Sefaria (n.d.) Deuteronomy 27:13. Available at: https://www.sefaria.org/Deuteronomy.27.13?lang=bi&aliyot=0
68 Thomas, Z. (2022) "Israel's Political and Administrative Structures in the Pre-Monarchic and Monarchic Periods." In: Keimer, K.H. and Pierce, G.A. (eds.) *The Ancient Israelite World*. New York: Routledge
69 Grabbe, L.L. (2022) *The Dawn of Israel: A History of Canaan in the Second Millennium BCE*. London: T&T Clark
70 Ibid.
71 Thomas, Z. (2022) "Israel's Political and Administrative Structures in the Pre-Monarchic and Monarchic Periods," in *The Ancient Israelite World*. 1st edn. London: Routledge
72 Eames, C. and Reinsch, W. (2019) "Moabite Altar Inscription: Earliest Reference to Hebrews," *Armstrong Institute*, September 18. Available at: https://armstronginstitute.org/191-moabite-altar-inscription-earliest-reference-to-hebrews
73 Sefaria (n.d.) Numbers 32:34. Available at: https://www.sefaria.org/Numbers.32.34?lang=bi&aliyot=0
74 Thomas, Z. (2022) "Israel's Political and Administrative Structures in the Pre-Monarchic and Monarchic Periods." In: Keimer, K.H. and Pierce, G.A. (eds.) *The Ancient Israelite World*. New York: Routledge
75 Ibid.
76 Sefaria (n.d.) Genesis 49:5. Available at: https://www.sefaria.org/Genesis.49.5?lang=bi&aliyot=0
77 Sefaria (n.d.) Deuteronomy 33:7. Available at: https://www.sefaria.org/Deuteronomy.33.7?lang=bi&aliyot=0
78 Sefaria (n.d.) Judges 5:16. Available at: https://www.sefaria.org/Judges.5.16?lang=bi
79 Jewish Virtual Library (n.d.) "The Twelve Tribes of Israel." Available at: www.jewishvirtuallibrary.org/the-twelve-tribes-of-israel
80 Grabbe, L.L. (2022) *The Dawn of Israel: A History of Canaan in the Second Millennium BCE*. London: T&T Clark
81 Ibid.
82 Dever, W.G. (2017) *Beyond the Texts: An Archaeological Portrait of Ancient Israel and Judah*. Atlanta: Society of Biblical Literature

83 Sefaria (n.d.) 1 Samuel 8:5. Available at: https://www.sefaria.org/I_Samuel.8.5?ven=Tanakh:_The_Holy_Scriptures,_published_by_JPS&lang=bi&with=all &lang2=en
84 Albright Live (2021) *Episode Nineteen: The Patriarchs: The Jacob Cycle*. Available at: https://www.youtube.com/watch?v=0BDBrAmdOYQ
85 Grabbe, L.L. (2022) *The Dawn of Israel: A History of Canaan in the Second Millennium BCE*. London: T&T Clark
86 Sefaria (n.d.) 2 Kings 3:4. Available at: https://www.sefaria.org/II_Kings.3.4?lang=bi
87 Biblical Archaeology Society (2024) *The Tel Dan Inscription: The First Historical Evidence of the King David Bible Story*. Available at: https://www.biblicalarchaeology.org/daily/biblical-artifacts/the-tel-dan-inscription-the-first-historical-evidence-of-the-king-david-bible-story/
88 Keimer, K.H. (2021) "Evaluating the 'United Monarchy' of Israel: Unity and Identity in Text and Archaeology," *Journal of Jewish Studies*. Available at: https://jjar.huji.ac.il/sites/default/files/jjar/files/keimer_2021_jjar_1_68-101.pdf
89 Ortiz, S.and Wolff, S. (2024) "Solomon's Powerplay: Gezer's Royal Complex Confirmed," *Biblical Archaeology Review*, Summer. Available at: https://library.biblicalarchaeology.org/article/solomons-powerplay-gezers-royal-complex-confirmed
90 Keimer, K.H. (2021) "Evaluating the 'United Monarchy' of Israel: Unity and Identity in Text and Archaeology," *Journal of Jewish Studies*. Available at: https://jjar.huji.ac.il/sites/default/files/jjar/files/keimer_2021_jjar_1_68-101.pdf
91 Finkelstein, I. (2013) *The Forgotten Kingdom: The Archaeology and History of Northern Israel*. Atlanta: Society of Biblical Literature
92 Ibid.
93 Finkelstein, I. (1996) "The Archaeology of the 'United Monarchy': An Alternative View," *Levant*, 28
94 Ibid.
95 Armstrong Institute (n.d.) *New Evidence for King David's Kingdom: An Interview with Prof. Yosef Garfinkel*. Available at: https://armstronginstitute.org/931-newevidence-for-king-davids-kingdom-an-interview-with-prof-yosef-garfinkel
96 Ibid.
97 Keimer, K.H. (2021) "Evaluating the 'United Monarchy' of Israel: Unity and identity in Text and Archaeology", *Journal of Jewish Studies*, pp. 68–101. Available at: https://jjar.huji.ac.il/sites/default/files/jjar/files/keimer_2021_jjar_1_68-101.pdf
98 Armstrong Institute (n.d.) *New Evidence for King David's Kingdom: An Interview with Prof. Yosef Garfinkel*. Available at: https://armstronginstitute.org/931-newevidence-for-king-davids-kingdom-an-interview-with-prof-yosef-garfinkel
99 Ibid.
100 Ibid.
101 Ibid.
102 Ibid.
103 Ibid.
104 Ibid.
105 Margalit, R. (2020) "In Search of King David's Lost Empire," *The New Yorker*, June 22. Available at: of-king-davids-lost-empire?utm_source=twitter&utm_medium=social&utm_campaign=onsite-share&utm_brand=the-new-yorker&utm_social-type=earned
106 David, A. (2023) "Israeli Archaeologist Claims He Has Found David's Kingdom, but Fellow Researchers Cry Foul," *Haaretz*, July 4. Available at: https://www.haaretz.com/archaeology/2023-07-04/ty-article-magazine/israeli-archaeologist-claims-hehas-found-davids-kingdom-but-fellow-researchers-cry-foul/00000189-2015-d145a1e9-3377458a0000

107 Finkelstein, I. (2003) *One God – One Cult – One Nation: Archaeological and Biblical Perspectives*. Available at: https://israelfinkelstein.wordpress.com/wp-content/uploads/2013/07/um-one-god-one-cult-book.pdf
108 Amihai Mazar (ed.) (2001) "Jerusalem in the Tenth and Seventh Centuries BCE: From Administrative Town to Commercial City," *Studies in the Archaeology of the Iron Age in Israel and Jordan*. JSOTSup, 331; Sheffield: Sheffield Academic Press), pp. 280–88
109 Grabbe, L.L. (2017) *Ancient Israel: What Do We Know and How Do We Know It?* Revised Edition. London: Continuum-3PL
110 Cahill, J.M. (2003) "Jerusalem at the Time of the United Monarchy: The Archaeological Evidence." In: Vaughn, A.G. and Killebrew, A.E. (eds.) *Jerusalem in Bible and Archaeology: The First Temple Period*. Atlanta: Society of Biblical Literature
111 Mazar, E. (2024) "Did I Find King David's Palace?", *Biblical Archaeology Society*, May 11. Available at: https://www.biblicalarchaeology.org/daily/biblical-topics/hebrew-bible/did-i-find-king-davids-palace/
112 Ibid.
113 Fox, R.G. (1977) *Urban Anthropology: Cities in Their Cultural Settings*. Englewood Cliffs: Prentice-Hall
114 Thomas, Z. (2022) "Israel's Political and Administrative Structures in the Pre-Monarchic and Monarchic Periods." In: Keimer, K.H. and Pierce, G.A. (eds.) *The Ancient Israelite World*. London: Routledge
115 Barbosa, L. (2021) "The two concepts of patrimonialism in Max Weber: From the domestic model to the organizational model," *Sociologia & Antropologia*, 11(2)
116 Thomas, Z. (2022) "Israel's Political and Administrative Structures in the Pre-Monarchic and Monarchic Periods." In: Keimer, K.H. and Pierce, G.A. (eds.) *The Ancient Israelite World*. London: Routledge
117 Keimer, K.H. (2021) "Evaluating the 'United Monarchy' of Israel: Unity and Identity in Text and Archaeology," *Journal of Jewish Studies*. Available at: https://jjar.huji.ac.il/sites/default/files/jjar/files/keimer_2021_jjar_1_68-101.pdf
118 Ibid.

Chapter 2

1 Sefaria (n.d.) I Kings 11:4. Available at: https://www.sefaria.org/I_Kings.11.4?lang=bi&with=all&lang2=en
2 Sefaria (n.d.) I Kings 12:4. Available at: https://www.sefaria.org/I_Kings.12.4?lang=bi&with=all&lang2=en
3 Sefaria (n.d.) I Kings 12:10. Available at: https://www.sefaria.org/I_Kings.12.10?lang=bi
4 Römer, T.C. (ed.) (2020) *Saul, Benjamin, and the Emergence of Monarchy in Israel*. Atlanta: SBL Press
5 Hasegawa, S., Levin, C. and Radner, K. (eds.) (2018) *The Last Days of the Kingdom of Israel*. Berlin: Walter de Gruyter GmbH & Co KG
6 Finkelstein, I. (2008) *The Forgotten Kingdom: The Archaeology and History of Northern Israel*. Atlanta: Society of Biblical Literature
7 Broshi, M. and Finkelstein, I. (1992) "The Population of Palestine in Iron Age II," *BASOR* 287: 47–60. BASOR
8 Finkelstein, I. (2008) *The Forgotten Kingdom: The Archaeology and History of Northern Israel*. Atlanta: Society of Biblical Literature

9 Finkelstein, I. (2006) "The Last Labayu: King Saul and the expansion of the first North Israelite territorial entity." In: Amit, Y., Ben Zvi, E., Finkelstein, I. and Lipschits, O. (eds.) *Essays on Ancient Israel in its Near Eastern Context: A Tribute to Nadav Na'aman.* Winona Lake: Eisenbrauns

10 Edelman, D. (1996) "Saul ben Kish in History and Tradition." In: Fritz, F. and Davies, P.R. (eds.) *The Origins of the Ancient Israelite States.* JSOTSup 228. Sheffield: Sheffield Academic Press

11 Sefaria(n.d.) I Kings 14:26. Available at: https://www.sefaria.org/I_Kings.14.26?lang=bi

12 Finkelstein, I. and Na'aman, N. (2005) "Shechem of the Amarna period and the rise of the Northern Kingdom of Israel," *Israel Exploration Journal*, 55(2). Available at: http://www.jstor.org/stable/27927106

13 Sefaria (n.d.) I Kings 11:26. Available at: https://www.sefaria.org/I_Kings.11.26?lang=bi

14 Sefaria (n.d.) I Kings 15:28. Available at: https://www.sefaria.org/I_Kings.15.28?lang=bi

15 Sauter, M. (2024) "The palace of the kings of Israel—in the Bible and Archaeology: Samaria's Iron Age Palace," *Biblical Archaeology Review*, March 19. Available at: https://www.biblicalarchaeology.org/daily/biblical-sites-places/biblical-archaeology-sites/the-palace-of-the-kings-of-israel-in-the-bible-and-archaeology/

16 Sergi, O. and Gadot, Y. (n.d.) "Omride Palatial Architecture as Symbol in Action: Between State Formation, Obliteration, and Heritage," *Journal of Near Eastern Studies.* Available at: https://www.journals.uchicago.edu/doi/full/10.1086/690651

17 Nagtegaal, B. (2020) "Naboth's Vineyard Found in Jezreel? Archaeologists have uncovered an ancient winery connected to Naboth's vineyard," *Armstrong Institute*, July 21. Available at: https://armstronginstitute.org/267-naboths-vineyard-found-in-jezreel

18 Niccacci, A. (1994) "The Stele of Mesha and the Bible: Verbal system and narrativity," *Orientalia*, 63(3). Available at: http://www.jstor.org/stable/43076168

19 Naveh, J. (1963) "Old Hebrew inscriptions in a burial cave," *Israel Exploration Journal*, 13(2)

20 Hadley, J.M. (1987) "The Khirbet El-Qom inscription," *Vetus Testamentum*, 37(1). Available at: https://doi.org/10.2307/1517810

21 Davies, P.R. (2015) *The History of Ancient Israel: A Guide for the Perplexed.* London: T&T Clark

22 Ibid.

23 Ngo, R. (2024) "10 things to know about the Assyrian Empire: Who were the Assyrians?" *Biblical Archaeology Review*, July 21. Available at: https://www.biblicalarchaeology.org/daily/ancient-cultures/ancient-near-eastern-world/10-things-to-know-about-the-assyrian-empire/

24 Davies, P.R. (2015) *The History of Ancient Israel: A Guide for the Perplexed.* London: T&T Clark

25 Ibid.

26 Ibid.

27 Center for Online Judaic Studies (n.d.) *Tel Dan Stele: c. 840 BCE.* Available at: https://cojs.org/tel_dan_stele-_c-_840_bce/

28 Alanne, M. (2017) "Tel Dan – Biblical Dan: An Archaeological and Biblical Study of the City of Dan from the Iron Age II to the Hellenistic Period." Available at: https://core.ac.uk/download/pdf/84363234.pdf

29 Miller, J.M. and Hayes, J.H. (2006) *History of Ancient Israel and Judah.* London: SCM Press

30 Baker, H.D. (2023) "The Assyrian Empire: A view from within". In: Radner, K., Moeller, N. and Potts, D.T. (eds.) *The Oxford History of the Ancient Near East Volume IV: The Age of Assyria.* New York: Oxford University Press (online edn. Oxford Academic, March 23, 2023). Available at: https://doi.org/10.1093/oso/9780190687632.003.0038

NOTES

31 Sefaria (n.d.) II Kings 16:3. Available at: https://www.sefaria.org/II_Kings.16.3?lang=bi&with=all&lang2=en
32 Sefaria (n.d.) II Kings 16:7. Available at: https://www.sefaria.org/II_Kings.16.7?lang=bi&with=all&lang2=en
33 Sefaria (n.d.) II Kings 17:6. Available at: https://www.sefaria.org/II_Kings.17.6?lang=bi&with=all&lang2=en
34 Sefaria (n.d.) II Kings 17:9. Available at: https://www.sefaria.org/II_Kings.17.9?lang=bi&with=all&lang2=en
35 Finkelstein, I. and Silberman, N. A. (2001) *The Bible Unearthed: Archaeology's New Vision of Ancient Israel*. New York: Free Press
36 Although archeologist Nadav Na'aman disagrees.
37 Sefaria (n.d.) II Chronicles 31:8. Available at: https://www.sefaria.org/II_Chronicles.31.8?lang=bi
38 Borschel-Dan, A. (2017) "Jerusalem welcomed Jewish refugees 2,700 years ago, new finds show," *Times of Israel*, September 4. Available at: https://www.timesofisrael.com/jerusalem-welcomed-jewish-refugees-2300-years-ago-archaeological-finds-show/
39 Finkelstein, I. (2015) "Migration of Israelites into Judah after 720 BCE: An Answer and an Update," *Zeitschrift für die alttestamentliche Wissenschaft*, Vol. 127 (Issue 2). Available at: https://doi.org/10.1515/zaw-2015-0011
40 Mazar, A. (2010) "Archaeology and the Biblical Narrative: The Case of the United Monarchy," in *One God – One Cult – One Nation*. Available at: www.academia.edu/2503754/Archaeology_and_the_Biblical_Narrative_the_Case_of_the_United_Monarchy_2010_0
41 Na'aman, N. (2019) "Samaria and Judah in an Early Eighth-Century Assyrian Wine List," *Tel Aviv*, 46
42 Gilad, E. (2017) "Why are Jews called Jews?," *Haaretz*, February 15. Available at: jews/0000017f-dbeb-d856-a37f-ffeb3f760000
43 Deutsch, R. (n.d.) "First Impression: What We Learn from King Ahaz's Seal," *Archaeological Center*. Available at: https://web.archive.org/web/20170922075154/http://www.archaeological-center.com/en/monographs/m1/
44 Eisenbud, D.K. (2015) "First-ever seal impression of an Israelite or Judean king exposed near Temple Mount," *Jerusalem Post*, December 2. Available at: www.jpost.com/Israel-News/Culture/First-ever-seal-impression-of-an-Israelite-or-Judeanking-exposed-near-Temple-Mount-436061
45 Finkelstein, I. (2008) *The Forgotten Kingdom: The Archaeology and History of Northern Israel*. Atlanta: Society of Biblical Literature
46 Finkelstein, I. (2001) "The rise of Jerusalem and Judah: The missing link," *Levant*, 33
47 Ibid.
48 Garfinkel, Y. (2023) "The 10th century BCE in Judah: Archaeology and the Biblical Tradition". In: Faust, A., Garfinkel, Y. and Mumcuoglu, M. (eds.) "State formation processes in the 10th century BCE Levant," *Jerusalem Journal of Archaeology*, 1. Available at: https://jjar.huji.ac.il/sites/default/files/jjar/files/garfinkel_2021_jjar_1_126-154.pdf
49 Bible Archaeology.org (n.d.) *Akkadian document from 14th century BCE discovered in Jerusalem*. Available at: akkadian-document-from-14th-century-bc-discovered-in-jerusalem
50 Ibid.
51 Ngo, R. (2023) "King David's Palace and the Millo," *Biblical Archaeology Review*, January 14. Available at: https://www.biblicalarchaeology.org/daily/biblical-sites-places/jerusalem/king-davids-palace-and-the-millo/
52 Armstrong Institute (2022) *Let the Stones Speak*. September-October, Volume 1, No. 5. Available at: https://armstronginstitute.org/magazine_issues/5

53 Na'aman, N. (2007) "When and How Did Jerusalem Become a Great City? The Rise of Jerusalem as Judah's Premier City in the Eighth-Seventh Centuries B.C.E.," *Bulletin of the American Schools of Oriental Research*, 347, pp. 21–56. Available at: https://www.academia.edu/11658784/When_and_How_Did_Jerusalem_Become_a_Great_City_The_Rise_of_Jerusalem_as_Judahs_Premier_City_in_the_Eighth_Seventh_Centuries_B_C_E_BASOR_347_2007_pp_21_56
54 i24news (2024) "Breakthrough study dates First Temple period findings in Jerusalem." Available at: https://www.i24news.tv/en/news/israel/archeology/artc-breakthrough-study-dates-first-temple-period-findings-in-jerusalem
55 Na'aman, N. (2019) "Samaria and Judah in an early 8th-century Assyrian wine list." *Tel Aviv*, 46(1). Available at: https://doi.org/10.1080/03344355.2019.1586380
56 Ibid.
57 Although this is disputed by Nadam Na'aman.
58 Finkelstein, I. (2001) "The rise of Jerusalem and Judah: The missing link," *Levant*, 33
59 Coogan, M. (2008) "Hezekiah and Sennacherib: another deep probe." In *The Old Testament: A Very Short Introduction*. Very Short Introductions. New York: Oxford University Press. Online edn. Oxford Academic, September 24. Available at: https://doi.org/10.1093/actrade/9780195305050.003.0009
60 National Geographic Education (n.d.) "Water works." Available at: https://education.nationalgeographic.org/resource/water-works/
61 Deutsch, R. (1999) *Messages from the past*. Tel Aviv: Archaeological Center Publications
62 Lubetski, M. (2001) "King Hezekiah's seal revisited: Small object reflects big geopolitics," *Biblical Archaeology Review*, July/August. Available at: https://library.biblicalarchaeology.org/article/king-hezekiahs-seal-revisited/
63 Fridman, J. (2016) "Hezekiah Seal Proves Ancient Jerusalem was a Major Judahite Capital," *Haaretz*, January 4. Available at: https://www.haaretz.com/archaeology/2016-01-04/ty-article/what-the-hezekiah-seal-proves-jerusalemstatus/0000017f-ef78-df98-a5ff-effd370b0000
64 Amir, A., Finkelstein, I., Shalev, Y., Uziel, J., Chalaf, O., Freud, L., Neumann, R., and Gadot, Y. (2022) "Residue analysis evidence for wine enriched with vanilla consumed in Jerusalem on the eve of the Babylonian destruction in 586 BCE," *PLoS One*, 17(3), p.e0266085. Available at: https://doi.org/10.1371/journal.pone.0266085
65 Van De Mieroop, M. (2017) "The sack of Nineveh in 612." In: Petit, L. and Morandi Bonacossi, D. (eds.) *Nineveh: The Great City. Symbol of Beauty and Power*. Leiden: Dutch National Museum of Antiquities, pp. 243–247. Available at: https://www.academia.edu/35268906/2017_The_sack_of_Nineveh_in_612_Nineveh_The_Great_City_Symbol_of_Beauty_and_Power_edited_by_Lucas_Petit_and_Daniele_Morandi_Bonacossi_Leiden_Dutch_National_Museum_of_Antiquities_2017_243_247
66 Josiah is said to be responsible for the evolution of ancient Israelite monotheism when he enacted reforms which banned the worship of other gods.
67 Bible Archaeology.org (n.d.) *Megiddo: The Place of Battles*. Available at: https://biblearchaeology.org/research/conquest-of-canaan/3084-megiddo-the-place-of-battles?highlight=WyJqb3NpYWgiLCJqb3NpYWgncyJd
68 New World Encyclopedia (n.d.) *Jehoiakim*. Available at: https://www.newworldencyclopedia.org/entry/Jehoiakim
69 Albright Live, Finkelstein, I. (2021) *Episode Twenty-five: Persian and Early Hellenistic Jerusalem*. Available at: https://www.youtube.com/watch?v=qwGq7-35VGQ
70 Sefaria (n.d.) II Kings 24:17. Available at: https://www.sefaria.org/II_Kings.24.17?lang=bi
71 British Museum (n.d.) *Object W_1896-0409-51*. Available at: www.britishmuseum.org/collection/object/W_1896-0409-51

72 Sefaria (n.d.) II Kings 24:13. Available at: https://www.sefaria.org/II_Kings.24.13?lang=bi
73 Sefaria (n.d.) Jeremiah 50:17. Available at: https://www.sefaria.org/Jeremiah.50.17?lang=en
74 Sefaria (n.d.) II Kings 24:18. Available at: https://www.sefaria.org/II_Kings.24.18?lang=bi
75 Sefaria (n.d.) II Kings 25:3. Available at: https://www.sefaria.org/II_Kings.25.3?lang=bi&with=all&lang2=en
76 Lee, L. (2016) *Mapping Judah's fate in Ezekiel's oracles against the nations*. Documento de investigación. Centro de Estudios de Historia del Antiguo Oriente, Facultad de Ciencias Sociales, Society of Biblical Literature. Available at: https://www.sbl-site.org/assets/pdfs/pubs/9780884141808_0a.pdf
77 Sefaria (n.d.) II Kings 24:18. Available at: https://www.sefaria.org/II_Kings. 24.18?lang=bi
78 Sefaria (n.d.) II Kings 25:9. Available at: https://www.sefaria.org/II_Kings.25.9?lang=bi&with=all&lang2=en
79 Amir, A., Finkelstein, I., Shalev, Y., Uziel, J., Chalaf, O., Freud, L., Neumann, R. and Gadot, Y. (2022) "Residue analysis evidence for wine enriched with vanilla consumed in Jerusalem on the eve of the Babylonian destruction in 586 BCE," *PLoS One*, 17(3), p.e0266085. doi: 10.1371/journal.pone.0266085. PMID: 35349581; PMCID: PMC8963535
80 Judahites in rural areas and in some cities such as Mizpah (which may have replaced Jerusalem as the centre of worship until the return to Zion) remained even after the exile.
81 Sefaria (n.d.) II Kings 25. Available at: https://www.sefaria.org/II_Kings.25?lang=bi
82 Lipschits, O. (2005) *The Fall and Rise of Jerusalem: Judah under Babylonian Rule*. University Park: Penn State University Press. Available at: https://doi.org/10.5325/j. ctv1bxh5fd
83 New World Encyclopedia (n.d.) *Gedaliah*. Available at: https://www.newworld encyclopedia.org/entry/Gedaliah
84 Ibid.
85 Satlow, M.L. (2014) "The Second Commonwealth: Babylonia, Persia, and Yehud, 586–520 BCE." In: *How the Bible Became Holy*. New Haven: Yale University Press. Available at: https://doi.org/10.12987/9780300206852-006
86 Sefaria (n.d.) Psalms 137. Available at: https://www.sefaria.org/Psalms.137?lang=bi
87 Fishman-Duker, R. (2019) "The Cyrus debate ironically confirms the truth of Jewish history in Jerusalem," Jerusalem Center for Security and Foreign Affairs (JCFA), November 3. Available at: https://jcpa.org/the-cyrus-debate-ironically-confirmsthe-truth-of-jewish-history-in-jerusalem/
88 Satlow, M.L. (2014) "The Second Commonwealth: Babylonia, Persia, and Yehud, 586–520 BCE." In: *How the Bible Became Holy*. New Haven: Yale University Press. Available at: https://doi.org/10.12987/9780300206852-006
89 Adler, Y. (2020) "The Archaeology of Second Temple Judaism." In: Klawans, J. and Wills, L.M. (eds.) *The Jewish Annotated Apocrypha*. Oxford: Oxford University Press
90 Albright Live, Finkelstein, I. (2021) *Episode Nineteen: The Patriarchs: The Jacob Cycle*. Available at: https://www.youtube.com/watch?v=0BDBrAmdOYQ
91 Sefaria (n.d.) II Kings 22:8. Available at: https://www.sefaria.org/II_Kings.22.8?lang=bi&with=all&lang2=en
92 Sefaria (n.d.) II Kings 22:8. Available at: https://www.sefaria.org/II_Kings.22.8?vhe=Tanach_with_Ta%27amei_Hamikra&lang=en&with=Topics&lang2=he
93 Leith, M.J. (2020) "New perspectives on the return from exile and Persian-period Yehud". In: Kelle, B.E. and Strawn, B.A. (eds.) *The Oxford Handbook of the Historical Books of the Hebrew Bible*. Oxford: Oxford University Press
94 Albright Live, Finkelstein, I. (2021) *Episode Nineteen: The Patriarchs: The Jacob Cycle*. Available at: https://www.youtube.com/watch?v=0BDBrAmdOYQ

95 Leith, M.J. (2020) "New perspectives on the return from exile and Persian-period Yehud." In: Kelle, B.E. and Strawn, B.A. (eds.) *The Oxford Handbook of the Historical Books of the Hebrew Bible.* Oxford: Oxford University Press

96 Schama, S. (2014) *The Story of the Jews: Finding the Words (1000 BCE–1492 CE).* London: Vintage

97 Ibid.

98 Ibid.

99 Albright Live, Finkelstein, I. (2021) *Episode Nineteen: The Patriarchs: The Jacob Cycle.* Available at: https://www.youtube.com/watch?v=oBDBrAmdOYQ

100 Sefaria (n.d.) II Chronicles 33:9. Available at: https://www.sefaria.org/II_Chronicles.33.9?lang=bi&with=all&lang2=en

101 Barber, M. (2006) *Loose Canons: The Development of the Old Testament (Part 1).* Available at: https://www.catholicfidelity.com/apologetics-topics/bible/old-testament-canon-by-michael-barber/

102 Josephus, F. (n.d.) *Against Apion.* Translated by W. Whiston. Available at: https://www.gutenberg.org/files/2849/2849-h/2849-h.htm#link2H_4_0001

103 Satlow, M.L. (2014) *How the Bible became holy.* New Haven: Yale University Press. Available at: http://www.jstor.org/stable/j.ctt5vm45s

104 Ibid.

105 Coogan, M.D. (ed.) (1999) *The Oxford History of the Biblical World.* New York: OUP USA

106 Berlejung, A. (n.d.) *New life, new skills, and new friends in exile: The loss and rise of capitals of the Judeans in Babylonia.* Available at: https://www.academia.edu/31965367/NEW_LIFE_NEW_SKILLS_AND_NEW_FRIENDS_IN_EXILE_THE_LOSS_AND_RISE_OF_CAPITALS_OF_THE_JUDEANS_IN_BABYLONIA

107 Ibid.

108 Pearce, L.E. (2016) "How bad was the Babylonian exile?", *Biblical Archaeology Review,* September/October. Available at: https://library.biblicalarchaeology.org/article/how-bad-was-the-babylonian-exile/

109 Ibid.

110 Ibid.

111 We are able to identify these individuals as Judahites through their names. Their names are considered to be Yahwistic, which have the ending of "yah" or "iah," so Josiah, Isaiah, or Hezekiah as examples.

112 Pearce, L.E. (2016) "How bad was the Babylonian exile?", *Biblical Archaeology Review,* September/October. Available at: https://library.biblicalarchaeology.org/article/how-bad-was-the-babylonian-exile/

113 Ibid.

114 Sefaria (n.d.) II Chronicles 36:19. Available at: https://www.sefaria.org/II_Chronicles.36.19?lang=bi

115 Sefaria (n.d.) Lamentations 1:5. Available at: https://www.sefaria.org/Lamentations.1.5?lang=bi

116 Leith, M.J. (2020) "New perspectives on the return from exile and Persian-period Yehud". In: Kelle, B.E. and Strawn, B.A. (eds.) *The Oxford Handbook of the Historical Books of the Hebrew Bible.* Oxford: Oxford University Press

117 Kelle, B.E. and Strawn, B.A. (eds.) (2020) *The Oxford Handbook of the Historical Books of the Hebrew Bible.* Online edn. Oxford Academic, Nov 10, 2020. Available at: https://doi.org/10.1093/oxfordhb/9780190261160.001.0001

Chapter 3

1. Farrokh, K. (2015) "Israel Post issues Cyrus Declaration stamp," April 16. Available at: https://www.kavehfarrokh.com/news/israel-post-issues-cyrus-declaration-stamp/
2. Becking, B. (2006) "We all returned as one!": Critical notes on the myth of the mass return". In: Lipschits, O. and Oeming, M. (eds.) *Judah and the Judeans in the Persian Period*. University Park, U.S.A: Penn State University Press, pp. 1–18. Available at: https://doi.org/10.1515/9781575065618-003
3. Sefaria (n.d.) II Chronicles 36:23. [online] Available at: https://www.sefaria.org/II_Chronicles.36.23?lang=bi
4. Sefaria (n.d.) II Chronicles 36:23. [online] Available at: https://www.sefaria.org/II_Chronicles.36.23?lang=bi
5. Hess, R., Klingbeil, G.A. and Ray Jr., P.J. (eds.) (2008) "The Persian Period and the Origins of Israel: Beyond the 'Myths'". In: *Critical Issues in Early Israelite History*. Winona Lake, IN: Eisenbrauns
6. Encyclopaedia Iranica (n.d.) "Jerusalem and Iran," *Encyclopaedia Iranica*. Available at: https://www.iranicaonline.org/articles/jerusalem-and-iran
7. Garsiel, M. (1999) "The Crisis of Israelite Religion: Transformation of Religious Tradition in Exilic and Post-Exilic Times," *Oudtestamentische Studiën*, 42. Leiden: Brill
8. Ibid.
9. Satlow, M. (2014) "The Second Commonwealth: Babylonia, Persia, and Yehud, 586–520 BCE." In: *How the Bible Became Holy*. New Haven: Yale University Press, pp. 52–68. Available at: https://doi.org/10.12987/9780300206852-006
10. Schama, S. (2014) *The Story of the Jews: Finding the Words (1000 BCE–1492 CE)*. London: Vintage
11. Friends of the Israel Antiquities Authority (2020) "A seal and a seal impression discovered in the City of David bears witness to the restoration of the city in the period of Ezra and Nehemiah," *Friends of the IAA*. June 30. Available at: www.friendsofiaa.org/news/2020/6/30/a-seal-and-a-seal-impression-discovered-in-the-city-of-david-bears-witness-to-the-restoration-of-the-city-in-the-period-of-ezra-and-nehemiah
12. Leith, M.J. (2020) "New perspectives on the return from exile and Persian-period Yehud." In: Kelle, B.E. and Strawn, B.A. (eds.) *The Oxford Handbook of the Historical Books of the Hebrew Bible*. Oxford: Oxford University Press
13. Lipschits, O. (2009) "Persian Period Finds from Jerusalem: Facts and Interpretations," *The Journal of Hebrew Scriptures*, 9(20). Available at: https://jhsonline.org/index.php/jhs/article/view/7232
14. Sefaria (n.d.) Ezra 10:3. Available at: https://www.sefaria.org/Ezra.10.3?lang=bi&with=all&lang2=en
15. Leith, M.J. (2020) "New Perspectives on the Return from Exile and Persian-period Yehud". In: Kelle, B.E. and Strawn, B.A. (eds.) *The Oxford Handbook of the Historical Books of the Hebrew Bible*. Oxford: Oxford University Press
16. Ibid.
17. Sefaria (n.d.) Ruth 1:16. Available at: https://www.sefaria.org/Ruth.1.16?ven=Tanakh:_The_Holy_Scriptures,_published_by_JPS&lang=bi&with=all&lang2=en
18. Segal, B. (2021) "The Book of Ruth: The tale of King David's ancestry is a taste of perfection", *The Jerusalem Post*. Available at: holidays/the-book-of-ruth-the-tale-of-king-davids-ancestry-is-a-taste-of-perfection-668028
19. Sefaria (n.d.) Nehemiah 1:1. Available at: https://www.sefaria.org/Nehemiah.1.1? lang=bi
20. Shanks, H. (2024) *Ancient Jerusalem. Biblical Archaeology*. Available at: www.biblicalarchaeology.org/daily/biblical-sites-places/jerusalem/ancient-jerusalem/

21 Albright Live, Finkelstein, I. (2024) *Episode Twenty-five: Persian and Early Hellenistic Jerusalem*. Available at: https://www.youtube.com/watch?v=[Video_ID]
22 Harvard Divinity School (n.d.) *Destruction of the Second Temple (70 CE)*. Available at: https://rpl.hds.harvard.edu/faq/destruction-second-temple-70-ce
23 Sefaria (n.d.) Ezra 3:12. Available at: https://www.sefaria.org/Ezra.3.12?lang=bi&with=all&lang2=en
24 Wyssmann, P. (2014) "The coinage imagery of Samaria and Judah in the late Persian period." In: Frevel, C. et al. (eds.) *A "Religious Revolution" in Yehûd? The Material Culture of the Persian Period as a Test Case."* Orbis Biblicus et Orientalis, 267. Fribourg/Göttingen: Academic Press
25 Josephus, F. (n.d.) *Antiquities of the Jews*, Book 11. Available at: https://penelope.uchicago.edu/josephus/ant-11.html
26 Rose, J. (n.d.) *The "Persian" Period*. Oxford Bibliographies. Available at: www.oxfordbibliographies.com/display/document/obo-9780195393361/obo-9780195393361-0194.xml
27 Jewish History (n.d.) *Alexander the Great*. Available at: https://www.jewishhistory.org/alexander-the-great/
28 Encyclopædia Britannica, Inc (n.d.) "From Alexander the Great to 70 CE," *Encyclopædia Britannica*. Available at: https://www.britannica.com/place/Palestine/From-Alexander-the-Great-to-70-ce
29 Encyclopædia Britannica, Inc (n.d.) "Alexander the Great," *Encyclopædia Britannica*. Available at: https://www.britannica.com/biography/Alexander-the-Great
30 Encyclopædia Britannica, Inc (n.d.) "Ptolemy I Soter," *Encyclopædia Britannica*. Available at: https://www.britannica.com/biography/Ptolemy-I-Soter
31 Encyclopædia Britannica, Inc (n.d.) "Seleucus I Nicator," *Encyclopædia Britannica*. Available at: https://www.britannica.com/biography/Seleucus-I-Nicator
32 University of Michigan Library (n.d.) "Zenon Archive." Available at: https://apps.lib.umich.edu/reading/Zenon/index.html
33 Finkelstein, I. (2010) "The territorial extent and demography of Yehud/Judea in the Persian and early Hellenistic periods," *Revue Biblique*, 117(1). Available at: http://www.jstor.org/stable/44090976
34 Sefaria (n.d.) Jerusalem Talmud Avodah Zarah 2:2:12. Available at: www.sefaria.org/Jerusalem_Talmud_Avodah_Zarah.2.2.12?lang=bi
35 LeFebvre, M. (2019) *Collections, Codes, and Torah: The Re-characterization of Israel's Written Law*. Bloomsbury
36 Reinhard, G. and Kratz, G. (2016) "The Books of the Hebrew Bible." In: Kurtz, P.M. (ed.) *Historical and Biblical Israel: The History, Tradition, and Archives of Israel and Judah*. Oxford: Oxford University Press. Available at: https://doi.org/10.1093/acprof:oso/9780198728771.003.0008
37 Biblical Cyclopedia (n.d.) "Alexandria: Jews," *Biblical Cyclopedia*. Available at: https://www.biblicalcyclopedia.com/A/alexandria-jews-in.html
38 Encyclopædia Britannica, Inc (n.d.) "Septuagint," *Encyclopædia Britannica*. Available at: https://www.britannica.com/topic/Septuagint
39 Ross, W.A. (2021) "The most important Bible translation you've never heard of," *Text and Canon*. Available at: https://textandcanon.org/the-most-important-bible-translation-youve-never-heard-of/
40 Wright, B. (2015) *The Letter of Aristeas: "Aristeas to Philocrates" or "On the Translation of the Law of the Jews."* Berlin, München, Boston: De Gruyter. Available at: https://doi.org/10.1515/9783110431346
41 Aristeas (n.d.) *The Letter of Aristeas to Philocrates: Sections 1 to 182*. Translated by Charles, R.H. (1913). Available at: https://www.attalus.org/translate/aristeas1.html

NOTES

42 Bible.ca (n.d.) "Alexandria Great Basilica Colonnaded: Ancient Synagogues of Alexandria," *Bible.ca*. Available at: https://www.bible.ca/synagogues/Alexandria-Great-Basilica-Colonnaded-Egypt-ancient-synagogues-first-century-oldest-pre70AD-archeology-top-plan-double-columns-71-gold-chairs-Philo-Talmud-280bc

43 Van der Horst, P.W. (2002) "The first pogrom: Alexandria 38 CE," *European Review*, 10(4). doi:10.1017/S1062798702000388

44 The Metropolitan Museum of Art (n.d.) *The Seleucid Empire. The Metropolitan Museum of Art*. Available at: https://www.metmuseum.org/essays/the-seleucid-empire-323-64-b-c

45 Rooke, D.W. (2003) *The Hasmonean Dynasty: John Hyrcanus and His Successors*. In: *Zadok's Heirs: The Role and Development of the High Priesthood in Ancient Israel*. Oxford: Oxford University Press. Available at: https://doi.org/10.1093/0198269986.003.0013

46 Ginzberg, L. (n.d.) "Antiochus III the Great." *Jewish Encyclopedia*. Available at: https://www.jewishencyclopedia.com/articles/1588-antiochus-iii-the-great

47 However, from 192–188 BCE, Rome and the Seleucids fought the Aetolian war, which resulted in the submission of the Seleucid Empire to Rome. It resulted in the handover of all Seleucid territories in Europe and west of the Taurus Mountains in Turkey. In response, the weakened Antiochus would try and maintain his grip over the Eastern part of his empire, until Rome—and the Parthians—also encroached on that.

48 Gruen, E.S. (2016) *The Construct of Identity in Hellenistic Judaism: Essays on Early Jewish Literature and History*. 1st edn. Berlin: De Gruyter. Available at: www.jstor.org/stable/j.ctvbkjxph

49 Ibid.

50 Schwartz, D.R. (2023) *Judea versus Judaism: Between 1 and 2 Maccabees. The Torah*. Available at: 2-maccabees

51 Ibid.

52 Ibid.

53 Ibid.

54 Liddell, H.G. and Scott, R. (n.d.) *An Intermediate Greek-English Lexicon*. Available at: https://archive.org/details/intermediategree002716mbp/page/n7/mode/2up

55 Meaning "Hellenism," which had previously been in reference to a language. Maccabees II, however, referred to it in a new, more holistic way.

56 Gruen, E.S. (2016) "Hellenism and Persecution: Antiochus IV and the Jews." In *The Construct of Identity in Hellenistic Judaism: Essays on Early Jewish Literature and History*. De Gruyter. Available at: https://www.jstor.org/stable/j.ctvbkjxph.2

57 Gruen, E.S. (1993) "Hellenism and Persecution: Antiochus IV and the Jews." In Green, P. (ed.) *Hellenistic History and Culture*. University of California Press

58 Ibid.

59 Josephus, F. (n.d.) *Antiquities of the Jews 12.237–12.264*. Translated by Whiston, W. Available at: https://lexundria.com/j_aj/12.237-12.264/wst

60 A significant part of Greek society. Men would gather together and exercise in the gymnasium, but also it was a social and business environment. All activities were done naked. This caused Jewish men to engage in epispasm (reversal of circumcision) as the Greeks looked down on circumcision, and to enter the gymnasium and take part in Greek society, Jewish men tried to reverse their circumcisions to be accepted.

61 Gruen, E.S. (1993) "Hellenism and Persecution: Antiochus IV and the Jews." In Green, P. (ed.) *Hellenistic History and Culture*. University of California Press

62 Ibid.

63 Sefaria (n.d.) The Book of Maccabees II 4:48. Available at: https://www.sefaria.org/The_Book_of_Maccabees_II.4.48?lang=bi

64 Gruen, E.S. (2016) "Hellenistic Judaism." In *Hellenistic Judaism: Essays on Early Jewish Literature and History*. pp. 333–358. Available at: https://www.jstor.org/stable/j.ctvbkjxph.20

65 Mittag, P.F. (2019) "Chapter 6: Antiochus IV Epiphanes's Policy towards the Jews." In *Intolerance, Polemics, and Debate in Antiquity*. Available at: https://doi.org/10.1163/9789004411500_008

66 Gruen, E.S. (1993) "Hellenism and Persecution: Antiochus IV and the Jews." In Green, P. (ed.) *Hellenistic History and Culture*. University of California Press

67 Sefaria (n.d.) The Book of Maccabees II. Available at: https://www.sefaria.org/The_Book_of_Maccabees_II?tab=contents

68 Ibid.

69 Ibid.

70 Sefaria (n.d.) The Book of Maccabees II 5:5. Available at: https://www.sefaria.org/The_Book_of_Maccabees_II.5.5?lang=bi

71 Gruen, E.S. (1993) "Hellenism and Persecution: Antiochus IV and the Jews." In Green, P. (ed.) *Hellenistic History and Culture*. University of California Press

72 Ibid.

73 Sefaria (n.d.) The Book of Maccabees II 6. Available at: https://www.sefaria.org/The_Book_of_Maccabees_II.6?lang=bi

74 Sefaria (n.d.) The Book of Maccabees I 1:17. Available at: https://www.sefaria.org/The_Book_of_Maccabees_I.1.17?lang=bi

75 Josephus, F. (n.d.) *The Wars of the Jews*, 1.31–1.47. Translated by Whiston, W. Available at: https://lexundria.com/j_bj/1.31-1.47/wst

76 Sefaria (n.d.) Genesis 17:12. Available at: https://www.sefaria.org/Genesis.17.12?lang=bi&aliyot=0

77 Jewish Virtual Library (n.d.) *Mattathias ben Johanan*. Available at: www.jewishvirtuallibrary.org/mattathias-ben-johanan

78 Sefaria (n.d.) The Book of Maccabees I 2:28. Available at: https://www.sefaria.org/The_Book_of_Maccabees_I.2.28?lang=bi

79 Sefaria (n.d.) The Book of Maccabees I 2:40. Available at: https://www.sefaria.org/The_Book_of_Maccabees_I.2.40?lang=bi

80 Sefaria (n.d.) The Book of Maccabees I 2:49. Available at: https://www.sefaria.org/The_Book_of_Maccabees_I.2.49?lang=bi

81 DBpedia (n.d.) *Battle of the Ascent of Lebonah*. Available at: https://dbpedia.org/page/Battle_of_the_Ascent_of_Lebonah

82 Sefaria (n.d.) The Book of Maccabees I 3. Available at: https://www.sefaria.org/The_Book_of_Maccabees_I.3?lang=bi

83 Sefaria (n.d.) The Book of Maccabees I 3:39. Available at: https://www.sefaria.org/The_Book_of_Maccabees_I.3.39?lang=bi&with=all&lang2=en

84 Sefaria (n.d.) The Book of Maccabees I 4:26. Available at: https://www.sefaria.org/The_Book_of_Maccabees_I.4.26?lang=bi&with=all&lang2=en

85 Vidal-Naquet, P. (n.d.) "Maccabean Revolt." *My Jewish Learning*. Available at: https://www.myjewishlearning.com/article/maccabean-revolt/

86 Jewish Virtual Library (n.d.) "Judah Maccabee'. Available at: https://www.jewishvirtuallibrary.org/judah-maccabee-2

87 Bickerman, E. (2007) "Elias Bickerman on the Hellenizing Reformers: A Case Study of an Unconvincing Case." *The Jewish Quarterly Review*, 97(2). doi: 10.1353/jqr.2007.0009

88 Ponet, J. (2005) "Hanukkah as Jewish Civil War." *Slate*. Available at: https://slate.com/human-interest/2005/12/hanukkah-as-jewish-civil-war.html

NOTES

89 Schultz, J.P. (1979) *Judaism and the Gentile Faiths: Comparative Studies in Religion.* UNKNO
90 Hall, R.G. (1992) "Epispasm: Circumcision in Reverse." *Bible Review.* Available at: https://www.cirp.org/library/restoration/hall1/
91 *The Judean* (2022) "The Hasmonean Dynasty: Unifying the Israelites (140BC)." Available at: https://thejudean.com/index.php/history/79-the-hasmonean-dynastyunifying-the-israelites-140-bc
92 Sefaria (n.d.) The Book of Maccabees I 16:1. Available at: https://www.sefaria.org/The_Book_of_Maccabees_I.16.1?lang=bi&with=all&lang2=en
93 Shapira, D. (2021) "Who Were the Hasmoneans?" *Tablet Magazine.* Available at: https://www.tabletmag.com/sections/history/articles/who-were-the-hasmoneans
94 Ibid.
95 Shanks, H. (2024) "Ancient Jerusalem." *Biblical Archaeology Review.* Available at: https://www.biblicalarchaeology.org/daily/biblical-sites-places/jerusalem/ancient-jerusalem/
96 Albright Live, Finkelstein, I. (2024) *Episode Twenty-five: Persian and Early Hellenistic Jerusalem.* Available at: https://www.youtube.com/watch?v=qwGq7-35VGQ
97 Adler, Y. (2023) *The Origins of Judaism: An Archaeological-Historical Reappraisal.* Yale University Press
98 Kratz, R.G. (2015) *Historical and Biblical Israel: The History, Tradition, and Archives of Israel and Judah.* Translated by Kurtz, P.M. Oxford University Press
99 Adler, Y. (2023) *The Origins of Judaism: An Archaeological-Historical Reappraisal.* Yale University Press
100 Kratz, R.G. (2015) *Historical and Biblical Israel: The History, Tradition, and Archives of Israel and Judah.* Translated by Kurtz, P.M. Oxford University Press
101 Shapira, D. (2021) "Who Were the Hasmoneans?" *Tablet Magazine.* Available at: https://www.tabletmag.com/sections/history/articles/who-were-the-hasmoneans
102 Ibid.
103 Babota, V. (2020) "Alexander Janneus as High Priest and King: Struggling between Jewish and Hellenistic Concepts of Rule." *Religions,* 11(1), p. 40. Available at: https://doi.org/10.3390/rel11010040
104 Dąbrowa, E. (ed.) (2009) *The Hasmoneans and their State: A Study in History, Ideology, and the Institutions.* Volume 16. Jagiellonian University Press
105 Encyclopædia Britannica (n.d.) "Antiochus VII Sidetes." Available at: www.britannica.com/biography/Antiochus-VII-Sidetes
106 Dąbrowa, E. (ed.) (2009) *The Hasmoneans and their State: A Study in History, Ideology, and the Institutions.* Volume 16. Jagiellonian University Press
107 Oxford Reference (n.d.) "Forced Conversion." Available at: https://www.oxfordreference.com/display/10.1093/acref/9780199730049.001.0001/acref-9780199730049-e-0734
108 Adler, Y. (2023) *The Origins of Judaism: An Archaeological-Historical Reappraisal.* Yale University Press
109 Ibid.
110 Encyclopædia Britannica (n.d.) "Sadducee." Available at: https://www.britannica.com/topic/Sadducee
111 Lendering, J. (n.d.) "Sadducees." Available at: https://www.livius.org/articles/people/sadducees/
112 Jewish Virtual Library (n.d.) "Pharisees, Sadducees, and Essenes." Available at: https://www.jewishvirtuallibrary.org/pharisees-sadducees-and-essenes
113 Ibid.
114 Ibid.
115 Biblical Archaeology Society (n.d.) *Who Wrote the Dead Sea Scrolls?* Available at: https://library.biblicalarchaeology.org/collections/who-wrote-dead-sea-scrolls/

116 Shapira, D. (2021) "Who Were the Hasmoneans?" *Tablet Magazine*. Available at: https://www.tabletmag.com/sections/history/articles/who-were-the-hasmoneans

117 Jewish Virtual Library (n.d.) "Pharisees, Sadducees, and Essenes." Available at: https://www.jewishvirtuallibrary.org/pharisees-sadducees-and-essenes

118 Dąbrowa, E. (ed.) (2009) *The Hasmoneans and their State: A Study in History, Ideology, and the Institutions*. Volume 16. Jagiellonian University Press

119 Ibid.

120 Josephus, F. (n.d.) *Queen Alexandra. Antiquities of the Jews*. Available at: https://josephus.org/QueenAlexandra.htm#jannaeusFreed

121 Dąbrowa, E. (ed.) (2009) *The Hasmoneans and their State: A Study in History, Ideology, and the Institutions*. Volume 16. Jagiellonian University Press

122 Ibid.

123 Gottheil, R. and Broydé, I. (n.d.) *Hyrcanus II*. Available at: www.jewishencyclopedia.com/articles/7973-hyrcanus-ii

124 Josephus, F. (n.d.) *Antiquities of the Jews—Book XIV*. Available at: https://penelope.uchicago.edu/josephus/ant-14.html

125 Ibid.

126 Gibson, D. (2002, 2022) *The History of Nabataea*. Available at: https://nabataea.net/explore/history/history/

127 Josephus, F. (n.d.) *Antiquities of the Jews—Book XIV*. Available at: https://penelope.uchicago.edu/josephus/ant-14.html

128 Ibid.

129 Ibid.

130 Ibid.

131 Lendering, J. (n.d.) *Roman-Jewish Wars*. Available at: https://www.livius.org/articles/concept/roman-jewish-wars/

132 Josephus, F. (n.d.) *Antiquities of the Jews—Book XIV*. Available at: https://penelope.uchicago.edu/josephus/ant-14.html

133 Lendering, J. (n.d.) *Herod the Great*. Available at: https://www.livius.org/articles/person/herod-the-great/

134 Encyclopædia Britannica (n.d.) "Antigonus Mattathias." Available at: www.britannica.com/biography/Antigonus-Mattathias

135 Ginzberg, L. (n.d.) "Antigonus Mattathias." *Jewish Encyclopedia*. Available at: https://www.jewishencyclopedia.com/articles/1580-antigonus-mattathias

136 Russell, J. and Cohn, R. (eds.) (2012) *Antigonus II Mattathias*. Book on Demand

137 Cassius Dio (n.d.) *Roman History*. Available at: https://penelope.uchicago.edu/Thayer/e/roman/texts/cassius_dio/49*.html

138 The Israel Bible (2021) "The truth about the Hasmonean dynasty." Available at: https://theisraelbible.com/the-truth-about-the-hasmonean-dynasty/

139 Josephus, F. (n.d.) "Antiquities of the Jews—Book XVII: Chapter 1." *Christian Classics Ethereal Library*. Available at: https://www.ccel.org/j/josephus/works/ant-17.htm

Chapter 4

1 Lendering, J. (2023) "Herod the Great." *Livius.org*. Available at: https://www.livius.org/articles/person/herod-the-great/

2 Ibid.

3 Encyclopædia Britannica (n.d.) "Judaea." Available at: https://www.britannica.com/place/Judaea

4   Josephus, F. (n.d.) *Antiquities of the Jews, Book 14*. Available at: https://penelope.uchicago.edu/josephus/ant-14.html
5   Lendering, J. (2023) "Herod the Great." *Livius.org*. Available at: https://www.livius.org/articles/person/herod-the-great/
6   Jewish Agency (n.d.) *Jerusalem: Historical Overview*. Available at: https://archive.jewishagency.org/jerusalem/content/23697/
7   Josephus, F. (n.d.) *Antiquities of the Jews, Book 14*. Available at: https://penelope.uchicago.edu/josephus/ant-14.html
8   Jewish Virtual Library (n.d.) *Antigonus*. Available at: https://www.jewishvirtuallibrary.org/antigonus
9   McCarthy, L. (2024) *Hellenistic Worlds*. In: *Women in the Ancient Mediterranean World*. Cambridge University Press
10 Jewish History (n.d.) "Herod." Available at: https://www.jewishhistory.org/herod/
11 Josephus, F. (n.d.) *Antiquities of the Jews, Book 15*. Available at: https://penelope.uchicago.edu/josephus/ant-15.html
12 Ibid.
13 Ibid.
14 Lendering, J. (2023) "Battle of Actium, 31 BCE." *Livius.org*. Available at: www.livius.org/articles/battle/actium-31-bce/
15 Cohen, S.J.D. (1999) "Roman Domination: the Jewish Revolt and the Destruction of the Second Temple." In: Shanks, H. (ed.) *Ancient Israel: from Abraham to the Roman destruction of the Temple*. Revised ed. Washington, D.C.: Biblical Archaeology Society
16 Simple to Remember (n.d.) "Herod the Great." Available at: www.simpletoremember.com/articles/a/herod3_the_great/
17 Perowne, S. (2003) *The Life and Times of Herod the Great*. Sutton Publishing Ltd
18 Lendering, J. (2023) "Herod the Great." *Livius.org*. Available at: https://www.livius.org/articles/person/herod-the-great/
19 Ritmeyer, K. and Ritmeyer, L. (1989) "Reconstructing Herod's Temple Mount in Jerusalem." *Biblical Archaeology Review*, November/December
20 Josephus, F. (n.d.) *The Jewish War, Book 5*. Available at: https://penelope.uchicago.edu/josephus/war-5.html
21 Rubin, M. (2022) "The Jewish View of Herod: Between History and Tradition." *Hakirah: The Flatbush Journal of Jewish Law and Thought*, 26
22 Encyclopædia Britannica (n.d.) "Herod, king of Judaea." Available at: www.britannica.com/biography/Herod-king-of-Judaea
23 Lendering, J. (2020) "Judaea." *Livius.org*. Available at: https://www.livius.org/articles/place/judaea/
24 Josephus, F. (n.d.) *The Jewish War, Book 2*. Available at: https://penelope.uchicago.edu/josephus/war-2.html
25 Lendering, J. (2020) "Herod Archelaus." *Livius.org*. Available at: https://www.livius.org/articles/person/herod-archelaus/
26 Ibid.
27 Ben-Sasson, H.H. (ed.) (1976) *A History of the Jewish People*. Harvard University Press
28 Green, A. (2003) "Herod and the Kingdom of the Jews." In: *The Jewish War*. Cambridge University Press
29 Josephus, F. (n.d.) *Antiquities of the Jews, Book 18*. Available at: https://penelope.uchicago.edu/josephus/ant-18.html
30 Skarsaune, O. (2008) *In the Shadow of the Temple: Jewish Influences on Early Christianity*. Downers Grove, IL: IVP Academic

31 Josephus, F. (n.d.) *Antiquities of the Jews, Book 18*. Available at: https://penelope.uchicago.edu/josephus/ant-18.htm

32 Ibid.

33 Isaac, B. (2020) "Judaea-Palaestina." In: *The Oxford Research Encyclopedia of Classics*. Oxford University Press. Available at: https://oxfordre.com/classics/display/10.1093/acrefore/9780199381135.001.0001/acrefore-9780199381135-e-3500?d=%2F10.1093%2Facrefore%2F9780199381135.001.0001%2Facrefore-9780199381135-e-3500&p=emailAMvrJnAB2Pkyg

34 Marcomisano, M. (2019) "Ancient Rome and Judea: Caligula and the Temple of Jerusalem." *Roman Jews*. Available at: https://romanjews.com/ancient-rome-and-judea-caligula-and-the-temple-of-jerusalem/

35 Ibid.

36 Blanchetière, F. (2001) *Enquête sur les racines juives du mouvement chrétien*. Paris: Cerf.

37 Josephus, F. (n.d.) *Antiquities of the Jews, Book 19*. Available at: https://penelope.uchicago.edu/josephus/ant-19.html

38 Ibid.

39 Goodblatt, D. (1987) "Agrippa I and Palestinian Judaism in the First Century." *Jewish History*, 2(1). Springer Nature. Available at: https://www.jstor.org/stable/20101031

40 Schwentzel, C.-G. (2011) *Hérode le Grand*. Paris: Pygmalion

41 Josephus, F. (n.d.) *Antiquities of the Jews, Book 19*. Available at: https://penelope.uchicago.edu/josephus/ant-19.html

42 Ibid.

43 Mason, S. (1997) "Will the Real Josephus Please Stand Up?" *Biblical Archaeology Review*, September/October. Available at: https://library.biblicalarchaeology.org/article/will-the-real-josephus-please-stand-up/

44 Schuster, R. (2023) "Yodfat: The Jewish Town Attacked by 60,000 Roman Soldiers." *Haaretz*. Available at: https://www.haaretz.com/archaeology/2023-03-21/ty-article/yodfat-the-jewish-town-attacked-by-60-000-roman-soldiers/00000187-03d4-dbfb-adf7-73d506330000

45 Mason, S. (1997) "Will the Real Josephus Please Stand Up?" *Biblical Archaeology Review*, September/October. Available at: https://library.biblicalarchaeology.org/article/will-the-real-josephus-please-stand-up/

46 Mason, S. (n.d.) "How Reliable Is Josephus?" *Biblical Archaeology Review*. Available at: https://library.biblicalarchaeology.org/sidebar/how-reliable-is-josephus/

47 Skarsaune, O. (2008) *In the Shadow of the Temple: Jewish Influences on Early Christianity*. Downers Grove, IL: IVP Academic

48 Goodman, M. (1987) *The Ruling Class of Judaea: The Origins of the Jewish Revolt Against Rome, A.D. 66–70*. Cambridge University Press Online

49 Rogers, G.M. (2024) *For the Freedom of Zion: The Great Revolt of Jews against Romans, 66–74 CE*. Yale University Press

50 Ibid.

51 Josephus, F. (n.d.) *The Jewish War, Book 5*. Available at: https://penelope.uchicago.edu/josephus/war-5.html

52 Savir, A. (2022) "4,000-Year-Old Israelite Settlement Discovered in Binyamin." *Israel Today*. Available at: https://www.jewishpress.com/news/israel/4000-year-old-israelite-settlement-discovered-in-binyamin/2022/08/30/

53 Josephus, F. (n.d.) *The Jewish War, Book 6*. Available at: https://penelope.uchicago.edu/josephus/war-6.html

54 Ibid.

55 Schäfer, P. (2012) *The History of the Jews in the Greco-Roman World*. Routledge
56 Bunson, M. (2005) *A Dictionary of the Roman Empire*. Oxford University Press
57 Josephus, F. (n.d.) *The Jewish War, Book 6*. Available at: https://penelope.uchicago.edu/josephus/war-6.html
58 Ibid.
59 The Colosseum (n.d.) "Facts About the Colosseum." Available at: www.thecolosseum.org/facts/
60 Josephus, F. (n.d.) *The Jewish War, Book 6*. Available at: https://penelope.uchicago.edu/josephus/war-6.html
61 Dospěl, M. (2023) "Where Did the Temple Menorah Go?" *Biblical Archaeology Review*. Posted on November 23, 2023. Available at: https://www.biblicalarchaeology.org/daily/biblical-sites-places/temple-at-jerusalem/where-did-the-temple-menorah-go/
62 Ibid.
63 Brandfon, F.R. (2017) "Did the Temple Menorah Come Back to Jerusalem?" *Biblical Archaeology Review*, September/October. Available at: https://library.biblicalarchaeology.org/article/did-the-temple-menorah-come-back-to-jerusalem/
64 Prokopios (2015) *The Wars of Justinian*. Translated by Dewing, H.B. Hackett Publishing Company
65 Brandfon, F.R. (2017) "Did the Temple Menorah Come Back to Jerusalem?" *Biblical Archaeology Review*, September/October. Available at: https://library.biblicalarchaeology.org/article/did-the-temple-menorah-come-back-to-jerusalem/
66 Josephus, F. (n.d.) *The Jewish War, Book 7*. Available at: https://penelope.uchicago.edu/josephus/war-7.html
67 Richmond, I.A. (2012) "The Roman Siege-Works of Masàda, Israel." *Journal of Roman Studies*, Published online by Cambridge University Press
68 Mason, S. (2016) *A History of the Jewish War: ad 66–74*. Cambridge University Press
69 Ibid.
70 Ibid.
71 Herr, M.D. (1984) "The History of Eretz Israel." In: Stern, M. (ed.) *The History of Eretz Israel, vol. 4, The Roman-Byzantine Period: The Roman Period from the Conquest to the Bar Kokhba War, 63 BCE–135 CE*. Ben-Zvi Institute
72 Schwartz, S. (2014) *The Ancient Jews from Alexander to Muhammad*. Cambridge University Press
73 Lendering, J. (n.d.) "Yohanan ben Zakkai." *Livius.org*. Available at: www.livius.org/articles/person/yohanan-ben-zakkai/
74 Sefaria (n.d.) Ketubot 112a:15. Available at: https://www.sefaria.org/Ketubot.112a.15?lang=bi
75 Mishnah Yomit (n.d.) *Kedushat Eretz Yisrael*. Available at: www.mishnahyomit.com/articles/Keilim/Kedushat%20Eretz%20Yisrael
76 History in the Bible (n.d.) *Jewish-Roman Wars*. Available at: https://www.historyinthebible.com/supplementary_pages/jewish_roman_wars.html
77 Ibid.
78 Jewish Virtual Library (n.d.) *The Bar Kokhba Revolt (132–135 ce)*. Available at: https://www.jewishvirtuallibrary.org/the-bar-kokhba-revolt-132-135-ce
79 Rodman, D. (2019) "The Bar Kokhba War ad 132–136: The Last Jewish Revolt Against Imperial Rome." *Israel Affairs*, 25(2), pp. 403–405. doi: 10.1080/13537121.2019.1577604
80 Hofman, M.B.Z. (2019) "Eusebius and Hadrian's Founding of Aelia Capitolina in Jerusalem." *Electrum*, 26, pp. 119–128. doi: 10.4467/20800909EL.19.007.11210
81 Ibid.

82 Ibid.
83 Eck, W. (2020) "Judaea-Palaestina." In *The Oxford Research Encyclopedia of Classics*. Oxford University Press. Available at: https://oxfordre.com/classics/classics/abstract/10.1093/acrefore/9780199381135.001.0001/acrefore-9780199381135-e-1056
84 Israeli Government (2024) "Rare coin from the time of the Bar Kokhba Revolt discovered in the Judean Desert." Available at: https://www.gov.il/en/departments/news/rare-coin-from-the-time-of-the-bar-kokhba-revolt-discovered-in-the-judean-desert-4-mar-2024
85 Yadin, Y. (1961) "The Secret in the Cliffs: The Discovery of the Bar-Kochba Letters." *The Atlantic*, November. Available at: https://www.theatlantic.com/magazine/archive/1961/11/the-secret-in-the-cliffs-the-discovery-of-the-bar-kochba-letters/657736/
86 Ibid.
87 Holmes, R.C.L. (2022) "The Bar Kokhba Revolt: The Jewish War against Rome." *The Collector*. Available at: https://www.thecollector.com/bar-kokhba-revolt-war/
88 Rosenberg, D. (n.d.) "False Messiahs RR." Available at: https://www.sefaria.org/sheets/370723?lang=bi
89 Sefaria (n.d.) Numbers 24:17. Available at: https://www.sefaria.org/Numbers.24.17?lang=bi&with=all&lang2=en
90 Holmes, R.C.L. (2022) "The Bar Kokhba Revolt: The Jewish War against Rome." *The Collector*. Available at: https://www.thecollector.com/bar-kokhba-revolt-war/
91 Biblical Archaeology Society. (2016) "A new document dated to four years after the Second Jewish Revolt." *Biblical Archaeology Review*, August 27. Available at: document-dated-to-four-years-after-the-second-jewish-revolt/
92 Hofman, M.B.Z. (2019) "Eusebius and Hadrian's founding of Aelia Capitolina in Jerusalem." *ELECTRUM*, 26
93 Jewish Virtual Library (n.d.) "Roman rule (63 BCE–313 CE)." Available at: https://www.jewishvirtuallibrary.org/roman-rule-63bce-313ce
94 Judaica.ru (n.d.) "Memoranda timeline." Available at: http://www.judaicaru.org/rembrandt_rus/pdf/MemorandaTimeline.pdf
95 However, as part of the Byzantine–Sasanian War of 602–628, in 614 CE, with the Persian conquest of Jerusalem, Jews were allowed to return to home after nearly 500 years of exile. This did not last long, however, as the Jews and Christians fought one another until Jerusalem was conquered once more, this time by Muslim armies.
96 Jewish Virtual Library (n.d.) "The Muslim Empire (636–1099)." Available at: https://www.jewishvirtuallibrary.org/the-muslim-empire-636-1099
97 Engelmayer, J. (2022) "The Crusades (1099–1291)." *The Judean*. Available at: https://thejudean.com/index.php/history/60-the-crusades-1099-1291
98 Jewish Virtual Library (n.d.) "Mamluk rule timeline (1291–1516)." Available at: https://www.jewishvirtuallibrary.org/mamluk-rule-timeline-1291-1516
99 Luz, N. (2023) "The Holy Land from the Mamluk Sultanate to the Ottoman Empire (1260–1799)." In: Hoyland, R.G. and Williamson, H.G.M. (eds.) *The Oxford History of the Holy Land*, Oxford University Press. Available at: https://doi.org/10.1093/oso/9780192886866.003.0010
100 University of Central Arkansas (n.d.) "British Palestine (1917–1948)." Available at: https://uca.edu/politicalscience/home/research-projects/dadm-project/middle-east north-africa-persian-gulf-region/british-palestine-1917-1948/
101 Rabbi Menachem Levine (n.d.) "The Jewish history of Rome." Available at: https://aish.com/the-jewish-history-of-rome/
102 Berg, N.E. (1996) *Exile from Exile: Israeli Writers from Iraq*. State University of New York Press

103 Brenner, M. and Reuveni, G. (n.d.) "Emancipation through Muscles: Jews and Sports in Modern Europe." Available at: https://www.semanticscholar.org/paper/Emancipation-through-Muscles%3A-Jews-and-Sports-in-Brenner-Reuveni/d36987bc27d41abc42af0b542c98020f77f71a29

104 Klein, Z. (2022) "Israel receives 70,000 new immigrants in 2022, highest rate in decades." *The Jerusalem Post*, August 26

Chapter 5

1 United Nations (2007) "United Nations Declaration on the Rights of Indigenous Peoples." Available at: https://www.un.org/development/desa/indigenouspeoples/wp-content/uploads/sites/19/2018/11/UNDRIP_E_web.pdf

2 United Nations (n.d.) "Situation in Occupied Palestine and Israel: History." Available at: https://www.un.org/en/situation-in-occupied-palestine-and-israel/history

3 Lightfoot, S. (2016) *Global Indigenous Politics: A Subtle Revolution*. Routledge. Available at: https://www.routledge.com/Global-Indigenous-Politics-A-Subtle-Revolution/Lightfoot/p/book/9781138477858

4 Lightfoot, S. and MacDonald, D. (2020) "The UN as both foe and friend to Indigenous peoples and self-determination." *E-International Relations*, March 12. Available at: https://www.e-ir.info/2020/03/12/the-un-as-both-foe-and-friend-to-indigenous-peoples-and-self-determination/

5 Ibid.

6 Rich, D. (2016) *The Left's Jewish Problem—Updated Edition: Jeremy Corbyn, Israel and Anti-Semitism*. Biteback Publishing

7 Office of the United Nations High Commissioner for Human Rights (n.d.) "Declaration on the Granting of Independence to Colonial Countries and Peoples." Available at: https://www.ohchr.org/en/instruments-mechanisms/instruments/declaration-granting-independence-colonial-countries-and-peoples

8 Lightfoot, S. and MacDonald, D. (2020) "The UN as both foe and friend to Indigenous peoples and self-determination." *E-International Relations*, March 12. Available at: https://www.e-ir.info/2020/03/12/the-un-as-both-foe-and-friend-to-indigenous-peoples-and-self-determination/

9 Watson, I. (2011) "The 2007 Declaration on the Rights of Indigenous Peoples: Indigenous Survival—Where to From Here?" *Griffith Law Review*, 20(3), p. 507. Available at: https://www.tandfonline.com/doi/abs/10.1080/10383441.2011.10854707

10 Institute for Jewish Policy Research (n.d.) "Grounding Jewishness: How attached do Jews feel to Israel, Europe, and the countries in which they live?" Available at: https://www.jpr.org.uk/reports/grounding-jewishness-how-attached-do-jews-feel-israel-europe-and-countries-which-they-live

11 City, University of London (2015) "Attitudes of British Jews towards Israel revealed in new study." Available at: https://www.city.ac.uk/news-and-events/news/2015/11/attitudes-of-british-jews-towards-israel-revealed-in-new-study

12 Institute for Jewish Policy Research (n.d.) "Committed, concerned and conciliatory: The attitudes of Jews in Britain towards Israel." Available at: https://www.jpr.org.uk/reports/committed-concerned-and-conciliatory-attitudes-jews-britain-towards-israel

13 Campaign Against Antisemitism (2023) "Almost 70% of British Jews are hiding their identity and almost half have considered leaving Britain since 7th October, new CAA polling shows." Available at: https://antisemitism.org/almost-70-of-british-jews-are-hiding-their-identity-and-almost-half-have-considered-leaving-britain-since-7th-october-new-caa-polling-shows/

14 United Nations (n.d.) "Indigenous Peoples, Indigenous Voices: Factsheet." Available at: https://www.un.org/esa/socdev/unpfii/documents/5session_factsheet1.pdf
15 Orthodox Judaism is matrilineal while Reform Judaism states "a child of one Jewish parent, who is raised exclusively as a Jew and whose Jewish status is 'established through appropriate and timely public and formal acts of identification with the Jewish faith and people' is Jewish."
16 Reform Judaism (n.d.) "How does Reform Judaism define who is a Jew?" Available at: https://www.reformjudaism.org/learning/answers-jewish-questions/how-does-reform-judaism-define-who-jew
17 Seidenberg, D.M. (2020) "The Third Promise." *Tikkun*, June 25. Available at: https://www.tikkun.org/the-third-promise/
18 Montefiore, S.S. (2011) *Jerusalem: The Biography*. London: Weidenfeld & Nicolson
19 Goodblatt, D. (2006) "The political and social history of the Jewish community in the Land of Israel." In: Davies, W.D., Finkelstein, L., and Katz, S.T. (eds.) *The Cambridge History of Judaism: Volume 4, The Late Roman-Rabbinic Period*. Cambridge: Cambridge University Press
20 Bar-Asher, M. (1999) "Mishnaic Hebrew: An Introductory Survey." *Hebrew Studies*, 40
21 Kessler, E. (2010) *An Introduction to Jewish-Christian Relations*. Cambridge: Cambridge University Press
22 Schein, S. (1996) "Between East and West: The Latin Kingdom of Jerusalem and Its Jewish Communities as a Communication Center (1099–1291)." In: Menache, S. (ed.) *Communication in the Jewish Diaspora: The Pre-Modern World*. Leiden: E. J. Brill
23 Ibid.
24 Bahat, D. (1976) *Twenty Centuries of Jewish Life in the Holy Land: The Forgotten Generations*. Tel Aviv: The Israel Economist
25 Ron Marvin, T. (2023) "The Aliyah of 300 Rabbis in 1211." *Stories from Jewish History*
26 Maimonides, A., *The Wars of the Lord*. The Maimo Hardcover Edition
27 The others being Jerusalem, the site of the Temple; Tiberias the city where the Mishna was compiled; and Hebron where the Cave of Machpelah can be found, resting place of the matriarchs and patriarchs.
28 Branovsky, Y. (2008) "400 olim arrive in Israel ahead of Independence Day." *Ynet News*, June 5. Available at: https://www.ynetnews.com/articles/0,7340,L-3539874,00.html
29 BJE (n.d.) "Judaism and Israel." *BJE*. Available at: https://bje.org.au/knowledge-centre/basic-judaism/judaism-and-israel/
30 Sefaria (n.d.) Psalms 122:8. Available at: https://www.sefaria.org/Psalms.122.8?lang=bi
31 Institute of Jewish Studies (IJS) (n.d.) "The Significance of Jerusalem in Judaism." *Institute of Jewish Studies*. Available at: https://ijs.org.au/the-significance-of-jerusalem-in-judaism/
32 Cain, A. and Lenski, N. (eds.) (1991) *The Power of Religion in Late Antiquity*. London: Routledge
33 Conder, C.R., Kitchener, H.H., Palmer, E.H. & Besant, W. (1881–1883) *The Survey of Western Palestine: Memoirs of the Topography, Orography, Hydrography, and Archaeology, Vol. 3*. London: Committee of the Palestine Exploration Fund
34 United Nations (2007) "United Nations Declaration on the Rights of Indigenous Peoples." Available at: https://www.un.org/development/desa/indigenouspeoples/wp-content/uploads/sites/19/2018/11/UNDRIP_E_web.pdf
35 Winer, S. (2020) "Kissing the ground: Hundreds of Ethiopian immigrants welcomed to Israel." *The Times of Israel*. Available at: https://www.timesofisrael.com/kissing-the-ground-hundreds-of-ethiopian-immigrants-welcomed-to-israel/

NOTES

36 Chabad.org (n.d.) *Melachim uMilchamot,* Chapter 5. Available at: www.chabad.org/library/article_cdo/aid/1188349/jewish/Melachim-uMilchamotChapter-5.htm

37 Rav Kook Torah (n.d.) "Shlach: Parshat Shlach—65." Available at: https://ravkooktorah.org/SHLACH_65.htm

38 Gilad, E. (2023) "The surprising ancient origins of Passover." *Haaretz,* April 7. Available at: https://www.haaretz.com/israel-news/2023-04-07/ty-article/the-surprising-ancient-origins-of-passover/0000017f-e155-d38f-a57f-e757d8510000

39 Prosic, T. (2004) *The Development and Symbolism of Passover.* London: Bloomsbury

40 Sefaria (n.d.) Deuteronomy 16:5-6. Available at: https://www.sefaria.org/Deuteronomy.16.5-6?lang=bi&aliyot=0

41 Chabad.org (n.d.) *Orlah.* Available at: https://www.chabad.org/search/keyword_cdo/kid/1427/jewish/Orlah.htm

42 Sefaria (n.d.) Exodus 23:11. Available at: https://www.sefaria.org/Exodus.23.11?lang=bi&with=all&lang2=en

43 Sefaria (n.d.) Genesis 15:10. Available at: https://www.sefaria.org/Genesis.15.10?lang=bi&aliyot=0

44 Sefaria (n.d.) Sheet: 523752. Available at: https://www.sefaria.org/sheets/523752?lang=bi

45 Sefaria (n.d.) Psalms 126:3. Available at: https://www.sefaria.org/Psalms.126.3?lang=bi&with=Talmud&lang2=en

46 Jewish Virtual Library (n.d.) "My Heart Is in the East"—Yehuda Halevi." Available at: https://www.jewishvirtuallibrary.org/quot-my-heart-is-in-the-east-quot-yehuda-halevi

47 Knesset (n.d.) *Declaration of Independence.* Available at: https://m.knesset.gov.il/en/about/pages/declaration.aspx

48 Sefaria (n.d.) Sheet: 267613. Available at: https://www.sefaria.org/sheets/267613?lang=bi

49 Zur, Y. (2017) "Jews abroad are just dying to be buried in Israel." *Haaretz,* February 5. Available at: https://www.haaretz.com/israel-news/2017-02-05/ty-article-magazine/.premium/jews-abroad-are-just-dying-to-be-buried-in-israel/0000017f-e338-d804-ad7f-f3faa9d40000

50 Chabad.org (n.d.) "Why Do Some Put Earth from Israel in the Coffin?" Available at: https://www.chabad.org/library/article_cdo/aid/5052511/jewish/Why-Do-Some-Put-Earth-From-Israel-in-the-Coffin.htm

51 Jewish Telegraphic Agency (JTA) (1950) "Sacred soil from Jerusalem is sent to Jewish burial societies in United States." *Jewish Telegraphic Agency.* Available at: https://www.jta.org/archive/sacred-soil-from-jerusalem-is-sent-to-jewish-burial-societies-in-united-states

52 Cohen, S.J.D. (2001) "The Beginnings of Jewishness: Boundaries, Varieties, Uncertainties." *Hellenistic Culture and Society,* vol. 31. Berkeley: University of California Press

53 My Jewish Learning (n.d.) "Community Focused." Available at: www.myjewishlearning.com/article/community-focused/

54 Ibid.

55 Schlank, M. (2023) "One day at a time." *The Times of Israel.* Available at: https://blogs.timesofisrael.com/one-day-at-a-time/

56 Jewish Care (n.d.) "Jewish Care." Available at: https://jewishcare.org/?gclid=CjwKCAi AvoqsBhB9EiwA9XTWGYuS5JVC62B4QOF6WPE3N4GKou6PURnNplji8uoC6R2k kzFl2FQD-hoCy7IQAvD_Bw

57 Philpot, R. (2023) "Gone, not forgotten: Margaret Thatcher, our honorary Jew." *The Jewish Chronicle,* April 4. Available at: https://www.thejc.com/lets-talk/gone-not-forgotten-margaret-thatcher-our-honorary-jew-n5k6ou24

58 Jewish Communal Structures Around the World (n.d.). Available at: https://www.bjpa.org/content/upload/bjpa/jewi/JEWISH%20COMMUNAL%20STRUCTURES%20 AROUND%20THE%20WORLD.pdf

59 Ibid.
60 World Union for Progressive Judaism (WUPJ) (n.d.) "*Kol Yisrael Arevim Zeh Ba-Zeh or Is It Zeh La-Zeh? Parashat Behar-Bechukotai.*" Available at: https://wupj.org/library/the-weekly-portion/1095/kol-yisrael-arevim-zeh-ba-zeh-or-is-it-zeh-la-zeh-parashat-behar-bechukotai/
61 The Jewish concept of charity, although translating to justice.
62 Sefaria (n.d.) Leviticus 23:22. Available at: https://www.sefaria.org/Leviticus.23.22?lang=bi&aliyot=0
63 Religion shmita (n.d). *Time.* Available at: https://time.com/archive/6619465/religion-shmita-5712/
64 "When is the next Sabbatical year?" *Chabad.org.* Available at: https://www.chabad.org/library/article_cdo/aid/538797/jewish/When-is-the-next-Sabbatical-year.htm
65 My Jewish Learning (n.d.) "Pe'ah: The Corners of Our Fields." Available at: https://www.myjewishlearning.com/article/peah-the-corners-of-our-fields/
66 Ibid.
67 Sefaria (n.d.) Sheet: 76024. Available at: https://www.sefaria.org/sheets/76024?lang=bi
68 Vallely, P. (n.d.) "Tzedakah: a concept that changed the world." *The Jewish Chronicle.* Available at: https://www.thejc.com/life-and-culture/tzedakah-a-concept-that-changed-the-world-maf8ump4
69 Chabad.org (n.d.) "Maimonides' Eight Levels of Charity." Available at: https://www.chabad.org/library/article_cdo/aid/45907/jewish/Eight-Levels-of-Charity.htm
70 Ibid.
71 Bar Nissim, H.S. (2017) "American Jews and charitable giving: An enduring tradition." *The Conversation*, February 15. Available at: https://theconversation.com/american-jews-and-charitable-giving-an-enduring-tradition-87993
72 Cambridge Dictionary (2024) "Politics." Available at: https://dictionary.cambridge.org/dictionary/english/politics
73 Adler, Y. (2023) *The Origins of Judaism: An Archaeological-Historical Reappraisal.* Yale University Press
74 Ibid.
75 From the Second Temple period, Torah came to be the name for all the laws surrounding the Pentateuch (the Five Books of Moses).
76 An important discussion laid out by Yonatan Adler in *The Origins of Judaism.*
77 Sanders, E.P. (2016) *Judaism: Practice and Belief, 63 BCE–66 CE.* Minneapolis: 1517 Media. Available at: https://doi.org/10.2307/j.ctt17mcs1x
78 Kedem, Berman, J. (2023) *Created equal: How the Bible Broke with Ancient Political Thought.* Available at: https://www.youtube.com/watch?v=IMTzGn74YWE
79 Berman, J.A. (2008) *Created Equal: How the Bible Broke with Ancient Political Thought.* Oxford: Oxford University Press
80 United Nations (n.d.) "Factsheet on the United Nations Permanent Forum on Indigenous Issues." Available at: https://www.un.org/esa/socdev/unpfii/documents/5session_factsheet1.pdf
81 Sefaria (n.d.) Exodus 34:21. Available at: https://www.sefaria.org/Exodus.34.21?lang=bi&aliyot=0
82 Sefaria (n.d.) Numbers 15:32. Available at: https://www.sefaria.org/Numbers.15.32?lang=bi&aliyot=0
83 Sefaria (n.d.) Exodus 35:3. Available at: https://www.sefaria.org/Exodus.35.3?lang=bi&aliyot=0
84 Chabad.org (n.d.) *The 39 Melachot.* Available at: https://www.chabad.org/library/article_cdo/aid/102032/jewish/The-39-Melachot.htm
85 Adler, Y. (2023) *The Origins of Judaism: An Archaeological-Historical Reappraisal.* Yale University Press

86 Ibid.
87 Ibid.
88 Ibid.
89 Weiss, H. (1998) "The Sabbath in the writings of Josephus." *Journal for the Study of Judaism in the Persian, Hellenistic, and Roman Period*, 29(4), pp. 363–390. Available at: https://www.jstor.org/stable/24668810
90 Lew, J.D.M. (1976) "Jewish law—Its development and its coexistence in the non-Jewish world," *Rabels Zeitschrift für Ausländisches und Internationales Privatrecht / The Rabel Journal of Comparative and International Private Law*, 40(1)

Chapter 6

1 Daniels, P.T. (2021) *Hebrew script for Jewish languages: A unique phenomenon*. Available at: https://doi.org/10.1075/wll.00050.dan
2 Chabad.org (n.d.) "Why is Hebrew called the Holy Tongue (Lashon Hakodesh)?" Available at: https://www.chabad.org/library/article_cdo/aid/3354288/jewish/Why-Is-Hebrew-Called-the-Holy-Tongue-Lashon-Hakodesh.htm
3 Sefaria (n.d.) Ramban on Exodus 30:13. Available at: https://www.sefaria.org/Ramban_on_Exodus.30.13.1?lang=bi&with=all&lang2=en
4 Weinreich, M. (2008) *History of the Yiddish Language, Volume 1*. New Haven: Yale University Press
5 Huehnergard, J. and Pat-El, N. (eds.) (2019) *The Semitic Languages*. 2nd edn. United Kingdom: Taylor & Francis
6 Biblical Archaeology Society (n.d.) "What is Biblical Hebrew?" Available at: https://www.biblicalarchaeology.org/daily/ancient-cultures/ancient-israel/what_is_biblical_hebrew/
7 "The Qeiyafa Ostracon Relates the Birth of the Kingdom of Israel." 2018. *Biblical Archaeology Society*. Available at: https://www.biblicalarchaeology.org/daily/biblical-artifacts/inscriptions/the-qeiyafa-ostracon-relates-the-birth-of-thekingdom-of-israel/
8 Rollston, C.A. (2008) "The Phoenician Script of the Tel Zayit Abecedary and Putative Evidence for Israelite Literacy." In: Tappy, R.E. and McCarter, P.K. (eds.) *Literate Culture and Tenth-Century Canaan: The Tel Zayit Abecedary in Context*. Winona Lake, IN: Eisenbrauns
9 Reynolds, N.B. (2021) *A Brief History of Writing from the Perspective of Restoration Scripture*. [online] Brigham Young University. Available at: https://scholarsarchive.byu.edu/facpub/5591/
10 Sanders, S.L. (2011) *The Invention of Hebrew*. New York: Traditions
11 Orr-Stav, J. (1999) "The Transition from Paleo (Old) Hebrew to Aramaic." Available at: https://ancient-hebrew.org/ancient-alphabet/transition-from-paleo-hebrew-to-aramaic.htm
12 Abraham, K. and Sokoloff, M. (2011) "Aramaic Loanwords in Akkadian—A Reassessment of the Proposals." *Archiv für Orientforschung*, 52
13 Blum, S.T. (2017) "Typography and the Evolution of Hebrew Alphabetic Script: Writing Method of the Sofer." *Faculty and Staff Publications*, 49. Available at: https://digitalcommons.xula.edu/fac_pub/49
14 Orr-Stav, J. (1999) "The Transition from Paleo (Old) Hebrew to Aramaic." Available at: https://ancient-hebrew.org/ancient-alphabet/transition-from-paleo-hebrew-to-aramaic.htm
15 Cross, F.M. (2018) *Leaves from an Epigrapher's Notebook: Collected Papers in Hebrew and West Semitic Palaeography and Epigraphy*. Harvard Semitic Museum
16 Siegel, J.P. (1979) "The Evolution of Two Hebrew Scripts." *Biblical Archaeology Review*, May/June. Available at: https://library.biblicalarchaeology.org/article/the-evolution-of-two-hebrew-scripts/

17 My Jewish Learning (n.d.) "Yiddish." Available at: https://www.myjewishlearning.com/article/yiddish/
18 Sephardic Brotherhood (n.d.) "What is Ladino?" Available at: https://www.sephardic-brotherhood.com/what-is-ladino
19 Jewish Virtual Library (n.d.) "China: Virtual Jewish History Tour." Available at: https://www.jewishvirtuallibrary.org/china-virtual-jewish-history-tour#a
20 Brisman, S. (2000) *A History and Guide to Judaic Dictionaries and Concordances*. Hoboken, NJ: KTAV. (Jewish Research Literature; Vol. 3, Part 1)
21 Ibid.
22 Ibid.
23 Ibid.
24 Jewish Encyclopedia (n.d.) "Ben Ze'eb, Judah Löb." Available at: www.jewishencyclopedia.com/articles/2894-ben-ze-eb-judah-lob
25 Israel Ministry of Foreign Affairs (n.d.) "Hebrew Language Day: The revival of the language of the Bible." Available at: https://images.shulcloud.com/5061/uploads/Hebrew-Resources/Hebrew/HebrewLanguageDayHistoryofHebrewLanguage.pdf
26 Bensadoun, D. (2010) "This week in history: Revival of the Hebrew language." *The Jerusalem Post*. Available at: https://www.jpost.com/jewish-world/jewish-news/this-week-in-history-revival-of-the-hebrew-language
27 Halon, E. (2018) "The Israeli Academy: Continuing the unprecedented revival of the Hebrew language." *The Jerusalem Post*. Available at: https://www.jpost.com/israel-news/culture/the-israeli-academy-continuing-the-unprecedented-revival-of-the-hebrew-language-542822
28 Tylor, E.B. (1871) *Primitive Culture: Researches into the Development of Mythology, Philosophy, Religion, Art, and Custom*. London: J. Murray
29 Jewish Treats, 2021. "More than Shabbat." May 3. Available at: https://njop.org/more-than-shabbat-3/
30 Sefaria (n.d.) Genesis 17:1-14. Available at: https://www.sefaria.org/Genesis.17.1-14
31 Adler, Y. (2023) *The Origins of Judaism: An Archaeological-Historical Reappraisal*. Yale University Press
32 Ibid.
33 Ibid.
34 Bible Gateway (n.d.) "Galatians 5:2 (NIV)." Available at: https://www.biblegateway.com/passage/?search=Galatians%205%3A2&version=NIV
35 Rosner, F. (2003) *Encyclopaedia of Jewish Medical Ethics*. New York: Feldheim Publishers
36 Morris B.J., Wamai, R.G., Henebeng, E.B., Tobian, A.A., Klausner, J.D., Banerjee, J., Hankins, C.A. (2016) "Estimation of country-specific and global prevalence of male circumcision." Popul Health Metr. 2016 Mar 1;14:4. doi: 10.1186/s12963-0160073-5. Erratum in: Popul Health Metr. 2016 Apr 04;14:11. doi: 10.1186/s12963-0160080-6. PMID: 26933388; PMCID: PMC4772313
37 Morris, B.J., Wamai, R.G., Henebeng, E.B. et al. (2016) "Estimation of country-specific and global prevalence of male circumcision." *Population Health Metrics*, 14(4). Available at: https://doi.org/10.1186/s12963-016-0073-5
38 Sherwood, H. (2018) "Iceland to become first European country to ban male circumcision." *The Guardian*. Available at: https://www.theguardian.com/society/2018/feb/18/iceland-ban-male-circumcision-first-european-country
39 United Nations (2018) "United Nations Declaration on the Rights of Indigenous Peoples." Available at: https://www.un.org/development/desa/indigenouspeoples/wp-content/uploads/sites/19/2018/11/UNDRIP_E_web.pdf

40 Sefaria (n.d.) Leviticus 14. Available at: https://www.sefaria.org/Leviticus.14?lang=bi&aliyot=0
41 Ibid.
42 Jachter, C. (n.d.) "Gray Matter II: Building and Maintaining Mikva'ot, Part I; Community's Responsibility to Build a Mikvah." Available at: https://www.sefaria.org/Gray_Matter_II%2C_Building_and_Maintaining_Mikva'ot%2C_Part_I%3B_Community's_Responsibility_to_Build_a_Mikvah.6?lang=bi
43 Sefaria (n.d.) Mishnah Mikvaot. Available at: https://www.sefaria.org/Mishnah_Mikvaot?tab=contents
44 Sefaria (n.d.) Leviticus 15:19. Available at: https://www.sefaria.org/Leviticus.15.19?lang=bi&aliyot=0
45 Adler, Y. (2023) *The origins of Judaism: An Archaeological-Historical Reappraisal*. Yale University Press
46 Ibid.
47 Jewish Museum (n.d.) "Mikveh." Available at: https://jewishmuseum.org.uk/schools/asset/mikveh/
48 Wertheimer, J. (2018) *The New American Judaism: How Jews Practice Their Religion Today*. Princeton: Princeton University Press
49 Hoffman, A. (2012) "The new American mikveh." *Tablet Magazine*, August 13. Available at: https://www.tabletmag.com/sections/belief/articles/the-new-american-mikveh
50 Mayyim Hayyim (n.d.) "About us." Available at: https://www.mayyimhayyim.org/about/
51 ImmerseNYC (n.d.) "Testimonials." Available at: http://www.immersenyc.org/testimonials
52 Wertheimer, J. (2018) *The New American Judaism: How Jews Practice Their Religion Today*. Princeton: Princeton University Press
53 Sefaria (n.d.) Deuteronomy 6:4. Available at: https://www.sefaria.org/Deuteronomy.6.4?lang=bi&aliyot=0
54 Sefaria (n.d.) Deuteronomy 6:9. Available at: https://www.sefaria.org/Deuteronomy.6.9?lang=bi&with=all&lang2=en
55 Adler, Y. (2023) *The Origins of Judaism: An Archaeological-Historical Reappraisal*. Yale University Press
56 Encyclopædia Britannica (n.d.) "Marduk." Available at: https://www.britannica.com/topic/Marduk
57 Albertz, R. (1994) *A History of Israelite Religion in the Old Testament Period, Volume I: From the beginnings to the end of the monarchy*. Louisville, KY: Westminster/John Knox Press. (The Old Testament Library)
58 Jewish Virtual Library (n.d.) "The Bible on Jewish links to the Holy Land." Available at: https://www.jewishvirtuallibrary.org/the-bible-on-jewish-links-to-the-holy-land
59 Sefaria (n.d.) Deuteronomy 11:12. Available at: https://www.sefaria.org/Deuteronomy.11.12?lang=bi&with=all&lang2=en
60 Wesler, K.W. (2012) *An Archaeology of Religion*. London: RLPG/Galleys
61 Anderson, J.S. (2015) *Monotheism and YHWH's appropriation of Baal*. [pdf] Bloomsbury
62 Schniedewind, W.M. (2013) *A social history of Hebrew: Its origins through the Rabbinic period*. New Haven: Yale University Press
63 Smith, M.S. (2002) *The Early History of God: Yahweh and Other Deities in Ancient Israel*. Grand Rapids, MI: William B. Eerdmans Publishing Co. (Biblical Resource Series)
64 Sefaria (n.d.) II Kings 23:21. Available at: https://www.sefaria.org/II_Kings.23.21?lang=bi
65 Sefaria (n.d.) II Kings 23:5. Available at: https://www.sefaria.org/II_Kings.23.5?lang=bi

66 Sefaria (n.d.) Exodus 20:2. Available at: https://www.sefaria.org/Exodus.20.2?lang=bi&namedEntity=the-tetragrammaton&namedEntityText=%D7%99%D7%94%D7%95%D7%94&with=Lexicon&lang2=en

67 Sefaria (n.d.) Genesis 15:18. Available at: https://www.sefaria.org/Genesis.15.18?lang=bi&with=all&lang2=en

68 Sefaria (n.d.) Deuteronomy 11:12. Available at: https://www.sefaria.org/Deuteronomy.11.12?lang=bi&aliyot=0

69 Martin, J. (2022) "Chickahominy Tribe reacquires ancestral lands." *ICT News*, March 13. Available at: https://ictnews.org/news/chickahominy-tribe-reacquires-ancestral-lands

70 Poseidon Expeditions (n.d.) "People from Greenland." Available at: https://poseidonexpeditions.com/about/articles/people-from-greenland/

71 United Nations (n.d.) "Factsheet: United Nations Permanent Forum on Indigenous Issues, Fifth Session'. Available at: https://www.un.org/esa/socdev/unpfii/documents/5session_factsheet1.pdf

72 Adler, Y. (2023) *The origins of Judaism: An Archaeological-Historical Reappraisal*. University Press

73 Sefaria (n.d.) "Hypothetica 26–27." Available at: https://www.sefaria.org/Hypothetica.26-27?lang=bi

74 Josephus (n.d.) *Against Apion 2.174–178*. Available at: https://penelope.uchicago.edu/josephus/apion-2.html

75 Richard, S. (ed.) (2018) *Near Eastern Archaeology: A Reader*. Winona Lake, IN: Eisenbrauns

76 Ibid.

77 Jewish Policy Research (n.d.) "Synagogue membership in the United Kingdom in 2016." Available at: https://www.jpr.org.uk/sites/default/files/attachments/Synagogue_membership_in_the_United_Kingdom_in_2016.pdf

78 Schwartz, J., Scheckner, J. and Kotler-Berkowitz, L. (2001) "Census of U.S. synagogues." *Berman Jewish Policy Archive*. Available at: https://www.bjpa.org/content/upload/bjpa/cens/CensusOfUSSynagogues2001.pdf

79 Solomon, J. (2019) "So many synagogues in Jerusalem." *The Jerusalem Post*, October 10. Available at: jerusalem-604186#google_vignette

80 Pew Research Center (2021) "Jewish practices and customs." Available at: https://www.pewresearch.org/religion/2021/05/11/jewish-practices-and-customs/

81 Rosenberg, S.G. (2007) "The Jewish calendar is out of sync. Fix it." *The Jerusalem Post*, May 21. Available at: https://www.jpost.com/opinion/op-ed-contributors/the-jewish-calendar-is-out-of-sync-fix-it#google_vignette

82 Richardson, S. (2015) "Historical Sanhedrin." *Calendar Bias*. Available at: https://www.calendarbias.com/08-HISTORICAL-SANHEDRIN.htm

83 Rogovoy, S. (2024) "The secret Jewish history of leap year." *The Forward*, February 28. Available at: https://forward.com/culture/334125/the-secret-jewish-historyof-leap-year/

84 Sefaria (n.d.) Mishneh Torah, Sanctification of the New Month 3:12. Available at: https://www.sefaria.org/Mishneh_Torah%2C_Sanctification_of_the_New_Month.3.12?lang=bi&with=Talmud&lang2=en

85 Stern, S. (2001) *Calendar and community: A history of the Jewish calendar 2nd century B C E to 10th century C E*. Oxford: Oxford University Press

86 My Jewish Learning (n.d.) "Yom Ha'atzmaut: Israel Independence Day." Available at: https://www.myjewishlearning.com/article/yom-haatzmaut-israel-independence-day/

87 My Jewish Learning (n.d.) "Yom HaShoah: Holocaust Memorial Day." Available at: https://www.myjewishlearning.com/article/yom-hashoah-holocaust-memorial-day/

88 Sokol, S. (2024) "Cabinet approves national Remembrance Day for October 7 massacre, Gaza war." *The Times of Israel*, March 17. Available at: https://www.times ofisrael.com/cabinet-approves-national-remembrance-day-for-october-7-massacregaza-war/
89 Chabad.org (n.d.) "QA: The Holocaust's Jewish Calendars: Keeping Time Sacred, Making Time Holy." Available at: https://www.chabad.org/news/article_cdo/aid/4571234/jewish/QA-The-Holocausts-Jewish-Calendars-Keeping-Time-Sacred-Making-TimeHoly.htm
90 Sefaria (n.d.) Leviticus 16:34. Available at: https://www.sefaria.org/Leviticus.16.34?lang=en&with=all&lang2=en
91 Sefaria (n.d.) Leviticus 16:31. Available at: https://www.sefaria.org/Leviticus.16.31?lang=en&with=all&lang2=en
92 Sefaria (n.d.) Leviticus 17:4. Available at: https://www.sefaria.org/Leviticus.17.4?lang=bi&aliyot=0
93 Adler, Y. (2023) *The Origins of Judaism: An Archaeological-Historical Reappraisal*. Yale University Press

Chapter 7

1 Sefaria (n.d.) I Kings 5:15. Available at: https://www.sefaria.org/I_Kings.5.15?lang=en
2 Talmud (n.d.) *Massekheth Git.in*, 56b
3 Sefaria (n.d.) Mishneh Torah, Torah Study 1:6. Available at: https://www.sefaria.org/Mishneh_Torah%2C_Torah_Study.1.6?lang=bi
4 Sefaria (n.d.) Deuteronomy 33:4. Available at: https://www.sefaria.org/Deuteronomy.33.4?lang=bi&aliyot=0
5 Sefaria (n.d.) Deuteronomy 6:4. Available at: https://www.sefaria.org/Deuteronomy.6.4?lang=bi&aliyot=0
6 Smooha, S. (1978) *Israel: Pluralism and Conflict*. Berkeley: University of California Press
7 United Nations (2018) "United Nations Declaration on the Rights of Indigenous Peoples." Available at: https://www.un.org/development/desa/indigenouspeoples/wp-content/uploads/sites/19/2018/11/UNDRIP_E_web.pdf
8 Josephus, F. (1927) *The Jewish War*. Translated by Thackeray, H. St. J. Loeb Classical Library.
9 Tikkun Olam is more likened to the equity jurisdiction in common law systems. To read more about it, see M. Git.in 4:6 (discussed more in the Babylonian Talmud Git.in 45a).
10 United Nations (2018) "United Nations Declaration on the Rights of Indigenous Peoples." Available at: content/uploads/sites/19/2018/11/UNDRIP_E_web.pdf
11 U.S. History (n.d.) "The Pledge of Allegiance." Available at: https://www.ushistory.org/documents/pledge.htm
12 Choua, I. (2023) [Tweet]. April 27. Available at: https://x.com/ChouaIsaac/status/1759622882215260382

Chapter 9

1 At the turn of the century/at the time of the First Zionist Congress, there were over 20,000 Jews living in Gomel, constituting over 50% of the population. They were served by 30 synagogues. Like other Jewish population centers in the Pale of Settlement, the Jews of Gomel were periodically subjected to pogroms. For example, the 1903 Pogrom killed dozens of Jews, injured hundreds of others, and left hundreds of homes, businesses, and Jewish institutions torched, looted, and destroyed. Torah scrolls were torn up during the destruction of synagogues. After the 1917 revolution, Jewish religion and culture was

suppressed. The Rabbi of Gomel, R. Borishanski, was arrested by the communists for opposing anti-Jewish repression. Jewish schools and synagogues were gradually turned into clubs, movie theaters, etc. By the time the Nazis invaded in 1941, there remained only two synagogues (out of 30 in 1897).

2   The Nazis invaded Gomel on August 19, 1941. The remaining Jews (who hadn't fled/been evacuated) were corralled into four ghettoes, which were overcrowded and overrun with disease, and three work camps with brutal conditions. By the end of the year, 4,000 Jews were murdered. This included the use of the infamous gas vans. Within the next few months, the Nazis murdered the remaining Jews in Gomel. By the end of the war, nine out of every ten Jews in Belarus had been murdered.

3   Between 1959 and 1962, only six Yiddish books were produced (mostly for export and foreign consumption). In 1962, none were printed. By contrast, in 1961 alone, Soviet printing presses produced 62 books for the Maris (total pop 504,000) and 144 for the Yakut (pop 236,000), in their own languages. (Jews numbered around 3 million. Jews had one Yiddish newspaper as of 1961. The Maris have 17 newspapers; the Yakut have 28.)

4   About one-quarter of those sent to Gulags never returned, due to the brutal conditions within these labor camps.

5   United Nations (2018) "United Nations Declaration on the Rights of Indigenous Peoples." Available at: https://www.un.org/development/desa/indigenouspeoples/wp-content/uploads/sites/19/2018/11/UNDRIP_E_web.pdf

6   Blau, R. (2015) "What is the opium of the people?" *The Economist*, 5 January. Available at: https://www.economist.com/1843/2015/01/05/what-is-the-opium-of-the-people

7   No Hebrew bible had been printed since 1917. Not a single Jewish text of any other kind has appeared in print since the early 1920s. By contrast, in 1958, the Moslem Directorates in Ufa and Tashkent produced editions of 4,000 and 5,000 copies, respectively, of the Koran (in Arabic). The Baptists were authorized in 1956 to publish 25,000 hymnals; no single siddur for high holy days or other festivals have been authorized. Jews relied on photographed copies of hand-copied siddurim. Production of ritual items (like tallitot and tefillin) were banned. Various religions were allowed contact with and participation in global religious bodies. For example, Soviet Muslims were associated with the World Congress of Muslims. At the end of October 1962, a national conference of Moslem leaders, meeting in Tashkent, was authorized to establish a permanent department for international relations, with headquarters in Moscow, which would speak for all Muslim Boards in the country. Conversely, no Jewish religious delegation from the U.S.S.R. had ever been permitted to visit with Jewish institutions abroad or participate in Jewish summits. "Nor are synagogues in the U.S.S.R. allowed to have any kind of official contact, permanent ties or institutional relations with Jewish religious, congregational or rabbinic bodies outside their country."

8   Hebrew Songs (n.d.) "*Hineh matov umanayim.*" Available at: https://www.hebrewsongs.com/song-hinehmatov.htm

Chapter 11

1   Whose collection of writings is housed in the Leo Baeck Institute at the Jewish History Museum in New York.

2   Winston's PhD focused on a philological study of the word "To'evah" (Abomination) in the Hebrew Bible.

3   Sacks, J. (n.d.) "Join the journey." Available at: https://rabbisacks.org/quotes/join-the-journey/

Chapter 12

1. Australian Human Rights Commission (2009) "United Nations Declaration on the Rights of Indigenous Peoples." Available at: https://humanrights.gov.au/our-work/un-declaration-rights-indigenous-peoples-1
2. We must remember that the first Zionist Congress in 1897 was attended by a generation which had witnessed the unification of Italy and Germany within their lifetimes (1871), as well as countless national movements across Eastern and Central Europe.
3. Herzl, T. (1896) *The Jewish State*. Project Gutenberg. Available at: https://www.gutenberg.org/files/25282/25282-h/25282-h.htm#The_Jewish_State
4. Sefaria (n.d.) The Book of Maccabees I 15:36. Available at: https://www.sefaria.org/The_Book_of_Maccabees_I.15.36?lang=bi
5. Although also interpreted in the Talmud as rooted in the coming of the Moshiach (Messiah).
6. Sacks, J. (2009) *Future Tense*. Maggid Books. Available at: https://rabbisacks.org/books/future-tense/
7. Bogdanor, V. (2016) "Singling out Israel is a Very Modern Antisemitism." *The Israel Democracy Institute*. Available at: https://en.idi.org.il/articles/3229
8. Australian Human Rights Commission (2009) "United Nations Declaration on the Rights of Indigenous Peoples: Article 26." Available at: https://humanrights.gov.au/our-work/un-declaration-rights-indigenous-peoples-1
9. Canada and Indigenous Peoples (1998) "Sovereignty and Indigenous Peoples: A Legal Perspective." *Canadian Association for the History of Indigenous Peoples*. Available at: https://caid.ca/SovIndPeo1998.pdf
10. Waldron, J. (2003) "Settlement, Return, and the Supersession Thesis." Available at: https://www.degruyterbrill.com/document/doi/10.2202/1565-3404.1093/pdf
11. ICT News (2024) "Chickahominy Tribe reacquires ancestral lands." *ICT News*. Available at: https://ictnews.org/news/chickahominy-tribe-reacquires-ancestral-lands
12. Ibid.
13. Jewish Virtual Library (n.d.) "Excerpts from The Jewish State. Jewish Virtual Library." Available at: https://www.jewishvirtuallibrary.org/excerpts-from-quot-the-jewish-state-quot
14. Although later Maimonides used Dat to mean belief, in a theological sense, most thinkers did not.
15. Miller, J. (2020) "From Law to Religion." In: Cane, P. and Conaghan, M. (eds.) *Law as Religion, Religion as Law*. Cambridge: Cambridge University Press. Available at: https://www.cambridge.org/core/books/law-as-religion-religion-as-law/dat-from-law-to-religion/34AFF1D4D00ABBF8ADD88D9CB766D62A
16. Pailin, D.A. (1984) *Attitudes to Other Religions: Comparative Religion in Seventeenth and Eighteenth Century Britain*. Manchester: Manchester University Press
17. Simone Luzzatto (2013, p. 58, cited in Veltri, ed., 2013) notes: "Benche gli Hebrei erano differenti de religione dagli altri popoli, not gli era lectio mover Guerra a lor vicino per semplice cause di quella." Available at: https://library.oapen.org/bitstream/id/7303d462-96cf-46c2-ad82-2e9f6d83e682/1006590.pdf
18. Ruderman, D. (2000) *Jewish Enlightenment in an English Key*. Princeton and Oxford: Princeton University Press
19. Miller, J. (2020) "From law to religion." In: Cane, P. and Conaghan, M. (eds.) *Law as religion, religion as law*. Cambridge: Cambridge University Press. Available at: https://www.cambridge.org/core/books/law-as-religion-religion-as-law/dat-from-law-to-religion/34AFF1D4D00ABBF8ADD88D9CB766D62A
20. Merriam-Webster (n.d.) "Religion," *Merriam-Webster Dictionary*. Available at: https://www.merriam-webster.com/dictionary/religion

21 Israel Bible Center (2024) "Faith: A Biblical Idea," *Israel Bible Center*. Available at: https://weekly.israelbiblecenter.com/faith-biblical-idea
22 Buber, M. (1951) *Two Types of Faith*. New York: The Macmillan Company. Collection: Universal Library. Contributor: Universal Digital Library
23 Brigham Young University (n.d.) "Difference between faith and belief." Brigham Young University Humanities. Available at: https://hum.byu.edu/differencebetween-faith-and-belief
24 Buber, M. (1951) *Two Types of Faith*. New York: The Macmillan Company. Collection: Universal Library. Contributor: Universal Digital Library
25 Sefaria (n.d.) Pirkei Avot 5:23. Available at: https://www.sefaria.org/Pirkei_Avot.5.23?lang=bi
26 Kohler, K. and Hirsch, E.G. (n.d.) "Creed," *Jewish Encyclopedia*. Available at: https://www.jewishencyclopedia.com/articles/4734-creed
27 However, we must acknowledge that Maimonides wrote Shloshah Asar Ikkarim in Judeo-Arabic, and when discussing emuna (often translated as "faith"), he used the Arabic word *i'tiqād*. So, i'tiqād was then translated into emuna, which was subsequently translated into "faith." Indeed, we must consider translation issues when discussing all Jewish texts, as they are written in Ancient Hebrew or Aramaic. This argument is not whether Judaism contains ideas of emuna—it clearly does—but rather how we understand these ideas, where we take our cues from, and which terms we use to describe our culture and belief system.
28 Kohler, K. and Hirsch, E.G. (n.d.) "Creed," *Jewish Encyclopedia*. Available at: https://www.jewishencyclopedia.com/articles/4734-creed
29 Cotter, C. and Robertson, D.G. (2016a) "Preface." In: Cotter, C. and Robertson, D.G. (eds.) *After World Religions: Reconstructing Religious Studies*. London and New York: Routledge
30 Owen, S. (2011) "The World Religions Paradigm: Time for a Change," *Arts & Humanities in Higher Education*, 10(3)
31 Lokensgard, K.H. and Gonzalez, A.V. (2014) "Indigenous Religions." In: Leeming, D.A. (ed.) *Encyclopedia of Psychology and Religion*. Boston, MA: Springer. Available at: https://doi.org/10.1007/978-1-4614-6086-2_9019
32 Freeman, B.M. (2022) *Reclaiming Our Story: The Pursuit of Jewish Pride*. No Pasaran Media: London
33 White, M. (2023) X.com, July 12. Available at: https://twitter.com/michaelwhite/status/1782164072026325088
34 Freeman, B.M. (2023) X.com, July 12. Available at: https://twitter.com/BenMFreeman/status/1782288188263870782
35 Umebinyuo, I. (n.d.) "Diaspora Blues." *The Ijeoma Project*. Available at: https://www.scribd.com/document/533473946/462846398-OceanofPDF-Com-Questions-for-Ada-Ijeoma-Umebinyuo-PDF

INDEX

Abijam (King) 58
Abimelech (King) 45
Abraham (Avraham) 1, 29–30, 31, 41, 65, 74, 77, 139–40, 169, 171, 189
Academy of the Hebrew Language 160
Achaemenid Persian Empire 85
Acre (Akko) 100, 133–4, 137
Adad-Nirari III (King) 62
Adida (fortress of) 98
Adkins, Chief Wayne 173, 245
Adler, Yonatan (and *The Origins of Judaism: An Archaeological-Historical Reappraisal*) 98, 99, 148, 163, 166, 176
Adret, R. Solomon (Rashba) 134
Aelia Capitolina 117117
Agatharchides of Cnidus 151
agnostic Jews 162, 168, 192, 222
agricultural holidays/festivals 14, 137, 139, 178
Agrippa the Great (Herod Agrippa) 109–10
Ahab (King) 61, 62, 186
Ahaz (King) 63, 66
Akiva, Rabbi 116, 118
Akkadian 68
Akko (Acre) 100, 133–4, 137
Aklum, Ferede 203, 293
Alexander, Tiberius Julius 112
Alexander Jannaeus (King) 100
Alexander the Alabarch 191
Alexander the Great 89
Alexandra, Salome 100
Alexandria (Egypt) 89, 91, 100, 109, 112, 117, 120, 191
  Basilica Synagogue 91
Alexandrium 101
Al-harizi, Yehuda 134
Aliyah (immigration of Jews from Diaspora to Land of Israel/ Palestine region) 121, 130, 134, 140, 160, 181, 191, 219–20, 234, 261
allies (non-Jewish) as crucial to defeating antisemitism 5
alphabet 101
Alshich, Rabbi Moses: *Torat Moshe* 146
Al-Yahūdu 80
Am Yisrael (People of Israel) 18, 33, 75, 116, 145, 176

America (USA, and Americans) 12–13, 148, 155, 209
  cultural colonialism 6
  Native Americans *see* Native Americans
  synagogues 168
Amidah (Jewish prayer) 140, 141, 242
Amir, Ayala 70
Amun-Ra 35
Amzallag, Nissim 39
ancestry
  indigeneity and 15–19, 15–18
  resolve to maintain and reproduce their ancestral environments and systems as distinctive peoples and communities 150, 175–81
Andronicus 94
Anthony, Mark 106
Antigonus II Mattathias (King) 101–2
anti-Jewishness *see* antisemitism
Antiochus III 91, 92, 93
Antiochus IV Epiphanes 89, 91–7, 108, 163
Antiochus VII 99
Antipater the Idumaean 101, 105, 106
antisemitism (anti-Jewishness; Jew-hatred) 4, 208, 210, 240–1, 243, 253
  allies as crucial to defeating 5
  Diaspora and 254
  internalized 248, 258
  Jewish difference (notion of) and 155, 259
  Labour Party (UK) and 234
  as non-Jewish problem which impacts Jews 5–6
  Palestinian state and 8
  pogroms 21, 91, 109, 117
  Soviet Union and 207–16
  Zionism and 234
  see also Holocaust
antizionism 2, 4, 5, 158, 201, 242–3, 243
Arab(s) 119, 186
  colonization by 51, 86
  considered indigenous to the Land of Israel 125
  peace between Jews and xix

Arab Zionism xix
Aramaic 29, 47, 157, 158, 187
Aretas III 101
Aristobulus I (high priest) 100
Aristobulus II 101, 105
Ascent of Lebonah, Battle of the (167 BCE) 96
Asher, Jacob 146
Asherah 39, 41, 61, 160, 170
Ashi, Rav (Rabbi) 81
Ashkelon 32
Ashkenazi Jews 3, 4, 6, 13, 17, 120, 156, 181, 188, 197, 200
Ashurnasirpal II 62
Assyrian Empire 58, 62, 63–4, 70
Assyrian Wine List 66, 69
Ataroth 44
Athaliah 67
atheist Jews 22, 88, 168, 172–3, 192
Augustine of Hippo 8
Augustus (Emperor) 109, 177
Australians, indigenous 13, 244
Avraham (Abraham) 1, 29–30, 31, 41, 65, 74, 77, 139–40, 169, 171, 189
Avraham, R.: *Milchamot Hashem* 134

Baal 39, 41, 61, 169, 170
Baal ha Turim (Jacob Asher) 146
Baasha (King) 60
Babylon/Babylonians
  Babylonian Gemara 81
  Babylonian Talmud 81, 186
  exile to (from 586 BCE) 28, 71–3, 79–82, 97, 170
  Edict of Cyrus and choice of returning to Judah from 79, 85
  Psalm 137 and 72, 135, 140
  Jerusalem sieges and sackings of 70–2, 86, 98
"Bad Jew"/"Good Jew" model 253
Bahat, Dan: *Twenty Centuries of Jewish Life in the Holy Land: The Forgotten Generations* 134
Balfour Declaration (1917) 1, 2

Bamidbar (Numbers) 75, 118, 150
Bar-Mitzvah, author's 157, 179
Bar Kokhba (Shimon Ben Koseva) and revolt of 132 CE 112, 116–19, 135, 166
Barker, Joanne: *Native Acts* 11
Baxter, Richard: "The Reasons of the Christian Religion" 246
Beit David (House of David) 47, 48, 58, 75
Belarus, Gomel in 207
beliefs, central Jewish 149, 155, 168–72, 173, 192, 248, 249, 250
Belisarius 113–14
Bellerose, Ryan 10
Ben-Gurion, David 135, 181, 188, 219, 220
Ben-Yehuda, Eliezer 160
Ben-Ze(')ev, Judah Leib: *Talmud lashon Ivri* 159
Benjamin, tribe of 43, 45, 50, 57, 65, 86
Bereshit (Genesis) 1, 30, 31, 42, 45, 75, 95, 139, 150, 162, 170, 171
Berg, Nancy E.: *Exile from Exile: Israeli Writers from Iraq* 120–1
Berlejung, Angelika 80–1
Berman, Joshua 149, 150
Berurah, Mishnah 143
Beta-Yisrael Jews 4, 120, 199
Beth-Tsur 98
Bethsura (Battle of—164 BCE) 96
Bible
  Hebrew 29, 46, 48, 51, 53, 57, 59, 62, 65, 76, 90
  Septuagint 60, 91, 148
  Talmud and *see* Talmud
  Tanakh and *see* Tanakh
  Torah and *see* Torah
  see individual book names
Bickermann, Elias 96
biological racism 17
Black Obelisk 62
blood quantum 16–20
Bogdanor, Vernon 243
Bornstein, Carrie 167
brit milah (circumcision) 80, 95, 97, 144, 149, 162–5, 176, 211
British Mandate of Palestine 1, 2, 119, 135
Britishness (sense of)
  author 130, 254, 255, 256

Efrat Sopher 224
  see also United Kingdom
"Broken Mirror of Jewish Identity" 21, 189, 253
Bronze Age 32–3, 40
Buber, Martin 230, 231
  Zwei Glaubensweisen ("Two Types of Faith") 248, 249
Buck, Mary Ellen: *The Canaanites: Their History and Culture from Texts and Artifacts* 39
bulla (seal) 65, 66, 69, 70
bumiputera ("sons of the soil") 9
burials 141, 144
Byzantine period 113, 119

Caesar, Julius 105
Caesarea 106, 108
Cahill, J. M. 51
Calderwood Lodge Jewish Primary School 171
calendar (Hebrew/Jewish) 137, 178–80
Caligula 109
Campaign Against Antisemitism 130
Campaign for Soviet Jews 213
Canaan/Canaanites 9, 30, 32, 33, 34–5, 37, 38–9, 40–3, 45, 57, 169, 170, 171
  language 157–8
Canada, Tegegne family and Ethiopian Jews 197, 202, 203
Carchemish (Battle of—605 BCE) 171
Cassidy, Julie 244
Catholicism 229, 230
census, Quirinius 108
Central Europe 6, 120
Chalcolithic Era 38
Chanukah 90, 92, 93, 96, 97, 179, 199
charity 147–8
  Mishneh Torah ("Laws of Charity") 147, 187
Cherem (exclusion) 18
Chevra Kadisha 144
Chickahominy Tribe 173, 245
chicken (eating) 199
Choua, Rabbi Isaac 171, 181, 183–93
Christianity 246–7
  Constantine converts Roman Empire to 133
  conversion of Jews to 133, 243
  emergence of 78

Jesus 260
Jews and Judaism in Christian context 246, 248, 249, 257, 259
Old Testament 91
redefinition of Judaism and 246–53
Chronicles (*Divrei Hayamim*) 64–5, 77, 81
circumcision (brit milah) 80, 95, 97, 144, 149, 162–5, 176, 211
City of London School for Girls 223
civilization (Jewish) 146, 231
  continuity of 131, 132, 176, 242
  recording 73–8
Claudius (Emperor) 109, 110
Clermont-Tonnerre, Stanislas Marie Adélaïde (Comte de) 268
Cline, Eric: *The Year Civilization Collapsed* 40
Cobo, José Martínez: "Study of the Problem of Discrimination Against Indigenous Populations" 7
Cohen, Rabbi Shaye J. D. 27, 28
  "The Beginnings of Jewishness" 142
coins 88, 108, 112
  Jewish–Roman war 112, 117, 118, 119
Collins, John 98
colonialism and colonization 12, 126, 128, 132, 133, 143, 186, 191
  American cultural colonialism 6
  Arab 51, 186
  Greeks 96–7
  Israel/Zionists 3, 240
  mental colonization 186, 188, 203
  Romans 108, 111, 116
  Soviet Union 240
Commentary 3
"Committed, Concerned and Conciliatory: Attitudes of Jews in Britain towards Israel" (2010 study) 130
Common Judaism 149
community (communities; communal life) 143–5
  acceptance as member of community (first criterion for assessing indigeneity) 129–32

INDEX

distinctive communities 175–81
Constantine (Emperor) 133
constitution, Torah as 7, 78, 148
conversion
   from Judaism to Christianity 133, 243
   to Judaism 16, 17, 18, 87, 99, 131, 232, 235
Corbyn, Jeremy 234
Cotter, Christopher R. 250
Crusader Period 119
culture 14–15, 155, 161–2, 246–53
   American cultural colonialism 6
   continuity 132, 165, 209
   cultural genocide 94, 97, 208, 209, 258
   cultural Zionism 161
   indigenous 13, 27, 120, 172, 173, 186, 188, 209, 211, 246–53
   Judaism as a 28
   maintenance in modern times 14–15
   see also customs/traditions/practices
customs/traditions/practices 14–15, 18, 34, 64, 65, 76, 94, 120, 137, 138–9, 161, 162, 165, 192, 193, 197, 222, 260
   Ethiopian Jews 197–8
   maintenance in modern times 14–15
   Shabbat (sabbath) 22, 88, 95, 150–1, 161, 162, 180, 215, 222
   in USSR 215
   see also culture; festivals and holidays
Cyrus Cylinder 85
Cyrus the Great 72, 220
   Edict of Cyrus (539 BCE) 79, 85

Daily Rambam Study 147
Damascus 89, 101
   Hazael (King) of 48, 62–3, 69
Darius I 86
David (King) 30, 46, 47–8, 49, 50, 51, 53, 54, 68, 135
   Beit David (House of David) 65
David, Ariel 50
David and Solomon, Kingdom of *see* United Monarchy
Davidic dynasty 48, 65, 75, 85, 86
Dead Sea Scrolls 100, 159
Declaration of Independence, State of Israel (1948) 10, 140
Declaration on the Rights of Indigenous Peoples *see* United Nations
decolonization xix, 6, 9, 11, 121, 126, 127, 174, 175, 244, 259–63
Deuteronomy (Devarim) 40, 43, 45, 46, 74, 75, 76, 134–5, 138, 169, 171, 177
Devarim (Deuteronomy) 40, 43, 45, 46, 74, 75, 76, 134–5, 138, 169, 171, 177
Dever, William and *Beyond the Texts: An Archaeological Portrait of Ancient Israel and Judah* 37, 46
Diaspora (and the exile) 79–82
   antisemitism and 254
   Babylonian exile *see* Babylon
   "Bad Jew"/"Good Jew" model 253
   Bar Kokhba revolt and 116
   "Broken Mirror of Jewish Identity" and 253
   burials and 141, 144
   Campaign for Soviet Jews and 213
   circumcision and 164
   close connection to Israel within 4, 5, 6, 8, 20, 22, 116, 121, 129–32, 139, 141, 157, 167, 171, 189, 219, 225
   dual identity and loyalty 90, 220–1, 253–4
   duality faced by Jews in Diaspora 220–1, 254
   Edict of Cyrus and choice of returning home from Babylon to Judah 79, 85
   expulsion from Jerusalem 1, 79, 119, 176
   Galut (exile) and 79, 191
   Hebrew calendar and 179
   immigration to Land of Israel/Palestine region from (Aliya) 121, 130, 134, 140, 160, 181, 191, 219–20, 234, 261
   indigeneity and 23, 33, 155
   integration into non-Jewish societies 23, 253–6
Israelite evolution into modern Jews and 79
Jewish–Roman wars fought in 110, 115, 116, 120
language and 155–6, 157, 159
Levant and 186, 188
mental colonization 186
October 7th and 6, 128, 191
origins 79
two thousand years of 119–21
YHWH and 171
see also specific locations of exile
"Diaspora Blues" 23, 221, 254
dictionaries, Hebrew 159
Divrei Hayamim (Book of Chronicles) 64–5, 77, 81
dual identity and loyalty 90, 220–1, 253–4
Dymshits–Kuznetsov aircraft hijacking (1970) 214

Eastern Europe 6, 13, 120, 159, 209, 240
Ecbatana (Battle of—129 BCE) 99
economics (and economic systems) 145–8
   modern Israel 147–8, 155
Edelman, Diana 59
Edict of Cyrus (539 BCE) 79, 85
Egypt 34–5, 60, 63, 70, 77
   Egyptian names 36
   Exodus from (and Book of Exodus) 18, 30, 33–7, 41, 42, 75, 137, 138, 139, 150, 170
   hieroglyphs 32
   slavery 30, 33, 34, 36, 37
Eicha (Book of) 81–2
El (Canaanite deity) 32, 39, 41, 169–70
Elasa (Battle of—160 BCE) 96
Elazar, Daniel J. 4, 144–5
elephantine papyri and ostraca 86
Elohim 169
Emmaus (Battle of—165 BCE) 96
emuna (and faith) 248, 249, 250
endogamy 17
English–Hebrew dictionary 159
Episcopalianism 229, 230
Eretz Ysrael *see* Israel (Land of)
Essenes 78, 99, 100, 108, 148, 151
Esther (Queen) and Scroll of Esther 88, 246

Ethiopian Jews 120, 134, 137, 181, 197, 198–204
Europe
  Central 6, 120
  Eastern 6, 13, 120, 159, 209, 240
Eusebius 117, 119
exile *see* Diaspora; post-exilic period
Exodus (Book of, and Exodus story) 18, 30, 33–7, 41, 42, 75, 137, 138, 139, 150, 170
Ezra (Book of) 80, 81, 85, 86–7, 88

faith 248–50
Faitlovitch, Jacques 200
fascism 207–8
fasting 180
festivals and holidays 14, 88, 137–9, 141, 179–80, 185, 211, 214
  see also individual festival names
Finkelstein, Israel 31, 34, 47, 48, 49, 50, 51, 58, 59, 60, 62, 64, 65, 67, 68, 69, 74, 76–7, 87
First Temple 46, 54, 88, 138, 150
"firstness" and indigeneity 9–10
Flight, John W.: "The Nomadic Idea and Ideal in the Old Testament" 41–2
Florus, Gessius 111
Fortgang, Tal: *Commentary* 3
"fourth sect" of the Jews 108, 111
Fox, R. G. Urban: *Anthropology: Cities in their Cultural Settings* 51–2
Friedman, Richard Elliott: *The Exodus* 35–6

Gad (Tribe of) 30, 43, 44, 45, 64
Gadot, Yuval 68–9
Galilee 100, 105, 109, 110, 118, 119, 133, 166
Galut (Diaspora referred to as) 79, 191
Ganor, Sa'ar 49
Garfinkel, Yosef 49–50, 67
gay Jew, author as 255–6
Gaza 100
Gedaliah 72
Gemara 81, 100
Genesis (Bereshit) 1, 30, 31, 42, 45, 75, 95, 139, 150, 162, 170, 171

genetics 14, 16, 17, 38, 242
genocide 88, 208
  cultural 94, 97, 208, 209, 258
  Zionism as genocidal cult 21
Gerizim, Mount 94, 95
Geva, Hillel 87–8
Gezer 32, 48, 53
Gibbethon 60
Gibeon-Bethel area 59
gladiatorial battles 107, 113
God
  names 41
  promising Land of Israel 1, 31, 169, 171–3, 252
  Rabbi Choua's perceptions 189, 192
  wrath of 74, 77
  see also agnostic Jews; atheist Jews; monotheism; YHWH
gods 39, 40, 85, 169–70
  Canaanite 39
Golan 100, 133
Gomel (Belarus) 207
Gonzalez, Alejandro V. 251–2
"Good Jew"/"Bad Jew" model 253
Grabbe, Lester L. and *The Dawn of Israel* 43, 45–6, 47, 51
Greece/Greeks 88–97
  Hellenism/Hellenistic period 89–93, 96, 97, 98, 100, 107, 163
  Tanakh translation into Greek (Septuagint) 60, 91, 148
  see also Hellenism
Gruen, Erich S. 91–2, 93, 94

Ha'am, Ahad 161
Habakkuk, Book of (*Sefer Habakkuk*) 40
Hadrian 119, 135
Ha-Kohen, Rabbi Israel Meir 143
Halacha (Jewish law) 18, 98, 107, 109, 115, 116, 130, 139, 145–6, 148, 149, 150, 151, 167, 171, 178
Halevi, Rabbi Yehuda 140
HaMaccabee, Judah (Judah the Hammer) 95
Hamas and October 7th massacre (2023) 3, 4, 6, 21, 128, 179, 191, 235, 242, 257, 258, 260
ha-Nasi, Judah 100
Hasel, Michael 49

Haskalah (Jewish Enlightenment) 247
Hasmonean dynasty 89, 90, 91, 92, 96, 99–100, 101–2, 105, 106, 110, 120, 135, 158, 165
  map xiii
HaTarsi, Shimon (Simon Thassi) 97
Hazael of Damascus (King) 48, 62–3, 69
Head, Hands, and Heart model (Jewish Pride) 259
Hebrew (language) 39, 155–61
  Bible 29, 46, 48, 51, 53, 57, 59, 62, 65, 76, 90
  dictionaries 159
  Hebrew 137, 178–80
  as official language of newly established State of Israel 156, 160, 209
  origins of 39, 157–61
  significance to Jews of 156
  in USSR, and its banning 208–11, 215
  see also Paleo-Hebrew
Hebrew Immigrant Aid Society (HIAS) 214
Hebrew Union College—Jewish Institute of Religion 231
Hebron 31, 61
Hellenism/Hellenistic period 89–93, 96, 97, 98, 100, 107, 163
Henderson, James (Sa'ke'j) Youngblood 126–7
Henderson, Phil 126
Herod Agrippa (Agrippa the Great) 109–10
Herod the Great (King) 101–2, 105–7, 114
  maps of kingdom and its division xiv–xv
Herodian dynasty/tetrarchy 101, 107, 110
Herr, Moshe David 115
Herzl, Theodore 172, 198, 241, 246
Hezekiah (King) 62, 66, 68, 69–70
hieroglyphs 32
Hillel II 178
Hiram of Tyre 186
Hirsch, Emil G. 250
historic systems, maintenance in modern times 14–45
history and origins (of Jews) xviii, 7, 12, 25–122
  the beginnings 25–52

INDEX

continuity with pre-colonial and/or pre-settler societies 132–6
Efrat Sopher learning about 221
Hofman, Miriam Ben Zeev 117
holidays *see* festivals and holidays *and specific festivals*
Holocaust (Shoah) 21, 179–91, 207
  Commemoration Day 179
Hoshea of Israel (King) 63–4
House of David (Beit David) 47, 48, 58, 75
Hyrcanus I (King John Hyrcanus) 92, 99
Hyrcanus II (King) 101, 105, 106

Idumea 99, 101, 105
ImmerseNYC mikveh 167
immersion pools (mikveh) 165–8
Indian Blood Law (1705) 15
indigeneity xvii, xviii–xx, xxii–xxiv, 123–281
  ancestry and 15–18
  blood quantum and 15–19, 20
  culture and 13, 27, 120, 172, 173, 186, 188, 209, 211, 246–53
  definition 7, 8–15, 127, 132, 142, 155, 175, 225
  depoliticizing 8–12
  "firstness" and 9–10
  genetics and 16–18, 38, 242
  impact on us as Jews today 239, 253
  "indigenous" term 8, 11, 12, 174
  interviews 181–236
  Jews arguing against 19–20, 258
  study on 123–81
  tribal membership and 15–19
  United Nations' seven criteria for 7, 125–52
  see also Native Americans
Indigenous Foundation 16, 19
indigenous rights movement 3, 20, 121, 174, 240–6
Inquisition, Spanish and Portuguese 134
Institute for Jewish Policy Research 129, 130
integration (of Diaspora) into non-Jewish societies 23, 253–6
intermarriage 16, 86–7

International Labour Organisation: Indigenous and Tribal Peoples Convention (1989) 20–1
Ioudaismos 27–8, 92
Iran 99
  Efrat Sopher's family connections 219, 220
Iron Age 32, 58, 169
Isaac (biblical character) 30, 31, 41, 74, 77
Ishmael (son of Nethaniah) 72
Islam *see* Muslims
Israel (Land of—Eretz Ysrael) 30, 137
  Babylonian expulsion 28, 71, 72–3, 79, 97, 170
  connection to/relationship with (of Jews) 4, 5, 6, 8, 20, 22, 116, 121, 129–32, 139, 141, 157, 167, 171, 189, 219, 225, 260
  Diaspora and immigration to 121, 130, 134, 140, 160, 181, 191, 219–20, 234, 261
  Ethiopian Jews and 199–204
  group rooted in 13–14, 176, 239
  Hebrew calendar and 178
  history 25–121
  as "homeland" or "ancestral land" 2, 3, 129, 201
  indigenous to 6, 10, 11, 23, 24, 125, 127, 128, 229, 239, 240, 254, 258, 259
  Israelites entering 37–42
  kings 42–54
  origins of 27–54
  people of (Am Yisrael) 18, 33, 75, 116, 145, 176
  promised (by God) 1, 31, 169, 171–3, 252
  right of return to 200, 202–3
  Roman expulsion from 79, 110–20, 133, 142–3, 159, 176
  twelve tribes of 30, 43–4, 45, 57, 58, 61, 64
  visiting 23, 233
  as Western country (or not) 187–8
Israel (modern State of)
  burials 141, 144
  Declaration of Independence (1948) 10, 140

Jerusalem as capital of 135, 221
  Netanyahu government 254
  official language of Hebrew 156, 160, 209
  origins/rebirth (1948) 33, 72, 97, 102, 119, 121, 134, 135, 174–5, 176, 197, 219, 239, 244, 246
  wars/conflicts *see individual war names*
  Zionism and *see* Zionism
Israel (Northern Kingdom of) 27, 31, 34, 46, 47, 48–9, 49, 58–66, 67, 69, 72, 77, 221
  map xi
Israel (United Monarchy of) *see* United Monarchy
Israel Institute of Technology (Technion) 17
Israelites
  entering Eretz Yisrael 37–42
  evolution into modern Jews 79
  refugee 65, 69
Issachar (House of) 43, 45, 60, 64

Jacob (biblical character) 30, 31, 34, 35, 41, 43, 45, 65, 74, 77, 118, 135, 187
Jacob Cycle 31
Jahaz 61
Jason (King) (formerly known as Joshua) 83, 94
Jeconiah (King) 71, 72
Jehoahaz (King) 66, 70
Jehoiachin (King) 71, 80
Jehoram (King) 66, 67
Jehu (King—son of Omri) 62
Jericho 38, 107, 108
Jeroboam 58, 60
Jerusalem 51, 59, 67–70, 71, 75, 77, 86, 88, 93, 94, 98, 101, 112, 113–14, 117, 119, 133, 134–5, 138, 190, 221, 233, 242
  Antiochus IV and 94–5
  Antiochus VII and 99
  Assyrian siege (701 BCE) 70
  Babylonian siege (589 BCE) 71
  Babylonian siege (597 BCE) 71, 79
  central to Jewish identity and life 88, 168, 190, 221, 242
  declared capital of modern Jewish state 135

THE JEWS

evolution and expansion of 68–9
expulsions from 1, 79, 119, 176
facing in prayer 198, 242
First Temple in 46, 54, 88, 138, 150
Hadrian's temple to Jupiter 119, 135
Hasmoneans and 98, 99, 100, 101
Hellenization of 93–4
Herod and 105–7
Hyrcanus and 101
Judaea capital moved to Caesarea Maritima from 108
as Judah's capital 66, 67–9, 70
prayer (and synagogue) facing towards 135, 198
Priests of 86
rebuilding of during Persian period 86
renamed as Aelia Capitolina 117
return (post-exilic) 114, 198
Romans and 16, 79, 110–20
Saul and 59
Second Temple see Second Temple
Shalosh Regalim and 138
synagogues in 178
Temple Mount 51, 68, 88, 107, 119, 135
Torah and 74, 75
United Monarchy and 46, 48, 50, 51, 53, 67, 135
Western Wall 107
Zionism 198–9
Jesus 260
Jew(s) (Jewish people) 25–122
as a people (peoplehood, and acknowledging/identifying this) 1, 2, 28, 28–9, 33, 41, 62, 99, 143, 173, 192, 197, 214, 253, 256
agnostic 162, 168, 192, 222
arguing against Jewish indigeneity 19–20, 259
Ashkenazi 3, 4, 6, 13, 17, 120, 156, 181, 188, 197, 200
atheist 22, 88, 168, 172–3, 192
Babylonian exile see Babylon
"Bad Jew"/"Good Jew" model 253
central beliefs 149, 155, 168–72, 173, 192, 248, 249, 250
Diaspora see Diaspora
hatred of see antisemitism
Hellenized 90, 92, 96, 97, 163
indigeneity see indigeneity
"Jew"/"Jewish" term 27, 28, 87
lived experiences 181–236
non-Jewish definitions of Jewish identity 4, 240, 258
origins and history see history
Patriarchs 31, 75, 77
religion see Judaism
secular 28, 172
Sephardic 4, 120, 134, 147, 159, 181, 185
Jewish Board of Guardians 144
Jewish Care 144
Jewish Chronicle 148
Jewish Currents: "When Settler Becomes Native" 19
Jewish difference, antisemitism and notion of 155, 259
Jewish Enlightenment (Haskalah) 247
Jewish law (Halacha) 18, 98, 107, 109, 115, 116, 130, 139, 145–6, 148, 149, 150, 151, 167, 178
Jewish Museum of London 166
Jewish Policy Research 129, 130
Jewish Pride xvii, xxii, 4, 8, 20, 22, 45, 192–3, 256, 257–9
Jewish Pride trilogy xxii, 7, 243, 261
  Jewish Pride: Rebuilding a People xxiii, xxiv, 144, 181
  Reclaiming Our Story: The Pursuit of Jewish Pride 21, 97, 129, 163, 181, 243, 258
Jewish–Roman Wars 159
  final (Third—Kitos War) 116–17
  First (66–74 CE) 110–16
  Second (Bar Kokhba revolt of 132 CE) 112, 116–18, 135, 166
Jezebel (daughter of the King Tyre) 61, 186
Jezreel Valley 60
Joseph (biblical character) 30, 37, 38, 42

Josephus, Flavius 78, 92, 93, 95, 97, 102, 107, 110–15, 177, 180
  Against (Contra) Apion 78, 111
  Antiquities of the Jews 88, 97, 108, 111
  The Jewish War 107, 111
  The Wars of the Jews 97
Joshua (biblical character) 30, 37, 38
Joshua (Book of—*Sefer Yehoshua*) 75
Josiah (King) 70, 74, 75, 76, 77, 138, 170
Judah (Southern Kingdom) 34, 47, 58–65, 69, 72, 98, 178
  as Assyrian vassal state 63
  Babylonians and exile/expulsion from 28, 71, 72
  Greek rule 89
  Israelite refugee influx/absorbed into 65, 69
  Jerusalem and 67–8
  map xi
  Northern Kingdom and 58
  Persian Empire rules 73, 85
  renamed Judea 88, 101
  Southern Kingdom of 34, 47, 58, 59, 61, 63, 65, 69, 72, 98, 178
Judah the Hammer (Judah HaMaccabee) 95
Judahites 27, 61, 65, 67, 71, 72, 75, 80–1, 82, 85, 88
  exile/escape 71, 72, 80–1
Judaism (Jewish Religion)
  Bible and see Bible
  in Christian context 246, 248, 249, 257, 259
  "Common Judaism" 149
  conversion to 16, 17, 18, 87, 99, 131, 232, 235
  culture and indigeneity and 13, 27, 28, 120, 172, 173, 186, 188, 209, 211, 246–53
  as culture that contains religion 28
  definition and redefinition 246–53
  Haskalah (Jewish Enlightenment) and 247
  historical use of term 92, 248
  indigeneity and 246–53
  "Jewish religion" (religione hebrea and first use of term) 247

Liberal, recognizing equilineal descent 18
Muscular 121
nationality and 2–3
Orthodox *see* Orthodox Jews and Judaism
Rabbinic 100, 115, 116, 191
Reform 2, 34, 131, 166, 232, 234
reframing our understanding of 252
Talmud and *see* Talmud
Tanakh and *see* Tanakh
Torah and *see* Torah
world religions and 250–1
Judas of Galilee 108
Judea 105–19
Bar Kokhba revolt and 112, 116–19, 135, 166
circumcision and 163
identity changed from an ethno-geographic term to an ethno-religious identity 99
immersion pools in 166
Judea renamed as 98, 101
Roman rule 105–19
Judeo-Arabic languages 155
Judges (Book of—*Sefer Shoftim*) 43, 45, 46, 75
judges (Shoftim) 30–1, 42–6
Julian (Emperor) 135
Jupiter, Hadrian's temple to 119, 135

Kaddish 179, 248
Kagan, Yisrael Meir 165
Kahn, Rabbi Andrue 19
kashrut (kosher—dietary laws) 24, 149, 167, 199
Kaufmann, Yehezkel 79
Kehilla (community) 143, 144, 145
Keimer, Kyle 44, 46, 48, 52, 53
Kenite hypothesis 39
Kennedy, Titus 35
Kenyon College 232, 233, 320
Ketuvim (Writings) 18, 29, 78, 81
Kfar Batya 200
Khaykin, Vlad 181, 205–16, 224–5
Khirbet al-Ra'I 50
Khirbet Beit Lei 61
Khirbet ed-Dawwara 50
Khirbet el-Qom 61
Khirbet Qeiyafa 49, 50, 100
Kia, General Ali 220

Kings (Book of—*Sefer Melachim*) 47, 59, 60, 75, 170
kings (of Israel) 42–54
kissing the ground 137, 171
Kitos (Quietus) War (115–117 CE) 116–17
Kochubievsky, Boris 212–13
Kohler, Kaufmann 249–50, 250
Koseva, Shimon Ben (Bar Kokhba) and revolt of 132 CE 112, 116–19, 135, 166
kosher (kashrut—dietary laws) 24, 100, 149, 167
Kranes, Rabbi Charisse 234
Krauthammer, Charles 5, 233
Kullmann, Eugen 230–1, 232
Kurkh Stele 62
Kuznetsov and Dymshits aircraft hijacking (1970) 214

Labour Party (UK) and antisemitism 234
Lachish 67
Ladino 155, 159
Land of Israel *see* Israel (Land of)
language 155–61, 209–11
alphabet 159
distinct 155, 158, 159
Soviet Union 209, 211, 215
see also Hebrew *and other individual language names*
law 148–52
Halacha (Jewish Law) 18, 98, 107, 109, 115, 116, 130, 139, 145–6, 148, 149, 150, 151, 167, 171, 178
League of Nations 1, 126
Lebanon 30, 38, 185
LeFebvre, Michael 90
left-wing, new (New Left) 2, 3, 5, 9, 10, 19, 21, 125, 126, 174, 175, 187, 243
Leith, Mary Joan 75, 76, 82, 87
Leshon Hakodesh 156
Letter of Aristeas 91
Levant xviii, 3, 9, 10, 17, 33, 35, 38, 62, 157, 175, 185, 186–7, 188
Southern 23, 33, 35, 39, 58, 60, 63, 70, 71, 185, 186, 187, 229, 239, 260
Levi (Tribe of) 35, 43, 45
Levi, David: *Lingua Sacra* 159
Leviticus (Vayikra) 75, 146, 165, 166
Lew, Julian D. M. 151

Liberal, Judaism recognizing equilineal descent 18
Lightfoot, Sheryl 125
Lindo, Abigail 159
living systems (rules of Life) 14, 15, 127, 151, 155, 175
Lokensgard, Kenneth H. 251, 252
Low Chronology theory 49, 68
Luria, Rabbi Sara 167
Luzzatto, Moshe Chaim 299
Lysimachus 94

Maasai 9
Maccabean revolt (167–141 BCE) 91, 92, 95, 96, 97
Maccabees I 92, 95, 97, 241
Maccabees II 87, 92, 93, 94, 95, 97
Maimonides (Rambam; Moses ben Nachman) 137, 147, 150, 230
Shloshah Asar Ikkarim 250
Mamluks 119
Mamre 31, 77
Manasseh (King) 77
Manasseh (tribe of) 30, 45, 64
Mandate of Palestine (1922) 1, 2, 119, 135
Māori and New Zealand 9, 11
Mariamne 102, 106
Marlene Meyerson JCC Manhattan 167
Mary of Bethezuba 112
Masada 106, 110, 114, 177
Mason, Steve 111, 114
Mayyim Hayyim (Living Waters) 167
Mazar, Amihai 66
Mazar, Eilat 51, 68
Megiddo 49, 53
Battle of (609 BCE) 70, 77
Melachot 150–1
Melamed, Abraham 247
Menelaus 95
Menorah 113–14
menstruation 166
mental colonization 186, 188, 203
Merneptah Stele 31–2, 34, 41, 62
Mesha (King of Moab) and Mesha Stele 41, 44, 47, 61, 63
Meyers, Hannah E. 3
Middle (Near) East 3, 16, 17, 27, 37, 40, 44, 52, 53, 63, 89, 101, 120, 133, 172, 178, 185, 186, 260

mikveh 165–8
Mishnah (written collection of oral tradition) 81, 100, 116, 133, 139, 150, 165
Mishnah Berurah 143
Mishneh Torah 147, 187
mitzvah (mitzvot) 143, 145
Mizpah 86
Mizrahi (Beta-Yisrael) Jews 4, 120, 199
Modi'in 95
money, *see also* coins; economics
monolatrism 169
monolithic people 128, 131, 161
monotheism 41, 109, 168, 169, 170, 192, 198
see also God
Montefiore, Simon Sebag: *Jerusalem: The Biography* 133
Moses 18, 30, 33, 37, 41, 45, 73, 74–5, 90, 176
Five Books of Moses *see* Torah on Mount Sinai receiving Torah 30, 33, 73
see also Operation Moses
Moses ben Nachman *see* Maimonides
Murašû Archive 80
Muscular Judaism (Muskeljudentum) 121
Muslims (and Islam) xix, 3, 119, 164, 201, 210, 247, 250
peace between Jews and xix
Myers, Hannah E.: *Commentary* 3

Na'aman, Nadav 34–5, 66, 68, 69
Nachman, Moses ben 156
Nadab 60
Nahal Hever 118
names 22
Egyptian 36
for God 41
Soviet Union and 209–10
Native Americans 15–16, 209
Chickahominy Tribe 173, 245
natural resources, strong link to 136–41
Navajo Nation 15–16
Nazis 16, 17, 207, 208
see also Holocaust
Near (Middle) East 3, 16, 17, 27, 37, 40, 44, 52, 53, 63, 89, 101, 120, 133, 172, 178, 185, 186, 260
Nebuchadnezzar Chronicle 71
Nebuchadnezzar II 71, 72, 73, 82

Necho II (Pharaoh) 71
Nehemiah (Book of) 80, 81, 86, 87
neo-evolutionism 52
Nero 111, 112
Netanyahu government 254
Nevi'im (Prophets) 29, 78
New Left (Leftists) 2, 3, 5, 9, 10, 19, 21, 125, 126, 174, 175, 187, 243
New Zealand and Māori 9, 11
Niddah 166, 166–7
Niehr, Herbert 61
Nimrud slab 62
Nimrud Tablet 66
Nineveh (Battle of—612 BCE) 70
Noll, K. L.: *Canaan and Israel in Antiquity: A Textbook on History and Religion* 37
nomadic people 32, 33, 40, 41–2, 137
non-dominant groups of society, formation of (6th UN criterion for assessing indigeneity) 174–5
non-Jewish allies as crucial to defeating antisemitism 5
Nordau, Max 121
North America *see* America; Canada
Northam, Ralph 245
Northern Kingdom (of Israel) *see* Israel (Northern Kingdom of)
Northwest Semitic language 157, 158
Numbers (*Bamidbar*) 75, 118, 150
Nuremberg Laws (1935) 16

Octavian (Emperor) 106
October 7th massacre (10/7/2023) and Hamas 3, 4, 6, 21, 128, 179, 191, 235, 242, 254, 257, 258, 260
Old Testament 51, 91, 260
Omri (King) and Omride dynasty/family 60, 61, 62, 63, 67
Oniad family (and high priests) 93
Onias III 93, 94
Operation Moses 200, 201, 203
oral tradition 81, 100
see also Mishna
Orlah 139

Orthodox Jews and Judaism 131, 139, 141
conversion 232, 233
mikveh and 166–7
Ortiz, Steven 48
Ottoman Empire 119
Oven, Joshua van 247
Owen, Suzanne 251

Pahlavi, Mohammad Reza (Shah of Iran), and son 220
Pale of Settlement 207
Paleo-Hebrew 39, 157–9
Palestine
British Mandate of 1, 2, 119, 135
Diaspora and immigration to Land Of Israel and 121, 130, 134, 140, 160, 181, 191, 219–20, 234, 261
Jewish peoples' historical connection 1
Palestine Liberation Organization 185
Palestinian National Charter: Resolutions of the Palestine National Council (July 1–17, 1968) 2
Palestinian state (and Palestinians), and right to statehood 3, 8
Jews for 258
Parthians and Parthian Empire 95, 99, 101, 117
Passover (Pesach) 22, 30, 112, 135, 137, 138, 139, 141, 211, 214, 236, 247
Patriarchs, Jewish 31, 75, 77
peace (between Jews and Muslims/Arabs) xix
Pe'ah 146
Pearce, Laurie E. 81
Pekah (King) 63
Pentateuch *see* Torah
peoplehood (Jews as a people and acknowledging/identifying this) 1, 2, 28, 28–9, 33, 41, 62, 99, 143, 173, 192, 197, 214, 253, 256
Persian Empire 73, 76, 78, 85, 86, 87, 88–9
Pesach 22, 30, 112, 135, 137, 138, 139, 141, 211, 214, 236, 247
Petrie, Flinders 31
Petronius 109
Pharisees 78, 99–100, 108, 148
Phasaelus 105

INDEX

Philistia 60, 62
Philistines 37, 48, 60, 65
Philo 109, 163, 176, 177
Phoenecians and their language 39, 157, 185–6
Pickett, Dr. Winston 181, 227–36
Pikuach nefesh (saving a life) 180
Pirkei Avot (Chapters of the Fathers) 249
pogroms 21, 91, 109, 117
politics 148–52
   depoliticizing indigeneity 8–12
   distinct political systems 52, 142
   left-wing 2, 3, 5, 9, 10, 19, 21, 125, 126, 174, 175, 187, 243
pomegranates 176, 225
Pompey (Roman general) 101
Ponnet, Rabbi James 96
pork 73, 163
Portuguese Inquisition 134
post-exilic (Second Temple) period 78, 83–102, 170
practices *see* customs/traditions/practices; festivals and holidays
prayer (Jewish prayer) 14, 140, 177
   Amidah 140, 141, 242
   Shema 168, 171, 173, 187
pride *see* Jewish Pride
Priests of Jerusalem 86
Procopius of Caesarea 113
Prosic, Tamara: *The Development and Symbolism of Passover* 137
Protestantism 229
Psalm 122. 135
Psalm 126. 140
Psalm 137. 72, 135, 140
Ptolemaic dynasty 89, 90, 91
Ptolemy I Soter 89
Ptolemy II 91
Purim 81, 88, 199

Qeiyafa Ostracon 158
Quietus (Kitos) War (115–117 CE) 116–17
Quirinius (governor of Syria) 108

Rabbinic Judaism 100, 115, 116, 191
Rabin, Yitzhak 234
racism, biological 17
Ramallah 60

Rambam *see* Maimonides
Rambam Medical Center 17
Ramses II (Pharaoh) 30
Ravina II 81
Reclaiming Our Story: The Pursuit of Jewish Pride 21, 97, 129, 163, 181, 243, 258
Reform Judaism 2, 34, 81, 131, 166, 232
refugees (ancient) 72
   Israelite 65, 69
   Masada 114
refuseniks 213, 214
Rehoboam (King) 57, 58, 59, 60, 67
Reich, Ronny 114
religions (in general)
   indigenous 251–2
   Judaism as culture that contains 28
   Soviet Union 210
   in Torah, concept of 18
   Winston Pickett's experiences 229–30
   world, Judaism and 250–1
Remaliah of Israel 63
reversion (Cassidy's notion of) 244
Rezin (King of Aram) 63
Richards, Martin 17
Robertson, David G. 250
Rogers, Guy MacLean: *For the Freedom of Zion: The Great Revolt of Jews against Romans* 111
Roman Empire 105–20
   Bar Kokhba revolt (132 CE) 112, 116–19, 135, 166
   Constantine and conversion to Christianity in 133
   Jerusalem and Jerusalem 16, 79, 110–20
   Judea as client kingdom of 15–17
   wars with *see* Jewish–Roman Wars
Rome
   direct rule of Judaea from 107, 108–10
   Jews voluntarily moved to 120
Romer, Thomas 34, 35
roots
   Book of the (*Sefer ha-Shorashim*) 159
   in Land of Israel 13–14, 176, 239
   of modern Hebrew 157
Rosen, Avraham 180

Rosh Hashanah 22, 137, 176, 179
Rosh HaShanah La'Ilanot (Tu BiShvat) 14, 139
Rosner, Fred: *Encyclopedia of Jewish Medical Ethics* 163
Russia 197, 240
   see also Soviet Union
Rustin, Bayard 215
Ruth (and Book of Ruth) 18–19, 87

Sabbath (Shabbat—and laws/prohibitions/restrictions) 22, 88, 95, 150–1, 161, 162, 180, 215, 222
Sabra, Efrat Sopher as 219
Sabri, Ekrima 3
Sacks, Rabbi Jonathan 147, 236, 242
Sadducees 78, 99–100, 108, 111, 148
Salome (Queen—Salome Alexandra) 100, 101
Salome I (Herod's sister) 108
Samaria 43, 60, 62, 64, 94, 106, 118
Samuel (prophet) 46, 50
Sanders, E. P.: "Judaism: Practice & Belief" 149
Sanders, Seth L. 158
Sanhedrin (council of Jewish elders) 105, 106, 178, 179
Sappir 81
Sargon II 62
Satanow, Isaac: *Sefer ha-Shorashim* (Book of the Roots) 159
Satlow, Michael L. 79, 86
Saul (King) 30, 46, 47, 48, 49, 59, 65, 76, 158
Schama, Sir Simon 76
   The Story of the Jews: Finding the Words, 1000 B C – 1492 A D 29
Schein, Sylvia 133
Schniedewind, William M.: *How the Bible Became a Book: The Textualization of Ancient Israel* 64
Schultz, Joseph P. 96
Second Temple 73, 78, 88, 107, 110, 111, 135, 138, 147, 191
   period of (post-exilic period) 78, 83–102, 170
secularism 28, 172
Sefer ha-Shorashim (Book of the Roots) 40

Sefer Habakkuk (Book of Habakkuk) 40
Sefer Melachim (Book of Kings) 47, 59, 60, 75, 170
Sefer Shoftim (Book of Judges) 43, 45, 46, 75
Sefer Yehoshua (Book of Joshua) 75
Seidenberg, David Mevorach 133
Selassie, Emperor Haile 201
Seleucid Empire and Seleucids 89, 91, 92, 93, 95, 96, 96–7, 99, 101
Seleucus I Nicator 89
self-identification as indigenous peoples at the individual level 125–6, 129–32
Sennacherib 68–70
Sephardic Jews 4, 120, 134, 147, 159, 181, 185
Septuagint 60, 91, 148
Sesostris I (Pharaoh) 30
7/10 (Oct 7th, 2023) massacre and Hamas 3, 4, 6, 21, 128, 179, 191, 235, 242, 254, 257, 258, 260
sexual orientation, author's 255–6
Shabbat (Sabbath—and laws/ prohibitions/restrictions) 22, 88, 95, 150–1, 161, 162, 180, 215, 222
Shah of Iran (and son) 220
Shalmaneser III 62
Shalosh Regalim (pilgrimage festivals) 138
Shaphan (scribe) 72
Shapira, Dan 100
Sharpe, Fiona 234
Shasu 35, 40
Shavuot 22, 137, 138, 179, 180
Shechem 31, 33, 59, 60, 68
Shema prayer 168, 171, 173, 187
Shemini Atzeret 141
Shemot (Book of Exodus) and Exodus story 18, 30, 33–7, 41, 42, 75, 137, 138, 139, 150, 170
Shephelah 49–50, 67
Sheplah 31
Sheshbazzar ("Prince of Judah") 85
Shishak (King) 59
Shivat Haminim (seven species of fruit native to the Land of Israel as mentioned in the Torah) 176, 186, 225
Shmita (Sabbatical Year) 139, 146

Shoah *see* Holocaust
Shoah/Holocaust 179–91, 207
shofar 34, 140, 242
Shoftim (judges) 30–1, 42–6
shoresh (roots of modern Hebrew) 157
Shoshenq I (Pharaoh) 59, 60
Silberman, Neil Asher, *Bible Unearthed* 64
Silberstein, Abe: "Bio-Zionism: Why Claiming Jews Are Indigenous to Israel Is So Dangerous" 19–20
Sinai, Mount 30, 33, 73
Singh, Manvir, and "It's Time to Rethink the Idea of the Indigenous" 9, 10
Six Day War (1967) 2, 212
skin tone (author's) 6
slavery 36–7
 Egyptians and 30, 33, 34, 36, 37
 Romans and 113, 118
Smart, Ninian 251
Smith, Mark S.: *The Early History of God: Yahweh and the Other Deities in Ancient Israel* 38–9, 41, 169
society (ancient Israel) 43, 142–5
 forming non-dominant groups of 174–5
Soleb Inscription 35
Solomon (King) 39, 46, 48, 53, 54, 57, 59, 186, 201, 203
Solomon and David, Kingdom of *see* United Monarchy
Sopher, Dr. Efrat 181, 189, 217–26, 254
Southern Kingdom of Judah *see* Judah
sovereignty 89–102
 end/loss 103–21
 re-establishment/regaining/ rebirth (1948) 33, 72, 97, 102, 119, 121, 134, 135, 174–5, 176, 239, 244, 246
Soviet Union (USSR) 2, 201, 207–16, 240, 242, 255
Spanish Inquisition 134
Sperling, Rabbi S. David 34–5
Spinoza, Baruch 18
Stalin and Stalinism 207, 240
Sudan and Ethiopian Jews 201, 202, 203
Sukkot 22, 137, 138, 148
Supreme Islamic Council (Jerusalem) 3
Susa 81

synagogues 12, 91, 135, 149, 162, 176–8, 178, 242
 prayer facing towards Jerusalem 135, 198
Syria 30, 63, 107, 108, 109, 119, 219

Tal Jezreel 51
talmid haham (Torah scholar) 143
Talmud 100, 116, 121, 137, 143, 147, 159, 162, 198, 199, 236, 249
 Babylonian 81, 186
Tanakh 46, 60, 73–8
 codifying 73–8
 Ketuvim (Writings) 18, 29, 78, 81
 Nevi'im (Prophets) 29, 78
 Torah *see* Torah
 translation into Greek (Septuagint) 60, 91, 148
taxation 57, 80, 86, 93, 108, 111
Tcherikover, Victor 96
Technion (Israel Institute of Technology) 17
tefillin 168, 214
Tegegne, Yaffa (and her father Baruch) 181, 198–204
Tel Dan Stele 47, 48, 62, 66
Tel Keisan 39
Tell en-Nasbeh 50
Temple Mount (Jerusalem) 51, 68, 88, 107, 119, 135
territories
 pre-colonial presence in 125, 132–6
 strong link to (third UN criterion) 136–41
Thassi, Simon (Shimon HaTarsi) 97
Thatcher, Margaret 144
Theodotus 172, 177, 241
Tiglath-Pileser (King of Assyria) 63
Tikkun Olam 191
Tillich, Paul 230, 231
Titus 111, 112, 114
Tobin, Gary 162
Tomas, Zachary: *Israel's Political and Administrative Structures* 44, 52
Toorn, K. Van Der 39
Torah (Five Books of Moses; Pentateuch) 29, 81, 100, 260
 as constitution 7, 78, 148
 culture and 162–3

INDEX

Edict of Cyrus and 85
Hasmoneans and 98
Hellenistic period and 90, 91
Hezekiah in 70
as inheritance 187
Land of Israel and 171–4, 189
language and 156, 157, 158, 159, 160
law/politics and 7, 72, 73, 148–52, 198, 199
Mishneh Torah ("Laws of Charity") 147, 187
Moses on Mount Sinai receiving 30, 33, 73
origins and composition of 73–9
parsha/parashot (portion) 149, 157, 177–8
religion in, concept of 18
Roman census 108
scholar (talmid haham) 143
Septuagint 60, 91, 148
synagogue and 176–8
Temple destruction and 115
tribes of Israel and 46
United Monarchy and 46–9, 50
YHWH and 41, 169, 170
traditions *see* culture; customs/traditions/practices; festivals and holidays
tribes 15–19, 42–6
indigenous 15, 16, 18, 128
membership 15–19
neo-evolutionism and 52
twelve (of Israel) 30, 43–4, 45, 57, 58, 61, 64
Troen, Ilan and Carol 1–2
Tsfat 124
Tu BiShvat 14, 139
Tylor, Edward Burnett 161
Tzedakah 143, 145–6, 147, 148

UK *see* United Kingdom
Umebinyuo, Ijeoma: "Diaspora Blues" 23, 221, 254
UN *see* United Nations
United Kingdom (UK)
Efrat Sopher and family in 222–5
synagogues 168
see also Britishness
United Monarchy of Israel 30, 46–52, 57, 58, 61, 67, 135, 169
map xx

United Nations (UN—and Declaration on the Rights of Indigenous Peoples) 17, 125–9, 165, 180–1, 209, 241, 244
3rd Article 241
6th Article 126
8th Article 165
12th Article 189
13th Article 192, 209
25th Article 136
26th Article 244
criteria for indigeneity (seven) 7, 125–81
General Assembly Resolution 1514 (1960) 126
United States *see* America
Ur (modern-day Iraq) 29, 171
USA *see* America
USSR (Soviet Union) 2, 201, 207–16, 240, 242, 255

Vandal kingdom 113
vanilla 70
Varus, Publius Quinctilius 107
Vatroth 61
Vayikra (Leviticus) 75, 146, 165, 166
Vespasian (Emperor) 110, 112, 114
Virginia (Colony of) and Indian Blood law 15
Virginia (State of), returning land to Chickahominy tribe 245

Waldron, Jeremy 244–5
Weber, Max 52
Weill, Raymond 177
Weinreich, Max: *History of the Yiddish Language* 156
Wertheimer, Jack 166
West Bank 27, 31, 59
Western country, Israel as or not as a 187–8
Western Wall (Jerusalem) 107
White, Michael 254
Wiesel, Elie 202
Wilf, Dr. Einat xvii–xx
wine 66, 69, 70
Wolff, Samuel 48
women and the mikveh 165–6, 167, 176
world religions and Judaism 250–1
Wozaba, Baruch Tegegne born in 199
wrath of God 74, 77
Wrathall, Mark 77
Writings (Ketuvim) 18, 29, 78, 81

Yafo 98
Yahweh (YHWH), God of the Israelites 18, 32, 35, 39–40, 42, 57, 58, 61–2, 69, 73, 74, 79, 82, 168–71, 172
Yannai, Alexander 100
Yanoam 22
Yavne 115, 118
Yehud/Yehud Medinata (and yehudim) 72, 74, 85, 88, 108, 142
coinage 88
map xii
YHWH (Yahweh), God of the Israelites 18, 32, 35, 39–40, 42, 57, 58, 61–2, 69, 73, 74, 79, 82, 168–71, 172
Yiddish 13, 155, 156, 159, 160, 188
Soviet Union 209, 210–11
Yodfat, siege of (67 CE) 110
Yohai, Rabbi Simeon Ben 113
Yohanan, Mattityahu Ben 92, 95–6
Yom Kippur 180
Yonatan, Mattityahu haKohen Ben 97, 98

Zadok the Pharisee 108
Zakkai, Rabbi Yohanan Ben 115
Zayit Stone 158
Zealots 95, 96, 105, 108, 111, 114
Zedekiah (King) 71, 72
Zemaraim, Mount (battle of—913 BCE) 58
Zenon papyri 90
Zeredah 60
Zerubbabel 85
Zion, Mount 312
Zion, return to 85–9, 140
Zionism xviii, 240–6
Arab Zionism xix
cultural 161
decolonization and 6
emergence/origins 174–5, 241
as genocidal cult 21
goal 244
indigenous rights movement and 3, 21, 240–6
Muscular Judaism and 121
Zionist Congress, Second (1898) 121

Ben M. Freeman is the founder of the modern Jewish Pride movement and the author of *Jewish Pride: Rebuilding a People* (2021), *Reclaiming Our Story: The Pursuit of Jewish Pride* (2022), and *The Jews: An Indigenous People* (2025). A Holocaust scholar with nearly twenty years of experience, Freeman gained international prominence during the Corbyn Labour antisemitism crisis and is recognized as a leading Jewish thinker and public intellectual. Ranked number 8 on the inaugural 2023 "25 Young Vizionaries" list by *The Jerusalem Post* and JNF-USA, Ben also serves as a Jewish Diplomat for the World Jewish Congress and writes a column for *The Jerusalem Post*.